Running Applications on Oracle Exadata: Tuning Tips & Techniques

Joyjeet Banerjee

Mc
Graw
Hill
Education

New York   Chicago   San Francisco
Athens   London   Madrid   Mexico City
Milan   New Delhi   Singapore   Sydney   Toronto

Cataloging-in-Publication Data is on file with the Library of Congress

McGraw-Hill Education books are available at special quantity discounts to use as premiums and sales promotions, or for use in corporate training programs. To contact a representative, please visit the Contact Us pages at www.mhprofessional.com.

Running Applications on Oracle Exadata: Tuning Tips & Techniques

1 2 3 4 5 6 7 8 9 0   DOC DOC   1 0 9 8 7 6 5 4

ISBN 978-0-07-183312-7
MHID   0-07-183312-9

Sponsoring Editor
Paul Carlstroem

Editorial Supervisor
Janet Walden

Project Manager
Jigyasa Bhatia,
Cenveo® Publisher Services

Acquisitions Coordinator
Amanda Russell

Technical Editor
Chris Craft

Copy Editor
Lisa Theobald

Proofreader
Lisa McCoy

Indexer
Ted Laux

Production Supervisor
George Anderson

Composition
Cenveo Publisher Services

Illustration
Cenveo Publisher Services

Art Director, Cover
Jeff Weeks

This book is dedicated to my gurus Mahavatar Babaji, Paramahansa Yogananda, and Gyanswami for all the blessings, my mom and dad, my sisters Joyeeta and Tiya, my brothers-in-law Sagar and Riju, my little sweet niece Saanjh, and my lovely nephew Manav.

About the Author

Joyjeet Banerjee works as an enterprise architect with the Oracle Engineered System team in Redwood City, California, where he helps application customers (Oracle E-Business Suite [EBS], PeopleSoft, JD Edwards, Siebel, Oracle ATG, SAP, and other third-party applications) to migrate from legacy systems to engineered systems. So far, Joyjeet and his team have helped hundreds of OLTP customers implement engineered systems. Before joining the Engineered System team, Joyjeet was with Oracle Consulting, where he assisted Oracle Database, Real Application Clusters (RAC), and EBS customers implement Oracle products. Joyjeet has helped customers implement Oracle Exadata Database Machine since its inception. He joined Oracle in 2003 as a database administrator in the E-Business Suite development organization, where he specialized in application performance for Oracle Database.

Joyjeet is a regular guest speaker at Oracle Applications Users Group (OAUG), COLLABORATE, and Oracle OpenWorld. He serves on the panel of Oracle University that reviews course content and sets up questions for the OCP for the Oracle Database, RAC, and Oracle Applications tracks.

In addition to this book, Joyjeet has authored *Oracle Applications DBA* (McGraw-Hill Education India, 2007) and *Cracking the Applications DBA Interview* (McGraw-Hill Education India, 2008). His first book, *Oracle Applications DBA,* is a bestselling title.

Joyjeet earned an MBA in Systems and Operations Management from the University of Burdwan and has recently been honored as an Oracle Innovator (www.oracle.com/us/products/applications/ebusiness/conversations-with-innovators-070240.html).

About the Technical Editor

Chris Craft leads the Exadata Specialist team in St. Louis, Missouri, and has been involved with Exadata since its introduction in 2008. He and his team have conducted more than 500 Exadata Proof of Concept benchmarks, including Data Warehouse, Analytic Systems, online transaction processing (OLTP), and packaged applications including the Oracle E-Business Suite, PeopleSoft, Siebel, SAP, and other third-party applications. Chris led the development of the Exadata System sizing methodology and software tools used worldwide to size Exadata deployments at thousands of customer sites. He joined Oracle in 1995 as an Oracle Database Specialist in the Advanced Customer Services organization, where he specialized in database performance, Oracle application development, backup and recovery, and database replication, and he provided onsite diagnostic and debugging assistance to Fortune 100 customers. Chris has been a speaker at Oracle OpenWorld, Oracle AppsWorld, local Independent Oracle Users Group (IOUG) and AOUG events, and Oracle-hosted events in cities throughout North America. He holds a bachelor of science degree in Applied Computer Science from Illinois State University and studied abroad at Université de Grenoble in the French Alps.

Contents at a Glance

v

Contents

Acknowledgments

Many people have contributed a lot to the successful completion of this book. I would like to use this opportunity to thank all of you. Without all your help, it would have been difficult for me to finish this book.

I would like to thank Paul Carlstroem, senior content acquisitions editor at McGraw-Hill Professional, for his enthusiastic support and motivation throughout the book, helping me in all possible ways to make this book a reality; Amanda Russell, editorial coordinator at McGraw-Hill Professional, for managing this project; Lisa Theobald and Janet Walden for helping me in editing this book; Jigyasa Bhatia of Cenveo Publisher Services for helping me in all phases of the production of this book; Lisa McCoy for the proofreading; and Melinda Lytle for helping in editing all the images.

I would like to thank Christian Craft, sales consulting director of the Exadata team, for his technical review of this book and for providing his valuable feedback and advice at every step. It was a great honor to have this book technically reviewed by Chris. I would also like to thank Mahesh Subramaniam, director of Exadata development, for providing the valuable inputs for each chapter, for shaping the structure of this book, and for advising on the flow of each chapter.

I would like to thank my friend and colleague Sahil Thapar from the Exadata team for reviewing each chapter with a second pair of eyes and providing valuable input.

I would like to thank Hamidou Dia of the SVP Enterprise Architecture team and Andy Mendelsohn of EVP Database Server Technologies for quickly approving this project; Sheila Cepero for following up in getting me all the required approvals very quickly; Todd Alder, managing counsel; and Mark Schreier from the Oracle Legal team for providing all the necessary approvals.

Last, but not the least, I would like to thank all my friends and colleagues who, without fail, motivated and encouraged me to make this happen—Vebhhav Singh, for being my mentor and always guiding me and showing me the correct path; Timothy Davis, the best manager I ever had at Oracle; my buddies Murali Sriram, Ajay Arora, Dhanraj Pondicherry, Jayaraman Sampathkumar, Jagjeet Malhi, and Saumika Sarangi, for providing much valuable input for this book.

Introduction

When Exadata was launched in 2008, it was targeted primarily for Oracle Data Warehouse customers. The subsequent release was targeted for both data warehousing and OLTP customers, making it a general-purpose machine. Application customers started realizing the tremendous value of Exadata Machine and adopting it. Using Exadata, application customers can solve complex business problems without changing any application code. Using Exadata, an average OLTP application can perform up to five or six times faster, including faster month-end closing, quick forecasting, and so on. As a result, thousands of application customers are running their applications on Exadata.

I have been involved with Exadata since its inception. So far, I have helped hundreds of customers implement Exadata. The OLTP workload is totally different from that of Data Warehouse, as is the implementation strategy. In every customer engagement, I was asked whether a best-practice guide was available that focused exclusively on running applications on Exadata, and I realized that we needed a handbook on this topic, since one size does not fit all.

With this book, you will learn and perform the following:

- Understand Oracle Exadata architecture, hardware components, and software features.

- Achieve peak performance from OLTP systems.

- Size Oracle Exadata for applications using comparative and predictive methods.

- Migrate and consolidate applications to Oracle Exadata.

- Monitor, manage, and administer all Oracle Exadata components to ensure high availability and performance.

- Develop and implement a backup and recovery strategy.

- Learn best practices for running applications on Exadata.

This book comprises the following ten chapters.

Chapter 1: Exadata Architecture

In this chapter, you'll read a brief history of Exadata, and you'll learn about the Exadata architecture, various components of Exadata, Exadata configurations, and the advantages of Exadata.

Chapter 2: Exadata Hardware Features

This chapter explores the hardware components of Exadata—the processor and memory architecture for database compute nodes, all the hardware components of Exadata Storage Servers, InfiniBand architecture, Exadata networking, and power and environment details.

Chapter 3: Exadata Software Features

Here you will learn about some of the "secret sauce" of Exadata, including Hybrid Columnar Compression, Smart Scan, Exadata Smart Flash Cache, and Resource Manager.

Chapter 4: Leveraging Exadata Features for Applications

This chapter discusses the features of Exadata that OLTP benefits and shows you how to get the most out of Exadata in an OLTP system. You will learn about using Write-Back Flash Cache, Smart Flash Logging, and Smart Flash Cache compression; leveraging InfiniBand for database links and for traffic between the database and application tiers; and configuring HugePages.

Chapter 5: Sizing Exadata for Applications

In this chapter, you will learn how to size Exadata for applications. You will learn the comparative and predictive sizing methodology. You will also learn how to size Exadata for a production workload and a non-production workload. A case study is presented to help you understand more about sizing Exadata properly.

Chapter 6: Migrating Applications to Exadata

This chapter discusses the factors that govern the method for migrating applications to Exadata, how to plan for the migration, and the various paths available for migration, including Recovery Manager (RMAN), Data Pump Export and Import, transportable databases, transportable tablespaces, Oracle Data Guard, and GoldenGate.

Chapter 7: Application Consolidation in Exadata

In this chapter, you will learn about the advantages of consolidation, how to consolidate applications in Exadata, and how to consolidate production and non-production workloads in Exadata. You will learn about the consolidation planner and how to manage all the resources of Exadata—CPU, memory, I/O, and storage. You will also learn about the Database Resource Manager (DBRM) and I/O Resource Manager (IORM) in depth.

Chapter 8: Monitoring Exadata

Chapter 8 shows you how to monitor all the components of Exadata Machine, including the compute node, storage cells, InfiniBand switches, Integrated Lights Out Manager (ILOM), power distribution unit, and the Ethernet switch. You'll learn the important metrics that need to be monitored and how to monitor the machine using Enterprise Manager. You will also learn about the Exachk tool.

Chapter 9: Managing Exadata

In this chapter, you will learn how to administer all the components of Exadata, how to start and stop the Exadata Machine, how to manage all the services running in the database compute nodes including the operating system database and Grid Infrastructure, how to manage the InfiniBand network, and how to manage the storage cells. The chapter discusses the utilities Cell Command Line Interface (CellCLI) and Distributed Command Line Interface (DCLI) that you use to administer the storage servers, including sample CellCLI commands. You'll learn how to manage the disks and Flash, including creating the griddisk and celldisk.

Chapter 10: Exadata Backup and Recovery

In this chapter, you will learn how to back up the databases running in an Exadata Machine and how to back up various components of Exadata Machine, compute nodes, storage cells, the InfiniBand switch, and various restore methodologies.

Intended Audience

This book is suitable for the following readers:

- Database administrators and application DBAs

- UNIX system administrators who are going to implement Exadata

■ Application administrators whose applications will reside on Exadata

■ Technical managers or consultants who need to know about Exadata

This book assumes that the reader has a basic knowledge of Oracle Database, Real Application Clusters (RAC), and Automatic Storage Management (ASM) technology.

Code Available Online

All of the SQL scripts and code used in this book can be downloaded from the Oracle Press website at www.OraclePressBooks.com.

CHAPTER
1

Exadata Architecture

T he Oracle Exadata Database Machine provides extreme performance for both data warehousing and online transaction processing (OLTP) applications, making it the ideal platform for consolidating onto grids or private clouds. It is a complete package of servers, storage, networking, and software that is massively scalable, secure, and redundant. With Oracle Exadata Database Machine, customers can reduce IT costs through consolidation, manage more data on multiple compression tiers, improve performance of all applications, and make better business decisions in real time.

A Brief History

The Storage Appliance for Grid Environments (SAGE) project, the working name for Oracle Exadata Database Machine, began about three years before the product's final release in 2008. The main drivers behind SAGE were ever-increasing data volumes and sizes of Oracle databases, increasing disk drive capacities, disk speeds not increasing to match volumes, and the inability of Fibre Channel Storage Area Network (SAN) technology to keep up. Oracle's solution to these problems was to execute database management system (DBMS) logic closer to the disk drives by splitting the DBMS into two pieces, combining the conventional DB tier with a separate storage tier running DBMS logic.

The underlying technical innovations and technology decisions during initial development included the following:

- Development of the Cell Services (CELLSRV) software (CELLSRV is also called Cell Server)

- Decision to rely on InfiniBand for the backplane of SAGE

- Development of the Relational Database Service (RDS) and Remote Direct Memory Access (RDMA)

- Development of the Intelligent Database (iDB) protocol

- Implementation of Smart Scan fundamentals

- Implementation of Bloom filtering

- Implementation of an I/O resource manager

The development team decided to use commodity hardware based on the results Oracle had seen with Real Application Clusters (RAC). Using commodity hardware would provide the following benefits: lowest possible cost, high performance and scalability with RAC, compatibility with existing Oracle DBMS software, and fast hardware revisions with each new generation.

Using commodity hardware has allowed Oracle to leap ahead and then stay ahead of the competition with each release. This would not have been possible using proprietary hardware components. Instead, Oracle chose to invest in advancement of specific individual components such as InfiniBand technology, including contributions made to the open source community that helped advance the technology for the entire industry.

Oracle Database Machine V1

In September 2008, Oracle CEO Larry Ellison announced the world's first Oracle Database Machine V1 in a partnership with Hewlett-Packard. The sole purpose of the machine was for running data warehouse systems. The Exadata Storage Server was introduced to the market for the first time and was installed in a separate rack. The operating system for the database servers was Oracle Enterprise Linux 5.1 or Red Hat Linux and the Oracle database version was 11.1.0.7. The only configuration available at launch of version 1 was a full rack system. Smaller configurations were added later. A full rack included eight database servers, four InfiniBand switches, and fourteen Exadata storage servers. The database server nodes were based on HP Proliant DL360 G5 servers with two-socket Quad-Core Intel Xeon E5430 processors running at 2.66GHz; the Exadata storage servers were HP Proliant DL180 G5 servers with two-socket Quad-Core Intel Xeon E5430 processors running at 2.66GHz. The machine was sold and supported exclusively from Oracle.

Oracle Database Machine V1 was a very successful product that proved the viability in the market. It also proved the value of a prebuilt, pre-integrated system with a single stream of support. The version 1 HP/Oracle machines were phased out after version 2, when Oracle Corporation acquired Sun Microsystems.

Oracle Database Machine V2

In September 2009, the Database Machine V2 was introduced simultaneously with Oracle's announcement of the Sun acquisition. Instead of HP, this time, the partnership was with Sun Microsystems, which would soon become an important part of the Oracle family. The tagline became "Hardware from Sun and software from Oracle." Version 2 of the machine was greatly enhanced to include the ability to run both data warehouse as well as OLTP systems, making it a general-purpose machine. New features such as Flash Cache, Hybrid Columnar Compression (HCC), Smart Scan, and storage indexes were introduced with V2. The operating system for the database servers was Oracle Enterprise Linux 5.3. Support for Red Hat was deprecated with the release of version 2 in favor of an all-Oracle supported platform. The database version was upgraded to 11.2.0.1.

The machine was offered in three different configurations of quarter, half, and full rack. The quarter rack came with two database servers, three Exadata storage cells, and two InfiniBand switches. The half rack came with four database servers, seven Exadata storage cells, and two InfiniBand switches. And the full rack came with eight database servers, fourteen Exadata storage cells, and three InfiniBand switches. The DB server was based on Sun Fire X4170 with two-socket Quad-Core Intel Xeon E5540 processors running at 2.53 GHz. The Exadata Storage Server was based on Sun Fire X4275 with two-socket Quad-Core Intel Xeon E5540 processors running at 2.53 GHz. The major innovation in V2 was the introduction of the Flash Cache in the storage cells, which was the primary feature that enabled Exadata to also support OLTP workloads. A storage cell contained four Sun SLC flash cards of 96GB each, for a total of 384GB of flash in each cell.

Oracle Exadata Database Machine X2

The Exadata Database Machine X2 was introduced during Oracle OpenWorld in September 2010. The architecture was same as that of V2; however, the third generation of Exadata brought improvements in WRITE efficiencies with the introduction of Smart Flash Logging and Write-Back Flash Cache. The Database Machine X2 was launched in two varieties: X2-2 with eight database servers in a full rack and X2-8 with two database servers in a full rack. The operating system for the DB servers in both the models was Oracle Enterprise Linux 5.5 for Oracle Database 11*g* Release 2. X2-2, like V2, was offered in quarter, half, and full rack sizes, whereas X2-8 was available as only a full rack. The architecture of X2-2 remained the same as that of V2. The quarter rack came with two database servers, three Exadata storage cells, and two InfiniBand switches. The half rack came with four database servers, seven Exadata storage cells, and three InfiniBand switches. The number of InfiniBand switches was increased to three in X2-2 half-rack models. The full rack came with eight database servers, fourteen Exadata storage cells, and three InfiniBand switches. On the other hand, the X2-8 model came with two DB servers, fourteen Exadata storage cells, and three InfiniBand switches. The X2-2 database server is based out of two-socket, six-core Intel Xeon 5670 processors running 2.93 GHz, whereas the X2-8 database server is based on Sun Fire X4800 with two-socket, eight-core Intel Xeon X7560 processors running 2.26 GHz. The Exadata Storage server is the same for both the models containing two-socket, six-core Intel Xeon L5640 processors running 2.26 GHz.

Oracle Exadata Database Machine X3

Exadata Database Machine X3 was introduced in September 2012. The architecture was the same as that of X2. X3 was also launched in two varieties: X3-2 with eight database servers in a full rack and X3-8 with two database servers in a full rack. A choice of two operating systems was offered for the DB servers: Oracle Enterprise Linux 5 Update 8 with the Unbreakable Enterprise Kernel and Solaris 11. Oracle Database 11*g* Release 2 was also featured. X3-2 introduced eight-rack configuration along with quarter, half, and full, whereas X2-8 was available only as a full rack.

The architecture of X3-2 remained the same as that of X2-2. The quarter rack came with two database servers, three Exadata storage cells, and two InfiniBand switches. The half rack came with four database servers, seven Exadata storage cells, and three InfiniBand switches. The full rack came with eight database servers, fourteen Exadata storage cells, and three InfiniBand switches. The hardware configuration of eight racks is same as that of the X3-2 quarter rack, except half of the CPU cores in the database servers are enabled and half of the cores per server are disabled. Similarly, in the Exadata Storage Server, half of the CPU cores are enabled and half are disabled. In Flash Cache, half of the PCI flash cards are enabled and half of the flash cards are disabled. In addition, half of the disks in the storage cell are enabled and half are disabled. The X3-8 model came with two DB servers, fourteen Exadata storage cells, and three InfiniBand switches. The X3-2 database server is based on Sun Server X3-2 with two-socket, eight-core Intel Xeon E5-2690 processors running 2.9 GHz, whereas the X2-8 database server is based on Sun Server X4800 with two-socket, eight-core Intel Xeon X7560 processors running 2.26 GHz. The Exadata Storage server is the same for both the models, containing two-socket, six-core Intel Xeon L5640 processors running 2.26 GHz.

Oracle Exadata Database Machine X4

The current generation of Exadata is X4, released in November 2014. In this chapter, we will cover the architecture of Exadata X4 in a detailed manner. Our discussion throughout the book refers to X4 machines.

Exadata Architecture

What exactly is Exadata? Is it some new database from Oracle, is it hardware, is it an appliance, or is it storage? Figure 1-1 shows the components of Exadata to help answer these questions.

As shown in the figure, Exadata includes the following components:

- Database servers

- Exadata storage cells or Exadata storage servers

- InfiniBand switches

Database Servers

An Exadata Database Machine deployment consists of one to eight database servers, depending on the configuration you choose. Each database server includes the following components.

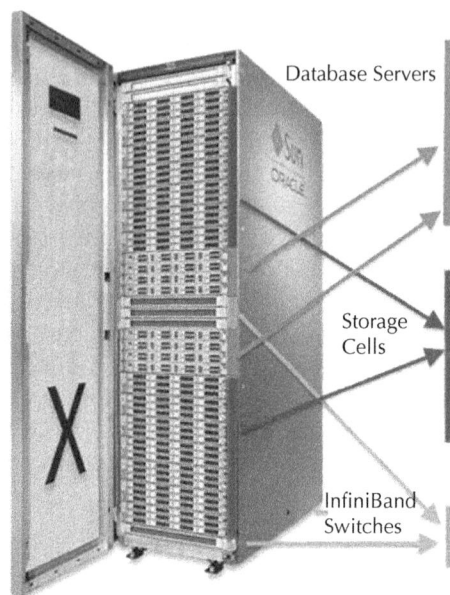

FIGURE 1-1. *Exadata components*

Operating System

Two operating systems are available with each X4 server deployment: Oracle Linux 5 and Solaris 11 update 1. You select the appropriate OS at the time of install. Following is the OS information from an X4 Exadata server running on Linux:

```
[oracle@exa6db01 ~]$ uname -a
Linux exa6db01.osc.us.oracle.com 2.6.39-400.126.1.el5uek #1 SMP Fri Sep
20 10:54:38 PDT 2013 x86_64 x86_64 x86_64 GNU/Linux
[oracle@exa6db01 ~]$
```

Oracle Home

An Exadata machine comes with two primary Oracle homes, one for the database and another for the grid infrastructure. The database Oracle home in an X4 machine supports both Oracle Database 11g Release 2 and Oracle Database 12c. A customer can run both 11g and 12c database in an X4 machine using two separate database Oracle homes. Oracle Database 12.1 can run alongside other databases running version 11.2 software in the same cluster. The grid infrastructure Oracle home supports Oracle Database versions 11.2.0.3, 11.2.0.4, and 12.1.0.1.

Exadata provides sufficient space for many Oracle homes. When planning to host multiple applications in an Exadata machine, you may want to separate the Oracle home. Depending on how the space is sliced, each node should be able to support in the range of 100 homes.

Real Application Clusters (RAC)

Oracle RAC is the foundation for the Exadata machines. In an Oracle RAC database, more than one instance concurrently runs and executes transactions against a shared database. In other words, multiple node instances access the same database at the same time. The instances are spread across multiple nodes, or servers, and each node hosts one instance of the database.

> **NOTE**
> *Although Exadata comes with RAC, if the database workload is small enough, you can run lots of small non-RAC single-instance databases as well.*

The independent servers are *clustered* to operate as if they were one server. Oracle Clusterware provides the foundation of clustering for all the nodes. In this way, the separate servers appear as if they are one server to applications and end users. You can also create multiple RAC clusters within a single rack of Exadata machines.

The data spread across the RAC is shared and stored centrally in the form of database files and is accessible from all the nodes all the time. Oracle RAC manages all the instances and coordinates each instance's access to shared data to provide data consistency and data integrity.

Following are the advantages of RAC:

■ **Scalability**   You can scale applications to meet increasing data processing demands without changing the application code. As you add resources such as nodes or storage, RAC extends the processing powers of these resources beyond the limits of the individual components.

■ **Parallel processing**   A large task divided into subtasks and distributed among multiple nodes can be completed sooner and more efficiently than if you processed the entire task on one node. Cluster processing also provides increased performance for larger workloads and for accommodating rapidly growing user populations. Exadata enables cross-instance parallelism, which can be dangerous on non-Exadata platforms.

■ **High availability**   RAC also provides high availability, so if an instance in an RAC database goes down, it does not impact the entire system to provide uninterrupted service. The application continues to run on the survived instance and there is no outage. (Note that some applications may have to disconnect/reconnect upon instance failure.)

■ **Transparency** Any application that runs as a single instance can usually be deployed in RAC without making many changes in the application code. The same applies for Exadata.

> **TIP & TECHNIQUE**
> *Any application that is certified to run on Oracle*
> *Database 11g R2 and 12.1 can run on Exadata.*

Oracle stores resources, such as data block information, in a buffer cache that resides in memory and helps reduce the disk I/O. In an RAC database, each instance has its own background process and memory structure. The data in the buffer cache of each instance is synchronized using the RAC cache fusion feature, which coordinates and moves the data block across database instances. This optimizes performance and expands the effective memory to be nearly equal to the sum of all memory in your cluster database. Cache fusion uses a diskless cache coherency mechanism that copies blocks directly from a holding instance's memory cache to a requesting instance's memory cache, using the interconnect, enabling the Oracle RAC database to access and modify data as if the data resided in a single buffer cache.

The high-bandwidth, low-latency interconnect in Exadata enables much more scalable RAC clusters. Exadata runs an entirely native InfiniBand (IB) communication stack, which is not the case on all other platforms.

The Global Cache Service (GCS) process implements Cache Fusion. GCS maintains the block mode for blocks in the global role. It is responsible for block transfers between instances. GCS employs various background processes such as the Global Cache Service Processes (LMSn) that manage remote messages and the Global Enqueue Service Daemon (LMD) that coordinates enqueues that are shared globally.

Automatic Storage Management (ASM)

Oracle Automatic Storage Management (ASM) is a volume manager for Oracle Database files. ASM supports both single-instance and RAC databases and is integrated with Exadata. Oracle ASM makes storage management easier and is based on the principle that a database, rather than an administrator, should manage storage. So instead of DBA managing thousands of database files, ASM does it automatically without any overhead. ASM is designed to provide the performance of raw I/O with the management capabilities of a file system.

Oracle ASM uses disk groups to store the database files. A disk group is a collection of disks that ASM manages as a single unit. ASM provides a file system interface for Oracle Database files within a disk group. Oracle automatically places the database files within the disk groups.

Exadata Machine includes two disk groups by default:

■ **DATA disk group** This disk group stores all the active database files, control files, online Redo log files, and server parameter file (SPFILE). It also stores the change tracking files used for incremental backups.

■ **Fast Recovery Area (RECO) disk group** This disk group stores all the ARCHIVELOG files, copies of current control files, Redo log files, SPFile, backup sets, Flashback log files, and all the recovery-related files.

NOTE
Although this is the standard configuration, you can change this if needed. It's not common to change it, but this is not a completely "fixed" configuration. You can choose the ratio of the DATA disk group versus the RECO disk group—it can be 80:20, 60:40, or any other custom configuration before the installation of Exadata.

In addition to DATA and RECO, you can create a database file system (DBFS) disk group, which provides file system capabilities. The DBFS database can be created on top of the DBFS disk group, but it can also be extended into the DATA disk group. DBFS is covered in the next section of this chapter.

The storage disks provisioned with ASM disk groups are called Automatic Storage Management (ASM) disks. ASM disks could be a disk or a partition from a disk, from a storage array, from logical volumes, and so on.

ASM provides the following benefits:

■ **Automatic rebalancing** Disks can be added or removed from a disk group while a database continues to access files from the disk group. When the files are added or removed, ASM automatically rebalances and redistributes the data without any downtime. Depending on the ASM rebalance power limit setting, there is no or minimal performance overhead. With Exadata, cells and disks can be added or dropped dynamically.

■ **Reduction of administration** ASM reduces the overhead of administration of managing the data files and volume. With ASM, the database file management does not require a DBA, and volume management does not require a UNIX system administrator.

■ **Striping** ASM distributes, or balances, the data across all the disks in a disk group to maximize performance. It helps in reducing I/O latency, and as a result, I/O performance tuning is not needed. Coarse-grained striping provides load balancing for disk groups, while fine-grained striping reduces latency by spreading the load more widely. To stripe the data, ASM separates files into stripes and spreads it evenly across all of the disks in a disk group. The stripes are equal in size to the effective allocation unit. The coarse-grained stripe size is always equal to the AU size. The fine-grained stripe size always equals 128 KB; this provides lower I/O latency for small I/O operations such as redo log writes. With Exadata, the database files are striped evenly across all the storage cells and disks for optimal performance. Exadata uses the SAME (Stripe And Mirror Everything) methodology.

■ **Mirroring** To prevent data loss in the event of disk failures, ASM mirrors the data by storing copies of data in multiple disks. The mirroring happens at the file level and not at the disk level. ASM provides the following levels of mirroring:

■ **Normal** Two-way mirroring, in which a copy of the data is kept in a separate disk

■ **High** Three-way mirroring, in which two copies of the data are kept in a separate disk

■ **External** Mirroring is chosen at the hardware or storage level using RAID or similar technologies; this is not applicable for Exadata because the storage is already built in

■ **Oracle Managed Files (OMF)** ASM uses OMF, which simplifies database file management. OMF automatically names the files when new database files are added to the database and creates files in the designated locations, thus reducing the DBA's overhead of naming the files and keeping track of the location of database files.

■ **Sharing** ASM allows multiple databases to share storage cells and disks.

Database File System

The database file system (DBFS) is not a feature of Exadata, but is often installed in Exadata as a shared network file system. Basically a file system that is stored in the database and has its own instance, DBFS is very similar to NFS and is used for staging temporary files such as extract, transform, load (ETL) files; temporary files; flat files; and so on. DBFS uses Oracle Database to store the objects. Files are stored as SecureFiles LOBs in database tables stored in Exadata and are protected like any database data, with mirroring, Data Guard, Flashback, and so on. Data is copied onto the DBFS in the Exadata storage servers using traditional OS utilities (such as ftp, scp, or rcp).

NOTE
DBFS is a FUSE (File System in User Mode) file system, which can contain data but not executables.

TIP & TECHNIQUE
Application deployments usually integrate with many third-party applications. DBFS should not be used as a mount point for third-party integrations because it's a file system within a database. Many applications need to have a common mount point between the database and application file system to store the PL/SQL output files and temporary files, and DBFS should not be used for that. For example, the Oracle E-Business Suite needs a UTL_FILE directory for storing the PL/SQL temporary output files. The UTL file system is mounted across the database and application tiers.

Exadata Storage Servers or Storage Cells

Traditionally, storage is used for storing data only and has no role in data processing. Disk arrays run CPUs, but they are typically low-power CPUs that are used for serving blocks of data. The database server always does the processing, and Exadata is very unique in this aspect. In an Exadata machine, storage plays an equal role in processing the data like the database servers. In Exadata machines, the data is stored in Exadata storage servers, also known as storage cells.

The Exadata Storage Server has comparatively high-powered CPUs (compared to traditional disk arrays), and that horsepower is used to perform Oracle Database processing. The Exadata Storage Server runs a portion of the Oracle DBMS processing logic within the storage layer. Exadata Storage Server executes a portion of the SQL processing, which frees a portion of the database tier CPU. In addition, the storage server processes a lot of data itself and returns only the relevant results rather than sending all the data to the database node for query processing, which frees up a large amount of I/O bandwidth. We will discuss this in detail in Chapter 3; for now, let's discuss some of the key characteristics of the storage server.

Intelligent Database (iDB) Protocol

The iDB protocol is used in Exadata Machine for all communications between database servers and storage servers. Whenever a query is run and the database kernel determines that the underlying storage is Exadata, it constructs an iDB command for sending the SQL and metadata information about the SQL to the storage cell and getting the data blocks from the cell.

iDB is built on Reliable Datagram Sockets (RDS), which in turn runs on InfiniBand. RDS is a high-performance, low-latency, reliable connectionless protocol for delivering datagrams. It was developed by Oracle. RDS also supports Remote Direct Memory Access (RDMA), in which the memory of a computer is accessed from another without involving both OSs. This mode doesn't need any CPU cycles and thus it's very useful in a parallel processing environment. Exadata storage cells use RDMA for sending and receiving data. With RDMA and RDS, high-bandwidth and low-latency communication to storage cells within Exadata is achieved.

Most of the Exadata-specific features such as query offload and resource management are leveraged by Oracle Database and ASM using iDB.

Software Components in the Storage Cell

A storage cell consists of the following software:

- **Operating system software** The Exadata storage software runs on Oracle Enterprise Linux. Here are the details of the OS running on the storage cell:

  ```
  [root@exa6cel01 ~]# uname -a
  Linux exa6cel01.osc.us.oracle.com 2.6.39-400.126.1.el5uek #1 SMP
  Fri Sep 20 10:54:38 PDT 2013 x86_64 x86_64 x86_64 GNU/Linux
  ```

- **Cell Server (CELLSRV)** CELLSRV handles all the iDB requests that come from the database server. It caters all the storage offload, I/O requests, predicates filtering at the cell level, and performs other tasks. It is a multi-thread process that does most of the heavy lifting in the storage cell and takes the maximum CPU cycle. CELLSRV can operate in block-server mode as well.

- **Management Server (MS)** The Management Server facilitates the management of the storage cell. It works in conjunction with the cell command-line interface (CellCLI) to manage the standalone storage cell. The CellCLI utility provides a CLI to the cell management functions, such as cell initial configuration, cell disk and grid disk creation, and performance monitoring. The CellCLI utility runs on the cell and is accessible from a client computer that has network access to the storage cell or is directly connected to the cell. We will discuss the CellCLI in more details in Chapter 9.

- **Restart Server (RS)** The Restart Server is responsible for monitoring the Cell Server and Management Server and restarts them whenever needed.

Exadata Smart Flash Cache

The Exadata Storage Server comes with massive flash storage capability, which is based on the PCI flash technology, known as the Exadata Smart Flash Cache. In a storage cell, the flash is placed on the PCI bus. Each storage cell contains four flash cards. The flash cache works in conjunction with Oracle Database to cache frequently accessed data in the most intelligent way. We discuss details of the Exadata Smart Flash Cache in Chapters 2 and 3.

Disk Layout in the Storage Cell

The backbone of any storage cell is the hard disk, and this is also the case for Exadata storage cells. An Exadata cell contains 12 physical disks.

Figure 1-2 shows a pictorial overview of the disk layout.

The information about the cell OS, cell binaries, swap space, various configuration files, and so on is stored in the first two disks in a specially reserved area known as the system area, where the system is mirrored across both drives. The remaining 10 disks don't have a system area and are used as is.

Logical Units (LUN) is the lowest level of the storage abstraction. LUN in an Exadata storage cell is created using the physical disk. After leaving the system area in the first two disks, the rest of the area is used for creating the LUN, and in the 10 disks left, the area in the physical disk is used to create a LUN.

So for the first two disks: LUN = Total Space in Disk – System Area
And for the remaining ten disks: LUN = Total Space in Disk

Free space in the LUN is used to create the Cell disk. The Cell disk is a higher-level abstraction of the data storage area on the physical disk. Exadata Storage Server manages the Cell disk. A part of the Cell disk is reserved for the cell system area that is used to store and capture the various metrics and statistics of the Storage Cell.

The Grid disk is created from the Cell disk and is available to ASM for creating the ASM disk groups. Single or multiple Grid disks can be created using a Cell disk. Often, the Cell disks are split based on slow or fast track to create different Grid disks (in a spinning hard drive, the outermost tracks are usually fast and innermost tracks are usually slow). The Grid disk on the fast track is used to create the DATA disk group, and the Grid disk on the slow track is used to create the FRA (Fast Recovery Area) disk group.

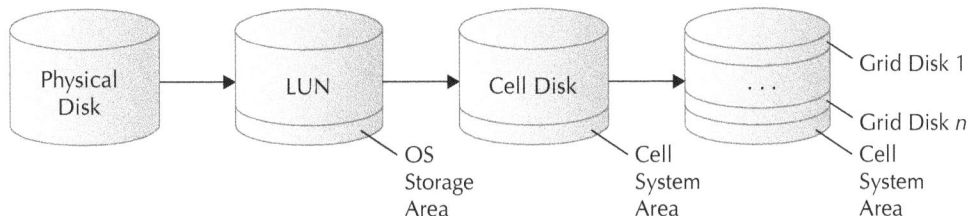

FIGURE 1-2. *Disk layout*

A disk group typically contains similar disk areas across all cells and across all disks within the cell. This is an important design to ensure that the entire disk group offers the same level of performance. ASM breaks up a file into small file segments and distributes file segments across the Grid disks for the disk group.

To summarize: Physical Disk > LUNS > Cell Disk > Grid Disk > ASM Diskgroup.

InfiniBand

The database nodes and the storage cells are connected via InfiniBand, which provides a massive speed of 40 Gbps in each direction. The interconnect across the RAC database node also uses InfiniBand for connectivity. InfiniBand uses *zero copy reservation*, wherein the data is transferred by bypassing the buffer copies in various layers of the network. InfiniBand also uses *buffer reservation* so that the hardware knows well ahead of time where to place the buffers.

Figure 1-3 depicts a pictorial overview of the Exadata architecture and InfiniBand network.

Exadata uses the Zero Data Loss UDP Protocol (ZDP) developed by Oracle. The ZDP protocol has very low CPU overhead. Its full technical name is Reliable Datagram

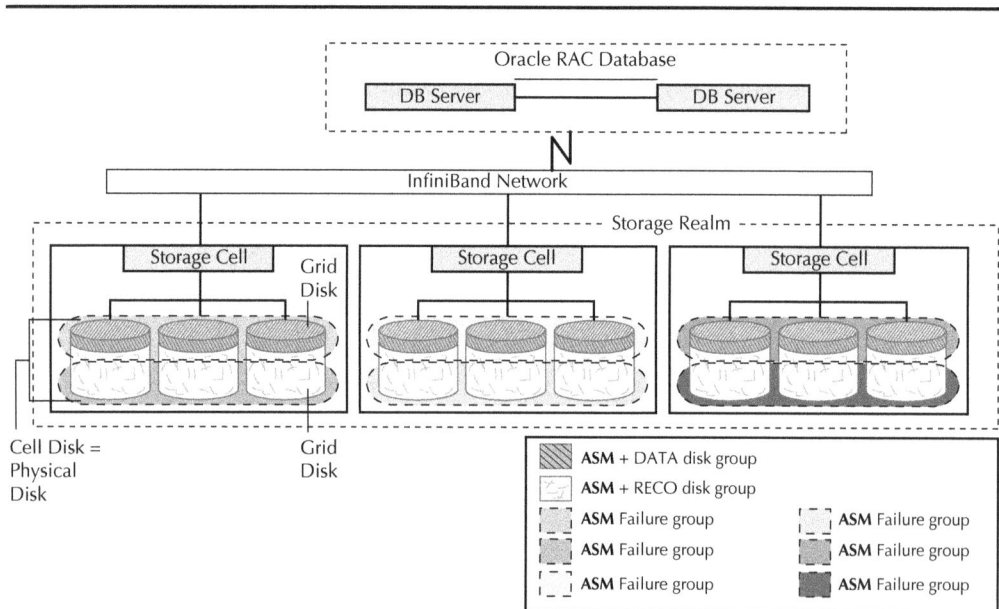

FIGURE 1-3. *Exadata architecture and the InfiniBand network*

Sockets (RDS). RDS is a high-performance, low-latency, reliable connectionless protocol for delivering datagrams.

We will cover InfiniBand in more detail in Chapter 2.

Exadata Configurations

Exadata comes in two variations: Xn-2 and Xn-8. Variation Xn-2 is available in four different rack configurations: eighth, quarter, half, and full. Variation Xn-8 is available in only one configuration: full rack. The current generation of Xn-2 is X4-2. The current generation of Xn-8 is X4-8.

Xn-2 Full Rack

A full-rack Xn-2 Exadata has eight database nodes, fourteen storage cells, three InfiniBand switches, and one Ethernet switch. The X4-2 database server consists of two 12-core 2.6-GHz Intel Xeon E5-2697 V2 processors, 256GB of memory that can be expanded to 512GB, and four 600GB 10K RPM SAS disks for local storage. The X4-2 storage server consists of two six-core 2.6-GHz Intel Xeon E-5 2360 v2 processors, 96GB memory, four Sun Flash Accelerator F80 PCIe cards of 800GB each, a choice of 12 1.2TB 10K RPM High Performance SAS 2.5-inch disks or 12 4TB 7.2 RPM High Capacity SAS 3.5-inch disks. Figure 1-4 shows the Exadata full rack.

FIGURE 1-4. *Exadata full rack*

Xn-2 Half Rack

An X4-2 half rack consists of four database nodes, seven storage cells, three InfiniBand switches, and one Ethernet switch. The specifications of the database nodes and storage server are exactly the same as those of the full-rack system. Figure 1-5 shows the Exadata half rack.

Xn-2 Quarter Rack

An X4-2 quarter rack consists of two database nodes, three storage cells, two InfiniBand switches, and one Ethernet switch. The specifications of the database nodes and storage server are exactly the same as those of the full-rack system. Figure 1-6 shows the Exadata quarter rack.

Xn-2 Eighth Rack

An X4-2 eighth rack consists of two database nodes, three storage cells, two InfiniBand switches, and one Ethernet switch, the same as that of the quarter rack. The only difference in an eighth rack is that 50 percent of the resource (CPU, storage, and flash) remains disabled. The specifications of the database nodes and storage server are exactly the same as those of the full-rack system.

FIGURE 1-5. *Exadata half rack*

FIGURE 1-6. *Exadata quarter rack*

Xn-8 Full Rack

A full-rack X4-8 Exadata has two database nodes, fourteen storage cells, three InfiniBand switches, and one Ethernet switch. The database server consists of eight 15-core 2.8-GHz Intel Xeon E7-8895 processors, 2TB of memory, and seven 600GB 10K RPM SAS disks for local storage. The X4-8 machine comes with the X4-2 storage server, which consists of two six-core 2.6-GHz Intel Xeon E-5 2360 v2 processors, 96GB memory, four Sun Flash Accelerator F80 PCIe cards of 800GB each, and a choice of twelve 1.2TB 10K RPM High Performance SAS 2.5-inch disks or twelve 4TB 7.2 RPM High Capacity SAS 3.5-inch disks. Figure 1-7 shows the Exadata Xn-8 full rack.

The various configurations of the machines are summarized in Tables 1-1 and 1-2.

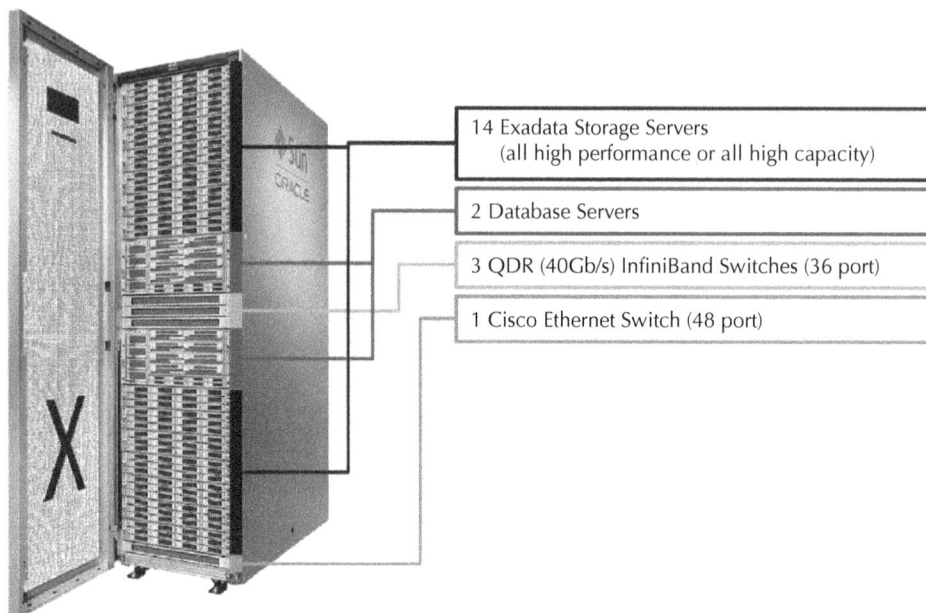

14 Exadata Storage Servers
(all high performance or all high capacity)

2 Database Servers

3 QDR (40Gb/s) InfiniBand Switches (36 port)

1 Cisco Ethernet Switch (48 port)

FIGURE 1-7. *Exadata Xn-8 full rack*

		X4-8 Full	X4-2 Full	X4-2 Half	X4-2 Quarter	X4-2 Eighth
Database servers		2	8	4	2	2
Database grid cores		240	192	96	48	24
Database grid memory (GB)		4096	2048 (max 4096)	1024 (max 2048)	512 (max 1024)	512 (max 1024)
InfiniBand switches		2	2	2	2	2
Ethernet switch		1	1	1	1	1
Exadata Storage Servers		14	14	7	3	3
Storage grid CPU cores		168	168	84	36	18
Raw flash capacity		44.8TB	44.8TB	22.4TB	9.6TB	4.8TB
Raw storage capacity	High Perf	200TB	200TB	100TB	43.2TB	21.6TB
	High Cap	672TB	672TB	336TB	144TB	72TB
Usable mirrored capacity	High Perf	90TB	90TB	45TB	19TB	9TB
	High Cap	300TB	300TB	150TB	63TB	30TB
Usable triple mirrored capacity	High Perf	60TB	60TB	30TB	13TB	6.3TB
	High Cap	200TB	200TB	100TB	43TB	21.5TB

TABLE 1-1. *Exadata Machine Configuration*

Version	Model	Disk Type	Allocation	Flash Cache	Total	Usable	DBFS_ DG	DATA_ DG	RECO_ DG
X4-8	Full	1.2TB H P	80/20	44800	190178	95089	2030	74447	18612
X4-8	Full	1.2TB H P	80/20	44800	192470	64157	1353	50243	12561
X4-8	Full	4TB H C	80/20	44800	625,070	208,357	1,353	165,603	41,401
X4-8	Full	4TB H C	80/20	44800	617628	308814	2030	245427	61357
X4-2	Eighth	1.2TB H P	80/20	4800	20570	6857	145	5370	1342
X4-2	Eighth	1.2TB H P	80/20	4800	19424	9712	218	7595	1899
X4-2	Eighth	4TB H C	80/20	4800	63259	31630	248	25106	6276
X4-2	Eighth	4TB H C	80/20	4800	66,984	22,328	165	17,730	4,433
X4-2	Full	1.2TB H P	80/20	44800	192470	64157	1353	50243	12561
X4-2	Full	1.2TB H P	80/20	44800	190178	95089	2030	74447	18612
X4-2	Full	4TB H C	80/20	44800	618284	309142	2310	245466	61366
X4-2	Full	4TB H C	80/20	44800	625,734	208,578	1,540	165,630	41,408
X4-2	Half	1.2TB H P	80/20	22400	96206	32069	677	25114	6278
X4-2	Half	1.2TB H P	80/20	22400	95060	47530	1015	37212	9303
X4-2	Half	4TB H C	80/20	22400	309109	154555	1155	122720	30680
X4-2	Half	4TB H C	80/20	22400	312,834	104,278	770	82,806	20,702
X4-2	Quarter	1.2TB H P	80/20	9600	41198	13733	290	10754	2689
X4-2	Quarter	1.2TB H P	80/20	9600	40052	20026	435	15673	3918
X4-2	Quarter	4TB H C	80/20	9600	134,034	44,678	330	35,478	8,870
X4-2	Quarter	4TB H C	80/20	9600	130309	65155	495	51728	12932

TABLE 1-2. *The Actual Space Allocations for Exadata*

Exadata Storage Expansion Rack

If the database size keeps growing, the storage cells may run out of space and there might be a need to add additional storage. If you need more space but don't need additional compute power, Exadata provides the capacity to add storage servers without adding database nodes for computing. With the Exadata Storage Expansion Rack, you can purchase additional storage cells.

The Exadata Storage Expansion rack comes in four different configurations: full rack, half rack, quarter rack, and single cell. Depending on the storage needs, you can purchase from a single cell to a full storage expansion rack. A full storage expansion rack has eighteen storage cells, three InfiniBand switches, and one Ethernet switch. The configuration of X4-2 storage cells is exactly the same as that of X4-2 Exadata machines. A half-storage expansion rack has nine storage cells,

		X4-2 Full	X4-2 Half	X4-2 Quarter	Single Cell
InfiniBand switches		3	3	2	-
Ethernet switch		1	1	1	-
Exadata Storage Servers		18	9	4	1
Storage grid CPU cores		216	108	48	12
Raw flash capacity		57.6TB	28.8TB	12.8TB	3.2TB
Raw storage capacity	High Perf	258TB	129TB	57TB	14.4TB
	High Cap	864TB	432TB	192TB	48TB
Usable mirrored capacity	High Perf	116TB	58TB	25TB	6TB
	High Cap	387TB	194TB	85TB	20TB
Usable triple mirrored capacity	High Perf	78TB	39TB	17TB	4.25TB
	High Cap	260TB	130TB	58 TB	14.5TB

TABLE 1-3. *Exadata Storage Expansion Rack Configuration*

three InfiniBand switches, and one Ethernet switch. A quarter storage expansion rack has four storage cells, two InfiniBand switches, and one Ethernet switch. A summary of the Exadata storage cells is shown in Table 1-3.

Up to eight Exadata machines can be connected without additional switches. Each eight additional Exadata machines require a separate InfiniBand switch. Thus, several Exadata machines can be connected to create an Exadata farm.

> **TIP & TECHNIQUE**
> *Consider the Exadata Storage Expansion Rack when the capacity of the machine gets full and you don't need to expand the CPU and memory. For example, instead of upgrading an Exadata quarter rack to an Exadata half rack, you can add a Storage Expansion Rack.*

Advantages of Exadata

Apart from the performance benefit, Exadata provides several other advantages, such as:

- **Time to market** Typically, any application's implementation cycle takes from six months to a few years. During the implementation cycle, there is always a need to provision environments very quickly during the development, Conference Room Pilot (CRP), User Acceptance Testing (UAT), and testing cycles. If an environment can't be provided on time, it increases the project costs because all the developers/testers sit idle, waiting for the environment. Even after go-live, new functionalities are added to applications, and thus the development cycle is always ongoing. Exadata is ready for use in any application implementation cycle on day one because it comes preconfigured with Oracle Database, RAC, and storage.

- **RAC ready**   An application's migration to an RAC environment is usually a two- or three-month project. For any new RAC implementation, all the components must be assembled and configured starting from storage, networking, OS install, and clusterware install. Exadata comes prebuilt with RAC databases, and applications can be migrated to Exadata the day it is installed. This easily saves two or three months and a lot of consulting money.

- **Proactive maintenance**   All customers running Exadata run the same configuration. All patches in Exadata are applied via Exadata bundle patches, which take care of patching the DB nodes, storage cells, and InfiniBand switches. The Exadata bundle patches are released periodically, and all customers upgrade to the Exadata bundle patch around the same time. Oracle monitors all the customer Exadata boxes, and if any customer faces an issue, Oracle immediately is alerted of that issue and provides a fix. Any other customer who is running a similar configuration is alerted immediately with the fix even before they hit the issue. Because all database machines are the same, each customer will not need to diagnose and resolve unique issues that occur only on their configuration. Performance tuning and stress testing performed at Oracle occur on the exact same configuration used by the customer to ensure better performance and higher quality. Also, the SR activity in Oracle Support is roughly half as much for Exadata compared to other legacy environments. SR resolution time is 30 percent faster.

- **Redundant at all levels**   All components in Exadata are redundant. Each database server, storage server, and InfiniBand switch has redundant hot-swappable power supplies. Disk drives and fans are hot-swappable, ASM provides protection against storage server failures, and RAC provides protection against database server failures. Two or three InfiniBand switches in every Exadata machine, depending on configuration, provide redundancy for the InfiniBand network. The system is highly resilient and can tolerate the loss of an entire switch or connection without affecting performance. Two Redundant Power Distribution Units provide rack-level power. Exadata uses up to six power cables, connecting to redundant data center power sources to eliminate single points of failure.

■ **Simpler administration** Exadata makes administration of database, storage, networking, and disks simple. From one single console, all the components of Exadata can be managed easily. More importantly, Exadata reduces the number of "working parts" and the amount of redundant administration required. For example, storage is administered once by the DBA without having to involve a separate storage administrator. We will discuss administration details in Chapter 9.

■ **Single vendor** All the layers, starting from disks to the database server, are provided by a single vendor, which makes support for Exadata convenient. Customers don't have to follow-up with multiple vendors, avoiding the typical "runaround."

■ **Auto Service Request (ASR)** ASR is a secure, scalable, customer-installable software solution available as a feature on Exadata. The ASR software helps to resolve problems faster by using auto-case generation when specific hardware faults occur. ASR automatically opens service requests (SRs) with Oracle Support when specific hardware faults occur either in the Exadata storage servers or the database servers. ASR is currently applicable only for hardware faults detected on the following server components: CPUs, disk controllers, disks, flash cards, flash modules, InfiniBand cards, memory modules, system boards, power supplies, and fans.

Platinum Services for Exadata

Exadata comes with Oracle Platinum Services, a special entitlement under Oracle Premier Support that is delivered at no additional cost. It's exclusively available on certified configurations of Exadata. Oracle continually updates the certified configuration, so refer to the Oracle Support portal for the latest certified configuration.
    Platinum Services provides the following benefits:

■ **Event and Certified Platinum Configuration Reporting** Oracle provides event reports to assist customers in identifying patterns that may help predict or identify improperly tuned components of the Certified Platinum Configuration. Oracle also provides Certified Platinum Configuration reports that include a list of targets, associated versions, and patch history.

■ **24/7 Oracle remote fault monitoring** Oracle will monitor the Certified Platinum Configuration 24 hours a day, seven days a week (24/7) to identify events that represent faults in the proper functioning of the Certified Platinum Configuration. The following components are monitored:

   ■ **Hardware system and integrated software monitoring** Oracle will monitor the hardware system and integrated software for faults in proper functioning.

■ **Operating system monitoring**   Oracle will monitor the operating system(s) for faults in proper functioning.

■ **Software monitoring**   Oracle will monitor the certified Platinum Services program releases for faults. Software monitoring services consist of monitoring the fault generated by the certified Platinum Services program release and capturing key configuration parameters using Oracle fault-monitoring tools.

■ **Oracle Database monitoring**   Oracle will monitor the Oracle Database for faults in proper functioning. Oracle Database monitoring consists of monitoring the event information provided by the Oracle Database as recorded to log files and detected by custom-tuned monitors, and capturing key database configuration parameters using Oracle fault-monitoring tools.

■ **Accelerated response times**   Response times consist of 5-minute fault notification, 15-minute restoration or escalation to development, and 30-minute joint debugging with development.

■ **Patch deployment**   Oracle Platinum Services includes patching services in which Oracle applies patches to covered systems up to four times per year via the Oracle Advanced Support Gateway. To leverage this service, customers must upgrade to the latest release of the patch bundle for the Certified Platinum Configuration within six months of its availability and may not be more than two patch bundle releases behind the latest release, except 11.2.0.4 customers. Customers running 11.2.0.4 need to upgrade only to the latest release of the patch bundle for the Certified Platinum Configuration within 12 months of its availability and may not be more than four patch bundle releases behind the latest release to stay compliant. Oracle deploys the patch remotely either by rolling upgrade or by shutting down the components, depending on the patch and customer preference.

NOTE
Remote patch installations do not include Oracle Database version upgrades (such as 11.x to 12.x) or the installation of application-specific patch bundles for the Oracle Database—for example, SAP-specific patch bundles or E-Business Suite–specific patch. Platinum Services limits the number of databases that will be patched to eight databases on a full rack and four databases on a half, quarter, or eighth rack. But that doesn't mean Oracle won't patch other databases. Oracle will also patch additional databases for a nominal fee.

Summary

Exadata has three main building blocks: database servers, Exadata storage servers, and InfiniBand. Exadata comes preinstalled and preconfigured with RAC and ASM. Any application that is certified to run on an 11g R2 and 12.1 database can run on Exadata. Exadata comes in two flavors: Xn-2 and Xn-8. The Xn-2 is available in four configurations: eight, quarter, half, and full rack. Xn-8 is available in only one configuration: full rack. Eight Exadata machines can be connected together without additional cable. Each additional eight machines can be connected using a InfiniBand switch. Finally, Exadata comes with Platinum Services and the ASR feature for free.

CHAPTER
2

Exadata Hardware
Features

Exadata is an engineered system that is optimized to run Oracle databases. It is prebuilt, preconfigured, and tested at all the layers, thus eliminating the complexity of deploying a high-performance database system. All the Exadata machines are the same, and they are delivered ready to run, are identical to the configuration used by Oracle Engineering, are highly supportable, and can run both online transaction processing (OLTP) and DW applications. In this chapter, we will learn the "secret sauce" of the hardware that makes Exadata an engineered system. We have already covered the Exadata hardware basics in Chapter 1. In this chapter, we will discuss the hardware components in more detail.

Database Servers

The Exadata database servers consist of either a two-socket or eight-socket Oracle Sun Server. The current generation as of this writing is X4-2 or X4-8, respectively. Sun Server X4-2 or X4-8 is one of the most versatile servers from Oracle's offering for clustered computing, packing the optimal balance of compute power, memory capacity, and I/O capability. It is an ideal server for a wide range of mission-critical business applications designed and engineered to achieve the highest reliability for maximizing uptime.

Exadata version refresh occurs about every 18 to 24 months. The fast refreshes of these servers has allowed Exadata to stay on the cutting edge and provide increases in "horsepower" from one version to the next.

X4-2 Servers

The new Oracle Sun Server X4-2 is based on the Intel Xeon processor E5-2697 v2 product family. Compared to the Oracle Sun Server X3-2 included in the previous version of Exadata, the new X4-2 offers 50 percent more cores (12 cores per processor), which provides up to a 35 percent performance gain. The cores are much more powerful compared to previous generations.

The X4-2 has two processors, at 2.7 GHz, 12-core, and 130W, with four integrated DDR3 memory controllers per processor. It supports up to eight dual inline memory modules (DIMMs) per processor for a maximum of 16 DDR3 DIMMs and a maximum of 512GB of memory. The memory is organized in four channels per processor with two DIMMs per channel.

The physical layout of the DIMMs and processor(s) is shown in Figure 2-1. When you view the server from the front, processor 0 (P0) is on the left and processor 1 (P1) is on the right.

DIMMs are installed into DIMM sockets starting with P0 D0 and then alternating between sockets associated with processor 0 (P0) and matching sockets for processor 1 (P1), first filling the blue sockets and then the white. As shown in Figure 2-1, each processor has four channels and can support two DIMMs per channel. Each

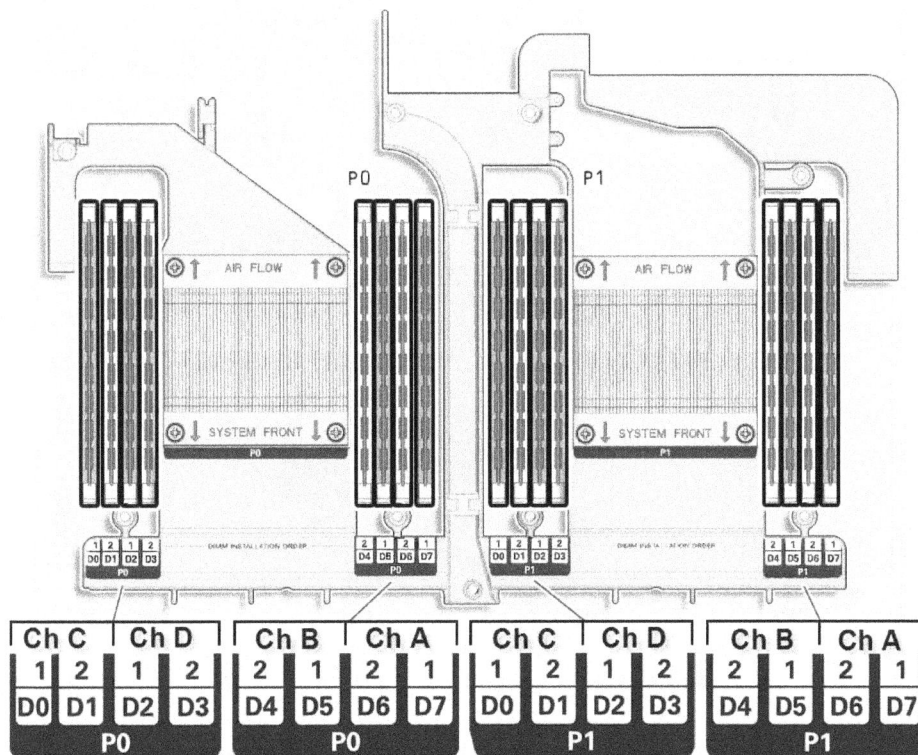

FIGURE 2-1. *Processor and memory in an X4-2 system*

processor (P0, P1) has eight associated DIMM sockets, numbered D0, D1, D2, D3, D4, D5, D6, and D7.

The default memory of the X4-2 is 256GB. Customers can optionally expand the memory by opting for the memory expansion kit, which changes memory configuration of the X4-2 database server from 256GB (16 × 16GB) to 512GB (16 × 32GB) and the DIMM size from 16GB to 32GB. The memory expansion kit is available for X4-2 full, half, quarter, and eighth racks.

Each of the 16 DDR3 DIMM sockets on the motherboard has an amber fault status indicator (LED) associated with it. If Oracle Integrated Lights Out Manager (ILOM) (discussed later in this chapter) determines that a DIMM is faulty, you can press the Fault Remind button, as shown in Figure 2-2, on the motherboard to signal the service processor to light the faulty LEDs, as shown in Figure 2-3 associated with the faulted DIMMs.

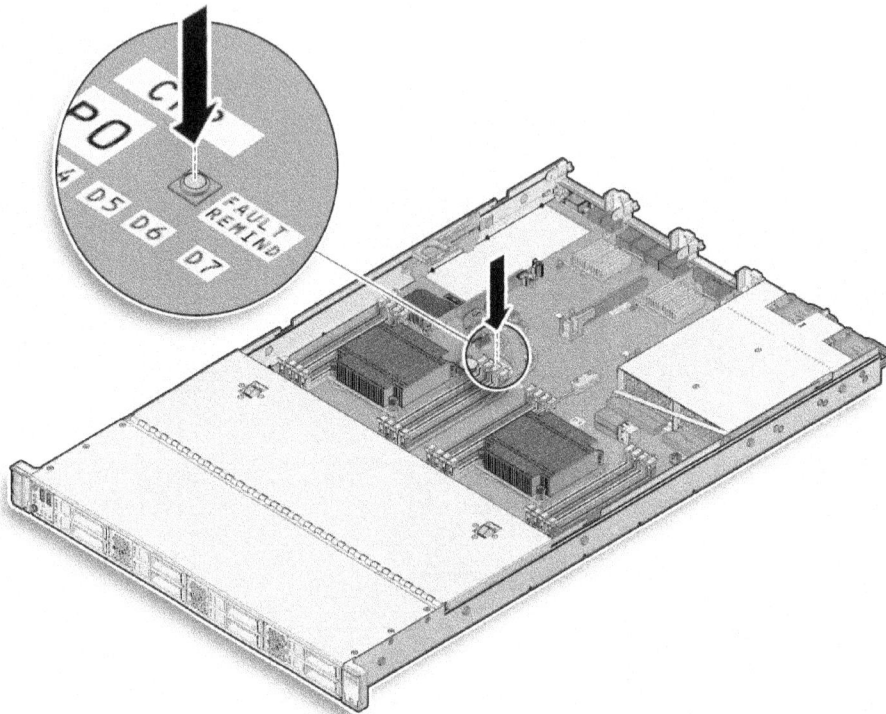

FIGURE 2-2. *Fault Remind button*

The motherboard includes a fault status indicator (LED) adjacent to each of the two processor sockets. These LEDs indicate when a processor is faulty. If it is determined that a processor is faulty, you can press the Fault Remind button on the motherboard to signal the service processor to light the faulty LED associated with the faulted processor. Figure 2-4 shows a faulty P1 processor in the motherboard.

TIP & TECHNIQUE
Because the Exadata machine has Intel-based processors, hyper-threading is turned on by default.

The X4-2 server has redundant hot-swappable power supplies and four 600GB 10K-RPM serial attached SCSI (SAS) disks (hot-swappable) hard drives, and a Disk Controller host bus adapter (HBA) with a 512MB battery-backed cache.

Table 2-1 shows a summary of the hardware of the X4-2 server.

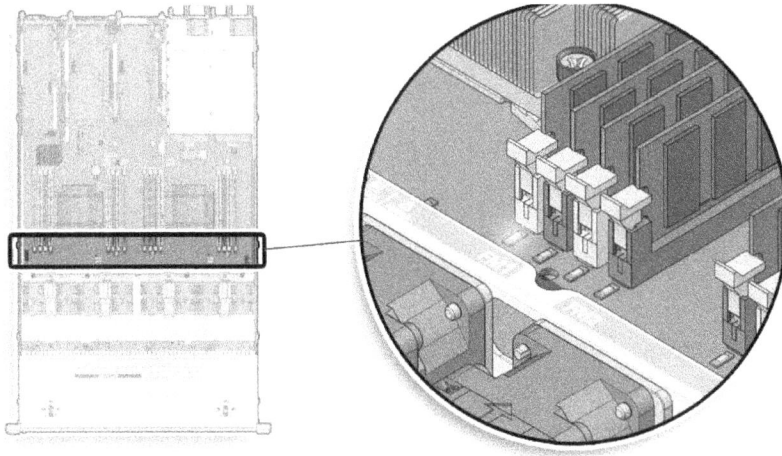

FIGURE 2-3. *Amber light for faulty DIMM*

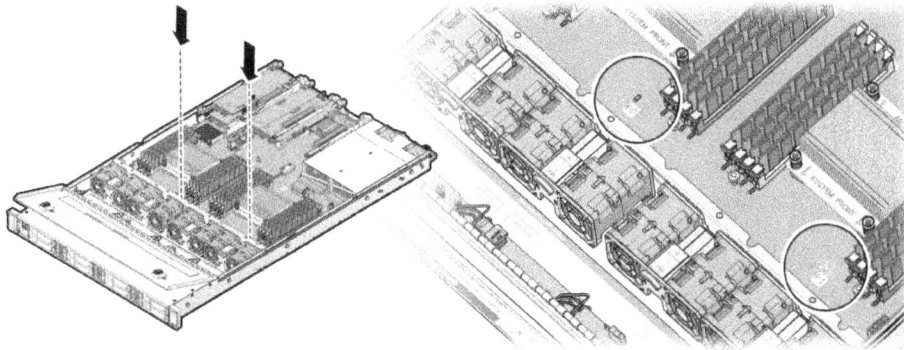

FIGURE 2-4. *Faulty processor*

Processors	Two 12-core Intel Xeon E5-2697 v2 processors (2.7GHz)
Memory	256GB (16×16GB), expandable to 512GB (16 × 32GB) via memory kits
Local Disks	Four 600GB 10K-RPM SAS disks (hot-swappable)
Disk Controller	Disk Controller HBA with 512MB cache – battery online replaceable
Network	Two InfiniBand 4X QDR (40 Gb/s) ports (PCIe 3.0) – both ports active Four 1GbE/10GbE Base-T Ethernet ports Two 10GbE Ethernet SFP+ ports (one dual-port 10GbE PCIe 2.0 network card based on the Intel 82599 10GbE Controller technology)
Remote Management	One Ethernet port (ILOM)
Power Supplies	Redundant hot-swappable power supplies and fans

TABLE 2-1. *X4-2 Hardware Summary*

X4-8 Servers

The CPU architecture for the X4-8 machines is bit different. X4-8 machines are bigger, more powerful machines with more processors. A compute node of an X4-8 machine contains eight processors, with fifteen core Intel Xeon E7-8895 processors (2.8 GHz) on each.

The X4-8 server comprises a chassis component, a CPU module (CMOD) component, and a subassembly module component. Figure 2-5 shows an X4-8 server subassembly module. The numbered elements are described in the text that follows.

Callout 1 identifies the chassis module, which contains the chassis, power supply, and the hard drives. The X4-8 server has four redundant hot-swappable power supplies and seven 600GB 10K-RPM SAS disks (hot-swappable) hard drives, and Disk Controller HBA with 512MB battery-backed cache.

Callout 2 identifies the CPU module, which contains the processing engines for the X4-8 server. Each CMOD contains two processors (CPUs), memory viz 32 DIMM slots, and I/O capabilities (Intel 7500 I/O Controller Hub [IOH]). Within this architecture, Intel QuickPath Interconnects (QPIs) support high-speed, low-latency communication between processors and from processors to IOHs. Four scalable memory interfaces on the die of Intel Xeon E7-8895 product family CPUs support fast data transfer to and from memory DIMMs. In addition, the Sun Server X4-8

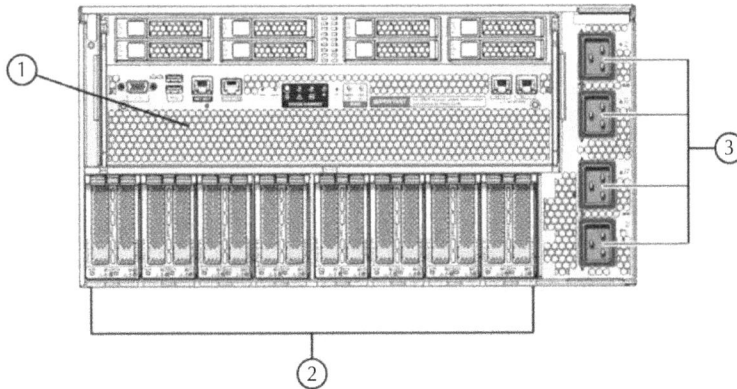

FIGURE 2-5.   *X4-8 subassembly module*

system uses the Intel Xeon chipset to establish connectivity to I/O components, including two network express modules (NEMs) and up to eight hot-swappable PCI express modules (EMs) for PCIe and Gigabit Ethernet.

The default memory of the X4-8 is 2TB. Customers can optionally expand the memory by opting for the memory expansion kit, which changes the memory configuration from 2TB (64 × 32GB) to 4TB (128 × 32GB) or 6TB (192 × 32GB).

The CMOD bay of the X4-8 server contains four CMODs. Callout 3 in Figure 2-5 indicates the subassembly module (SAM). The SAM provides the interconnect between the AC power input lines and the power supply. It also provides the midplane interconnect between the back-end components such as PCI express modules, network express modules, and so on, and the front-side components such as the hard drives and the CPU modules. The SAM also contains the cooling system for the CPU modules.

The CPU architecture of an X4-8 machine is shown in Figure 2-6. As discussed previously, the X4-8 system CPU module is a system board that supports two Intel Xeon E7-8895 product family CPUs and an I/O Controller Hub (IOH). The X4-8 system relies on a glueless design, eliminating any need for an interconnect switch between CMODs. The maximum distance between any two processors is two hops. Each CMOD includes a multiboard SMP Interconnect that plugs into a socket on the Sun Server X4-8 midplane to establish the QPI bus topology. An intelligent switch

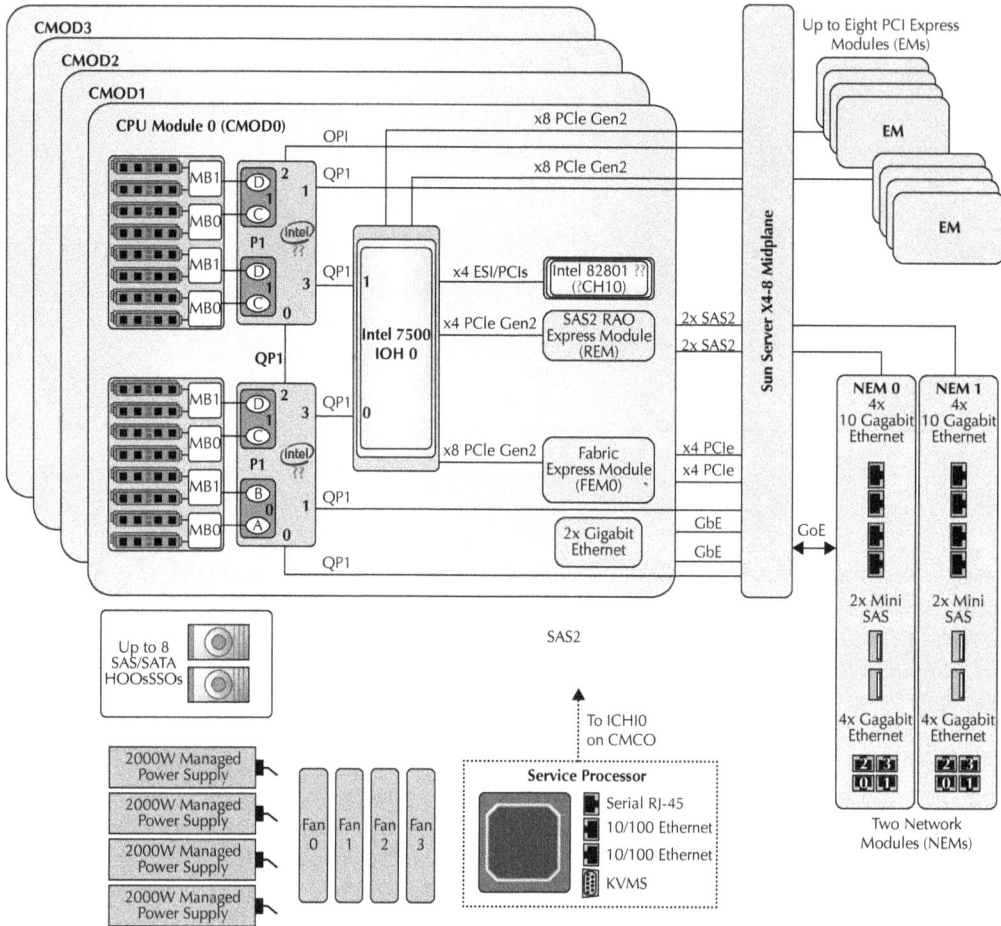

FIGURE 2-6. *CPU architecture of X4-8*

on each CMOD detects the current position of the CMOD within the X4-8 chassis. Based on this switching mechanism, the CMOD inserted into slot 0 gains connections that establish it as the master interface to the SAS-2 ports, the ILOM service processor, and the ICH10 chip that controls legacy interfaces.

Table 2-2 shows a summary of the hardware of the X4-8 server.

Processors	Eight 15-core Intel Xeon E7-8895 v2 processors (2.8 GHz)
Memory	2TB (64 × 32GB), expandable to 6TB (192 × 32GB)
Local Disks	Seven 600GB 10K-RPM SAS disks (hot-swappable)
Disk Controller	Disk Controller HBA with 512MB battery-backed cache – battery online replaceable
Network	Eight InfiniBand 4X QDR (40 Gb/s) Ports (PCIe 3.0) – both ports active Ten 1GbE Base-T Ethernet Ports (two Quad-port PCIe 2.0 network cards and two embedded ports based on the Intel I350 1GbE Controller technology) Eight 10GbE Ethernet SFP+ ports (four dual-port 10GbE PCIe 2.0 network cards based on the Intel 82599 10GbE Controller technology)
Remote Management	One Ethernet port (ILOM)
Power Supplies	Redundant hot-swappable power supplies and fans

TABLE 2-2.   *X4-8 Hardware Summary*

Storage Servers

The storage servers in an Exadata Machine are called Exadata Storage Servers or Storage Cells. The storage server works in conjunction with the database servers for processing the data. The hardware details of the storage server are given in the following sections.

Exadata Storage Server X4-2

The Exadata Storage Server is also based on Oracle Sun Server X4-2, which is the foundation for the X4-2 database compute nodes. The difference between the Database Server and the Storage Servers is the type of chipset in processor, the memory, and the number of physical disks. The Exadata Storage Server X4-2 consists of two, six-core Intel Xeon E5-2630 v2 processors (2.6 GHz) with 96GB of memory. The CPU architecture of the X4-2 Storage Server is exactly same as the compute nodes, so we won't discuss it again.

The Exadata Storage Server comes with two choices of disks—either high performance or high capacity. There are 12 hard drives in each Exadata Storage Server.

The high-performance SAS drive consists of 10K RPM of 1.2TB capacity each, whereas the high-capacity SAS drives are of 7.2K RPM with a capacity of 4TB in each drive. Both high-performance and high-capacity drives are hot-swappable. The high-performance drive is 2.5 inches in size, and the high-capacity drive is 3.5 inches in size. The disk controller HBA comes with a 512MB cache where the battery is online replaceable.

The Exadata Storage Server also comes with four PCI-based flash cards in each Storage Cell. The flash card that comes with the X4-2 Storage Server is a Sun Flash Accelerator F80. The Sun Flash Accelerator F80 PCIe card is a turnkey PCI-E 2.0, host bus adapter (HBA), low-profile, half-height, and half-length PCIe board form-factor flash memory storage card. These PCI-based flash cards are used for creating the Exadata Smart Flash Cache. Here are the important features of the F80 Flash Card:

- 800GB (1TB raw) capacity

- Over 155K read/133K write IOPS (8K)

- Over 2.1 GB/s throughput (1M)

- 84 microseconds write latency

- High write endurance

- End-to-end data integrity and power failure protection

- Proactive health and flash endurance monitoring

The Sun Flash Accelerator F80 PCIe card is a block storage device with block sizing optimization capabilities. The card offers high performance with low latency and a low CPU burden. The Sun Flash accelerator F80 PCIe card is designed with advanced enterprise multilevel cell NAND (eMLC) technology for high-level performance and write durability, providing higher capacity than SLC NAND cards.

The F80 card provides robust power failure protection and ensures data integrity after power failure events. The F80 cards have built-in arrays of capacitors that power the card in the event of system power failure. Figure 2-7 shows the F80 flash card. These capacitors can survive multiple consecutive power cycles. If there are any failures in the capacitor array, the embedded processor gets an interrupt and an event is sent to the host driver to indicate a backup rail monitor failure.

Table 2-3 shows a hardware summary of the Exadata Storage Server X4-2.

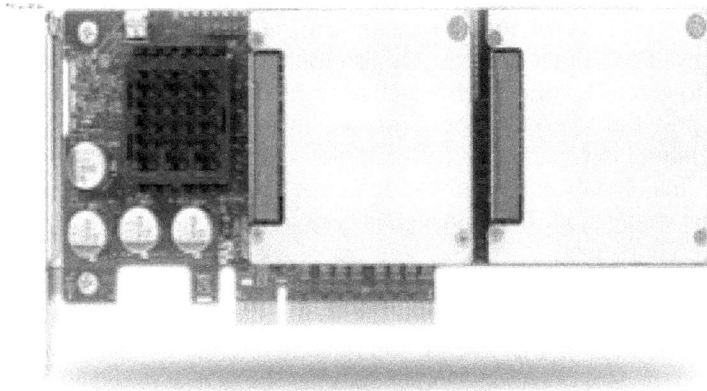

FIGURE 2-7.   *F80 flash card*

Processors	Two, six-core Intel Xeon E5-2630 v2 processors (2.6 GHz) – Faster clock
Memory	96GB (4 × 8GB + 4 × 16GB) – more memory needed to manage larger flash
Disks	Twelve 1.2TB 10K RPM high-performance SAS (hot-swap) – 2.5-inch disk size or Twelve 4TB 7.2K RPM high-capacity SAS (hot-swap) – 3.5-inch disk size
Flash	4 x 800GB Sun Flash Accelerator F80 PCIe cards – hardware compression
Disk Controller	Disk Controller HBA with 512MB cache – battery online replaceable
Network	Two InfiniBand 4X QDR (40Gb/s) ports (PCIe 3.0) – both ports active Embedded Gigabit Ethernet ports for management connectivity
Remote Management	One Ethernet port (ILOM)
Power Supplies	Redundant hot-swappable power supplies and fans

TABLE 2-3.   *Hardware Summary of Exadata Storage Server*

InfiniBand

The InfiniBand network is used for the connectivity between the database compute nodes and the Exadata Storage Servers. It is also used for the RAC interconnect traffic. It can be used to connect other systems such as Exalogic or ZFS storage appliances.

InfiniBand provides a very high-performance, low-latency network. The end-to-end latency in InfiniBand is equal to 1.07 microseconds. It provides 80 Gb/s bandwidth per link (40 Gb/s each direction). It provides SAN-like efficiency and zero-copy buffer reservation. The manageability of InfiniBand is very simple; it's just like managing an IP network.

InfiniBand runs on the Zero-copy Zero-loss Datagram Protocol (ZDP RDSv3). The Reliable Datagram Sockets (RDS) provide, in order, nonduplicating, highly reliable, highly available, low overhead, and reliable delivery of datagrams between hundreds of thousands of nonconnected endpoints. The RDS supports RDMA read and RDMA write.

The InfiniBand stack also runs Sockets Direct Protocol (SDP) and IP over InfiniBand Protocol (IPoIB). SDP is completely transparent to the application and uses SOCK_STREAM as a transport mechanism. It leverages the InfiniBand capabilities by providing transport offload for reliable connection, Zero copy using RDMA, kernel bypass, and very low latency. It uses the IBTA standard wire protocol. The SDP architecture is explained in Figure 2-8.

IPoIB is the IETF standard and does all the IP transmission over IB. It is not as efficient as SDP because it doesn't provide the Zero copy using RDMA. It maps the

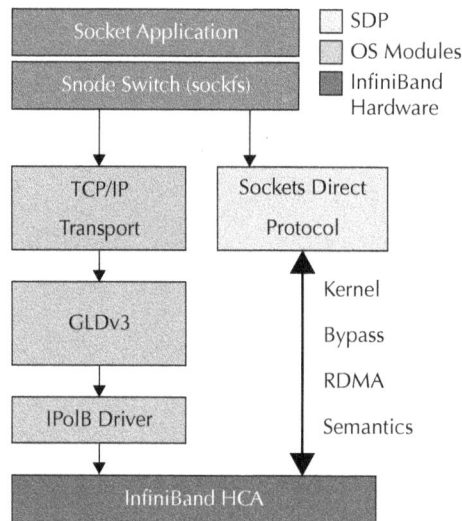

FIGURE 2-8. *SDP architecture*

IP subnet to the IB partition. It provides features such as TCP checksum offload and LSO (Large Send Offload) and uses IPMP (IP Network Multipathing) for high availability. The IPoIB architecture is shown in Figure 2-9.

The Exadata machine uses Sun Datacenter 36-port Managed QDR InfiniBand switches. The InfiniBand switches in the middle of the machines are called *leaf switches*. There are two leaf switches in each rack, which provide redundant connectivity of servers within the rack. The IB switch in the bottom of the rack is called a *spine switch*. There is only one spine switch per rack. The spine switch is used for switch-to-switch connectivity across racks.

TIP & TECHNIQUE
When you're connecting multiple racks of Exadata, both leaf switches and spine switches should be used to connect multiple racks, instead of using only the spine switches, to avoid single point of failure.

The Database Server Compute nodes and Exadata Storage Servers each have a dual-port QDR InfiniBand HCA for InfiniBand connectivity. The X4-8 server has four dual-port HCAs. It provides active-active bonding by assigning two IP addresses per dual-port HCA for the X4-2/X4-8 database and X4-2 storage servers. It is recommended that you connect one port from the HCA to one leaf switch and the other port to the second leaf switch for redundancy. By default, all the connections are prewired in the factory. Figures 2-10 and 2-11 show the leaf connections for the X4-2 and X4-8, respectively.

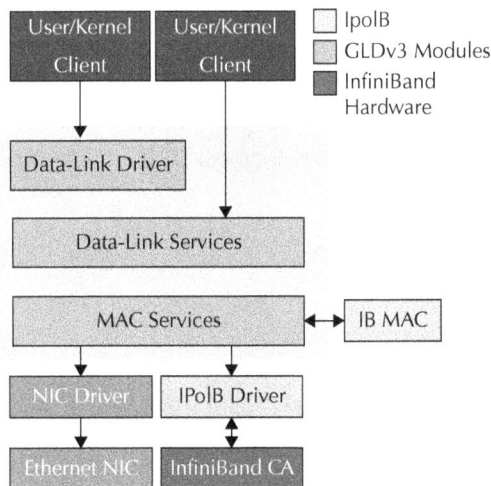

FIGURE 2-9. *IPoIB architecture*

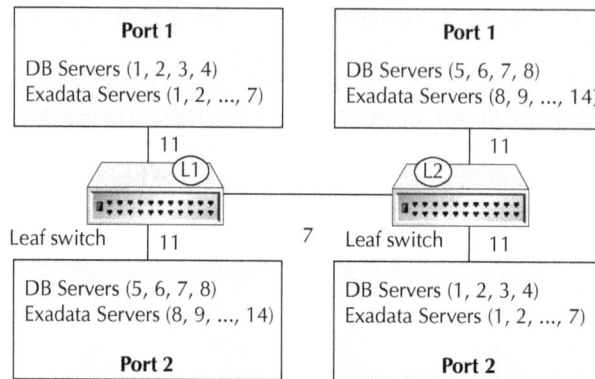

FIGURE 2-10. *X4-2 leaf connections*

As discussed previously, when connecting multiple racks, you need to use both the leaf switches and the spine switches. Oracle recommends both to connect multiple racks using the "fat tree" topology, which works like so:

- Every leaf switch is interconnected with every spine switch.

- Leaf switches are not connected with other leaf switches.

- Spine switches are not connected with other spine switches.

- Database and Exadata Server cabling is unchanged.

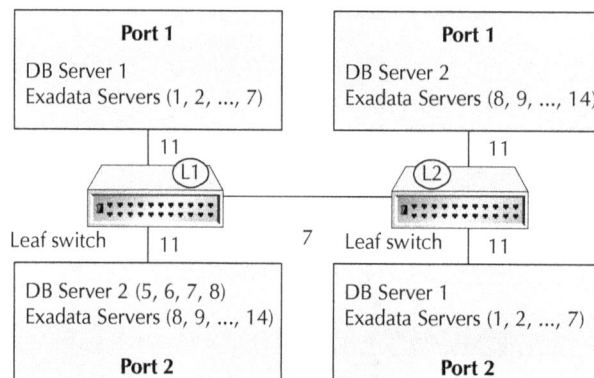

FIGURE 2-11. *X4-8 leaf connections*

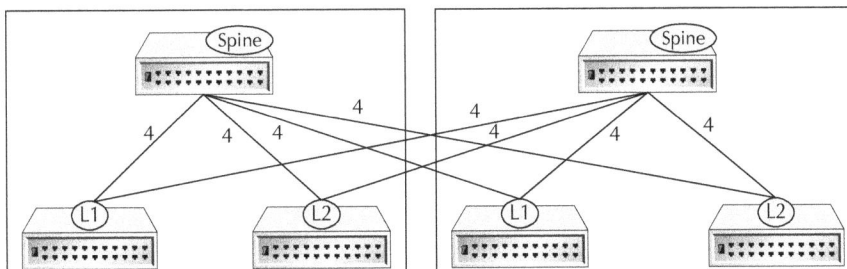

FIGURE 2-12. *Two-rack fat tree topology*

The fat tree topology is shown in the following two figures. Figure 2-12 depicts two racks connected together. If the spine switch doesn't exist, it needs to be installed before two racks can be connected together. In this figure, the leaf switch and spine switch are connected using four links per pair.

Figure 2-13 shows the fat tree topology when multiple racks (up to eight) are connected. The spine switch needs to be installed if it doesn't exist. In this case, the eight links need to be distributed from every leaf switch to every spine switch.

If you need to connect more than eight racks, additional InfiniBand switches are needed. The overall method and logic remain the same.

Six ports in each of the two leaf switches per Exadata rack are available for external connectivity, such as Exalogic, ZFS SA, Media Server, and so on. The port numbers are 5B, 6A, 6B, 7A, 7B, and 12A per leaf switch (total 12 per rack).

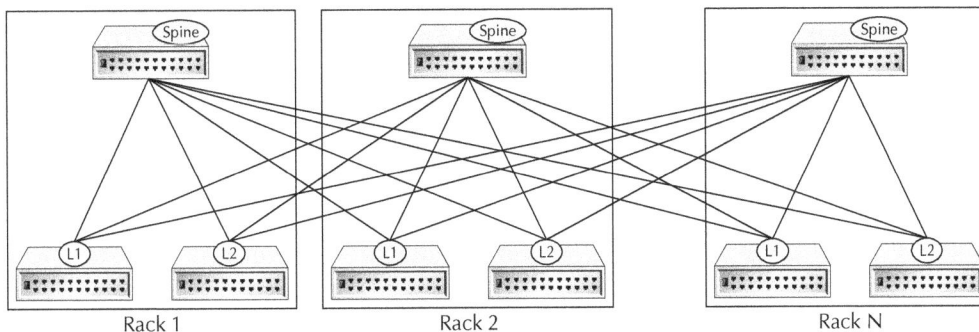

FIGURE 2-13. *Up to eight-rack fat tree topology*

Ethernet Network

One Cisco 1Gb Ethernet "Admin" switch is pre-installed and pre-cabled in each rack. This switch is connected to multiple ports:

- Connected to hardware management ports of each server
  - ILOM port on the Exadata Storage Servers and Database Servers
- Connected to software management ports of each server
  - eth0 on Exadata Storage Server
  - eth0 on the Database Server
  - For software admin, root access
- Connected to InfiniBand switch management ports
- Connected to the data center administration network (one port)

Power Distribution Units

Each rack comes with two redundant power distribution units (PDUs). Four different PDUs are available to choose from.

For X4-2 Machines

The low-voltage 15 kVA single-phase (Americas/Japan/Taiwan) machine comes with the following configuration:

- Two 72A 15 kVA PDUs
- Six power plugs (three 30A plugs per PDU)
- 200–240VAC
- NEMA L6-30R data center receptacle type

The low-voltage 15 kVA three-phase (Americas/Japan/Taiwan) machine comes with the following configuration:

- Two 69A 15 kVA PDUs
- Two power plugs (one 60A plug per PDU)

- 200–208VAC 3ph

- IEC309-3P4W-IP67 60A 250VAC 3ph (Hubbell equivalent is HBL460R9W) data center receptacle type

The high-voltage 15 kVA single-phase (EMEA/APAC, excluding Japan/Taiwan) machine comes with the following configuration:

- Two 72A 15 kVA PDUs

- Six power plugs (three 25A plugs per PDU)

- 220–240VAC

- IEC309-2P3W-IP44 32A 250VAC (Hubbell equivalent is HBL332R6W) data center receptacle type

The high-voltage 15 kVA three-phase (EMEA/APAC, excluding Japan/Taiwan) machine comes with the following configuration:

- Two 62.7A 15 kVA PDUs

- Two power plugs (one 25A plug per PDU)

- 220/380–240/415VAC

- IEC309-4P5W-IP44 32A 400VAC 3ph (Hubbell equivalent is HBL532R6W) data center receptacle type

For X4-8 Machines

The low-voltage 22 kVA single-phase (Americas/Japan/Taiwan) machine comes with the following configuration:

- Two 110.4A 22 kVA PDUs

- Six power plugs (three 36.8A plugs per PDU)

- 200–240VAC

- Hubbell CS8265C data center receptacle type

The low-voltage 24 kVA three-phase (Americas/Japan/Taiwan) machine comes with the following configuration:

- Two 120A 24 kVA PDUs

- Four power plugs (2 × 60A plug per PDU)

- 200–208VAC 3ph

- IEC309-3P4W-IP67 60A 250VAC 3ph (Hubbell equivalent is HBL460R9W) data center receptacle type

The high-voltage 22 kVA single-phase (EMEA/APAC, excluding Japan/Taiwan) machine comes with the following configuration:

- Two 96A 22 kVA PDUs

- Six power plugs (three 32A plugs per PDU)

- 220–240VAC

- IEC309-2P3W-IP44 32A 250VAC (Hubbell equivalent is HBL332R6W) data center receptacle type

The high-voltage 24 kVA three-phase (EMEA/APAC, excluding Japan/Taiwan) machine comes with the following configuration:

- Two 109A 24 kVA PDUs

- Four power plugs (two 25A plug per PDU)

- 220/380–240/415VAC

- IEC309-4P5W-IP44 32A 400VAC 3ph (Hubbell equivalent is HBL532R6W) data center receptacle type

Environment Information

The environment information for the Exadata Machines is provided in Tables 2-4, 2-5, and 2-6.

X4-2 High-Capacity Disks

		X4-2 Full HC	X4-2 Half HC	X4-2 Quarter HC	X4-2 Eighth HC
Power	Max	11.2 kW (11.4 kVA)	6.2 kW (6.3 kVA)	3.1 kW (3.2 kVA)	2.8 kW (2.9 kVA)
	Typical	7.9 kW (8.1 kVA)	4.3 kW (4.4 kVA)	2.2 kW (2.3 kVA)	2.0 kW (2.1 kVA)
Cooling	Max	38,300 BTU/hr 40,400 kJ/hr	21, 200 BTU/hr 22, 400 kJ/hr	10,600 BTU/hr 11,200 kJ/hr	9,500 BTU/hr 10,000 kJ/hr
	Typical	27,000 BTU/hr 28,500 kJ/hr	14,700 BTU/hr 15,500 kJ/hr	7,500 BTU/hr 7,900 kJ/hr	6,600 BTU/hr 7,000 kJ/hr
Airflow: front-to-back	Max (CFM)	1780	980	490	440
	Typical (CFM)	1250	680	350	310
Weight	Rack	1880 lbs (852.8 kgs)	1158 lbs (525.3 kgs)	806 lbs (365.6 kgs)	806 lbs (365.6 kgs)
	Shipping Wt	2064 lbs (936.2 kgs)	1273 lbs (577.4 kgs)	883 lbs (400.5 kgs)	883 lbs (400.5 kgs)
Acoustics		9.3B (operating)	8.9B (operating)	8.5B (operating)	8.5B (operating)
Dimensions		78.66" (H) × 23.62" (W) × 47.24" (D) [1998 mm (H) x 600 mm (W) × 1200 mm (D)]			
Operating Temperature		5°C to 32°C (41°F to 89.6°F), 10% to 90% relative humidity, non-condensing Altitude Operating: Up to 3048 m, max. ambient temperature is derated by 1°C per 300 m above 900 m			

TABLE 2-4. *X4-2 HC Environment*

Exadata X4-2 High-Performance Disk

		X4-2 Full HP	X4-2 Half HP	X4-2 Quarter HP	X4-2 Eighth HP
Power	Max	12.1 kW (12.4 kVA)	6.6 kW (6.8 kVA)	3.3 kW (3.4 kVA)	3.0 kW (3.1 kVA)
	Typical	8.5 kW (8.7 kVA)	4.7 kW (4.8 kVA)	2.4 kW (2.5 kVA)	2.1 kW (2.2 kVA)
Cooling	Max	41,300 BTU/hr 43,600 kJ/hr	22,500 BTU/hr 23,750 kJ/hr	11,300 BTU/hr 11,900 kJ/hr	10,200 BTU/hr 10,700 kJ/hr
	Typical	29,000 BTU/hr 30,600 kJ/hr	16,000 BTU/hr 16,900 kJ/hr	8,200 BTU/hr 8,700 kJ/hr	7, 100 BTU/hr 7, 500 kJ/hr
Airflow: front-to-back	Max (CFM)	1900	1050	520	470
	Typical (CFM)	1350	750	365	325
Weight	Rack	1880 lbs (852.8 kgs)	1158 lbs (525.3 kgs)	806 lbs (365.6 kgs)	806 lbs (365.6 kgs)
	Shipping Wt	2064 lbs (936.2 kgs)	1273 lbs (577.4 kgs)	883 lbs (400.5 kgs)	883 lbs (400.5 kgs)
Acoustics		9.3B (operating)	8.9B (operating)	8.5B (operating)	8.5B (operating)
Dimensions		78.66" (H) x 23.62" (W) × 47.24" (D) [1998 mm (H) × 600 mm (W) × 1200 mm (D)]			
Operating Temperature		5°C to 32°C (41°F to 89.6°F), 10% to 90% relative humidity, non-condensing. Altitude Operating: Up to 3048 m, max. ambient temperature is derated by 1°C per 300 m above 900 m			

TABLE 2-5. *X4-2 HP Environment*

Exadata X4-8 High-Performance and High-Capacity Drive

		X4-8 Full HP	X4-8 Full HC
Power	Max	15.0 kW (15.3 kVA)	14.4 kW (14.7 kVA)
	Typical	10.5 kW (10.7 kVA)	10.1 kW (10.3 kVA)
Cooling	Max	51,200 BTU/hr 54,000 kJ/hr	49,110 BTU/hr 52,000 kJ/hr
	Typical	36,400 BTU/hr 38,400 kJ/hr	34,400 BTU/hr 36,300 kJ/hr
Airflow: front-to-back	Max (CFM)	2410	2280
	Typical (CFM)	1700	1600
Weight	Rack	1912 lbs (867.3 kgs)	2063 lbs (935.8 kgs)
	Shipping Wt	2097 lbs (951 kgs)	2247 lbs (1019.2 kgs)
Acoustics		9.3B (operating)	9.3B (operating)
Dimensions		78.66" (H) × 23.62" (W) × 47.24" (D) [1998 mm (H) × 600 mm (W) x 1200 mm (D)]	
Operating Temperature		5°C to 32°C (41°F to 89.6°F), 10% to 90% relative humidity, non-condensing. Altitude Operating: Up to 3, m, max. ambient temperature is derated by 1°C per 300 m above 900 m	

TABLE 2-6. *X4-8 HC and HP Environment*

Summary

This chapter has presented the hardware details for all the components of an Exadata Machine:

- X4-2 Database Server has two processors with 12 cores, each with 256GB RAM.

- X4-8 Database Server has eight processors with 15 cores, each with 2TB RAM.

- X4-2 Storage Server has two processors with six cores, each with 96GB RAM.

- Each Exadata Storage Server contains four flash cards with 800GB capacity.

- The InfiniBand switches in the middle of the machines are called leaf switches; there are two leaf switches in a machine. The IB switch in the bottom of the machine is called the spine switch. There can be only one spine switch per machine.

- A Cisco switch comes with the Exadata Machine and can be connected to the management network.

CHAPTER
3

Exadata Software Features

Oracle Exadata is the latest database machine from Oracle and has been the fastest growing product in Oracle's history. Today, Exadata is being used everywhere for data warehousing, online transaction processing (OLTP), database consolidation, Real Application Clusters (RAC), and even enterprise resource planning (ERP) systems like Oracle E-Business Suite and Siebel. Exadata is optimized to achieve enterprise performance levels that are unmatched in the industry. Faster time to production is achieved by implementing pre-engineered and pre-assembled hardware and software bundles. With an inclusive "in-a-box" strategy, Oracle's Exadata systems combine best-of-breed hardware and software components with game-changing technical innovations. Designed, engineered, and tested to work best together, Oracle's Exadata systems can power the cloud or streamline data center operations to make traditional deployments even more efficient. Exadata is pre-assembled for targeted functionality and then—as a complete system—optimized for extreme performance. By taking the guesswork out of these high-availability, purpose-built solutions, Oracle delivers a sophisticated simplicity that's completely integrated throughout every layer of the technology stack—a simplicity that translates into less risk and lower costs for the business. In this chapter we will go through the features of Exadata software that make it unique and different from all the competitors' products.

Hybrid Columnar Compression (HCC)

Compressing data can provide dramatic reduction in the storage consumed by large databases. Exadata provides a very advanced compression capability called Exadata Hybrid Columnar Compression (HCC). Exadata HCC enables the highest levels of data compression and provides enterprises with tremendous cost savings and performance improvements due to reduced I/O. In an organization, HCC helps reduce the data storage footprint.

Its name specifies that it's a hybrid—that is, it's not pure columnar compression. In purely columnar storage, grouping is accomplished at the columnar level—for example, all the values for column 1 for all the rows will be stored together, all the values for column 2 for all the rows will be stored together, and so on. In HCC, a subset of a row is chosen, and within that subset, each column is stored separately. It's also called a hybrid because it allows updates by placing updated rows into uncompressed blocks.

HCC is a second-generation columnar technology that combines the best of row and column formats to provide compression levels that match full columnar, excellent scan times that are as good as full columnar, and good single-row lookup.

The subset of rows into which the physical data is organized are called *compression units* (CUs). Within a CU, the data is organized by column instead of by row, and then the data is compressed. Organizing the data by column brings

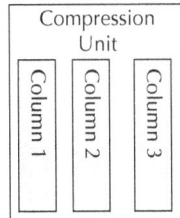

FIGURE 3-1. *Compression unit*

similar values close to each other and thus enhances the compression. Figure 3-1 shows a compression unit.

Let's examine in more detail how HCC works. Table 3-1 shows data for the inventory of three major components in three company stores.

The rows from the inventory table will be stored as one unit. HCC stores each unique value from the column Store_Code with metadata that maps the values to the rows. Thus, the compressed value after implementing HCC will look like this:

CALIFORNIA001CALIFORNIA002CALIFORNIA003

The database then compresses the repeated word CALIFORNIA in this value by storing it once and replacing each occurrence with a reference. If the reference is smaller than the original word, then the database achieves compression. The compression benefit is particularly evident for the Date column, which contains only one unique value.

Store_Code	Item_Code	Date	Quantity
CALIFORNIA001	5350	26-Apr-14	982218
CALIFORNIA002	5350	26-Apr-14	88182
CALIFORNIA003	5350	26-Apr-14	199010
CALIFORNIA001	2296	26-Apr-14	399299
CALIFORNIA002	2296	26-Apr-14	290300
CALIFORNIA003	2296	26-Apr-14	923012
CALIFORNIA001	3109	26-Apr-14	22112
CALIFORNIA002	3109	26-Apr-14	23940
CALIFORNIA003	3109	26-Apr-14	33491

TABLE 3-1. *Inventory Table*

A compression unit can span multiple data blocks. The values for a particular column may or may not span multiple blocks. Figure 3-2 shows compression unit spanning multiple data blocks.

These CUs are larger than the database blocks—usually 32K in size. The type of compression algorithm chosen mainly governs the size of the CU.

Any operation of work, such as loading, reading, inserting, updating, deleting, and so on, happens in a CU. It is possible to access a particular row within a CU, but for that we first need to read the CU and then fetch that particular row from the CU. So it's an abstraction at a higher level than a block. A CU is a self-contained unit of one or more rows. Thus, a CU has information about all the rows contained in it. There is no need to look for the information about those rows anywhere outside the CU. The CU looks like a very long row.

CUs are stored like a chained row. Suppose the size of the CU is 32K and the block size is 8K. The CU is stored in a single column across multiple blocks. The row has an appropriate header already, so there is no need to change the row header for HCC. A flag in the row header indicates whether a single column does not fit in a block and spills over to the next block. In HCC, the flag is reused.

Given a small set of rows, the creation of the CU involves the following steps:

1. Buffer this subset of rows.

2. Divide them by column.

3. A column is selected for the set of rows and they are compressed using a certain algorithm.

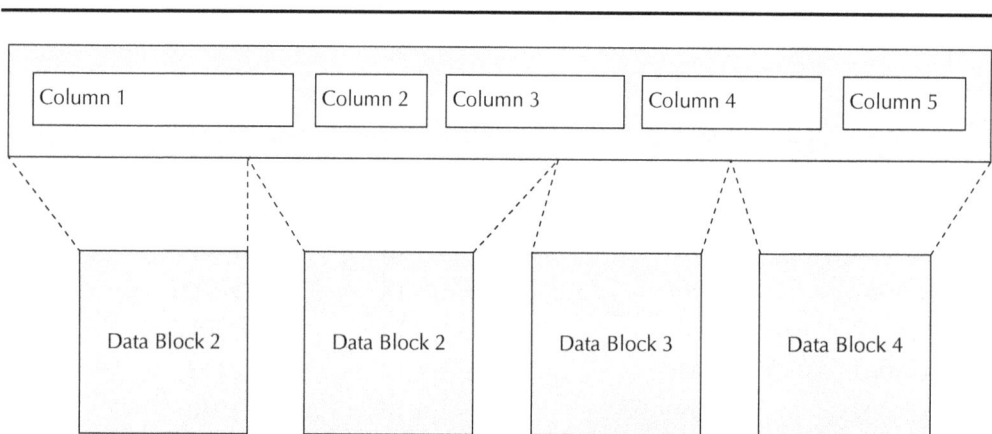

FIGURE 3-2. *Compression unit spanning multiple data blocks*

4. The next column is selected, and then the values of the next column, say column 2, are selected from the set of rows and compressed using a compression algorithm. The compression algorithm used in the second column can be different from the compression algorithm used in the first column.

5. The same steps are repeated until all the columns' CUs are stored.

When all the columns are compressed, the top-level compression unit (CU header) and the offsets to the column CU pointing to each column are updated. The CU header and the offsets to the column CU are stored uncompressed. The offsets of the column CU are used for the random access of data. If the data is requested only for one or two columns, then during data fetch, the offsets are used to obtain the information, and a data scan happens only for the requested columns instead of scanning all the column CUs.

For each column, an initial transformation to the data is applied, followed by a standard compression algorithm. Depending on the data, in some cases, transformation or compression may not be applied at all. The following list shows the transformations that are typically applied to the data before the compression algorithm is implemented. Transformation of data helps to increase the compression ratio for standard algorithms.

- **Length/Value**   Separation of length and value may not by itself result in any compression. Since the length could be the same or could be in a small range, by storing all the lengths together, the standard compression algorithm can do a much better job. This is a standard Oracle column format.

- **Length Separated**   The length of each column is stored separately, and the value of each column is stored separately. Thus, there will be a length vector for each column and a corresponding value. If the length is constant for a large run, then the length is stored just once, thereby providing very good compression.

- **Run-Length Encoded**   If a single value is repeated multiple times, the value is stored only once and a note of the occurrence (run) of that value is noted. This provides a very good compression ratio when the runs are very large, and provides very good decompression results as well.

- **Delta**   Delta doesn't provide compression by itself, since the number of bytes stored does not change, but it helps to improve the efficiency of the compression algorithm. The delta used in transformation is a byte-wise delta and not number-wise.

- **Length-Separated Delta**   In a length-separated delta, the length and the value are stored separately, and then the delta is applied on each individually.

HCC uses three compression algorithms internally:

- **LZO** LZO (Lempel-Ziv-Oberhumer) is a portable lossless data compression library written in ANSI C. LZO offers pretty fast compression and extremely fast decompression. Decompression requires no memory. LZO provides lower compression ratios compared to other compression algorithms. The LZO algorithms and implementations are copyrighted open source applications distributed under the GNU General Public License. For more information about LZO, see www.oberhumer.com/opensource/lzo/.

- **zlib** The zlib compression library provides in-memory compression and decompression functions, including integrity checks of the uncompressed data (www.zlib.net). The compression speed of zlib is lower than that of LZO but higher than BZ2, and the compression ratio is better than that of LZO but lower than BZ2.

- **bzip2, or BZ2** BZ2 compresses files using the Burrows-Wheeler block-sorting text compression algorithm and Huffman coding. It provides slower compression and decompression speed than zlib and LZO but offers higher compression ratios than either. For more information about BZ2 compression, see www.bzip.org.

HCC is fully supported with the following operations:

- B-Tree, bitmap indexes, text indexes

- Materialized views

- Exadata server and cells, including offload

- Partitioning

- Parallel query, Packet Details Markup Language (PDML), Planning Domain Definition Language (PDDL)

- Schema evolution support, online, metadata-only add/drop columns

- Data Guard physical standby support

The HCC can be implemented at the table level, partition level, and tablespace level. While data in Hybrid Columnar compressed tables can be modified using conventional Data Manipulation Language (DML) operations—Insert, Update, Delete—performing such operations could result in a reduction of the HCC compression ratio. It is recommended that HCC be enabled on tables or partitions with no or infrequent DML operations. If frequent DML operations are planned on a table or partition, the Oracle Advanced Compression Option is better suited for such data.

Exadata offers two types of compression: warehouse compression and online archival compression. You can choose either of them depending on your requirements and the type of application you will be running.

Warehouse Compression

Warehouse compression, also known as query compression, is optimized for query performance, and is intended for data warehouse applications. This mode is known as Query mode. COMPRESS FOR QUERY is useful in data warehousing environments. Valid values are LOW and HIGH, with HIGH (the default) providing a higher compression ratio. The increased storage savings may cause data load times to increase modestly. Therefore, warehouse compression LOW should be chosen for environments where load time service levels are more critical than query performance.

The CU size, compression algorithm, and transformations used for warehouse compression are shown in Table 3-2.

The warehouse compression syntax is

```
CREATE TABLE emp        (…)
COMPRESS FOR QUERY      [LOW |      HIGH];
```

Online Archival Compression

COMPRESS FOR ARCHIVE uses higher compression ratios than COMPRESS FOR QUERY and is useful for compressing data that will be stored for long periods of time. Valid values are LOW (the default) and HIGH, with HIGH providing the highest possible compression ratio. In contrast to warehouse compression, archive compression is a pure storage-saving technology. Tables or partitions using archive compression typically experience a decrease in performance—a factor of the compression algorithm being optimized for maximum storage savings. Therefore, archive compression is intended for tables or partitions that store data that is rarely

Level	Target CU Size	Algorithm	Transformations
Query Low	32K	LZO	Len/Val, Len Sep, RLE
Query High	32–64K	ZLIB	Len/Val, Len Sep, RLE, Delta, Len Sep Delta

TABLE 3-2.   *Warehouse Compression Details*

Level	Target CU Size	Algorithm	Transformations
Archive Low	32–256K	ZLIB	Len/Val, Len Sep, RLE, Delta, Len Sep Delta
Archive High	256K	BZ2	Len/Val, Len Sep, RLE, Delta, Len Sep Delta

TABLE 3-3. *Online Archival Compression Details*

accessed. It benefits any application with data retention requirements and is the best approach for Information Lifecycle Management (ILM) and data archival.

The CU size, compression algorithm, and transformations used for online archival compression are shown in Table 3-3.

The online archival compression syntax is

```
CREATE TABLE emp       (…)
COMPRESS FOR ARCHIVE  [LOW  |  HIGH];
```

Implementing HCC

Let's use an example to see how easy it is to create compressed tables and evaluate the compression ratio. In this example we will take a uncompressed table and apply HCC to it and will evaluate the compression ratio.

```
SQL>select segment_name , sum(bytes)/1024/1024 MB
2   from user_segments
3   where segment_name ='CUSTOMER';

SEGMENT NAME         MB
--------------------- ----
CUSTOMER             8822

SQL>select table_name, compression from user_tables where
2   table_name='CUSTOMER';

TABLE_NAME           COMPRESSION
--------------------- -----------
CUSTOMER             DISABLED
```

You can see that the current size of the table is 8822MB, and currently the compression is not enabled in this table. Let's enable the compression in this table and compress it using both methodologies.

Exadata HCC achieves its highest level of compression with data that is direct-path inserted. The `alter session` commands ensure the use of direct-path inserts later, when the compression tables are created.

```
SQL> alter session force parallel query;

Session altered.

SQL> alter session force parallel dml;

Session altered.

SQL> alter session force parallel ddl;

Session altered.
```

The next statements create compressed copies of the CUSTOMER table using Exadata HCC. The first statement uses the QUERY HIGH warehouse compression mode. The second statement uses the ARCHIVE HIGH archive compression mode.

```
SQL> Create table CUSTOMER_QUERY compress for query high
2     parallel 16 as select * from CUSTOMER;

Table Created

SQL> Create table CUSTOMER_ARCHIVE compress for archive high
2     parallel 16 as select * from CUSTOMER;

Table Created
```

The column `COMPRESS_FOR` confirms compression and indicates the type of compression being used.

```
SQL> select table_name , compression , compress_for from
2     from user_tables
3     where tablename like 'CUST%';

TABLE_NAME               COMPRESS    COMPRESS_FOR
----------------------   ---------   ------------
CUSTOMER_QUERY           ENABLED     QUERY HIGH
CUSTOMER_ARCHIVE         ENABLED     ARCHIVE HIGH
CUSTOMER                 DISABLED
```

Here is the comparison showing the space used by the uncompressed and compressed tables.

```
SQL> select segment_name,sum(bytes)/1024/1024 MB
2     from user_segments
```

```
3    where segment_name like 'CUST%'
4    group by segment_name;

SEGMENT_NAME                          MB
----------------------------------- --------
CUSTOMER_QUERY                      773.875
CUSTOMER                            8822
CUSTOMER_ARCHIVE                    501.937
```

With the data used in this example, the following compression ratios are achieved:

```
QUERY compression      11.3:1
ARCHIVE compression    17.5:1
```

Compression ratios are data dependent and will vary significantly based on the data in the table. All the internal benchmarks show that an average customer gets around a 10X compression ratio.

As discussed previously, HCC can be implemented at the table level, partition level, and tablespace level. The tables can be created as HCC tables, and once the data is loaded in the table, it is automatically compressed as per the compression definition. If the table is not created with the compression clause initially, then the data can be compressed in the existing tables at a later stage. The following statement will change the attribute of existing tables and will enable HCC in it:

```
SQL> alter table sales compress for query|archive low|high;
```

Doing this won't compress the data, however. For that, we need to move the table.

```
SQL> alter table sales move;
```

The HCC can be implemented at the partition level as well. In the same table, different partitions can use different compression algorithms. A table can also have both compressed and uncompressed partitions. An example is shown here:

```
SQL> CREATE TABLE sales (item varchar(2)not null, inv_code  number not
null,    sales_dt  date  not null)
PARTITION BY RANGE (sales_dt)
( partition sale01 VALUES LESS THAN(TO_DATE('2013-01-01', 'yyyy-mm-
dd')) COMPRESS FOR archive high,
 partition sale02 VALUES LESS THAN(TO_DATE('2013-02-01', 'yyyy-mm-dd'))
COMPRESS FOR archive low,
 partition sale03 VALUES LESS THAN(TO_DATE('2013-03-01', 'yyyy-mm-dd'))
COMPRESS FOR query high,
 partition sale04 VALUES LESS THAN(TO_DATE('2013-04-01', 'yyyy-mm-dd'))
COMPRESS FOR query low,
 partition sale05 VALUES LESS THAN(TO_DATE('2013-05-01', 'yyyy-mm-dd'))
NOCOMPRESS
);
```

If HCC is not enabled in a partition, it can be enabled at a later stage. To change the compression method for new data only, use the following command:

```
ALTER TABLE ... MODIFY PARTITION ... COMPRESS..
```

To change the compression method for both new and existing data, use the following command:

```
ALTER TABLE ... MOVE PARTITION ... COMPRESS..

ALTER TABLE sales MOVE PARTITION sales06 COMPRESS FOR ARCHIVE LOW;
```

If you use the MOVE statement, the local indexes for partition sales06 become unusable. It needs to be rebuilt.

```
ALTER TABLE sales  MODIFY PARTITION sales06 REBUILD UNUSABLE LOCAL INDEXES;
```

Similarly, a tablespace can be created with HCC enabled. Any tables created in that tablespace will inherit the compression attribute of the tablespace.

```
create bigfile tablespace sales  datafile '+DATA' compress for  query low;
```

Thus, any table created under the sales tablespace will have "compressed for query low" enabled automatically. However, the data in those tables will be compressed with the HCC algorithm only if they are loaded in "bulk" (insert/append, direct path load, and so on).

In the DBA_TABLES and USER_TABLES data dictionary views, compressed tables have been ENABLED in the COMPRESSION column. For partitioned tables, this column is null, and the COMPRESSION column of the DBA_TAB_PARTITIONS or USER_TAB_PARTITIONS views indicates the partitions that are compressed. In addition, the COMPRESS_FOR column indicates the compression method in use for the table or partition.

```
SQL> SELECT table_name, compression, compress_for FROM user_tables;
TABLE_NAME         COMPRESSION   COMPRESS_FOR
---------------- ------------ -----------------
TABLE1             DISABLED
TABLE2             ENABLED       BASIC
TABLE3             ENABLED       OLTP
TABLE4             ENABLED       QUERY HIGH
TABLE5             ENABLED       ARCHIVE LOW
```

Similarly, the compression information on the partition can be obtained using this query:

```
SQL> SELECT table_name, partition_name, compression, compress_for
FROM user_tab_partitions;
```

When Exadata HCC tables are updated, the rows change to a lower level of compression, such as from COMP_FOR_QUERY_HIGH to COMP_FOR_OLTP or COMP_NO COMPRESS. To determine the compression level of a row, use the following query:

```
DBMS_COMPRESSION.GET_COMPRESSION_TYPE
( ownname    IN    VARCHAR2,
  tabname    IN    VARCHAR2,
  row_id     IN    ROWID)
RETURN NUMBER;
```

An example is shown here:

```
SELECT DECODE(DBMS_COMPRESSION.GET_COMPRESSION_TYPE(
ownname => 'INV',
tabname => 'ITEM_MASTER',
row_id => 'AAAVEIAAGAAAABTAAD'),
1, 'No Compression',
2, 'Basic or OLTP Compression',
4, 'Hybrid Columnar Compression for Query High',
8, 'Hybrid Columnar Compression for Query Low',
16, 'Hybrid Columnar Compression for Archive High',
32, 'Hybrid Columnar Compression for Archive Low',
'Unknown Compression Type') compression_type
FROM DUAL;
```

As you know, the compression level can be changed for a partition, table, or tablespace. For example, if warehouse compression is used for the sales table, but sales data older than one year is rarely accessed, and if the sales data is stored in a table that is partitioned based on the age of the data, then the compression level for the older data can be changed to archive compression to free up disk space.

If a table is partitioned, the DBMS_REDEFINITION package can be used to change the compression level of the table. This package performs online redefinition of a table by creating a temporary copy of the table that holds the table data while it is being redefined. The table being redefined remains available for queries and DML statements during the redefinition. The amount of free space for online table redefinition depends on the relative compression level for the existing table and the new table.

TIP & TECHNIQUE
Though OLTP systems do not leverage HCC, you can still use HCC for all the historical data where updates won't happen. For example, you can implement HCC for a few tables for all the data that is seven years old.

Export/Import of HCC Tables

HCC tables can be exported using the regular `expdp` utility, which preserves the table properties. When imported in a Exadata machine, the tables automatically get compressed. If the import occurs at a non-Exadata machine, the import will fail with the following error:

ORA-64307: Exadata Hybrid Columnar Compression is not supported for tablespaces on this storage type.
Cause: An attempt was made to use Exadata Hybrid Columnar Compression on unsupported storage.
Action: Create this table in a tablespace residing on Oracle Exadata, Oracle's Sun ZFS or Pillar Axiom storage or use a different compression type.

To override this, the table needs to be imported as an uncompressed table using the `TRANSFORM:SEGMENT_ATTRIBUTES=n` option clause of the `impdp` command.

An uncompressed or OLTP-compressed table can be converted to Exadata HCC format during import. To convert a non-Exadata HCC table to an Exadata HCC table, do the following:

1. Specify default compression for the tablespace using the **ALTER TABLESPACE ... SET DEFAULT COMPRESS** command.

2. Override the SEGMENT_ATTRIBUTES option of the imported table during import.

Restoring an Exadata HCC Table

There may be times when an Exadata HCC table needs to be restored from a backup. The table can be restored to a system that supports HCC or to a system that does not support HCC. When restoring a table with HCC to a system that supports HCC, restore the file using Oracle Recovery Manager (RMAN) as usual.

When an HCC table is restored to a system that does not support HCC, you must convert the table from HCC to OLTP compression or a uncompressed format. To restore the table, do the following:

1. Use RMAN to restore the HCC tablespace. Make sure there is sufficient space.

2. Use the following command to change the data compression from HCC to NOCOMPRESS:

```
ALTER TABLE table_name MOVE NOCOMPRESS
```

3. Use the following command to change each partition:

```
ALTER TABLE table_name MOVE PARTITION partition_name NOCOMPRESS
```

Change each partition separately.

4. Use the following command to move the data in parallel:

```
ALTER TABLE table_name MOVE NOCOMPRESS PARALLEL
```

5. Use the following command to change the data compression from HCC to OLTP COMPRESS:

```
ALTER TABLE table_name MOVE COMPRESS for OLTP
```

Smart Scans

In traditional architecture, the database servers are connected to the Storage Area Network (SAN) infrastructure, where the Oracle Database files are stored. The SAN infrastructure is used for storing the data and does not play any role in processing the data. The conventional storage array does not understand the Oracle data format and hence cannot perform any intelligent operations, such as predicate evaluation, in the storage layer itself.

The connection between the storage arrays and the database tends to be small and hence sometimes limits the I/O bandwidth because the resources (i.e., the connection) are fixed. Finite resources can lead to oversubscription, which in turn causes performance bottlenecks. In modern computer systems, I/O is a true source of the bottlenecks that are caused by oversubscription.

There is a lack of scale-out architecture in traditional storage arrays. If the storage consumed in the array reaches the maximum capacity of the array, it is not simply a matter of just plugging in additional components and scaling out incrementally.

With Exadata, the storage has an equal role to play in processing the data. Each storage cell is equipped with CPUs and memory, which helps in processing the data. The Exadata Smart Scan feature of the Exadata Database Machine offloads the data search and retrieval processing to the storage cell. Smart Scan is designed to reduce the amount of data that flows from storage devices to the database server. This not only reduces the I/O bottleneck problem from the storage devices into the CPU, but also reduces the amount of processing that has to be done by the database node, resulting in performance improvements based on a reduction in demand for computing resources.

Let's look at the differences between the processing of traditional storage versus storage with Smart Scan. To appreciate the benefits of Smart Scan, let's look at a traditional scan processing. Let's say we have the following SQL statement:

```
select customer_name from customers where customer number IN ('6500 ,7500');
```

In this case, the SQL statement requests a group of 1000 records (6500–7500) from a 1TB table. With traditional processing, the SQL statement is parsed and the execution plan is prepared. The next step is to request the extents from the table, which are required to process this SQL statement. The storage system receives this request and proceeds to execute the I/Os required to retrieve 1TB of data, which is then returned to the DB server. The entire 1TB of data is sent back to the DB server. The DB server goes through that data in the buffer cache and selects the 1000 customer names, adds them to a result set, and returns this to the client.

All this for just 1000 records! Though the end client needs only 1000 records, in this case, 1TB of data had to travel from storage to DB server, wasting a lot of resources and serving lots of I/O requests with a limited bandwidth. Typically, the DB servers are connected to the SAN with either 1Gb Ethernet or 10Gb Ethernet or via Fibre Channel.

Let's take a look at the steps involved in this process in a bit more detail:

1. The client issues the SQL statement with a predicate to filter a table and return only the rows of interest to the user. In this case, the predicate is an IN clause and the request is for customer numbers between 6500 and 7500.

2. The database kernel maps this requests and identifies the extents for *all* of the data blocks belonging to the table.

3. The database kernel issues the I/O and requests all the table blocks from storage.

4. All the blocks for the table are fetched from storage into database server memory. During this step, actual data movement occurs from the storage to the database servers.

5. SQL processing occurs against those data blocks in the database buffer cache, searching for only those rows that satisfy the predicate—that is, customer numbers between 6500 and 7500.

6. The rows that satisfy the predicate clause are sent to the end user. The data stays in the database buffer cache and is wiped out based on the LRU algorithm.

Now let's look at the same process with Exadata Smart Scan. As soon as the query is parsed, the optimizer knows that an Exadata Storage Cell is attached to it. The request for the table extent is sent to the storage system along with the metadata about that SQL statement. This metadata is used to implement Smart Scan processing—for instance, some of that metadata could be selection criteria, and Smart Scan will use that to identify the rows that could be part of the result set, eliminating the need to send all the useless rows back to the database node for processing. Metadata also includes information such as which columns are requested, so the amount of information returned to the database nodes would be limited only to those columns required to process the query, and this limits the amount of data sent from the I/O to the database node. The net result of the Smart

Scan processing is that, instead of sending back 1TB of data for processing to the database node, only 100MB of data is sent. The database server uses this data to create the result set to return to the client. The Smart Scan process is much faster and is less resource intensive because less data requires parsing and the DB node performs much less work.

Let's take a detailed look at the steps involved:

1. The client issues the SQL statement with a predicate to filter a table and return only the rows of interest to the user. In this case, the predicate is an IN clause and the request is for customer numbers between 6500 and 7500.

2. The database kernel identifies that the data is stored in Exadata Storage Cells, so it constructs an iDB command and sends it to the Exadata Storage Cells. The iDB command actually contains a SQL *fragment*, or a portion of the original SQL statement. Each step in the Data Flow Operator (DFO) tree is expressed as a SQL statement or fragment.

3. The Exadata Storage Server starts scanning the data blocks and extracts only the relevant rows and columns that match the SQL query fragment.

4. Once the data scan is complete, the Exadata Storage Cells return the database server iDB messages containing the requested data. Exadata does row-and-column projection, so it returns only the requested rows and columns at this step. The data is sent from the Exadata Storage Cells to the database server. Exadata also returns data in row-source format, rather than a data block format. A row-source is a part of the DFO tree processing. Only the relevant 100MB of data will be sent.

5. The database server consolidates the results from all the Exadata Storage Cells.

6. The requested data is returned to the client.

The query is offloaded to the storage cells. The process of query offloading to the storage cell is the *Smart Scan*.

You can see that Smart Scan does Smart I/O rather than Block I/O. With Block I/O, the data is shipped to a location where it can be processed—the RDBMS or the database server. With Smart I/O, some of the processing is shipped to where data resides—the Exadata Storage Server. Results from the storage layer may then be further processed in the RDBMS.

Smart Scan uses direct reads, which involve reading the data into PGA buffers, as opposed to the buffer cache used for caching data blocks. Direct reads are useful when the ratio of cache to data to be read is very small.

Smart Scan is implemented by function shipping. The predicates and the block IDs are shipped to the cells, and filtered results are returned. Smart Scan block evaluation is implemented by fplib, a library that understands Oracle block format and can evaluate rows based on predicates to perform predicate evaluation, column selection, join filtering through bloom filters, and so on.

Smart Scan works only with the Exadata Storage Server. If any other storage exists, Exadata Smart Scan will not process the data. In Exadata Storage Servers, the ASM disk groups are created with a new attribute called **cell.smart_scan_capable**.

```
CREATE diskgroup datafile external redundancy disk
'o/140.87.2.120;140.87.2.120;140.87.2.120;140.87.2.120:46342/datafile0'
name DATAFILE_0000,
'o/140.87.2.120;140.87.2.120;140.87.2.120;140.87.2.120:46342/datafile1'
name DATAFILE_0001,
attribute 'compatible.asm' = '11.1.0.7',
'compatible.rdbms' = '11.1.0.7',
'cell.smart_scan_capable' = 'true'
```

If a database is created so that some of the database files of a tablespace reside in the Exadata Storage Servers and some of the database files reside in a traditional storage (not in Exadata Storage Cells), then Smart Scan will occur for the partition of tablespace residing in the Exadata Storage Servers, or Oracle's ZFSSA or Pillar storage. If a partition residing in a tablespace includes files on non-Exadata storage, the scan for that partition is not offloaded. In this case, the execution plan might indicate that a scan is being offloaded because there was at least one partition on Exadata storage.

In real life, it is not recommended to keep any database files outside the Exadata Storage Servers, since the Exadata Storage software can't work outside the Exadata Storage Cells. In some special cases, the database files can be stored on ZFS storage. For example, when you're planning an Information Lifecycle Management strategy, all the archived data can be stored in ZFS storage, or when using ZFS for the snapshot capabilities, the database files can be stored in the ZFS storage.

Smart Scan provides the following key benefits:

■ It eliminates lot of unproductive I/Os. For any application, the biggest bottleneck is I/O; with Smart Scan, this bottleneck is totally eliminated. Smart Scan reduces the network and disk I/Os by filtering the data with Smart I/O operations offloaded to the storage layer.

■ The DB sever can spend fewer CPU cycles processing the I/Os. When the I/O is reduced, the DB server CPU cycle is freed up, reducing the processing burden on the host. The freed CPU cycles can be used for serving other requests.

■ The data blocks are transferred from the Exadata Storage Cells to the DB server via InfiniBand, which provides 40 Gbps connectivity and has a much bigger pipe compared to 4GFC or 8GFC (Fibre Channel). In addition,

Exadata now runs in active/active configuration, so it delivers an 80 Gbps signaling rate.

■ Smart Scans correctly handle complex cases, including uncommitted data, locked rows and chained rows, compressed tables, national language processing, date arithmetic, regular expression searches, and partitioned tables.

■ Smart Scan can perform predicate filtering, column filtering, join processing, scans on encrypted data, scans on compressed data, data mining, creating/extending tablespace, and RMAN operations.

■ Smart Scans are transparent to the application—that is, no application or SQL changes are required, and returned data is fully consistent and transactional.

■ Smart Scans provide both horizontal and vertical parallelism. Horizontal parallelism is achieved by concurrent processing of the Smart I/O requests by many Exadata Storage Servers and concurrent processing of Smart I/O requests from a single database process by many threads within a single Exadata Storage Server. Vertical parallelism is obtained as Exadata Storage Servers process more results while the database is consuming results already returned.

Smart Scan SQL Operations

Let's look at the various SQL operations that benefit from the use of Exadata.

Predicate Filtering

Predicate filtering is enabled at the Exadata Storage Cells, which filter the data during the table scan. Exadata Storage Server filters out rows that are not of interest to the RDBMS and returns only those rows that are qualified by the scan predicates. The metadata sent to the storage server includes the information of predicates. Only those rows that match the filtered condition are returned to the database server, rather than all rows in a table. It supports all the conditional operators such as =,!=,<, >, <=, >=, IS [NOT] NULL, LIKE, [NOT] BETWEEN, [NOT] IN, EXISTS, IS OF type, NOT, AND, and OR. You can see the full list of functions that Exadata Storage Cells can evaluate by running the following query:

```
select * from v$sqlfn_metadata where offloadable='YES'
```

Column Projection

Smart Scan also does column filtering, known as *column projection*, for table scans, where only the requested columns are returned, instead of all the columns. This significantly reduces the I/O bandwidth. Columnar projection is very useful when a table has many columns.

In addition, column filtering applies to indexes, allowing for even faster query performance. Figure 3-3 shows columnar projection for the query select B,D from a table.

Join Processing

Smart Scan is capable of processing simple and complex joins. Exadata Storage Cells can perform joins between large tables and small lookup tables, which is the most common scenario for star schemas.

Joint filtering uses Bloom filtering, which was introduced in Oracle 10*g*. It was conceived by Burton Howard Bloom in 1970 in the paper "Space/time trade-offs in hash coding with allowable errors" (https://dl.acm.org/citation.cfm?doid=362686.362692). When two tables are joined via a hash join, the first table (typically the smaller table) is scanned, and the rows that satisfy the WHERE clause predicates for that table are used to create a hash table. During the hash table creation, a bit vector, or Bloom filter, is also created based on the join column. The bit vector is then sent as an additional predicate to the second table scan. After the WHERE clause predicates have been applied to the second table scan, the resulting rows will have their join column hashed, and this will be compared to values in the bit vector. If a match is found in the bit vector, that row will be sent to the hash join. If no match is found, then the row will be disregarded.

Bloom filters are used to reduce potential row candidates for a join, reducing the data sent to the database server for join processing. A Bloom filter corresponding to the smaller table is shipped to the Exadata Storage Server so that the join operation can be performed on the storage server itself, and the results of the join are returned. On Exadata, the Bloom filter or bit vector is passed as an additional predicate so it will be overloaded to the storage cells, making Bloom filtering very efficient.

Encrypted Data

Exadata Storage Cells are capable of performing Smart Scans on encrypted data residing in tablespaces and columns. Data is decrypted by Exadata cells before

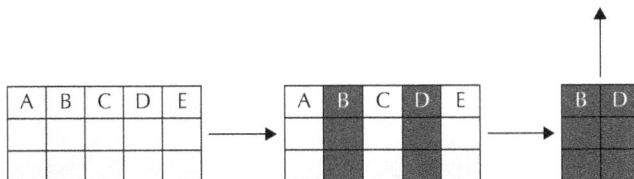

FIGURE 3-3. *Columnar projection*

being sent to the database servers. This increases performance when accessing the most confidential data in the enterprise.

Data Mining Model Offload

All data mining scoring functions (such as prediction_probability) are offloaded to Exadata Storage Cells, which reduces the CPU utilization on the database server and the I/O load between the database server and Exadata storage. An example of the data mining offload is shown here:

```
Select supplier_id from suppliers where region ='US' and prediction_
probability (churnmod,Y' using *) > 0.8;
```

From this SQL query, the scoring function is executed in the Exadata Storage Cells.

Smart Incremental Backup

In Exadata Storage Cells, RMAN does block change-tracking. It maintains a list of groups of blocks where data has changed. Any block whose System Change Number (SCN) is greater than the incremental SCN qualifies to be sent back to the RDBMS by CELLSRV. Incremental backup backs up only marked groups of blocks. Exadata Storage Server improves the granularity of tracking units, reducing the size of backups even more. This results in less I/O bandwidth being consumed for backups and faster running backups.

Smart File Creations

Smart Scans in Exadata Storage Cells kick in during file operations. During tablespace creation or extension in a Exadata machine, only metadata is sent by the database server to the Exadata Storage Server, and then initialization is done by the Exadata Storage Server software on the drives. The iDB protocol kicks in during the tablespace/data file creation/extension, offloading the work to the storage cells. With regular tablespace creation (non-Exadata), each block of the tablespace creation happens at the database server's memory and is written to storage. As a result, in an Exadata machine, there is a tremendous reduction in I/O between the database and storage system, which frees up the CPU cycle in serving the I/Os. Because the database server memory is not involved in this process, it frees up some memory as well. Smart file creation is enabled by default and cannot be disabled using a documented parameter.

Storage Index

Exadata Storage Cells maintain a storage index, which contains the summary of the distribution of the data in the hard drives. The storage index is very different from the database index. It is not maintained by the database; instead, it is very transparent to the Oracle Database. It is maintained automatically and can't be created/altered manually, unlike indexes in database objects.

An RDBMS index is a data structure that helps find data quickly. Exadata Storage Index is a data structure that helps filter out data very efficiently. Thus, storage index is a negative index, or anti-index, as opposed to database indexes, which use B-Tree or bitmap types of data structures in their implementation. An Exadata Storage Index is an array of structures that are stored in physical memory of Exadata Storage Cells. Each individual structure of the array is known as a region index (RIDX), and each RIDX stores summaries for up to eight columns. There is one RIDX for each 1MB of disk space.

Let's look at an example to see how the storage index works. The decision to store particular columns in RIDX is independent of other region indexes, making it highly scalable; thus, no latch contention occurs. As per Figure 3-4, column B stores the value of 1–9. Let's say the query requests the following:

```
select * from table where B=3
```

The Exadata Storage Cell divides the table into equal-sized logical portions, or regions. As shown in Figure 3-4, the first set of three rows is considered the first region, the second set of three rows is considered the second region, and so on. The minimum and maximum range of the column is stored in each region. So for the query, the value of the predicate B=3 lies in the first logical region; thus, the storage index will eliminate the second and the third regions for fetching the data. Storage indexes minimized the disk I/Os by using the minimum and maximum values, thereby eliminating unnecessary I/Os.

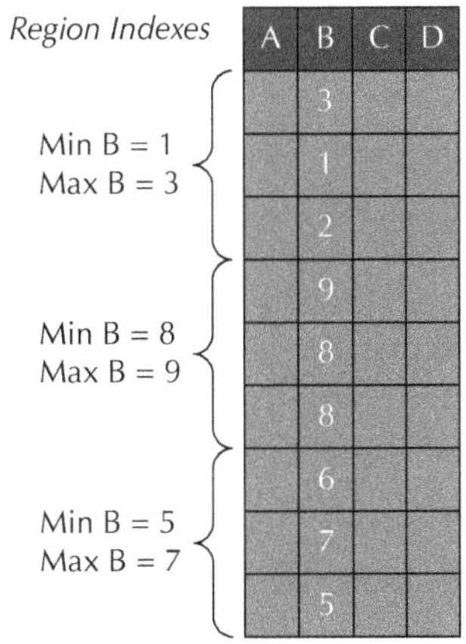

FIGURE 3-4. *Use of regional index*

Queries using the following comparisons benefit the most from the Exadata Storage Index:

- Equality (=)

- Inequality (<, !=, or >)

- Less than or equal (<=)

- Greater than or equal (>=)

- IS NULL

- IS NOT NULL

The Exadata Storage Index works in conjunction with Smart Scan and reduces the overall disk I/Os. Smart Scan helps reduce the overall network I/Os. When Smart Scan and Storage Indexes work together, both disk I/Os and network I/Os are reduced.

Exadata Storage Index avoids scanning unnecessary partitions of the table, providing partition pruning-like benefits. Exadata Storage Index also provides improvement in join performance because it allows table joins to skip unnecessary I/O operations.

The benefits from the Exadata Storage Index can be obtained by querying the V$SYSSTAT view. It tells the details of the I/Os that can be reduced with storage indexes. This view has many metrics, but the main metric, which gives the details related to storage indexes, is **cell physical IO bytes saved by storage index**. This metric shows the impact of storage index in saving the I/Os and tells us how many bytes of I/O elimination was done using the storage index.

```
SQL> select name, value from v$sysstat where name like '%storage%';

NAME                                               VALUE
-------------------------------------------------- ---------
cell physical IO bytes saved by storage index      754098176
```

The Exadata Storage Index can be enabled and disabled manually at the cell or database level. In both cases, use extreme caution, or do so at the recommendation of Oracle Support.

For enabling/disabling the Exadata Storage Index at the database, edit/modify the init.ora parameter:

```
_kcfis_storageidx_disabled = true |false
```

The default value of this parameter is false, which means Exadata Storage Index is enabled by default. Setting the value to true will disable the Exadata Storage

Index. Note that this parameter is a hidden parameter since it starts with an underscore. All the hidden parameters should be set only with supervision from Oracle Support.

To disable the Exadata Storage Index at the cell level, run the following command:

```
alter cell events = "immediate cellsrv.cellsrv_storidx('disable', 'ALL', 0, 0, 0)";
```

To enable the Exadata Storage Index, run the following command:

```
alter cell events = "immediate cellsrv.cellsrv_storidx('enable', 'ALL', 0, 0, 0)";
```

The Exadata Storage Index can also be manually purged. Use extreme caution while running this command:

```
alter cell events = "immediate cellsrv.cellsrv_storidx('purge', 'ALL', 0, 0, 0)";
```

Considerations that Affect Smart Scan

The following operations benefit the most from a Smart Scan:

- Full scan of a heap table

- Fast full scan of a B-Tree or bitmap index

- Direct reads—that is, reads to PGA (for example, parallel query processes generally use direct reads)

The following operations do not benefit from a Smart Scan:

- Scans of index-organized tables or clustered tables

- Index range scans

- Access to a compressed index

- Access to a reverse key index

- Secure enterprise search

- If the query is run serially and direct reads aren't chosen

For proper Smart Scan functioning, the following parameters/considerations must be in place:

- The initialization parameter **cell_offload_processing** should be set to TRUE. The default behavior for this parameter is TRUE.

    ```
    SQL> alter session set cell_offload_processing=TRUE;
    ```

- There should be no quarantines for any SQL ID. A SQL ID is normally quarantined if it is deemed to be problematic for the cell server. This is usually due to the statement or object generating an error in CELLSRV, such as ORA-600 or ORA-7445. If a quarantine for a statement is completed, the particular SQL ID, if executed again, will not use Smart Scan. This is a protection against failures of the CELLSRV process. To protect against future failures, the statement or object is quarantined. If a statement is quarantined, you may see a message like the following in the cell alert history:

```
alertMessage: "A SQL PLAN quarantine has been added. As a
result,Smart Scan is disabled for SQL statements with the
quarantined SQL plan.
Quarantine id : 1 Quarantine type : SQL PLAN Quarantine reason :
```

  The following command lists objects that have been quarantined in all the storage cells:

```
dcli -g cell_group -l root cellcli -e list quarantine
list quarantine <#> detail  -- run for each quarantine
```

- The **cell.smart_scan_capable** attribute of the disk group is set. This was discussed previously.

TIP & TECHNIQUE

If you are writing a brand-new application and the underlying database is in Exadata, you can try avoiding database indexes so that a Smart Scan can be leveraged as much as possible.

Querying for Smart Scan

For a particular query, whether or not Smart Scans are happening can be verified using the explain plan. When the Smart Scans are happening, the explain plan will provide information regarding table scans, index scans, bitmap index scans, and the Bloom filter, as discussed in the following sections.

Table Scan

If a table scan is being offloaded, the explain plan will show TABLE ACCESS STORAGE FULL instead of TABLE ACCESS FULL when the scan is not offloaded. A sample explain plan is shown next, without and with Smart Scan.

Here's the explain plan without Smart Scan:

```
| Id  | Operation              | Name      |
--------------------------------------------------------------------------
|   0 | SELECT STATEMENT       |           |           |
| * 1 | HASH JOIN              |           |           |
| * 2 | HASH JOIN              |           |           |
| * 3 | TABLE ACCESS FULL      | SALES     |           |
| * 4 | TABLE ACCESS FULL      | SALES     |           |
| * 5 | TABLE ACCESS FULL      | SALES     |           |
--------------------------------------------------------------------------

Predicate Information (identified by operation id):
--------------------------------------------------------------------------
1 - access("T"."CUST_ID"="T2"."CUST_ID" AND "T1"."PROD_ID"="T2"."PROD_ID"
AND "T1"."CUST_ID"="T2"."CUST_ID")
2 - access("T"."PROD_ID"="T1"."PROD_ID")
3 - filter("T1"."PROD_ID"<200 AND "T1"."AMOUNT_SOLD"*"T1"."QUANTITY_
SOLD">10000 AND "T1"."PROD_ID"<>45)
4 - filter("T"."PROD_ID"<200 AND "T"."PROD_ID"<>45)
5 - filter("T2"."PROD_ID"<200 AND "T2"."PROD_ID"<>45)
```

Here's the explain plan with Smart Scan (the words in boldface indicate Smart
Scan):

```
| Id  | Operation                    | Name      |
--------------------------------------------------------------------------
|   0 | SELECT STATEMENT             |           |           |
| * 1 | HASH JOIN                    |           |           |
| * 2 | HASH JOIN                    |           |           |
| * 3 | TABLE ACCESS STORAGE FULL    | SALES     |           |
| * 4 | TABLE ACCESS STORAGE FULL    | SALES     |           |
| * 5 | TABLE ACCESS STORAGE FULL    | SALES     |           |
--------------------------------------------------------------------------

Predicate Information (identified by operation id):
--------------------------------------------------------------------------
1 - access("T"."CUST_ID"="T2"."CUST_ID" AND "T1"."PROD_ID"="T2"."PROD_ID"
AND "T1"."CUST_ID"="T2"."CUST_ID")
2 - access("T"."PROD_ID"="T1"."PROD_ID")
3 - storage("T1"."PROD_ID"<200 AND "T1"."AMOUNT_SOLD"*"T1"."QUANTITY_
SOLD">10000 AND "T1"."PROD_ID"<>45)
     filter("T1"."PROD_ID"<200 AND "T1"."AMOUNT_SOLD"*"T1"."QUANTITY_
SOLD">10000 AND "T1"."PROD_ID"<>45)
4 - storage("T"."PROD_ID"<200 AND "T"."PROD_ID"<>45)
     filter("T"."PROD_ID"<200 AND "T"."PROD_ID"<>45)
5 - storage("T2"."PROD_ID"<200 AND "T2"."PROD_ID"<>45)
     filter("T2"."PROD_ID"<200 AND "T2"."PROD_ID"<>45)
```

Index Scan

If a B-Tree index fast full scan is being offloaded, it will show the words INDEX STORAGE FAST FULL SCAN instead of INDEX FAST FULL SCAN when the scan is not offloaded. A sample explain plan is shown next, without and with Smart Scan.

Here's the explain plan without Smart Scan:

```
---------------------------------------------------------------------
| Id  | Operation                      |      Name       |
---------------------------------------------------------------------
|   0 |  SELECT STATEMENT              |                 |
|   1 |   SORT AGGREGATE               |                 |
|*  2 |    INDEX FAST FULL SCAN        |      INDEX1      |
---------------------------------------------------------------------
Predicate Information (identified by operation id):
---------------------------------------------------------------------
2 - filter("P1"=10)
```

Here's the explain plan with Smart Scan (the words in boldface indicate Smart Scan):

```
---------------------------------------------------------------------
| Id  | Operation                      |      Name       |
|
---------------------------------------------------------------------
|   0 |  SELECT STATEMENT              |                 |
|   1 |   SORT AGGREGATE               |                 |
|*  2 |    INDEX STORAGE FAST FULL SCAN|      INDEX1      |
---------------------------------------------------------------------
Predicate Information (identified by operation id):
---------------------------------------------------------------------
2 - storage("P1"=10)
    filter("P1"=10)
```

Bitmap Index Scan

If a bitmap index full scan is being offloaded, it will show the words BITMAP INDEX STORAGE FAST FULL SCAN instead of BITMAP INDEX FAST FULL SCAN. A sample explain plan is shown next without and with Smart Scan.

Here's the explain plan without Smart Scan:

```
---------------------------------------------------------------------
| Id  | Operation                      |      Name       |
---------------------------------------------------------------------
|   0 |  SELECT STATEMENT              |                 |
|   1 |   SORT AGGREGATE               |                 |
|   2 |    BITMAP CONVERSION COUNT     |                 |
|*  3 |     BITMAP INDEX FAST FULL SCAN|      INDEX2     |
---------------------------------------------------------------------
Predicate Information (identified by operation id):
---------------------------------------------------------------------
3 - filter("P1"=10)
```

Here's the explain plan with Smart Scan (the words in boldface indicate Smart Scan):

```
-------------------------------------------------------------------
| Id  | Operation                              | Name          |
-------------------------------------------------------------------
|   0 | SELECT STATEMENT                       |               |
|   1 |  SORT AGGREGATE                        |               |
|   2 |   BITMAP CONVERSION COUNT              |               |
|*  3 |    BITMAP INDEX STORAGE FAST FULL SCAN | INDEX2        |
-------------------------------------------------------------------
Predicate Information (identified by operation id):
-------------------------------------------------------------------
3 - storage("P1"=10)
      filter("P1"=10)
```

Bloom Filter

If a query is running with a Bloom filter and the query is being offloaded, the explain plan will have the words TABLE ACCESS STORAGE FULL instead of TABLE ACCESS FULL INDEX. A sample explain plan is shown next without and with offload and Smart Scan.

Here's the explain plan without offload and Smart Scan:

```
-------------------------------------------------------------------
| Id  | Operation                     | Name          |
-------------------------------------------------------------------
|   0 | SELECT STATEMENT              |               |
|   1 |  SORT AGGREGATE               |               |
|   2 |   PX COORDINATOR              |               |
|   3 |    PX SEND QC (RANDOM)        | :TQ10002      |
|   4 |     SORT AGGREGATE            |               |
|*  5 |      HASH JOIN                |               |
|   6 |       JOIN FILTER CREATE      | :BF0000       |
|   7 |        PX RECEIVE             |               |
|   8 |         PX SEND HASH          | :TQ10000      |
|   9 |          PX BLOCK ITERATOR    |               |
|  10 |           TABLE ACCESS FULL   | EMPLOYEE      |
|  11 |       PX RECEIVE              |               |
|  12 |        PX SEND HASH           | :TQ10001      |
|  13 |         JOIN FILTER USE       | :BF0000       |
|  14 |          PX BLOCK ITERATOR    |               |
|* 15 |           TABLE ACCESS FULL   | DEPT          |
-------------------------------------------------------------------
Predicate Information (identified by operation id):
-------------------------------------------------------------------
   5 - access("E"."DEPT_ID"="D"."DEPT_ID")
  15 - filter(SYS_OP_BLOOM_FILTER(:BF0000,"D"."DEPT_ID"))
```

Here's the explain plan with offload and Smart Scan:

```
--------------------------------------------------------------------------
| Id  | Operation                            | Name      |
--------------------------------------------------------------------------
|   0 | SELECT STATEMENT                     |           |
|   1 |  SORT AGGREGATE                      |           |
|   2 |   PX COORDINATOR                     |           |
|   3 |    PX SEND QC (RANDOM)               | :TQ10002  |
|   4 |     SORT AGGREGATE                   |           |
|*  5 |      HASH JOIN                       |           |
|   6 |       JOIN FILTER CREATE             | :BF0000   |
|   7 |        PX RECEIVE                    |           |
|   8 |         PX SEND HASH                 | :TQ10000  |
|   9 |          PX BLOCK ITERATOR           |           |
|  10 |           TABLE ACCESS STORAGE FULL  | EMPLOYEE  |
|  11 |       PX RECEIVE                     |           |
|  12 |        PX SEND HASH                  | :TQ10001  |
|  13 |         JOIN FILTER USE              | :BF0000   |
|  14 |          PX BLOCK ITERATOR           |           |
|* 15 |           TABLE ACCESS STORAGE FULL  | DEPT      |
--------------------------------------------------------------------------

Predicate Information (identified by operation id):
--------------------------------------------------------------------------
   5 - access("E"."DEPT_ID"="D"."DEPT_ID")
  15 - storage(SYS_OP_BLOOM_FILTER(:BF0000,"D"."DEPT_ID"))
       filter(SYS_OP_BLOOM_FILTER(:BF0000,"D"."DEPT_ID"))
```

If the query has no predicate, is being offloaded, and includes Smart Scan, the explain plan will look like this:

```
--------------------------------------------------------------------------
|   0 | SELECT STATEMENT                     |           |
|   1 |  SORT AGGREGATE                      |           |
|   2 |   PX COORDINATOR                     |           |
|   3 |    PX SEND QC (RANDOM)               | :TQ10000  |
|   4 |     SORT AGGREGATE                   |           |
|   5 |      PX BLOCK ITERATOR               |           |
|   6 |       TABLE ACCESS STORAGE FULL      | LINEITEM  |
--------------------------------------------------------------------------
```

Note the following:

■ Smart Scan is using a Smart I/O code path instead of a Block I/O code path. This provides additional parallelism for the query on the storage server.

■ Some column projection may be occurring depending on the query.

Smart Scan Metrics

The Exadata Smart Scan statistics can be queried from the v$SYSSTAT, v$SQL, and DBA_HIST_SQLSTAT view to understand the efficiency of Smart Scan in terms of I/O processing avoided by the database host.

The following V$SYSSTAT metrics provide information on the Smart Scan:

- **cell physical IO interconnect bytes**   Amount of data returned from the cells.

- **physical IO disk bytes**   Amount of data read from the disk from the cells. This includes I/O performed for both Block I/O and Smart Scans.

- **cell physical IO bytes eligible for predicate offload**   Amount of disk I/O for Smart Scans.

- **cell physical IO bytes saved during optimized file creation**   Number of bytes of I/O saved by the database host by offloading the file creation operation to cells. This statistic shows the Exadata cell benefit due to optimized file creation operations.

- **cell physical IO bytes saved during optimized RMAN file restore**   Number of bytes of I/O saved by the host due to offloading the file restore. This statistic shows the Exadata cell benefit due to optimized RMAN file restore operations.

The following V$SQL metrics provide information on the Smart Scan:

- **IO_CELL_OFFLOAD_ELIGIBLE_BYTES**   Provides information on the bytes that are eligible for offload. If this has a value of zero, nothing was offloaded to the Exadata Storage Cells.

- **IO_CELL_UNCOMPRESSED_BYTES**   Provides information on the uncompressed bytes that were offloaded to the Exadata Storage Cells.

- **IO_CELL_OFFLOAD_RETURNED_BYTES**   Number of bytes returned by the Exadata Storage Cell by the virtue of Smart Scan.

The view DBA_HIST_SQLSTAT also provides information on Smart Scan. DBA_HIST_SQLSTAT displays historical information about SQL statistics. This view captures the top SQL statements based on a set of criteria and captures the statistics information from V$SQL. The total value is the value of the statistics since instance startup. The delta value is the value of the statistics from the BEGIN_INTERVAL_TIME to the END_INTERVAL_TIME in the DBA_HIST_SNAPSHOT view.

- **IO_OFFLOAD_ELIG_BYTES_TOTAL**   Provides information on the cumulative value of the number of bytes that are eligible for offload. If this has a value of zero, nothing was offloaded to the Exadata Storage Cells.

- **IO_OFFLOAD_ELIG_BYTES_DELTA** Provides information on the bytes that are eligible for offload of the delta.

- **IO_OFFLOAD_RETURN_BYTES_TOTAL** Cumulative value of number of bytes returned by the Exadata Storage Cell by the virtue of Smart Scan.

- **IO_OFFLOAD_RETURN_BYTES_DELTA** Delta of the number of bytes returned by the Exadata Storage Cell by the virtue of Smart Scan.

The metric related to smart incremental backup statistics can be queried from the view V$BACKUP_DATAFILE. It has the following columns pertaining to smart incremental backup:

- **BLOCKS_SKIPPED_IN_CELL** Number of blocks that were read and filtered by the cells to optimize the RMAN incremental backup.

- **BLOCKS** Size of the backup data file in blocks.

If block change tracking for fast incremental backups is used, then most of the filtering is done at the database using the change tracking file, and the blocks are skipped before making an I/O request to the cell. If block change tracking is not used, then all of the blocks are filtered at the cell.

TIP & TECHNIQUE
If Enterprise Manager is integrated with Exadata, you can get all these metrics in a very nice graphical presentation.

Queries to Capture Smart Scan

The following query can be used to determine whether the SQL query can take advantage of Smart Scan:

```
set pagesize 999
set lines 190
col sql_text format a70 trunc
col child format 99999
col execs format 9,999
col avg_etime format 99,999.99
col "IO_SAVED_%" format 999.99
col avg_px format 999
col offload for a7

select sql_id, child_number child, plan_hash_value plan_hash, executions execs,
```

```
(elapsed_time/1000000)/decode(nvl(executions,0),0,1,executions)/
decode(px_servers_executions,0,1,px_servers_executions/decode(nvl(execution
s,0),0,1,executions)) avg_etime,
px_servers_executions/decode(nvl(executions,0),0,1,executions) avg_px,
decode(IO_CELL_OFFLOAD_ELIGIBLE_BYTES,0,'No','Yes') Offload,
decode(IO_CELL_OFFLOAD_ELIGIBLE_BYTES,0,0,100*(IO_CELL_OFFLOAD_ELIGIBLE_
BYTES-IO_INTERCONNECT_BYTES)
/decode(IO_CELL_OFFLOAD_ELIGIBLE_BYTES,0,1,IO_CELL_OFFLOAD_ELIGIBLE_BYTES))
"IO_SAVED_%",
sql_text
from v$sql s
where upper(sql_text) like upper(nvl(q'[&sql_text]',sql_text))
and sql_text not like 'BEGIN :sql_text := %'
and sql_text not like '%IO_CELL_OFFLOAD_ELIGIBLE_BYTES%'
and sql_text not like '/* SQL Analyze(%'
and sql_id like nvl('&sql_id',sql_id)
order by 1, 2, 3
/
```

Save that script as file offload.sql. Then execute and provide the input for the information of the required query:

```
sql>@offload.sql
Enter value for sql_text: % test %
Enter value for sql_id:
Enter value for inst_id:

SQL> @offload
Enter value for sql_text: SELECT DISTINCT ORGANIZATION_ID FROM MTL_
MATERIAL_TRANSACTIONS WHERE COSTED_FLAG = 'N'
old  10: where upper(sql_text) like upper(nvl(q'[&sql_text]',sql_text))
new  10: where upper(sql_text) like upper(nvl(q'[SELECT DISTINCT
ORGANIZATION_ID FROM MTL_MATERIAL_TRANSACTIONS WHERE COSTED_FLAG =
'N']',sql_text))
Enter value for sql_id: 5m0b85phdybur
old  14: and sql_id like nvl('&sql_id',sql_id)
new  14: and sql_id like nvl('5m0b85phdybur',sql_id)

SQL_ID        CHILD PLAN_HASH EXECS AVG_ETIME AVG_PX OFFLOAD IO_SAVED_%
SQL_TEXT
------------- ----- --------- ----- --------- ------ ------- ---------- ---
----------------------------------------------------------------
5m0b85phdybur 0    103113867 2,247 2.76      0      Yes     95.30
SELECT DISTINCT ORGANIZATION_ID FROM MTL_MATERIAL_TRANSACTIONS WHERE C
```

You can see that the value for offload is Yes, which indicates that cell offload is happening, and IO_SAVED is 95.30, which means that around 95 percent of the query is being offloaded to the Exadata Storage Cells.

To find out the total impact of a complex large query, run the following SQL before and after running the SQL query to capture the Smart Scan metrics:

```
select b.name, a.value from v$mystat a, v$statname b
   where a.STATISTIC# = b.STATISTIC# and
         (b.name = 'cell session smart scan efficiency' or
          b.name = 'cell physical IO bytes saved by storage index' or
          b.name = 'cell physical IO bytes eligible for predicate offload' or
          b.name = 'cell physical IO interconnect bytes returned by smart scan'
          or
          b.name = 'cell IO uncompressed bytes'
          or
          b.name like '%cell blocks processed%');
```

Save this query as stats.sql:

```
SQL> select name, value from v$mystat s, v$statname n
  where n.statistic#=s.statistic#
  and name like 'cell scans';  2    3

NAME                        VALUE
--------------------------- ----------
cell scans                      1
```

Run the stats.sql before running the complex SQL query to find out the existing metric:

```
SQL> @stats.sql

NAME                                                         VALUE
------------------------------------------------------------ ----------
cell physical IO bytes eligible for predicate offload        1081237504
cell physical IO bytes saved by storage index                1067909120
cell physical IO interconnect bytes returned by smart scan         6856
cell blocks processed by cache layer                               1627
cell blocks processed by txn layer                                 1627
cell blocks processed by data layer                                1627
cell blocks processed by index layer                                  0
cell IO uncompressed bytes                                     13328384

8 rows selected.
```

Let's run a complex SQL now:

```
SQL>@run_a_SQL_query.sql
```

Now run the stats.sql one more time to see the impact of running the SQL:

```
SQL> @stats.sql

NAME                                                             VALUE
---------------------------------------------------------- ----------
cell physical IO bytes eligible for predicate offload      2162475008
cell physical IO bytes saved by storage index              2135818240
cell physical IO interconnect bytes returned by smart scan      13712
cell blocks processed by cache layer                             3254
cell blocks processed by txn layer                               3254
cell blocks processed by data layer                              3254
cell blocks processed by index layer                                0
cell IO uncompressed bytes                                   26656768

8 rows selected.

SQL> select name, value from v$mystat s, v$statname n
  where n.statistic#=s.statistic#
  and name like 'cell scans';  2    3

NAME                       VALUE
-------------------------- ----------
cell scans                 2
```

When you compare the before and after metrics, you can see the impact of the Smart Scan for a particular query.

Exadata Smart Flash Cache

Today's multi-core, multi-socket application server designs are increasingly impeded by slow storage. When requesting data, the server spends most of its time waiting for storage. Hard disk drives (HDDs), even the fastest at 15K RPM, cannot feed the servers fast enough. They are much slower than what today's servers are capable of, so a lot of time is spent waiting for data after a request. Application performance remains sluggish regardless of the server CPU horsepower.

Exadata Smart Flash Cache bridges this gap by sitting between the server and spinning hard disks. The flash cards are placed directly in the Exadata Storage Server. This allows applications to get the fastest response time required from flash, while storing infrequently used data on slower HDD technology. This happens automatically without the user having to take any action. Exadata Smart Flash Cache is "smart" because it monitors the data usage and stores only frequently used data in the flash cache. If the data is not reused frequently, then Exadata Smart Flash Cache avoids caching that data. Exadata Smart Flash Cache helps to enable a full-rack Oracle Exadata Machine to process up to 2,660,000 random I/O operations per second (IOPS), with scan data at a rate of up to 100 GB/second.

Each Exadata Storage Server comes preconfigured with Exadata Smart Flash Cache. The Exadata Smart Flash Cache is built on Sun's Open Flash Module - Sun Flash Accelerator F80 cards. This low-latency, solid-state flash storage is packaged on a PCI card. There are four flash cards in each Exadata Storage Server, and each card has a capacity of 800GB of flash, totaling 3.2TB.

> **NOTE**
> *The flash cards that are used in the Exadata Storage Cells are not flash disks. These cards are placed directly in the PCI slots, which are connected directly to the bus—hence, the performance of the flash cards is not bottlenecked by the slow disk controllers and neither the bandwidth nor IOPS is compromised.*

Exadata Smart Flash Cache offers two behaviors: write-through and write-back. With write-through, frequently accessed data is cached into the Exadata Smart Flash Cache; with write-back cache, the Exadata Smart Flash Cache also caches database block writes. Write caching eliminates disk bottlenecks in large-scale OLTP and batch workloads. The Exadata write cache is transparent, persistent, and fully redundant. The default behavior of the Exadata Machine is write-through cache. Write-back cache must be manually enabled on the Exadata Database Machine.

Next, let's see how the Exadata Smart Flash Cache works for read and write operations.

Exadata Smart Flash Cache and Read Operations

There are two main types of read operations: read operation on non-cached data and read operation on cached data.

Read Operation on Non-Cached Data

Whenever a data block is accessed by query, it is not immediately stored in Exadata Smart Flash Cache. There are some criteria that CELLSRV uses to determine if the data block can be stored in the Exadata Smart Flash Cache. When a query requests the data from the Exadata Storage Servers, all the data blocks that are scanned and returned by the query are updated with a numeric value called "touch count." Every time the same data block is accessed by any query, the touch count is increased by 1. Thus, if a data block is accessed five times, the touch count for that data block will be equal to 5. When the touch count for any data block becomes more than 1, i.e., when it is accessed twice, it is automatically cached in the Exadata Smart Flash Cache.

The Exadata server process (CELLSRV) maintains a hash table that it uses to store the touch count for each data block. This hash table is stored in the grid disks, which apart from storing the touch count, also record the last access time. The hash table is not persistent; that means whenever the CELLSRV is rebooted, this information is lost.

Exadata Smart Flash Cache uses the Least Recently Used (LRU) algorithm for keeping and replacing data blocks in the Exadata Smart Flash Cache. There are three main types of LRU that Exadata Smart Flash Cache maintains:

- **Auxiliary**   This LRU is used to keep the cold cache (cold cache refers to data that is residing in Exadata Smart Flash Cache but is not being used actively and can be flushed from the Exadata Smart Flash Cache anytime) and free cache lists. Whenever the data is kept in Exadata Smart Flash Cache, free cache list for keeping the data block is obtained from Auxiliary.

- **Main**   This is the LRU where active/hot data is stored in the Exadata Smart Flash Cache. Whenever a free cache list is obtained from the Auxiliary LRU, the corresponding data is stored in the Main LRU. The hot buffer stays in the Main LRU as long as it has been accessed frequently. The Main LRU also contains the cold data (cold data refers to the data block that is not accessed frequently), which eventually is moved to the Auxiliary LRU.

- **Keep**   This LRU is used to keep only the data blocks that have the keep flag enabled. We are going to learn more about this in the upcoming section "CELL_FLASH_CACHE Setting and Cache Hint." The keep flag is used if you want to explicitly pin any table in the Exadata Smart Flash Cache. If the keep flag is enabled for a particular table, the data blocks are not impacted by the LRU algorithm.

Whenever the touch count of a particular data block is increased by 1, a process called "replenish" moves it in front of the LRU. This process also moves the coldest data into the AUX LRU.

For OLTP and DW, these three LRUs are maintained separately. Thus, we have DW AUX, OLTP AUX, DW MAIN, and OLTP MAIN and DW KEEP AND OLTP KEEP.

Every I/O that comes to Exadata Smart Flash Cache has the information if it is a DW I/O or DW I/O. DW, and OLTP information is tracked in the cache header, and thus the data block is cached in the appropriate LRUs.

By default, 50 percent of the total flash cache is reserved for OLTP. You can change this setting by changing the parameter (_cell_fc_oltp_resv_pcntg) in the cellinit.ora file.

The following is the order of priority when a data block is cached in the Exadata Smart Flash Cache:

1. KEEP (OLTP KEEP or DW KEEP) gets top priority. Any table that has the KEEP flag enabled is kept on the Exadata Smart Flash Cache.

2. The OLTP reserved percentage gets the next priority for keeping the data blocks in the Exadata Smart Flash Cache.

3. Any other OLTP or DW I/O.

When an OLTP I/O needs a free cache line for keeping a data block in the Exadata Smart Flash Cache, it checks both the OLTP and DW AUX LRUs to see which LRU has the oldest data block. It compares the timestamp and touch count to find the oldest data block. Once it finds the oldest data block, it replaces, it irrespective of DW or OLTP. Similarly, if a DW IO needs a free cache line for keeping a data block in the Exadata Smart Flash Cache, it also checks both the OLTP and DW AUX LRUs to see which LRU has the oldest data block and replaces it accordingly. The only difference here is DW cannot use/replace OLTP AUX LRU if the OLTP used size is less than the OLTP reserved size.

Read Operation on Cached Data

For cached data, the database sends a read request to the Exadata Storage Server in the same way it sends a request for non-cached data. As soon as the request comes to CELLSRV, it checks the in-memory hash table to see if the data is residing in the Exadata Smart Flash Cache. If it exists, it updates the touch count and the last update stamp for that particular data block. If CELLSRV finds the data in the Exadata Smart Flash Cache, then cache lookup is used to satisfy the I/O request and the requested data is returned to the database. Since the touch count got bumped up by one, the replenish process moves the data block ahead in the LRU algorithm.

To optimize resources, smart table scans are usually stored to disks directly unless the object has a CELL_FLASH_CACHE setting of KEEP. In that case, the reads may be serviced by the Exadata Smart Flash Cache.

Exadata Smart Flash Cache and Write Operations

When the database requests that a data block be written to the disk, depending on the kind of flash algorithm (write-through or write-back), the Exadata Storage Server takes appropriate action.

When write-through flash is enabled, as soon as the write request comes, CELLSRV writes the data to the physical disks; as soon as the write operation is complete, CELLSRV sends that acknowledgment to the database. After writing to the disk, the data may be staged back to the cache if the software determines it is likely to be subsequently reread.

When write-back cache is enabled, as soon as the write request comes, the data is written to the Exadata Smart Flash Cache and marked as "dirty." The data continues to remain in the Exadata Smart Flash Cache. The LRU algorithm and CELL_FLASH_CACHE setting determine when the data needs to be flushed out of the Exadata Smart Flash Cache and written to the physical disk. All the writes that happen to the Exadata Smart Flash Cache are mirrored to protect the data against flash card failures.

CELL_FLASH_CACHE Setting and Cache Hint

All the database read and write I/O operations are tagged with additional information in the request about whether the data is likely to be read again and therefore whether it should be cached. The I/O is tagged with two main information CELL_FLASH_ CACHE settings, which determine whether to keep the data in the Exadata Smart Flash Cache, and a cache hint, which governs the reason for the I/O.

CELL_FLASH_CACHE has three settings:

- **KEEP**   Specifies that the object should be kept in Exadata Smart Flash Cache

- **DEFAULT**   Specifies that Exadata Smart Flash Cache should cache the object normally using its standard LRU algorithm

- **NONE**   Specifies that the object should not be cached in the Exadata Smart Flash Cache

Objects with a CELL_FLASH_CACHE setting of KEEP are subject to a different cache retention policy than objects with a CELL_FLASH_CACHE setting of DEFAULT. KEEP objects have priority over DEFAULT objects, so that new data from a DEFAULT object will not push out cached data from any KEEP objects. To prevent KEEP objects from monopolizing the cache, they are allowed to occupy no more than 80 percent of the total cache size. Also, to prevent unused KEEP objects from indefinitely occupying the cache, they are subject to an additional aging policy that periodically purges from the cache unused KEEP object data.

If a table with a KEEP attribute is spread across several Oracle Exadata Storage Servers, each one will cache its part of the table in its own Exadata Smart Flash Cache. If caches are of sufficient size, the table is likely to be completely cached over time.

The cache hint also has three settings:

- **CACHE**   Indicates that the I/O should be cached in the Exadata Smart Flash Cache.

- **NOCACHE**   Indicates that the I/O should not be cached in the Exadata Smart Flash Cache.

- **EVICT**   Indicates that the data should be removed from the Exadata Smart Flash Cache. In systems where the write-back cache is enabled, a cache hint of EVICT writes the data from the Exadata Smart Flash Cache to the physical disks.

Because Exadata Smart Flash Cache is intelligent, it knows what data to cache and what data not to cache. It helps to use the flash cache in full to maximize the performance potential of the Exadata Smart Flash Cache. It keeps and skips the following operations. All the cache operations have a CACHE hint, whereas all the skip caching operations have a NOCACHE hint.

- Skips caching I/Os to mirror copies

- Skips caching backups

- Skips caching data pump I/O

- Skips caching tablespace formatting

- Skips full table scans unless CELL_FLASH_CACHE setting is KEEP

- Caches control file reads and writes

- Caches file header reads and writes

- Caches data blocks and index blocks

Pinning Objects in Flash Cache

Exadata Smart Flash Cache provides additional flexibility and control to users to determine if they want to manually keep any object in the Exadata Smart Flash Cache and which ones should not be cached at all. This feature is very useful for OLTP customers since it provided greater flexibility; for example, during quarter end, all the financial tables can be kept in the Exadata Smart Flash Cache so that all the batch jobs related to quarter close can finish quickly.

The CELL_FLASH_CACHE storage clause attribute allows the override of the automatic caching policy when the COMPATIBLE parameter is greater than or equal to 11.2.0.0. This storage clause attribute can be used to specify how DB objects are cached in Exadata Smart Flash Cache. The storage clause can be provided during the **CREATE** and **ALTER** commands for a table or other objects. A table can be pinned into the Exadata Smart Flash Cache by running the command. As discussed previously, the parameter CELL_FLASH_CACHE has three settings: KEEP, DEFAULT, and NONE.

```
ALTER TABLE <table_name> STORAGE (CELL_FLASH_CACHE KEEP);
```

Similarly, if a table should not be kept in the Exadata Smart Flash Cache, then the command would be

```
ALTER TABLE <table_name> STORAGE (CELL_FLASH_CACHE NONE);
```

The storage clause CELL_FLASH_CACHE can be provided during the table creation itself:

```
CREATE TABLE SALES_DATA (inventory number, item varchar(100) )
TABLESPACE SALES
STORAGE (CELL_FLASH_CACHE KEEP));
```

In a partitioned table, different partitions can have different storage clauses for CELL_FLASH_CACHE KEEP:

```
CREATE TABLE test (c1 number, c2 clob) TABLESPACE TBS_1
PARTITION BY RANGE(c1) (PARTITION p1 VALUES LESS THAN (100) TABLESPACE
TBS_2 STORAGE (CELL_FLASH_CACHE DEFAULT),PARTITION p2 VALUES LESS THAN
(200) TABLESPACETBS_3 STORAGE (CELL_FLASH_CACHE KEEP));
```

The USER_TABLES can be checked to query the CELL_FLASH_CACHE_SETTING for a particular table. Similarly, other objects such as indexes will have information in ALL_INDEXES, LOB columns in ALL_LOB_PARTITIONS, partitions in ALL_TAB_PARTITIONS, and so on.

```
SQL> SELECT CELL_FLASH_CACHE FROM USER_TABLES WHERE TABLE_NAME='SALES_DATA';
```

TIP & TECHNIQUE
Pinning the objects in the Exadata Smart Flash Cache does not move the data from the disks to the flash queue. When you run a query for a table that has KEEP as the storage clause, the data is pinned to the flash cache.

Exadata Smart Flash Cache and Flash Grid Disks

Flash modules are exposed and accessed as Linux block devices. When an Exadata cell is installed, by default, cell disks are created on flash block devices, and all available space on these flash-based cell disks is assigned to be used as Smart Flash Cache. User data is automatically cached using the default caching behavior. By default, the Exadata Smart Flash Cache uses all the available space.

Optionally, a portion or all space on flash-based cell disks can be reserved and used as grid disks. Flash-based grid disks are assigned to an Automatic Storage Management (ASM) disk group in a way similar to non-flash grid disks. The best practice would be to reserve the same amount of flash on each Exadata cell for flash grid disks and have the ASM disk group spread evenly across the Exadata cells in the configuration, just as you would do for regular Exadata grid disks. This will evenly distribute the flash I/O load across the Exadata cells and flash.

After the introduction of Write-Back Flash Cache, creating separate flash grid disks doesn't make sense, since flash write-back does the same thing. Moreover, creation of flash-based grid disks requires advance planning to ensure that adequate space is reserved for the tablespaces stored on them. In addition, backup of the data on the flash disks must be done in case media recovery is required. This shrinks the size of the Exadata Smart Flash Cache.

The Write-Back Flash Cache eliminates some of the practices customers used to follow in previous versions of Exadata. Previously, customers used to create TEMP files on flash to handle high levels of write activity, such as heavily written tables. With Write-Back Flash Cache, there is no need to create a separate TEMP file on flash.

When an Exadata cell is installed, by default, the **CREATE CELL** command, which is run as part of one command to configure the Exadata Storage Server, creates flash cell disks on all flash cards; then it creates an Exadata Smart Flash Cache on the flash cell disks. To change the size of the Exadata Smart Flash Cache or create flash grid disks, you need to remove the flash cache and then create the flash cache with a different size, or create flash grid disks.

You can also create a flash cache by explicitly using the **CREATE FLASHCACHE** command. This command uses the celldisk attribute to specify which flash cell disks will contain a cache in case the Exadata Smart Flash needs to be created with a few flash cell disks. Alternatively, ALL can be specified to indicate that all flash cell disks will be used. The SIZE attribute is used to specify the total size of the flash cache to be allocated, and the allocation is evenly distributed across the flash cell disks. If SIZE is not specified, then all available space on the flash cell disks is used for flash cache.

Steps to Reconfigure the Exadata Smart Flash Cache and Create a Flash-Based Disk Group

To query the details of the existing Exadata Smart Flash Cache on a storage cell, run the following command:

```
CellCLI> LIST FLASHCACHE DETAIL
```

It will give the information about configured Smart Flash Cache size, current status, on which flash-based cell disks it is located, and other information.

```
CellCLI> LIST FLASHCACHE DETAIL
        name:                   exa10cel02_FLASHCACHE
        cellDisk:               FD_10_exa10cel02,FD_00_exa10cel02,FD_13_
exa10cel02,FD_15_exa10cel02,FD_05_exa10cel02,FD_14_exa10cel02,FD_08_
exa10cel02,FD_02_exa10cel02,FD_07_exa10cel02,FD_06_exa10cel02,FD_09_
exa10cel02,FD_03_exa10cel02,FD_04_exa10cel02,FD_11_exa10cel02,FD_12_
exa10cel02,FD_01_exa10cel02
        creationTime:           2014-03-25T14:15:41-07:00
        degradedCelldisks:
        effectiveCacheSize:     2978.75G
        id:                     d002af24-de1c-4c86-b644-0b31c8dc22a5
```

```
        size:                   2978.75G
        status:                 normal

CellCLI>
```

In the preceding code, the status can be normal, warning, or critical.

You can see that all the usable flash memory is configured as Exadata Smart Flash Cache. This is the default behavior whenever a new machine is installed.

```
CellCLI> list celldisk attributes name, freeSpace, size where
diskType=FlashDisk
        FD_00_exa10cel02        0       186.25G
        FD_01_exa10cel02        0       186.25G
        FD_02_exa10cel02        0       186.25G
        FD_03_exa10cel02        0       186.25G
        FD_04_exa10cel02        0       186.25G
        FD_05_exa10cel02        0       186.25G
        FD_06_exa10cel02        0       186.25G
        FD_07_exa10cel02        0       186.25G
        FD_08_exa10cel02        0       186.25G
        FD_09_exa10cel02        0       186.25G
        FD_10_exa10cel02        0       186.25G
        FD_11_exa10cel02        0       186.25G
        FD_12_exa10cel02        0       186.25G
        FD_13_exa10cel02        0       186.25G
        FD_14_exa10cel02        0       186.25G
        FD_15_exa10cel02        0       186.25G
```

The Flash Cache can be dropped at any time by running this command:

```
CellCLI> DROP FLASHCACHE
Flash cache exa10cel02_FLASHCACHE successfully dropped
```

Now let's run the command again to see how much free space is available:

```
CellCLI> list celldisk attributes name , freeSpace , size where
diskType=FlashDisk
        FD_00_exa10cel02        186.25G         186.25G
        FD_01_exa10cel02        186.25G         186.25G
        FD_02_exa10cel02        186.25G         186.25G
        FD_03_exa10cel02        186.25G         186.25G
        FD_04_exa10cel02        186.25G         186.25G
        FD_05_exa10cel02        186.25G         186.25G
        FD_06_exa10cel02        186.25G         186.25G
        FD_07_exa10cel02        186.25G         186.25G
        FD_08_exa10cel02        186.25G         186.25G
        FD_09_exa10cel02        186.25G         186.25G
        FD_10_exa10cel02        186.25G         186.25G
        FD_11_exa10cel02        186.25G         186.25G
```

```
FD_12_exa10cel02        186.25G        186.25G
FD_13_exa10cel02        186.25G        186.25G
FD_14_exa10cel02        186.25G        186.25G
FD_15_exa10cel02        186.25G        186.25G
```

You can see that the Exadata Smart Flash Cache has been dropped and all the flash is now available. Let's now take a part of celldisk and create the Exadata Smart Flash Cache. With the remaining <celldisk>, we will create the flash ASM disk groups.

Let's allocate 1600GB for the Exadata Smart Flash Cache. This cache can be re-created at any time by running this command:

```
CellCLI> CREATE FLASHCACHE ALL size 1600g
Flash cache exa10cel02_FLASHCACHE successfully created
```

Now let's query the space usage one more time:

```
CellCLI> list celldisk attributes name , freeSpace , size where
diskType=FlashDisk
        FD_00_exa10cel02         86.25G         186.25G
        FD_01_exa10cel02         86.25G         186.25G
        FD_02_exa10cel02         86.25G         186.25G
        FD_03_exa10cel02         86.25G         186.25G
        FD_04_exa10cel02         86.25G         186.25G
        FD_05_exa10cel02         86.25G         186.25G
        FD_06_exa10cel02         86.25G         186.25G
        FD_07_exa10cel02         86.25G         186.25G
        FD_08_exa10cel02         86.25G         186.25G
        FD_09_exa10cel02         86.25G         186.25G
        FD_10_exa10cel02         86.25G         186.25G
        FD_11_exa10cel02         86.25G         186.25G
        FD_12_exa10cel02         86.25G         186.25G
        FD_13_exa10cel02         86.25G         186.25G
        FD_14_exa10cel02         86.25G         186.25G
        FD_15_exa10cel02         86.25G         186.25G
```

You can see that 1600GB of the space has been allocated for the Exadata Smart Flash Cache. The total size of the flash cell disk is 186.25GB, and the free space available in each flash cell disk is 86.25GB. Thus, the Exadata Smart Flash Cache is spread across all the available flash-based cell disks, so the 1600GB of the Exadata Smart Flash Cache is made up of the 100GB (186.25GB – 86.25GB) on each of the 16 flash-based cell disks.

The remaining 1380GB of space is available for the creation of the flash-based ASM disk group. We need to create the flash disk first in order to use the free space for creating the flash-based ASM disk group.

To create the flash disk, run the following command. A unique prefix is given to distinguish the flash disk for ASM disk groups from the flash disks used for the Exadata Smart Flash Cache.

```
Cellcli> create griddisk all flashdisk prefix=set01flash size=40G
Griddisk set01flash_FD_00_exa10cel02 successfully created
Griddisk set01flash_FD_01_exa10cel02 successfully created
Griddisk set01flash_FD_02_exa10cel02 successfully created
Griddisk set01flash_FD_03_exa10cel02 successfully created
Griddisk set01flash_FD_04_exa10cel02 successfully created
Griddisk set01flash_FD_05_exa10cel02 successfully created
Griddisk set01flash_FD_06_exa10cel02 successfully created
Griddisk set01flash_FD_07_exa10cel02 successfully created
Griddisk set01flash_FD_08_exa10cel02 successfully created
Griddisk set01flash_FD_09_exa10cel02 successfully created
Griddisk set01flash_FD_10_exa10cel02 successfully created
Griddisk set01flash_FD_11_exa10cel02 successfully created
Griddisk set01flash_FD_12_exa10cel02 successfully created
Griddisk set01flash_FD_13_exa10cel02 successfully created
Griddisk set01flash_FD_14_exa10cel02 successfully created
Griddisk set01flash_FD_15_exa10cel02 successfully created
```

You can create as many flash disk groups as you want. In this example, we will create a second set of flash-based grid disks that will consume the remaining free space on the flash-based cell disks:

```
CellCLI> create griddisk all flashdisk prefix=set02flash
Griddisk set02flash_FD_00_exa10cel02 successfully created
Griddisk set02flash_FD_01_exa10cel02 successfully created
Griddisk set02flash_FD_02_exa10cel02 successfully created
Griddisk set02flash_FD_03_exa10cel02 successfully created
Griddisk set02flash_FD_04_exa10cel02 successfully created
Griddisk set02flash_FD_05_exa10cel02 successfully created
Griddisk set02flash_FD_06_exa10cel02 successfully created
Griddisk set02flash_FD_07_exa10cel02 successfully created
Griddisk set02flash_FD_08_exa10cel02 successfully created
Griddisk set02flash_FD_09_exa10cel02 successfully created
Griddisk set02flash_FD_10_exa10cel02 successfully created
Griddisk set02flash_FD_11_exa10cel02 successfully created
Griddisk set02flash_FD_12_exa10cel02 successfully created
Griddisk set02flash_FD_13_exa10cel02 successfully created
Griddisk set02flash_FD_14_exa10cel02 successfully created
Griddisk set02flash_FD_15_exa10cel02 successfully created
```

Let's check the status of these disks:

```
CellCLI>list griddisk attributes name , size , ASMModeStatus where
disktype=flashdisk
set01flash_FD_00_exa10cel02 40G UNUSED
set02flash_FD_00_exa10cel02 46.25G UNUSED
```

In this example, the results have been truncated to show only one set of flash disks instead of 16 sets. You can see that two sets of flash disks have been created and now we are ready to create the ASM disk groups.

Now log in to the ASM instance as sysasm and query for the flash-based grid disks inside the ASM:

```
sqlplus '/ as sysasm'

SQL> select path , header_status from v$asm_disk where path like 'o/%/set01flash%';

PATH                                              HEADER_STATUS
------------------------------------------------- ---------------
o/192.168.10.9/ set01flash_FD_00_exa10cel02       CANDIDATE
```

The status CANDIDATE indicates that the disks are available for creation of the ASM disk group. (In this example, results of the query are truncated.)

Create the first set of flash ASM disk groups with the command shown in this example:

```
SQL> create diskgroup FLASH1 normal redundancy disk 'o/*/set01flash*'
attribute 'compatible.rdbms'='11.2.0.0.0', 'compatible.asm'='11.2.0.0.0',
'cell.smart_scan_capable'='TRUE', 'au_size'='4M';

Diskgroup created.
```

Similarly, create additional flash-based ASM disk groups like this:

```
SQL> create diskgroup FLASH2 normal redundancy disk 'o/*/set02flash*'
attribute 'compatible.rdbms'='11.2.0.0.0', 'compatible.asm'='11.2.0.0.0',
'cell.smart_scan_capable'='TRUE', 'au_size'='4M';

Diskgroup created.
```

ASM automatically takes care of mirroring the data. The flash-based disks on different Exadata Storage Cells are automatically grouped into separate failure groups.

TIP & TECHNIQUE

With the introduction of Write-Back Flash Cache, there is no need to create flash-based ASM disk groups. Customers used to do this in previous generations of Exadata, where the size of Exadata Smart Flash Cache was small and there were no flash write-back capabilities.

Monitoring Flash Usage

From the database and the Exadata Storage Cells it can be easily found out if the data is being cached into the Exadata Smart Flash Cache or not. In order to find the statistics for a particular table, run the command as shown in this example:

```
SQL> SELECT data_object_id FROM DBA_OBJECTS
  2            WHERE object_name=SALES_DATA;
  OBJECT_ID
  ---------
  4194432
```

Query for the object_id in the Exadata Storage Server to get the details. The **LIST FLASHCACHECONTENT** command provides caching statistics for individual DB objects:

```
CellCLI> LIST FLASHCACHECONTENT where objectNumber=4194432 detail
  cachedKeepSize:      0
      cachedSize:      19660891
      dbID:            3353184300
      dbUniqueName:    DEMANTRA
      hitCount:        9972
      missCount:       0
      objectNumber:    4194432
      tableSpaceNumber: 3
```

You can see that 19,660,891 bytes of the data of the SALES_DATA table are cached into the Exadata Smart Flash Cache. This data has been intelligently cached by the Exadata Smart Flash Cache and not manually cached, since the cachedKeepSize is zero. The cachedKeepSize parameter shows the bytes of the data that have been cached by running the command **CELL_FLASH_CACHE.KEEP**. The hitCount parameter denotes how many times the object has been accessed from the Exadata Smart Flash Cache, and missCount denotes how many times the object was requested from the Exadata Smart Flash Cache but could not be found.

NOTE
*If the command **FLASH_CACHE.KEEP** is run instead of the **CELL_FLASH_CACHE.KEEP**, you won't see any activity in the flash cache.*

The previous example shows the statistics for the SALES_DATA table only from one storage cell. The aggregate statistics from all the storage cells can be obtained from the database as well by running this query:

```
SQL> SELECT statistic_name, value
  2      FROM V$SEGMENT_STATISTICS
  3      WHERE dataobj#= 4194432 AND ts#=3 AND
```

```
4       statistic_name='optimized physical reads';

STATISTIC_NAME                  VALUE
----------------------          ------
optimized physical reads        43660891
```

optimized physical reads reflects the number of disk I/Os saved by the Exadata Storage Index along with I/Os satisfied from the cell flash cache.

The overall statistics for Smart Flash Cache on a cell can be obtained by running this command:

```
LIST METRICCURRENT WHERE objectType='FLASHCACHE'

        FC_BY_USED                      FLASHCACHE 1,084,765 MB
        FC_IO_BYKEEP_R                  FLASHCACHE 15,298 MB
        FC_IO_BYKEEP_R_SEC              FLASHCACHE 0.000 MB/sec
        FC_IO_BYKEEP_W                  FLASHCACHE 61,304 MB
        FC_IO_BYKEEP_W_SEC              FLASHCACHE 0.000 MB/sec
        FC_IO_BY_ALLOCATED_OLTP         FLASHCACHE 612,473 MB
```

FLASHCACHE metrics provide overall cell-level statistics for Smart Flash Cache. You can see how much data is currently cached, the total number of cache hits and cache misses, the current rates (per second) for cache hits and cache misses, the number of flash I/O errors, and other information. More than 30 various flash-related metrics are available.

The detail information about each metric can be obtained by running this query:

```
CellCLI> LIST METRICDEFINITION FC_BY_USED DETAIL
    name:          FC_BY_USED
    description:   "Number of megabytesused on FlashCache"
CellCLI> LIST METRICDEFINITION FC_IO_BYKEEP_R DETAIL
    name:          FC_IO_BYKEEP_R
    description:   "Number of megabytes read from FlashCache for keep
objects"
```

For a DB, the cumulative number of I/O requests satisfied from a flash cache on all participating cells is available in V$SYSSTAT. All the metrics that provide the flash-related information from V$SYSSTAT are given next. Similar statistics are also available in V$SESSTAT and V$MYSTAT.

```
cell writes to flash cache
cell overwrites in flash cache
cell partial writes in flash cache
physical read flash cache hits
flash cache inserts
flash cache eviction: invalidated
flash cache eviction: buffer pinned
```

```
flash cache eviction: aged out
flash cache insert skip: not current
flash cache insert skip: DBWR overloaded
flash cache insert skip: exists
flash cache insert skip: not useful
flash cache insert skip: modification
flash cache insert skip: corrupt
physical reads for flashback new
flashback cache read optimizations for block new
flashback direct read optimizations for block new
flashback log writes
flashback log write bytes
cell flash cache read hits

SQL> SELECT name, value FROM V$SYSSTAT WHERE NAME IN ('cell writes to
flash cache','cell flash cache read hits');

NAME                                               VALUE
-------------------------------------------------- ----------
cell writes to flash cache                          44139080
cell flash cache read hits                          85213533
```

More Exadata Smart Flash Cache Features

Exadata Smart Flash Cache provides three additional features:

- Flash cache compression

- Smart flash logs

- Flash write-back

We will discuss these features in detail in Chapter 4.

Resource Manager

Storage is often shared by different workloads on multiple databases. Shared storage, however, is not a perfect solution. Running multiple types of workloads and databases on shared storage often leads to performance problems. For example, large parallel queries on one production data warehouse can impact the performance of critical queries on another production data warehouse. Also, a data load on a data warehouse can impact the performance of critical queries also running on it. You can mitigate these problems by over-provisioning the storage system, but this diminishes the cost savings of shared storage. You can also avoid running non-critical tasks at peak times, but manually achieving this is laborious.

When databases have different administrators who do not coordinate their activities, the task is even more difficult.

I/O Resource Manager (IORM) enables workloads and databases to share Exadata I/O resources automatically according to user-defined policies. To manage workloads within a database, you can define intra-database resource plans using the Database Resource Manager (DBRM), which has been enhanced to work in conjunction with Exadata. To manage workloads across multiple databases, you can define IORM plans. IORM is an extension of the Resource Manager capabilities, so it's fully integrated and doesn't have to be managed separately. IORM inherits the same consumer groups that are set up in DBRM.

For example, if a production database and a test database are sharing an Exadata cell, you can configure resource plans that give priority to the production database. In this case, whenever the test database load would affect the production database performance, IORM will schedule the I/O requests such that the production database I/O performance is not impacted. This means that the test database I/O requests are queued until they can be issued without disturbing the production database I/O performance. Similarly, if you have multiple databases in the same Exadata machine, IORM can be created to distribute the I/O resources across multiple databases.

Resource Manager will be covered in depth in Chapter 7.

Summary

Exadata is an engineered system that is optimized at all levels to maximize performance. In this chapter, we have covered the following features of Exadata:

- Hybrid Columnar Compression
- Smart Scan
- Exadata Smart Flash Cache
- Resource Manager

CHAPTER
4

Leveraging Exadata
Features for Applications

E xadata was initially launched as a data warehouse machine. Subsequent generations of Exadata are leveraged for online transaction processing (OLTP) customers as well. Many OLTP customers have adopted Exadata, and more and more customers are considering it for running their application because of the tremendous benefits it offers. This chapter describes characteristics of an OLTP system and then discusses how the features of Exadata can be used to maximize performance of OLTP systems.

Characteristics of an OLTP System

Following are the characteristics of an OLTP system:

- **Concurrent users** An OLTP system can accommodate a very large number of concurrent users and database sessions. It is not uncommon to see more than several hundred users connected in the system at any point in time—for example, a small E-Business Suite application customer has around 300 to 500 concurrent users, a midsize customer typically has around 500 to 2000 concurrent users, and a large customer can have more than 2000 concurrent users. In comparison, a PeopleSoft system accommodates around 2000 customers for a small to medium application footprint, 10,000 for large, and 20,000 for extra-large customers. Concurrent users are different from the total number of users. Concurrent users are those users who are connected to the system. Thus, the total number of concurrent users at any point in time is equal to users who are connected to the system at that point in time.

- **Quick response time** Response time is very crucial for any OLTP system. The quicker the response times, the faster the system. An important attribute while designing any OLTP system is a very fast I/O response time. A fast OLTP system usually offers an I/O response time of less than a few milliseconds.

- **Busy system** An OLTP system is usually busy all the time. In addition to performing online transactions, an OLTP system is used for running batch jobs and reports. It's not uncommon for reporting programs to run in the background as online users are simultaneously accessing the system and performing their day-to-day tasks. Sometimes the jobs running in the background require large data processing requirements that can impact the performance of the online users. Any OLTP is often integrated with lots of other systems. For example, an order management system may be integrated with an accounts payable system, a financial system may be integrated with a tax payment system, and so on. The integrated systems can also kick off several jobs into the OLTP system, making even more work for the system.

- **Larger population** OLTP systems typically have very large user populations, with many users trying to access the same data at the same time. For example, in an order management system, hundreds of people must simultaneously input data from customers' telephone orders. A sales person who is processing an order over the phone must also check the inventory to make sure the item is in stock. The nature of the system is such that at any time, a large number of users are querying against the same set of inventory tables and the same data set.

- **Primarily small transactions** OLTP systems typically read and update highly selective and small amounts of data. The data processing is usually simple in nature, without involving complex joins—such as changing the status of the inventory, adding new items, and so on. Though the transactions are small, many transactions occur simultaneously in the system, making for a very busy system.

- **Data retention** Depending on the nature of the application, the data retention in OLTP can sometimes become very large. Many financial customers store data in their enterprise resource planning (ERP) system for more than 15 years. Government legislation usually dictates the data retention policy for any OLTP system, which can differ from system to system; some OLTP systems may have the flexibility to purge old data, while some may not.

- **Different lifecycle data usage** OLTP systems often require different data access patterns. For example, a financial company closes its book of accounts every quarter and at the end of the year. The quarter-or year-end activities run only during those specified periods. Similarly, other lifecycle patterns, such as those for payroll, run biweekly; taxes are paid annually; and so on.

- **Highly available** Critical OLTP systems must always be highly available. All the mission-critical business of any company runs on OLTP systems; thus, it is very important that the systems are always up and running. A system outage can cause major revenue loss. Most OLTP systems are designed to be always available, and any downtime, other than maintenance downtime, requires the highest levels of approval. There may be some exceptions to this as well—for example, some internal noncritical OLTP applications in an organization may not have to be highly available. But in an enterprise, all the most important systems must always be highly available.

- **Priority-one system** An OLTP system is always the first-priority system compared to any data warehouse system. An OLTP always gets priority in terms of support, resources, and staff. An OLTP system always has a stricter service level agreement (SLA) compared to a data warehouse system and must usually be available on a 24/7 basis.

Exadata Features

To get maximum benefit of an OLTP system, you need to consider several features of Exadata, irrespective of the nature of the OLTP system. The following features can benefit an OLTP system the most:

- Write-Back Flash Cache
- Smart Flash Logging
- Smart Flash Cache compression
- Leveraging InfiniBand for database links
- Routing traffic through InfiniBand between the application and database tiers
- Configuring HugePages

We will discuss these features in depth one by one.

Write-Back Flash Cache

As the name suggests, Write-Back Flash Cache (WBFC) enables write operations to go to flash disks instead of the hard drive. By default, WBFC is not enabled in Exadata. OLTP applications benefit a lot from the WBFC, however, so it's a best practice to enable it in any OLTP system.

Most writing in Oracle Database is done without the user waiting for those writes, as long as the Database Writer (DBWR) is keeping up. Some writing is synchronous to the end-user transaction, such as sorts, writes, or direct writes. Users wait for Log Writer (LGWR) writes at commit time.

How the Write-Back Flash Cache Works

Whenever a write operation occurs, the Cell Services (CELLSRV) process running on Exadata storage cells analyzes the write operation and determines if it can be written in the Flash Cache. If it finds that the data is a candidate for caching, it writes the data to the Flash Cache. Once the data is written to the Flash Cache, an acknowledgment is sent back to the database and the data is kept in the Flash Cache. The data retention policy in the Flash Cache uses the Least Recently Used (LRU) algorithm in which the least recently used data is flushed to the physical disk when the Flash Cache becomes full. Normally, a data block is kept in Flash Cache until it ages out, which could be in days, months, or years, depending on when the data block stopped being accessed. Eventually, the data will age out and be written to the physical disk. During any flash write operation, if CELLSRV finds that the Flash Cache is full, it immediately pushes the oldest data block to the physical disk to create more space in the Flash Cache.

Operations such as backups and data pump reads and writes are not written in the Flash Cache. Exadata smartly caches only the important data into the Flash Cache to make the most of the space. For any OLTP system, typically I/O is the biggest bottleneck, and smart caching the data also helps the OLTP system to maximize the I/Os needed for OLTP operation, bypassing the noncritical I/Os to physical disk and thereby providing maximum performance.

The data in the Flash Cache is persistent and is not affected by storage cell reboots, power outages, and shutdowns. Writes are duplicated across cells, so written blocks will be in Flash Cache on multiple cells. Reads are not duplicated across cells, so the contents of Flash Cache will be different across cells. The LRU algorithm applies to blocks within a cell, so even the written blocks won't necessarily always be mirrored across cells. In the event of flash card failure, there is no impact on the data or interruption in the application, since the read and write operations are serviced by the mirrored copy, which resides in a different storage cell.

When a flash card fails, the Exadata storage software reads the data from mirror copies on the surviving cells and then determines the data that needs to be remirrored, a process called "resilvering." Resilvering is an automated process and no manual intervention is required. The resilvering process kicks in when the disk_repair_time is reached.

When the WBFC is enabled, some of the data may be kept in Flash Cache, and since the data has not aged out, it is not written to physical disk. In this case, most of the data is in the physical disk and some of the data is still in flash. You might be wondering what happens if a database backup occurs at this time. Will the backup take care of the data residing in the Flash Cache? Recovery Manager (RMAN) takes care of backing up the latest data from the disk as well as from the Flash Cache, thereby ensuring that all the data is backed up. RMAN automatically determines where the latest copy of the data is being written and intelligently backs up the data either from the disk or flash.

Advantages of Write-Back Flash Cache

OLTP systems often include write-intensive portions of the application. For example, order management in a high-volume order processing environment is a write-intensive process. In a supply chain implementation, the data collection updates are a write-intensive process, and for financial implementations, all the postings to the general ledger are write-intensive. Enabling the WBFC benefits OLTP systems the most, since the database write operations become significantly fast compared to the write operation in spinning disks. The writes to Flash Cache always bypass the bottlenecks of the disk controller and provide approximately 20 times more I/O per second compared to spinning disks. These fast write operations have a cascading effect on the database, as the redo log files are written faster, affecting the performance of log switches and checkpoints.

Steps for Enabling WBFC

To enable WBFC, follow these steps:

1. Drop the existing write through Flash Cache (WTFC):

   ```
   CellCLI> drop flashcache all
   ```

2. Shut down CELLSRV:

   ```
   CellCLI> alter cell shutdown services cellsrv
   ```

3. Change the Flash Cache mode to write back:

   ```
   CellCLI> alter cell flashcachemode=writeback
   ```

4. Start CELLSRV:

   ```
   CellCLI> alter cell startup services cellsrv
   ```

5. Re-create Flash Cache:

   ```
   CellCLI> create flashcache all
   ```

Verify WBFC is configured by running the following command. It should return "WriteBack". If WBFS is not configured, it will return "WriteThrough".

```
CellCLI> list cell attributes flashcachemode
      WriteBack
```

Smart Flash Logging

As discussed previously, in an OLTP, faster response time is of upmost importance, and having a faster response time for database log writes is very critical. If the redo log write wait time is too long, it will have a negative impact on the system and the overall performance of the database will be impacted.

Smart Flash Logging provides a lot of benefits for the OLTP customer running Exadata machines. Typically, the log files are set up using multiple groups and are mirrored across multiple log files to provide maximum availability. Often, the database ends up waiting for log writes to the physical disks. You can easily verify the write time by running the following query:

```
SQL> select * from v$event_histogram where event='log file parallel write' ;

EVENT# EVENT                   WAIT_TIME_MILLI WAIT_COUNT LAST_UPDATE_TIME
------- ----------------------- --------------- ---------- ----------------
  134   log file parallel write    1              128998   17-APR-14 03.11.28.691323
                                                           AM -04:00
  134   log file parallel write    2                4420   17-APR-14 02.03.27.813620
                                                           PM -04:00
  134   log file parallel write    4                9615   17-APR-14 89.12.29.137408
                                                           AM -04:00
  134   log file parallel write    8                   0
  134   log file parallel write   16                   0
  134   log file parallel write   32                   0
  134   log file parallel write   64                   0
  134   log file parallel write  128                   0
  134   log file parallel write  256                   0
  134   log file parallel write  512                  13   17-APR-14 04.05.23.212608
                                                           PM -04:00
  134   log file parallel write 1024                 890   06-APR-14 08.18.17.823009
                                                           PM -04:00
  134   log file parallel write 2048                 388   07-APR-14 03.05.27.212098 PM
                                                           -04:00
  134   log file parallel write 4096                 198   07-APR-14 04.06.27.212998 PM
                                                           -04:00
```

The output of the query indicates that the wait time for the log file parallel write went up to 4096ms, which indicates that there is a bottleneck in writing to the log files in the existing system. In this case, configuring Smart Flash Logging will provide tremendous benefits to the system as it relieves the bottleneck.

To implement Smart Flash Logging, you need implement no change at the database level. This feature is completely transparent to the database.

Here's how Smart Flash Logging works:

1. Whenever the request for writing the redo log file arrives, Exadata starts writing to the redo logs in parallel, not only to the on-disk redo logs, but also to the space reserved in the flash hardware.

2. The database gets notified when the write activity is completed, whether it is in the disk or in the flash hardware.

3. If the disk drives hosting the logs experience slow response times, then the Exadata Smart Flash Cache will provide a faster log write response time.

The Exadata Smart Flash Cache does not store the redo data permanently; it stores the data temporarily to provide faster response times to redo the write operations. The data of the redo log files is stored in the Smart Flash Cache until the data is safely written to the physical disks.

Using Smart Flash Logging does not change anything else in the Smart Flash Cache. Only a small amount of memory is required for the Smart Flash Logging— by default, 512MB of the Exadata flash is allocated to Smart Flash Logging, which is sufficient for most implementations. The storage cell maintains all the statistics related to Smart Flash Logging, and you can get the details of redo writes serviced by flash or disk to determine whether the allocated size of the Smart Flash Log is enough or needs to be expanded. From a DBA's point of view, after implementing Smart Flash Logging, the system behaves in a completely transparent manner and doesn't require any maintenance for day-to-day operations. However, the DBA will notice that the wait event "log file parallel write" will not have consistently long latencies for redo log writes. Smart Flash Logging handles all crash and recovery scenarios without requiring any special configurations beyond what would normally be needed for recovering the database from the redo logs.

Smart Flash Logging requires Exadata Storage Software version 11.2.2.4 or later, Oracle Database version 11.2.0.2 with Bundle Patch 11, and Oracle Database version 11.2.0.3 with Bundle Patch 1, or a later version.

Steps for Configuring the Smart Flash Log

Follow these steps to configure the Smart Flash Log:

1. Log in to the storage cell and run the following query. If the query doesn't return any value, it means that the Smart Flash Log is not configured in that storage cell.

    ```
    CellCLI> list flashlog
    ```

    Check the flash cache of the storage cell by running the command below

    ```
    CellCLI> list flashcache
             exa10cel01_FLASHCACHE normal
    ```

2. Before creating the Smart Flash Log, you must drop the existing Flash Cache. Make sure the data is flushed to the disk before performing this operation:

    ```
    CellCLI> drop flashcache
    Flash cache exa10cel01_FLASHCACHE successfully dropped
    ```

3. Once the Exadata Smart Flash Cache is dropped, configure the Smart Flash Log by running this command:

    ```
    CellCLI> create flashlog all
    Flash log exa10cel01_FLASHCACHE successfully created
    ```

4. Next, re-create the Smart Flash Cache using this command:

    ```
    CellCLI> create flashcache all
    Flash cache exa10cel01_FLASHCACHE successfully created
    ```

5. Verify the Smart Flash Log by running the following queries:

```
CellCLI> list flashlog
        exa10cel01_FLASHLOG normal

CellCLI> list flashlog detail
        name:                  exa10cel01_FLASHLOG
        cellDisk:              FD_05_exa10cel01,FD_14_exa10cel01,FD_02_
exa10cel01,FD_04_exa10cel01,FD_00_exa10cel01,FD_11_exa10cel01,FD_09_
exa10cel01,FD_03_exa10cel01,FD_10_exa10cel01,FD_01_exa10cel01,FD_06_
exa10cel01,FD_08_exa10cel01,FD_07_exa10cel01,FD_15_exa10cel01,FD_13_
exa10cel01,FD_12_exa10cel01
        creationTime:          2014-03-05T11:32:14-08:00
        degradedCelldisks:
        effectiveSize:         512M
        efficiency:            100.0
        id:                    682f7a85-2c76-4569-a219-756a00f65a36
        size:                  512M
        status:                normal
```

The Smart Flash Log can be configured in all the storage cells at the same time by using the `dcli` tool. The sequence of operations remains the same.

6. Drop the existing Exadata Smart Flash Cache:

```
dcli -c exa10cel01,exa10cel02,exa10cel03 cellcli -e dropFlash Cache
exa10cel01: Flash cache exa10cel01_FLASHCACHE successfully dropped
exa10cel01: Flash cache exa10cel02_FLASHCACHE successfully dropped
exa10cel03: Flash cache exa10cel03_FLASHCACHE successfully dropped
```

7. Create the Smart Flash Log:

```
dcli -c exa10cel01,exa10cel02,exa10cel03 cellcli -e create flashlog all
exa10cel01: Flash log exa10cel01_FLASHLOG successfully created
exa10cel02: Flash log exa10cel02_FLASHLOG successfully created
exa10cel02: Flash log exa10cel02_FLASHLOG successfully created
```

8. Re-create the Exadata Smart Flash Cache in all the cells:

```
dcli -c exa10cel01,exa10cel02,exa10cel03 cellcli -e create flashcache all

exa10cel01: Flash log exa10cel01_FLASHCACHE successfully created
exa10cel02: Flash log exa10cel02_FLASHCACHE successfully created
exa10cel02: Flash log exa10cel02_FLASHCACHE successfully created
```

9. Once the Smart Flash Log is implemented, check to see how the database behaves. Run the same query again with the Smart Flash Log enabled:

```
SQL> select * from v$event_histogram where event='log file parallel write';

 EVENT# EVENT                  WAIT_TIME_MILLI WAIT_COUNT LAST_UPDATE_
TIME
------- ---------------------- --------------- ---------- --------------
------------------------
```

```
  134    log file parallel write    1              7440282   22-APR-14
12.15.06.309584 PM -04:00
  134    log file parallel write    2                19113   22-APR-14
12.00.36.329095 PM -04:00
  134    log file parallel write    4                 9615   22-APR-14
10.39.27.517408 AM -04:00
  134    log file parallel write    8                 2737   22-APR-14
01.59.38.294171 AM -04:00
  134    log file parallel write   16                 1909   22-APR-14
06.00.12.351405 AM -04:00
  134    log file parallel write   32                  188   22-APR-14
06.00.12.340929 AM -04:00
  134    log file parallel write   64                  182   21-APR-14
03.11.20.717699 AM -04:00
  134    log file parallel write  128                   23   21-APR-14
03.11.28.691323 AM -04:00
  134    log file parallel write  256                   22   21-APR-14
01.03.27.612620 PM -04:00
  134    log file parallel write  512                   13   21-APR-14
06.09.29.222698 PM -04:00
  134    log file parallel write 1024                   12   21-APR-14
08.18.17.834319 PM -04:00

11 rows selected.
```

You can see that there is no 4088ms wait, which was shown previously. The performance of the system has massively improved.

Let's look at some of the metrics of the Smart Flash Log:

```
CellCLI> list metriccurrent where name like 'FL_.*'
          FL_ACTUAL_OUTLIERS              FLASHLOG    0 IO requests
          FL_BY_KEEP                      FLASHLOG    0
          FL_DISK_FIRST                   FLASHLOG    12,978,600 IO requests
          FL_DISK_IO_ERRS                 FLASHLOG    0 IO requests
          FL_EFFICIENCY_PERCENTAGE        FLASHLOG    100 %
          FL_EFFICIENCY_PERCENTAGE_HOUR   FLASHLOG    100 %
          FL_FLASH_FIRST                  FLASHLOG    3,297,208 IO requests
          FL_FLASH_IO_ERRS                FLASHLOG    0 IO requests
          FL_FLASH_ONLY_OUTLIERS          FLASHLOG    0 IO requests
          FL_IO_DB_BY_W                   FLASHLOG    912,957 MB
          FL_IO_DB_BY_W_SEC               FLASHLOG    0.010 MB/sec
          FL_IO_FL_BY_W                   FLASHLOG    952,734 MB
          FL_IO_FL_BY_W_SEC               FLASHLOG    0.016 MB/sec
          FL_IO_W                         FLASHLOG    16,275,808 IO requests
          FL_IO_W_SKIP_BUSY               FLASHLOG    0 IO requests
          FL_IO_W_SKIP_BUSY_MIN           FLASHLOG    0.0 IO/sec
          FL_IO_W_SKIP_LARGE              FLASHLOG    0 IO requests
          FL_IO_W_SKIP_NO_BUFFER          FLASHLOG    0 IO requests
          FL_PREVENTED_OUTLIERS           FLASHLOG    1,286 IO requests
```

You can see from this example that more than 16,275,808 log write I/Os were serviced by the storage cell (FL_IO_W), out of which 12,978,600 I/O requests were serviced by the disks (FL_DISK_FIRST) and 3,297,208 I/O requests were serviced by the Smart Flash Log (FL_FLASH_FIRST). OUTLIERS represents the redo log write that exceeds half a second, or the latency is half a second. FL_ACTUAL_OUTLIERS tells the number of actual outliers that have occurred, and FL_PREVENTED_OUTLIERS represents the numbers of OUTLIERS the Exadata Smart Flash Log has prevented. From this example, you can also see that FL_ACTUAL_OUTLIERS is zero and FL_PREVENTED_OUTLIERS is 1286. So we can say that for this example, the Smart Flash Log has prevented 1286 outliers. In addition, you can see that FL_EFFICIENCY_PERCENTAGE is 100 percent, which is another level of validation that the outlier is zero.

FL_IO_W_SKIP_BUSY is zero, which means that the Flash Log was never bypassed due to slow disk writes. FL_IO_W_SKIP_NO_BUFFER is also zero, which means the Smart Flash Log was never bypassed due to lack of buffers.

Flash Cache Compression

Exadata X4 comes with a new feature called Flash Cache Compression. Flash Cache Compression not only compresses the data at the Flash Cache level, but also provides performance benefits. The Flash Cache size doubles or more depending on the compression ratio, without adding any hardware. Flash Cache Compression leverages a built-in compression engine, a feature provided by an F80 flash card. As and when the data is written into the Flash Cache, it is compressed and uncompressed during reads at runtime, with no performance overhead.

During any write operation in Flash Cache, the actual data that's being written is equivalent to the logical space that is being used in the Flash Cache. When Flash Cache Compression is not used, the logical space is equal to the physical space, where the actual data is being written in the flash drive. When the data is compressed in the Flash Cache, the amount of physical space needed to write that data is much less than required in the logical space. For example, if 2GB of user data is written in Flash Cache, the amount of logical space needed for that write operation is 2GB; but when the actual write happens in the Flash Cache, the amount of physical space needed is only 1GB or less, depending on the compression ratio and the type of data. If there is no compression at the Flash Cache, then, for our example, the 2GB of user data would have needed 2GB of logical space, which in turn translates to 2GB of physical space in the flash card. Because of the compression ratio, the logical size of the flash disk looks much larger. For example, if the size of the raw flash card were 180GB, then the logical size would be presented in the storage cell as 360GB. Thus, Flash Cache Compression increases the logical Flash Cache size by double or more. This is a great benefit for OLTP customers that offers performance benefits, extra space, and a better compression ratio.

The following Flash Compression ratio benchmarks have been observed by Oracle development:

- Uncompressed tables between 1.3x and 4x

- Index between 1.3x and 4x

- E-Business Suite uncompressed tables to 4x

- OLTP compressed tables 1.2x to 2x

Customers using OLTP compression can still use Flash Cache Compression to compress their data further and get performance benefits. Note that Flash Cache Compression does not apply to Hybrid Columnar Compressed tables because the tables are already highly compressed.

Exadata Smart Flash Cache Compression can be implemented for both "write back" and "write through" Flash Cache. It can be implemented in the F40 and F80 flash cards—that is, with the X3 and X4 hardware. The F20 flash card does not support the Exadata Smart Flash Compression, and the older X2 hardware does not support this feature. It is supported on Exadata Storage Server running on software version 11.2.3.3.0 and later.

By default, Flash Cache Compression is not enabled on the storage cells. It can be enabled very easily, however. Before the Flash Cache Compression is turned on, all the data from the Flash Cache needs to be flushed. When this feature is enabled, the logical address for data within the Flash Cache changes and the overall logical size of the Flash Cache doubles (at least) in size. This process internally formats the device. This operation doesn't impact the data, since all the data is already flushed to the disk before starting this operation.

If you have enabled WBFC, you need to drop the Flash Cache and the cell disks, which are made up of flash, before you can enable Flash Cache Compression. That means any grid disks that have been created in flash need to be dropped, and you need to copy that data to a spinning disk before reformatting the flash.

The data in the Flash Cache can be flushed by issuing the following command:

```
CellCLI> Alter flashcache all flush
```

And all the Flash Cache can be dropped with the following:

```
CellCLI> drop flashcache all
```

If you have enabled Smart Flash Logging, that also needs to be dropped:

```
CellCLI> drop flashlog all
```

And if you have created the cell disk using Flash Cache, it needs to be dropped as well:

```
CellCLI> drop celldisk all flashdisk
```

Steps for Enabling the Flash Cache Compression

For existing storage cells, issue the following command to enable Flash Cache Compression:

```
CellCLI> Alter cell flashCacheCompress=true
```

If you are creating a new cell, use the following command:

```
CellCLI> Create cell <Cell_Name> flashCacheCompress=true
```

In an X3 machine, you need to run an additional command to enable Flash Cache Compression. In X3, the Exadata Storage Cell software version must be 11.2.3.3.0 or later to enable this feature. To use the Flash Cache Compression, Advanced Compression must be licensed.

```
CellCLI> Alter cell flashCacheComX3Support=true
```

Note that in X3 machines, this command needs to be run first before issuing the **<alter cell flashCacheCompresss=true>** command.

To disable Flash Cache Compression, use the following command:

```
CellCLI> Alter cell flashCacheCompress=false
```

After changing the attribute, it can be checked by running this command:

```
CellCLI> List cell attributes =flashCacheCompress
TRUE
```

As discussed previously, after enabling this feature, the logical size of the Flash Cache doubles or more. It can be easily verified from the storage cells by listing the Flash Cache.

```
CellCLI> LIST PHYSICALDISK ATTRIBUTES name, physicalSize WHERE diskType=flashdisk
        FLASH_1_0      186.26451539993286G
        FLASH_1_1      186.26451539993286G
        FLASH_1_2      186.26451539993286G
        FLASH_1_3      186.26451539993286G
        FLASH_2_0      186.26451539993286G
        FLASH_2_1      186.26451539993286G
        FLASH_2_2      186.26451539993286G
        FLASH_2_3      186.26451539993286G
        FLASH_4_0      186.26451539993286G
        FLASH_4_1      186.26451539993286G
        FLASH_4_2      186.26451539993286G
        FLASH_4_3      186.26451539993286G
        FLASH_5_0      186.26451539993286G
        FLASH_5_1      186.26451539993286G
        FLASH_5_2      186.26451539993286G
        FLASH_5_3      186.26451539993286G
```

Before enabling this feature, the size of the Flash Cache was

```
CellCLI> List flashcache attributes name, size
exa10cel01_flashcache 2978.75G
```

And after enabling this feature, the size of the Flash Cache is almost double in size:

```
CellCLI> List flashcache attributes name, size
exa10cel01_flashcache 5958.75G
```

TIP & TECHNIQUE
If you are planning to consolidate multiple databases or the existing size of Exadata Smart Flash Cache is not sufficient enough to keep your important table, consider using Exadata Smart Flash Compression.

Table 4-1 shows the size of the physical disks and Flash Cache after turning the compression on and off. The values have been rounded to the nearest whole number.

From the table, you can see that the size of the flash card (X4 machines/F80) when queried from the Exadata Storage Cell is 186GB, whereas the product data sheet shows the flash card size close to 256GB of raw flash. 60GB of space is maintained for overprovisioning. As discussed previously, the logical space is more than the physical space. The flash translation layer maps the data between the logical address and physical address, which uses the overprovisioning space. The overprovisioning space is used for bad data blocks. Approximately 30 percent of the space in the flash card is kept reserved for the overprovisioning space.

Database Links Over InfiniBand

OLTP systems are often integrated with other systems. For example, an E-Business Suite environment may be connected with an advanced supply chain planning (ASCP) environment. When the planning engine runs in an ASCP environment, it pulls all the data from the E-Business Suite environment; then, when the planning process completes, it updates the E-Business Suite environment. Similarly, an E-Business Suite environment may be connected with a PeopleSoft environment in which human resource information is maintained, while employees perform their day-to-day jobs using the E-Business Suite environment. Or perhaps the ASCP environment is connected with Demantra.

Disk Type	Compression Off X3 F40 Card	Compression On X3 F40 Card	Compression Off X4 F80 Card	Compression On X4 F80 Card
Flash Cache Size	1489GB	2979GB	2979GB	5959GB
Physical Flash Card Size	93GB	186GB	186GB	373GB

TABLE 4-1. *Flash Cache Size With and Without Compression*

Typically, these environments are connected via database links and rely on database links to transfer data from one environment to the other. A database link is a pointer that defines a one-way communication path from one database server to another. The link pointer is actually defined as an entry in a data dictionary table. To access the link, you must be connected to the local database that contains the data dictionary entry.

A database link connection is one-way in the sense that a client connected to local database A can use a link stored in database A to access information in remote database B, but users connected to database B cannot use the same link to access data in database A. If local users on database B want to access data on database A, then they must define a link that is stored in the data dictionary of database B.

A database link connection allows local users to access data on a remote database. For this connection to occur, each database in the distributed system must have a unique global database name in the network domain. The global database name uniquely identifies a database server in a distributed system.

The great advantage of database links is that they allow users to access another user's objects in a remote database so that they are bound by the privilege set of the object owner. In other words, a local user can access a link to a remote database without having to be a user on the remote database.

Assume, for example, that employees submit expense reports to Accounts Payable (AP), using the E-Business Suite database and that a user using an AP application needs to retrieve information about employees from the PeopleSoft database. The AP users should be able to connect to the PeopleSoft database and execute a stored procedure in the remote PeopleSoft database that retrieves the desired information. The AP users should not need to be PeopleSoft database users to do their jobs; they should be able to access PeopleSoft information in a controlled way as limited by the procedure.

A database link is a single-threaded TCP/IP connection where data transfer occurs in a single-threaded fashion. In Exadata Machine, the database listener can be configured to run on the InfiniBand using the bigger pipe. If two or more OLTP systems reside on the Exadata box, then creating the database link over InfiniBand provides the maximum performance benefit.

Database links over InfiniBand can be created only if the InfiniBand Listener is running in the database. The InfiniBand Listener runs in both Socket Direct Protocol (SDP) and Transmission Control Protocol (TCP). Because the database link serves as the connection between two databases, using SDB provides the maximum performance benefit. To use this feature, both databases must reside on an Exadata Machine.

Enabling SDP on Database Nodes

To enable SDP on a database node, follow these steps:

1. Open /etc/infiniband/openib.conf in a text editor and add the following. Then save the file.

```
set: SDP_LOAD=yes
```

2. Open /etc/ofed/libsdp.conf in a text editor and edit the file as follows:

- To use both SDP and TCP, add both of the following rules:

```
use both server * :
use both client * :
```

- To exclude SDP (that is, to use only TCP), add the **use tcp** rule as follows:

```
use tcp server * *:*
use tcp client * *:*
```

- Similarly, SDP can be included in this command by replacing **tcp** with **sdp**. After making the changes, save the file.

3. Open /etc/modprobe.conf in a text editor, and add the following:

```
options ib_sdp sdp_zcopy_thresh=0 recv_poll=0
```

4. Save the file after making the changes. Reboot the database nodes after making the changes.

TIP & TECHNIQUE

For running applications on Exadata, it is recommended that you enable both SDP and TCP for InfiniBand. SDP can be leveraged for InfiniBand connectivity between two databases running on Exadata. If the application tier runs on an Exalogic machine, then either SDP or TCP can be used for the Exalogic and Exadata connectivity using InfiniBand.

Enabling SDP on an InfiniBand Network

To enable SDP on an InfiniBand network, follow these steps:

1. Edit /etc/hosts on each node in the cluster to add the virtual IP addresses you will use for the InfiniBand network:

```
192.168.13.30 exa10db01-ibvip.us.oracle.com   exa10db01-ibvip
192.168.13.31 exa10db02-ibvip.us.oracle.com   exa10db02-ibvip
```

2. On one of the database nodes, as the root user, create a network resource for the InfiniBand network, as shown in this example:

```
[oracle@exa10db01 bin]$ /u01/app/11.2.0.3/grid/bin/srvctl add
network -k 2 -S 192.168.13.0/255.255.255.0/bondib0
```

3. Validate that the network was added correctly by running the following command:

```
[oracle@exa10db01 bin]$ /u01/app/11.2.0.3/grid/bin/crsctl  stat res -t |
grep net
ora.net1.network
ora.net2.network
```

The output indicates the new network resource.
Alternatively, this can be validated using the **srvctl** command:

```
[oracle@exa10db01 bin]$ /u01/app/11.2.0.3/grid/bin/srvctl config network
-k 2
Network exists: 2/192.168.13.0/255.255.255.0/bondib0, type static
```

4. Add the Virtual IP (VIP) addresses for each node in the cluster:

```
srvctl add vip -n exa10db01 -A exa10db01-ibvip/255.255.255.0/bondib0 -k 2
srvctl add vip -n exa10db02 -A exa10db01-ibvip/255.255.255.0/bondib0 -k 2
```

5. As the owner of a grid infrastructure home, add a listener that will listen on the VIP:

```
srvctl add listener -l LISTENER_IB -k 2 -p TCP:1522,/SDP:1522
```

6. For each database, modify the listener_networks init parameter to allow load balancing and failover across multiple networks (Ethernet and InfiniBand). You can either enter the full tnsnames syntax in the initialization parameter or create entries in tnsnames.ora in the $ORACLE_HOME/network/admin directory. The example shows the entries in the tnsnames.ora in the first node of Exadata. Complete this step on each node in the cluster with the correct IP addresses for that node. LISTENER_IBREMOTE should list all other nodes that are in the cluster.

Sample the tnsnames.ora file after configuring the InfiniBand Listener. This example shows that the InfiniBand Listener is configured on both SDP and TCP:

```
EBS =
  (DESCRIPTION =
    (ADDRESS = (PROTOCOL = TCP)(HOST = exa10-scan.us.oracle.com)(PORT =
1521))
    (CONNECT_DATA =
      (SERVER = DEDICATED)
      (SERVICE_NAME = EBS)
    )
  )

EBSIB =
  (DESCRIPTION =
    (LOAD_BALANCE = on)
    (ADDRESS = (PROTOCOL = SDP)(HOST = exa10db01-ibvip)(PORT = 1522))
    (ADDRESS = (PROTOCOL = TCP)(HOST = exa10db01-ibvip)(PORT = 1522))
```

```
              (ADDRESS = (PROTOCOL = SDP)(HOST = exa10db02-ibvip)(PORT = 1522))
              (ADDRESS = (PROTOCOL = TCP)(HOST = exa10db02-ibvip)(PORT = 1522))
              (CONNECT_DATA =
                (SERVER = DEDICATED)
                (SERVICE_NAME = ebs.world)
              )
          )
    LISTENER_IBREMOTE =
      (DESCRIPTION =
        (ADDRESS_LIST =
          (ADDRESS = (PROTOCOL = SDP)(HOST = exa10db02-ibvip.us.oracle.com)
    (PORT = 1522))
          (ADDRESS = (PROTOCOL = TCP)(HOST = exa10db02-ibvip.us.oracle.com)
    (PORT = 1522))
        )
      )

    LISTENER_IBLOCAL =
      (DESCRIPTION =
        (ADDRESS_LIST =
          (ADDRESS = (PROTOCOL = TCP)(HOST = exa10db01-ibvip.us.oracle.com)
    (PORT = 1522))
          (ADDRESS = (PROTOCOL = SDP)(HOST = exa10db01-ibvip.us.oracle.com)
    (PORT = 1522))
        )
      )

    LISTENER_IPLOCAL =
      (DESCRIPTION =
        (ADDRESS_LIST =
          (ADDRESS = (PROTOCOL = TCP)(HOST = exa1001-vip.us.oracle.com)(PORT
    = 1521))
        )
      )

    LISTENER_IPREMOTE =
      (DESCRIPTION =
        (ADDRESS_LIST =
          (ADDRESS = (PROTOCOL = TCP)(HOST = exa10-scan.us.oracle.com)(PORT =
    1521))
        )
      )
```

7. Modify the listener_networks initialization parameter. Connect to the database instance as sysdba.

```
SQLPLUS> alter system set listener_networks='((NAME=network2)
(LOCAL_LISTENER=LISTENER_IBLOCAL)(REMOTE_LISTENER=LISTENER_
IBREMOTE))','((NAME=network1)(LOCAL_LISTENER=LISTENER_IPLOCAL)(REMOTE_
LISTENER=LISTENER_IPREMOTE))' scope=both;
```

8. Stop and start LISTENER_IB using the following command:

```
srvctl stop listener -l LISTENER_IB
srvctl start listener -l LISTENER_IB
```

Once InfiniBand Listener is configured, register each database running in Exadata Machine with the InfiniBand Listener. The entry for the InfiniBand Listener also needs to be put in the initialization parameter file or the SPFILE. Here's an example:

```
SQL> alter system set LOCAL_LISTENER='(ADDRESS = (PROTOCOL = SDP)(HOST =
exa10db01-ibvip.us.oracle.com)(PORT = 1522)))' scope=both;

System altered.

SQL> alter system register
System altered.
```

9. Once the InfiniBand Listener is registered with both databases, create the database link using the InfiniBand connect string:

```
create public database link ebsap connect to AP identified by AP using
'EBSIB';
```

In this example, the user is connected to the AP schema of the EBS database using the database link ebsap and using the connect string EBSIB. The connect string EBSIP is mapped to the InfiniBand network.

Exalogic-Exadata Connectivity Using InfiniBand

In some cases, Exalogic is used along with Exadata to host the middle tier or application tier services. The application tier normally resides on the Exalogic box. If an Exalogic server is used to host the middle tier services, then InfiniBand should be leveraged within the application tier for all the database connections since both machines are already connected with the InfiniBand cable.

Some applications support SDP, but others don't. If the application does not support SDP, then TCP over InfiniBand can be used for application connectivity between the Exalogic and Exadata machines. For example, the 9*i*AS infrastructure does not support SDP since it uses 32-bit binaries, whereas the WebLogic infrastructure supports SDP. If the 9*i*AS infrastructure is used in the middle tier, TCP over InfiniBand can be used to connect the Exalogic and the Exadata machines, whereas for WebLogic, SDP can be leveraged.

Connect Exalogic and Exadata Using InfiniBand

To connect Exalogic and Exadata using InfiniBand, follow these steps:

1. Configure the InfiniBand Listener in the Exadata machine, following the steps presented earlier in the chapter.

2. Register the database with the InfiniBand Listener.

3. In the middle tier, modify all connect strings to leverage the InfiniBand network. For example, if the application (such as WebLogic) uses JDBC to connect to the database, then change the JDBC URL to leverage InfiniBand. Also make sure that the SDP support for JDBC is enabled on the Exalogic Machine. (Refer to the Exalogic administration guide for the steps to enable SDP support for JDBC.) Once SDP is enabled, you will change the entries in the JDBC URL, as shown in an example that follows.

Here is the existing JDBC URL from the application tier:

```
<jdbc_url oa_var="s_apps_jdbc_connect_descriptor">jdbc:oracle:thin:@
(DESCRIPTION=(ADDRESS_LIST=(LOAD_BALANCE=YES)(FAILOVER=YES)
(ADDRESS=(PROTOCOL=sdp)(HOST= exa1001-vip.us.oracle.com)(PORT=1521))
(ADDRESS=(PROTOCOL=sdp)(HOST= exa1002-vip.us.oracle.com)(PORT=1521)))
(CONNECT_DATA=(SERVICE_NAME=VISOW)))</jdbc_url>
```

Modify it as follows:

```
<jdbc_url oa_var="s_apps_jdbc_connect_descriptor">jdbc:oracle:thin:@
(DESCRIPTION=(ADDRESS_LIST=(LOAD_BALANCE=YES)(FAILOVER=YES)
(ADDRESS=(PROTOCOL=tcp)(HOST= exa10db01-ibvip.us.oracle.com)
(PORT=1522))(ADDRESS=(PROTOCOL=tcp)(HOST= exa10db02-ibvip.us.oracle.
com)(PORT=1522)))(CONNECT_DATA=(SERVICE_NAME=VISOW)))</jdbc_url>
```

If the application (such as *i*AS infrastructure) uses the tnsnames.ora file for connecting to the database, change tnsnames.ora to reflect the InfiniBand Listener entries. Some applications manage the tns entries using specific tools, and if you manually update tnsnames.ora, it may revert back to the old entries with the tool that manages it. In such a case, modify the file to reflect the InfiniBand tns entries.

Configuring HugePages

HugePages is an operating system feature on Exadata systems that allows the Linux kernel to use the multiple page-size capabilities of modern hardware architectures. *Pages* are the basic unit of memory in a Linux operating system. All the physical memory is partitioned and accessed using a page.

Currently, in any x86-based architecture, the default size of a page is 4096 bytes. The name "HugePages" implies that page size becomes huge or the unit of memory of becomes large; thus, configuring HugePages allows utilization of a large amount of memory and can improve system performance by reducing the amount of system resources required to access page table entries. It also doesn't swap, so performance is improved. If the default page size is used with a large amount of physical memory, the transaction lookaside buffers (TLBs) in Linux, which map virtual memory to actual physical address, add a lot of processing overhead.

If the page size is higher, there will be less overhead in managing the pages with TLB, and the Linux kernel can set aside a portion of physical memory to be addressed using a larger page size. In the Linux kernel, HugePages is enabled using the CONFIG_HUGETLB_PAGE feature when the kernel is built. Systems with large amounts of memory can be configured to use the memory more efficiently by setting aside a portion dedicated for HugePages. The actual size of the page is dependent on the system architecture.

Following are some features of HugePages:

■ **Page table** A data structure of a virtual memory system in an operating system that stores the mapping between virtual addresses and physical addresses. This means that on a virtual memory system, the memory is accessed by first accessing a page table and then accessing the actual memory location implicitly.

■ **TLB** A buffer (or cache) in a CPU that contains parts of the page table. This is a fixed-size buffer used to perform virtual address translation faster.

■ **hugetlb** An entry in the TLB that points to a HugePage (a large/big page larger than the regular 4K and predefined in size). HugePages are implemented via HugeTLB entries—we can say that a HugePage is handled by a "HugeTLB page entry." The "HugeTLB" term is also (and mostly) used synonymously with HugePage.

■ **hugetlbfs** A new in-memory file system like tmpfs that is presented by the 2.6 Linux kernel. Pages allocated on a hugetlbfs-type file system are allocated in HugePages.

HugePages offer several advantages:

■ **Larger page size** The default page size is 4K, whereas the HugeTLB size is 2048K. If HugePages is not configured, the system would need to handle 512 times more pages.

- **Reduced page table walking** Since a HugePage covers a larger contiguous virtual address range than a regular-sized page, the probability of getting a TLB hit per TLB entry with HugePages is higher than with regular pages. This reduces the number of times page tables are walked to obtain a physical address from a virtual address.

- **Less overhead for memory operations** On virtual memory systems, each memory operation is actually two abstract memory operations. With HugePages, since there are fewer pages to work on, the possible bottleneck on page table access is avoided.

- **Less memory usage** From the Oracle Database perspective, with HugePages, the Linux kernel will use less memory to create page tables to maintain virtual-to-physical mappings for SGA address ranges, in comparison to regular-size pages. This makes more memory available for process-private computations or PGA usage.

- **No swapping** Swapping should be avoided in a Linux OS. Regular pages are swappable, whereas HugePages are not. Therefore, there is no page replacement mechanism overhead. HugePages are universally regarded as pinned.

- **No kswapd operations** kswapd will get very busy if there is a very large area to be paged (such as 2.5 million page table entries for 10GB memory) and will use an incredible amount of CPU resources. When HugePages are used, kswapd is not involved in managing them.

Steps for Configuring HugePages
Follow these steps to configure HugePages:

1. Query for the memlock setting in the /etc/security/limits.conf file. The value (in KB) needs to be set slightly less than the available RAM in the system.

```
[root@exa10db01 ~]$ cat /etc/security/limits.conf | grep memlock
#        - memlock - max locked-in-memory address space (KB)
oracle     soft      memlock      74136726
oracle     hard      memlock      74136726
[root@exa10db01 ~]$
```

2. Log in as the Oracle software owner and check the memlock setting:

```
[oracle@exa10db01 ~]$ ulimit -l
74136726
[oracle@exa10db01 ~]$
```

3. Because Automatic Memory Management (AMM) cannot be used in conjunction with HugePages, you need to unset the MEMORY_TARGET and MEMORY_MAX_TARGET parameters for each database instance.

```
SQL> show parameter memory%target% ;

NAME                    TYPE          VALUE
--------------------    -----------   -----
memory_max_target       big integer       0
memory_target           big integer       0
```

4. Determine the HugePages settings for your environment. MOS note 401749.1 provides a shell script, hugepages_settings.sh, that can be run in your environment for finding the correct HugePages settings.

```
./ hugepages_settings.sh
…
Recommended settings: vm.hugetlb_pool=24576
```

5. Edit the file /etc/sysctl.conf and set the vm.nr_hugepages parameter there:

   - In the database, set the initialization parameter USE_LARGE_PAGES='only' for each instance so that the instance will start only if sufficient HugePages are available.

   - The USE_LARGE_PAGES parameter has four possible values: true (default), only, false, and auto (11.2.0.3 and later). The default value of true preserves the current behavior of trying to use HugePages if they are available on the OS. Setting it to false means "do not use HugePages." A setting of only means it does not start up the instance if HugePages cannot be used for the whole memory (to avoid an out-of-memory situation). Auto was introduced in version 11.2.0.3, where the OS HugePages are dynamically adjusted based on the instance.

6. Stop all the databases and reboot the server.

7. Validate the settings by querying the /proc/meminfo file:

```
[oracle@exa10db01 ~]$  cat /proc/meminfo|grep Huge
HugePages_Total:   24576
HugePages_Free :    9080
HugePages_Rsvd :     563
HugePages_Surp :       0
Hugepagesize   :    2048 kB
[oracle@exa10db01 ~]$
```

The alertlog also shows the HugePages information:

```
****************** Large Pages Information ******************
Total Shared Global Region in Large Pages = 20 GB (100%)
Large Pages used by this instance: 10241 (20 GB)
Large Pages unused system wide = 10351 (20 GB) (alloc incr 64 MB)
Large Pages configured system wide = 24576 (48 GB)
Large Page size = 2048 KB
```

Summary

Exadata provides a lot of features. Out of those features, there are some that help an OLTP system to get the best out of an Exadata machine. Those features are

- **Write Back Flash Cache**   Once enabled, all the eligible write I/Os go to flash and the data is kept in the Flash Cache until it gets phased out using the LRU algorithm. This speeds up the entire write process in the database.

- **Smart Flash Logging**   Once enabled, the redo log file is written to Exadata Smart Flash Cache and disks simultaneously. The database gets notified when the write activity is completed, whether it is in the disk or in the Flash hardware. Almost all the time, the acknowledgment comes from Exadata Smart Flash Cache first, thus accelerating the performance.

- **Smart Flash Cache Compression**   Once enabled, this provides 1.5 to 4 times more compression depending on the application. It should be used when the database size is bigger than flash or if you are planning to consolidate multiple databases into Exadata, since cumulative size of all the databases may be bigger than available flash.

- **Leveraging InfiniBand for DB links**   When there are multiple applications hosted in Exadata and all these applications need to talk to each other, the best way is to create the DB links between the InfiniBand listener so that all the inter database communication happens over the 40G pipe.

- **Routing traffic through InfiniBand between the application and DB tier**   When Exadata and Exalogic are connected together, then InfiniBand should be used so that all the data transfer between the database node and application tier goes via the 40G pipe.

- **Configuring HugePages**   It allows the Linux kernel to use the multiple page-size capabilities of modern hardware architectures. HugePages allows utilization of a large amount of memory and can improve system performance by reducing the amount of system resources required to access page table entries.

CHAPTER
5

Sizing Exadata for Applications

As every application is different, so are each application's characteristics: for example, some are very write-intensive, whereas others are very much read-intensive; some need a lot of computing power, while others require high amounts of memory consumption; some need a lot of I/O, and others require very fast response times.

It's important that you determine the appropriate sized Exadata Database Machine that you'll need to run a particular application. Underestimating your sizing needs will have a negative impact on system performance—your business won't be able to maintain its service level agreements (SLAs), jobs will slow down, and all this can potentially impact the revenue of the company. On the other hand, oversizing will incur additional expenditure for the company.

In this chapter you will learn how to size Exadata for a particular application, what the methodology is behind sizing Exadata, and what areas should be your focus as you determine the appropriate size.

Following are example scenarios for which you'd need to size an Exadata Machine:

- You are currently running your applications on a different hardware platform and plan to migrate them to Exadata.

- You are running multiple applications on a different hardware platform and plan to consolidate them to Exadata.

- You are deploying brand-new applications on Exadata.

- You are planning for an application upgrade and considering Exadata as a new platform.

- The hardware running the application is getting saturated at every level (CPU, I/O, memory, and so on) and you are considering Exadata.

- Your business is not able to meet its SLAs and you are considering Exadata to improve performance.

- You are expanding to different geographies and considering Exadata for the new expansion.

- You are planning for global single-instance and application consolidation and want to use Exadata as a target.

- You want to implement additional modules in your enterprise resource planning (ERP) system and are considering Exadata.

Here are the main methodologies for sizing an Exadata system:

- **Comparative sizing**   The application is already deployed and is currently running on some hardware.

- **Predictive sizing**   A new application needs to be deployed, the application is currently not running anywhere, and you are running the application for the first time and you need to predict what size hardware is the right fit for your application.

- **Comparative and predictive sizing**   Suppose, for example, that today you are running an E-Business Suite application with financials and procurement modules implemented. You will upgrade your E-Business Suite to a new release, and after upgrade, you want to implement new modules—say, Order Management, Inventory, and Logistics. In this case, you need a mix: comparative sizing for the existing modules and system and predictive sizing for the new modules being planned.

Comparative Sizing

In the comparative sizing methodology, you are already running your application on existing hardware and want to migrate to Exadata. You need to size the Exadata in comparison with the existing hardware. This method of sizing is very simple: you map the details of each component of the existing hardware to Exadata, and then you determine the final sizing number.

Comparative sizing is based on the following rules:

- You are not making any significant changes at the application level. The application will continue to run as it is with the same number of users and modules.

- There will be no significant changes in the workload.

- No new third-party integrations are being planned. (If, on the other hand, new third-party integrations are expected and are going to add greater workload to the database, a predictive sizing of the new workload needs to occur.)

- The hardware specifications from the existing environment need to be considered when determining the Exadata size. For example, you can't size a production Exadata system based on the data from quality assurance or test hardware. Production Exadata sizing needs to be determined by comparing it to existing production hardware.

Server Models

Use the existing server model(s) to determine the actual horsepower that is being used to service the application. Several factors can influence the size of the actual CPU:

- Number of actual processors in the machine
- Number of cores per processor
- Chip model and clock speed of the chip
- Use of hardware or software virtualization
- Use of chip-level hyper-threading

One way of finding the CPU information is to get the exact machine make and model and then read the product data sheet to determine the exact CPU and core count and clock speed of the processor. Otherwise, your UNIX system administrator should be able to provide that information.

Various operating system utilities can also provide CPU information. The following table lists the utilities you can use to find CPU information.

OS/Platform	Utility
Linux	/proc/cpuinfo
AIX	lsconf, prtconf
Solaris	prtconf, cpu_info
HP UX	ioscan -kfC processor, machinfo, getconf
Solaris SPARC	corestat
IBM Power systems	sar

NOTE
You can also get the CPU information from the Automatic Workload Repository (AWR), but you need to understand what it means.

You need to determine whether the system is using any kind of virtualization, such as logical partitions (LPARs) in IBM hardware or zones on Solaris systems, or if the hardware uses VMware or Oracle Virtual Machine (OVM). If so, the actual resources allocated must be accounted for while calculating the CPU and core. The UNIX system administrator should be able to provide this information.

In case of Intel chipsets where hyper-threading is turned on as per Intel documentation (http://software.intel.com/en-us/articles/performance-insights-to-intel-hyper-threading-technology), the second thread is equivalent to 25 percent of the first thread. Take special care while calculating the cores in case of hyper-threaded processors, since most of the OS utilities and performance measurement tools count both the threads as the same power.

For a hyper-threaded Intel chipset, use the following logic to find the true CPU utilization:

- Count the second thread as 20 percent of the first thread

- For CPU utilization less than 50 percent, multiply by 1.7

- For CPU utilization more than 50 percent, assume 85% + (util − 50%) × 0.3

Thus,

```
If (util < 50%) then
     true_util = util * 1.7
else
     true_util = 85% + (util - 50) * 0.3
```

Once you have determined the information for the CPU, your next task is to determine the CPU utilization. Sometimes the server has lot of cores but always remains idle, or CPU utilization stays at just 20 or 30 percent. Sometimes there might be a large variation between high and low CPU utilization. In such cases, it is advisable to take the higher number, as the system should be able to handle the busiest workload. If there are multiple databases and little overlap, choose the number of CPUs between the calculated values based on peak and high activity average utilization. If no analysis is possible, or to be conservative, always use the higher number based on peak utilization.

Here is the actual measure:

number of CPUs × CPU utilization

CPU growth is another important factor when determining comparative sizing. The CPU growth should include the number of years you plan to use the system. So, for example, if you are sizing the hardware for the next three years, you need to plan for the CPU growth for the next three years.

The CPU number for the server is calculated by multiplying the cores used by the specified CPU utilization percent. That result is multiplied by the expected CPU growth. The resulting number needs to be compared with the Exadata cores. The sizing example presented at the end of the chapter (see "Comparative Sizing Case Study") demonstrates a real-life case study.

You can compare the core of a server with the core of another server in several ways. Following are the widely known benchmarks:

- SPECint_rate
- TPC-C
- SPECjbb
- SAP SD
- Oracle Applications Standard Benchmark

All of these benchmarks provide data points. It's fine to use the benchmarks for comparative sizing, but you shouldn't use them in isolation. The benchmark results can be used for comparing cores across various server models.

SPECint_rate Benchmark The Standard Performance Evaluation Corporation (SPEC) was formed to standardize benchmarks for testing high-end computers and servers. SPEC has various benchmarks that can be used to compare various servers. You can even use those benchmarks to compare the parts of a server, such as the processor, memory, and so on. One of their most popular benchmarking suites is CPU2006, which is often used to compare the horsepower across different servers. It takes into account the systems processor, number of cores, the clock speed of each processor, memory of the machine, and the compiler. Each server is rated based on all these factors; this rating is called SPECint_rate.

TPC-C Benchmark Similar to SPEC, TPC is a non-profit corporation that was formed to standardize benchmarks. The TPC-C benchmark is totally different from SPECint_rate. TPC-C is used mainly for OLTP systems. In a TPC-C benchmark, transactions are executed in a system database and measured according to the number of transactions per minute. In a typical TPC-C benchmark, a "create sales order" workload is executed in a database and run for a few hours. Then the systems are compared in terms of how many sales orders were created per minute.

SPECjbb Benchmark SPECjbb is a Java Server benchmark. The SPECjbb2013 benchmark is used for any application that uses Java. This benchmark captures all the Java-related metrics such as Java virtual machine (JVM) performance, Java performance, and so on. If an application uses Java plus some other components, only those parts that use Java are included in this benchmark.

SAP SD Benchmarks The SAP Sales and Distribution (SD) benchmarks were developed by SAP. A workload is run against Oracle Database to test hardware, software, and RDBMS. During the workload execution, all metrics related to system, user experience, database, and business process are captured and are compared across different platforms. The SAP SD benchmark is used mainly to test the SAP performance across various hardware systems.

The Oracle Applications Standard Benchmark   The Oracle Applications Standard Benchmark is a comparable standard workload that demonstrates the performance and scalability of Oracle applications and provides metrics for the comparison of Oracle applications, performance on different system configurations.

Oracle has now moved to a more accurate measure using M-Values, which are based on a wide variety of benchmarks. Oracle M-Values use a variety of source benchmarks to determine an appropriate horsepower measurement for each server. The specific details behind M-Value measurements are proprietary and aren't available outside of Oracle. However, since the M-Value measures are based on publicly available benchmarks, and because Oracle applies the M-Value methodology consistently across all platforms, the M-Values measure is the most accurate measure available.

NOTE
You know that Exadata has computing power at the storage cells. So do you need to take these into account when sizing the Exadata? The answer is no, because that is where Exadata provides the performance advantage.

Memory

Memory need is a critical consideration when sizing a system. The operating system allocates virtual memory—or, more correctly, for our purposes, Oracle Database processes request the virtual memory from the OS. A physical system can have a very large amount of memory, but for our sizing purposes, we need to find out how much memory is required for Oracle Database processes.

Figure 5-1 shows the objects that run in Oracle Database memory.

The memory Oracle uses usually equals the sum of the sizes of System Global Area (SGA) and Program Global Area (PGA). The SGA used is much less than the maximum allocation of the SGA. The initialization parameter sga_target determines the SGA allocated to the system, and sga_max_size determines the maximum size the SGA can stretch to. The pga_aggregate_target parameter determines the PGA allocation in the server, but the memory used for PGA can go beyond the pga_aggregate_target size. Thus, pga_aggregate_target may not necessarily provide the true picture of the memory usage by the PGA.

Memory used by Oracle = (sga_target + pga_aggregate_target)

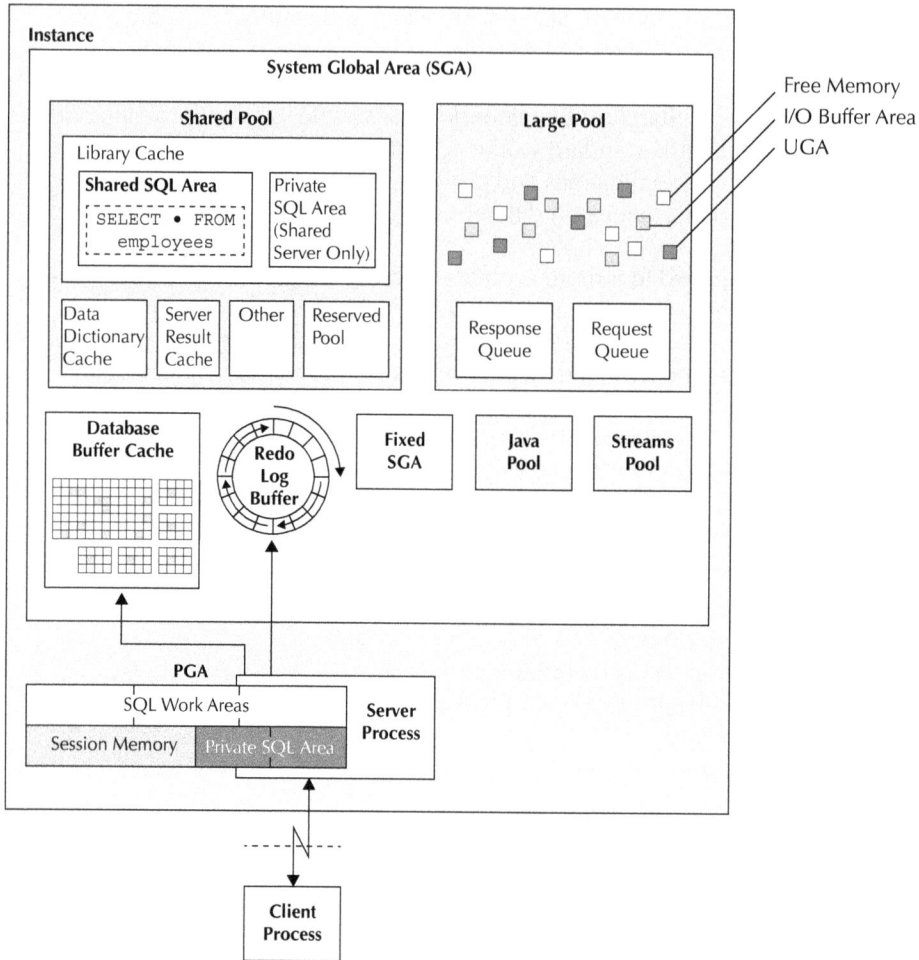

FIGURE 5-1. *Objects that run in Oracle Database memory*

The actual usage of the PGA and SGA can also be determined from the v$ views, which are v$pgastat (maximum PGA allocated, max processes count) and v$sgastat. If multiple databases are running on the system, all the databases need to be factored in when calculating the total memory requirement. In that case, the estimated memory usage would be

Sum of OLTP databases (pga_aggregate_target + sga_target) + Max DB processes × 4MB

You should also consider the memory growth factor for sizing the memory. So sizing the equivalent memory for Exadata would be very simple:

Current memory × growth factor = Target memory for Exadata

You can also look for the "SGA Target Advisory" in the AWR reports. The SGA advisory covers from half to twice the SGA size. If the SGA target advisory consistently recommends that "by increasing the SGA size, the estimated physical reads are reduced," then you need to adjust the memory according to the recommendation.

Figure 5-2 shows an SGA target advisory table. It can be seen that when SGA Target Size (M) = 32768MB, which is equal to 32GB, the estimated physical reads is 62033564, and when SGA Target becomes 53248, which is equal to 52GB, the estimated physical reads goes down to 52008940. You can see that just by adding 20GB to the SGA size—from 32GB to 52GB—you can obtain an 18 percent benefit straight out of the box. The figure also shows that decreasing the SGA too much would be detrimental.

SGA Target Size (M)	SGA Size Factor	Est DB Time (s)	Est Physical Reads
12,288	0.38	40,617,680	95,630,942
16,384	0.50	40,274,038	77,479,921
20,480	0.63	40,170,146	73,205,809
24,576	0.75	40,074,246	68,360,988
28,672	0.88	40,010,313	65,042,192
32,768	1.00	39,958,367	62,033,564
36,864	1.13	39,918,409	60,755,673
40,960	1.25	39,886,442	58,770,599
45,056	1.38	39,858,471	57,995,179
49,152	1.50	39,834,496	56,649,051
53,248	1.63	39,762,571	52,008,940
57,344	1.75	39,734,600	52,008,940
61,440	1.88	39,730,604	52,008,940
65,536	2.00	39,730,604	52,008,940

FIGURE 5-2. *SGA Target Advisory table*

If SGA and PGA calculations seem too complicated for you, you can compare the actual memory of the existing server against Exadata to make things simple.

TIP & TECHNIQUE
The cumulative memory of all the databases should never exceed the physical memory of the machine.

RAC or Non-RAC DB

For Exadata sizing, we assume that the current application is running on Oracle Database and not in any other database such as DB2, Sybase, and so on. If the application is currently running on a database other than Oracle and you plan to migrate to Oracle and Exadata at the same time, then you'll undertake a much bigger exercise than sizing. The entire application needs to be tested against the new database, which may involve redesigning the database, extensive testing, redeveloping some of the functionalities, and so on. It has a much bigger scope that is outside the scope of this book.

If the current application is running on a non-RAC database and your plan is to migrate to Exadata and RAC, you need to add 5 to 7 percent CPU for the cluster overhead. Again, this number is a good rule of thumb—but nothing more. This number will vary based on the application.

In addition, a lot depends on how well your applications behave with RAC. Some applications integrate well in the RAC database, while others result in diminished returns as you add more nodes. Suppose, for example, that you deploy application XYZ, which does not really leverage RAC capabilities, and you are currently running your XYZ application on an 84-core box. After sizing Exadata, you decide to go with a 4-node RAC with 24 cores on each box. In this case, you may find that you'll get diminishing returns as you add nodes. In this case, the recommended architecture would be to go with a 2-node RAC and use RAC for high availability, and use Xn-8 machines, which have more cores, instead of Xn-2 machines, which have fewer cores.

Storage

Storage plays an important role in sizing the machine. It's interesting to note that disk drive capacities are measured in powers of 10, whereas most other storage capacity measurements are in powers of 2. Disk drive manufacturers say that 1KB = 1000 bytes, 1MB = 1,000,000 bytes, and so on. Virtually all other measures use 1KB = 1024 bytes, 1MB = 1,048,576 bytes, and so on. In 2002, the IEEE adopted the 1541-2002 standard for prefixes of binary multiples, so KiB = 1024 bytes, MiB = 1,048,576 bytes, and so on. The International Electrotechnical Commission (IEC) adopted the same naming convention in 1998. Refer to http://physics.nist.gov/cuu/Units/binary.html for more information.

This has been a source of confusion for decades, and these standards have not been fully adopted by the industry. The use of KB = 1024 is deeply embedded in manuals, code, and other standards.

A 600GB disk drive stores 600,000,000,000 bytes, which equals 600,000,000,000 / 1024 / 1024 / 1024 = 558GiB (which is also ambiguously referred to as 558GB because of this issue of the standard definition of binary multiples).

Lots of factors affect the storage sizing, as described in the following sections.

Database Size   The size of the database governs the size of the machine. The size of the database includes the size of the database files and the temp files. These files are stored in the disk group DATA_DG in the Exadata Machine. In Exadata, the space management is simplified by storing the whole database in a single disk group. The database size also includes the online redo log files and the archived redo log files, which are stored in the RECO_DG group of the Exadata Machine. There might be differences in the physical database size and the logical database size—for example, the physical size includes all the data as well as the free space in the database, whereas logical size includes only the size of the data stored in the database.

Use the following query to find the DB size:

```
select      round(sum(used.bytes) / 1024 / 1024 / 1024 ) || ' GB' "Total
Database Size"
, round(sum(used.bytes) / 1024 / 1024 / 1024 ) -      round(free_space.s /
1024 / 1024 / 1024) || ' GB' "Used space"
, round(free_space.s / 1024 / 1024 / 1024) || ' GB' "Free space"
from     (select      bytes
     from      v$datafile
     union     all
     select      bytes
     from      v$tempfile
     union     all
     select      bytes
     from      v$log) used
,    (select sum(bytes) as s
     from dba_free_space) free_space
group by free_space.s
/

SQL> @dbsize.sql

Total Database Size         Used space          Free space
-------------------- -------------------- --------------------
552 GB                       511 GB              41 GB
```

Data Redundancy The data-mirroring requirement is important mostly for business data. Exadata provides two-way and three-way mirroring of data, known as *normal* and *high* redundancy, respectively. In normal mirroring, the data is mirrored across two hard drives, whereas in high redundancy, the data is mirrored across three hard drives. Most customers use normal redundancy, but customers in industries such as banking and other financial sectors typically choose high redundancy. The data redundancy in Exadata Machines is handled by Automatic Storage Management (ASM), which stripes and mirrors the data at different hard drives and cells depending on the type of coverage chosen.

Disk vs. Cell Failure Coverage Failure coverage refers to the amount of space in a disk group that will be used to remirror data in the event of some storage failure. Depending on what level of failure protection is needed, sizing can be impacted— that is, more free space means greater failure coverage.

Disk failure coverage refers to having enough free space to allow data to be remirrored (rebalanced) after a single disk failure in a normal redundancy disk group, or single or dual disk failure in a high-redundancy disk group. *Cell failure coverage* refers to having enough free space to allow data to be remirrored after the loss of one entire cell. Exadata cells can provide both levels of protection. Depending on the type of protection needed, ASM disk groups can be created accordingly. The disk failure and cell failure can be accomplished in parallel with high and normal redundancies in ASM. When using high-redundancy disk groups, it makes sense to plan for disk failure coverage to maximize capacity, since the disk group already has three copies of data allocated to withstand failures. If you choose disk failure coverage, you need no special sizing; if you choose cell failure coverage, sizing gets impacted because you need to account for extra storage cells.

Backup Requirements Backup requirements impact the sizing of the Exadata Machine. If your organizational policy is to keep one or two copies of the database backup in the Exadata Machine, the sizing of the storage is impacted. You need to account for the space required to store one or two copies of the backup in the Exadata Machine. Depending on your recovery time objective (RTO) and recovery point objective (RPO), you can also keep the backup as a compressed backup set, which can save a lot of space in the machine. If the plan is to do online backups, the RECO_DG (the Fast Recovery Area) is sized equal to 60 percent of the total space. This allows for one full (uncompressed) backup or at least two full compressed backups, plus archived redo.

Fast Recovery Area (FRA) If you are planning to turn on the flashback area, you need to account for the space needed for FRA in the Exadata Machine. FRA size typically depends on the number of days you want to flashback the database. More days equals greater FRA size. FRA is stored in the RECO_DG disk group in the Exadata Machine. If you will not do online backup, the size of the RECO_DG goes down.

Compression   You can implement compression in an OLTP system in several ways, such as by using advanced compression, OLTP compression, and so on. You can also implement Hybrid Columnar Compression (HCC) in OLTP systems, but you need to use it carefully. In an OLTP system, if the data becomes "dormant" and stops being updated, you can move it to an HCC partition. Implementing any kind of compression can definitely reduce the storage needs for the Exadata Machine. The compression ratio can be applied to the entire database or to a few specific tables, depending on the type of the compression mechanism you choose.

ETL Landing Pad Space   If you need to provide space for an Extract, Transform, and Load (ETL) landing pad, this can impact the sizing of the Exadata Machine. The ETL landing pad space is the DBFS file system in the Exadata Machine, which is mounted across all the nodes of the database. Since the DBFS file system is a ASM disk group (DBFS_DG) in Exadata Machine, it can take away a considerable amount of space from the DATA_DG and the RECO_DG disk groups of the machine. The DBFS is used to store temporary files, flat files, and so on. OLTP customers usually need a placeholder that the database can process to keep the flat files. DBFS can be used for that purpose.

Growth   Growth has a direct impact on sizing. Whenever an organization plans for new hardware, it always accounts for at least three to five years of data growth. The growth of the data is always compounded year over year. Table 5-1 provides an overview of data growth with 10 percent, 20 percent, and 25 percent annual growth.

You can see from the table that the data volume doubles in just four years, with 20 percent growth rate, and triples in five years, with 25 percent growth rate.

	10% Annual	**20% Annual**	**25% Annual**
Starting Size	1TB	1TB	1TB
End of Year 1	1.1TB	1.2TB	1.25TB
End of Year 2	1.21TB	1.44TB	1.56TB
End of Year 3	1.33TB	1.73TB	1.95TB
End of Year 4	1.46TB	2.07TB	2.44TB
End of Year 5	1.61TB	2.49TB	3.05TB

TABLE 5-1.   *Data Growth*

Use the following formula for the basic mathematical calculation for compounded growth. The formula assumes a constant rate of growth from year to year.

$$S = P(1 + j)^t$$

- S = future size
- j = growth rate
- P = present size
- t = number of years

I/O

I/O plays an important role in sizing an Exadata Machine. For OLTP sizing in Exadata, it is assumed that the current application is already running in an Oracle Database. To calculate the I/O needed for the Exadata system, we need to determine the current I/O request from the database for the existing application. There are mainly two categories of I/O requests: read I/O requests and write I/O requests. The Oracle AWRs or the DBA history tables are the best places to look for the I/O requests from the database. Examine the AWR during the peak workload of the system; otherwise, you won't capture the correct metric. One way to easily find the peak period is to run a shell script in the background that prints **vmstat** output. Save that to a file with a timestamp, and you'll be able to determine when the system is busiest. If there are multiple RAC nodes, then consider I/O requests from each node.

AWR reports like the one shown in Figure 5-3 show numerous data points for I/O calculations. These values were added in Oracle 10g to provide a single number that represents all read and write I/O calls. "Physical read total I/O requests" represents the approximate read input/output operations per second (IOPS) of an instance, and "Physical write total I/O requests" represents the approximate write IOPS of an instance.

Alternatively, you can use the following SQL query to find out the read and write I/O requests from the database:

```
SQL> select METRIC_NAME, avg(AVERAGE) as AVG_VAL, max(MAXVAL) as MAX_VAL
  2  from dba_hist_sysmetric_summary
  3  where METRIC_NAME in
  4  ('Physical Read Total IO Requests Per Sec',
  5  'Physical Write Total IO Requests Per Sec')
  6  group by METRIC_NAME;


METRIC_NAME                                      AVG_VAL     MAX_VAL
----------------------------------------------------------------------

Physical Write Total IO Requests Per Sec  227.0463485 5238.947193
Physical Read Total IO Requests Per Sec   21.39278912 1792.389675
```

You can also grab the MAX of the averages and the AVERAGE of the MAX in this query and compare the results.

Once you have the data for the read and write I/O requests, you can sum them up to find out the total I/O request from the database. You need to map that number to the data sheet of Exadata Machine to determine what configuration can handle

Physical read requests optimized	2,712,753	4,514.50	1.34
Physical read total I/O requests	2,735,164	4,551.79	1.35
Physical read total bytes	41,470,320,640	69,013,910.25	20,496.02
Physical read total bytes optimized	22,222,872,576	36,982,770.08	10,983.29
Physical read total multiblock requests	18,312	30.47	0.01
Physical reads	2,714,113	4,516.76	1.34
Physical reads cache	2,714,710	4,516.09	1.34
Physical reads cache prefetch	1	0.00	0.00
Physical reads direct	403	0.67	0.00
Physical reads direct (lob)	0	0.00	0.00
Physical reads direct temporary tablespace	403	0.67	0.00
Physical reads prefetch warmup	0	0.00	0.00
Physical write I/O requests	7,287,160	12,127.12	3.60
Physical write bytes	61,185,802,240	101,823,940.57	30,240.08
Physical write total I/O requests	7,727,634	12,860.14	3.82

FIGURE 5-3. *AWR showing I/O request*

the requested I/Os. The data sheet shows the I/O rates for Exadata in terms of tested results, not theoretical results.

For write operations, with ASM normal redundancy, the data is written at two different hard drives resulting in two I/O operations and similarly with ASM high redundancy, the data is written at three different hard drives resulting in three I/O operations.

So, for example, if your application has a requirement of 100 write I/O, then when sizing for Exadata with ASM normal redundancy, you need to account for 200 write I/O, and when sizing for Exadata with high ASM redundancy, you need to account for 300 write I/O.

Exadata comes with lot of Flash known as Exadata Smart Flash Cache, and lots of I/O requests are handled by the Exadata Smart Flash Cache itself. To understand how much I/O will be handled by Exadata Smart Flash Cache, you need to understand the I/O characteristics of the application. Exadata Smart Flash Cache can process all the random I/Os. Segments that have high physical reads generally have random I/O. In an OLTP, you can assume 50–60 percent of the I/O requests can be handled by Exadata Smart Flash Cache. This assumption is valid when the size of the database is less than or equal to the total size of Exadata Smart Flash Cache across all storage cells. On the other hand, if the size of database(s) is greater than the total size of Exadata Smart Flash Cache, you need to be conservative and should assume that only 30 percent of I/O requests would be handled by Exadata Smart Flash Cache.

Comparative Sizing Attributes to Consider

The following example shows the minimum attributes typically required for a comparative sizing in two categories: server and database.

Server:

- Server make and model
- Chip count
- Cores per chip
- Peak CPU utilization
- Planned CPU growth
- System memory (RAM)
- Memory utilization
- Planned memory growth

Database

- Database name
- Database version
- RAC or non-RAC
- Database size
- Data growth rate
- ASM redundancy (normal, high)
- Landing space
- Number of disk backups
- Backup mechanism (full/incremental) (compressed or uncompressed)
- Flashback enabled (if yes, then for how many days)
- Compression ratio
- SGA size
- PGA size

- Physical read total I/O requests per second from AWR

- Physical write total I/O requests per second from AWR

Predictive Sizing

Predictive sizing is usually done when a new application is being deployed or new functionalities are added to the existing application. Predictive sizing requires that you understand the future needs of the application—for example, if the planned application needs to process millions of lines of general ledger entries in a day, you should be able to translate that to the number of cores, I/O, and memory requirements. Similarly, if the application needs to process 10,000 orders in an hour, you should be able to translate that to the number of cores, I/O, and memory requirements. Every application is different: some are very read intensive, whereas some are write intensive. Some need a lot of CPU power, while some are memory hogs. Typically, all financial applications need a lot of computing power, while supply chain applications need huge amounts of memory.

Predictive sizing is done in the following scenarios:

- When a new application is being deployed.

- When new functionalities/modules are added to an existing application. For example, if today your application system is running financials and tomorrow you want to implement manufacturing along with the financials, you need to do predictive sizing for the new manufacturing module.

- When you are planning to upgrade an application. In this case, you need to do a mix of predictive and comparative sizing when an application upgrade requires additional horsepower and the horsepower differs from application to application. For example, if you're planning to upgrade Oracle E-Business Suite from 11*i* to Release 12, Oracle recommends that you expand the computing capacity of the hardware by 30 percent. This recommendation is application-specific, and similar rules apply for different applications.

- When you're planning to update an application with the addition of new modules.

The following information is typically needed when undertaking predictive sizing.

Users

In any application, the users can be categorized as follows:

- **Total number of uses**   Denotes the total number of uses that are registered with the application.

- **Concurrent/active users** The users who are actively accessing the application at any point in time. Typically, the active users average from 5 to 30 percent of the total number of users, depending on the application. Active users are always a subset of named users. Active users are divided into three subcategories:

  - **Heavy concurrently active users** Power users who complete one transaction every 2 minutes. Faster transaction rates may also be included in this category. Based on industry standards, heavy users perform 6–15 business events per user per hour. A business event consists of a complete set of user actions, such as adding a journal entry, inquiring about an account, or creating an order.

  - **Medium concurrently active users** Users work at the rate of one transaction every 3 minutes. Based on industry standards, medium users perform 4–8 business events per hour.

  - **Light concurrently active users** Occasional users who complete one transaction every 4 or more minutes. Based on industry standards, light users perform 2–4 business events per hour.

Functionalities

Functionalities play an important role in predicting the application size. Application sizing depends on the number of functionalities being deployed. The more functionalities, the more CPU and memory are required. Concurrent users are divided across various functions to size the application. Some functions are very high in CPU and memory requirements, while other modules have very low requirements. The CPU and memory requirements for 100 order management users will be completely different from those of 100 CRM users, for example.

With packaged applications such as E-Business Suite, PeopleSoft, and JD Edwards, there is often a need to customize the standard application. This typically happens when the standard package application does not provide the functionality the business requires. In that case, custom modules are added in the system, which adds more overhead, which must be considered while sizing. In addition to customization, there can be requirements for extensions, custom reports, or external or internal interfaces in the application system.

Application Services

Every application uses different services to host the application tier. Some applications such as E-Business Suite use Apache, others use forms, other applications such as Demantra and JD Edwards use WebLogic, and applications such as PeopleSoft use Tuxedo. The database-processing requirements will also be completely different depending on the application services. For example, in an E-Business Suite environment, a forms user creates two connections in the database, whereas an Apache user creates only one connection in the database. Some applications such as JD Edwards may use connection pooling for connecting to the database, whereas other applications will make a direct connection to the database. The sizing requirements will depend on what service is used to host the application and how it is connecting to the database.

Batch Jobs

Any OLTP system has online users and batch jobs. Online users use the system for performing day-to-day activities. They normally work during business hours and work interactively with the system—taking an order over the phone and entering it in the system, creating a shipping method, approving a purchase requisition, and so on. Batch jobs, on the other hand, run in the background—such as an online request or a scheduled job. Batch jobs may impact the online users and must be taken into account when sizing the application. If a large number of users are logged into the system and suddenly a big batch job kicks in, the system may slow down and affect the online users. A ratio of online users to batch jobs is normally considered when sizing the application. Batch job can be divided into the following categories:

- **Daily batch job** The total number of jobs running per day, which can differ from day to day.

- **Weekly batch job** Special jobs that run weekly.

- **Month-end/quarter-end/year-end jobs** Jobs that run only during the specified period. For example, when a company closes its quarterly book of accounts, it runs a quarter-end job.

- **Jobs coming from integrations/third-party systems** An OLTP system is always integrated with lots of third-party systems, and these systems often submit jobs in the OLTP system. This adds a lot of overhead to the database and must be considered while sizing the application.

A batch job can have different work shifts depending on the nature of the application. Some work shifts coincide with the online user activity, while others don't. The sizing varies depending on the work shift.

Reporting

Most applications require that reports be run periodically. In some OLTP systems, the reports are run directly from the production instance, whereas in other OLTP systems, a separate reporting environment is created either by replicating the production environment or by creating a clone of the production environment as per the business need. If the report is run from the production environment, the reporting needs must be taken into the account when sizing the application. Two types of reports are usually run in a OLTP system:

- **Regular reports** These are standard reports included as a part of the OLTP system.

- **Ad hoc reports** These are custom reports built by the users for specific needs. A standard report can also be modified to create an ad hoc report for a specific analysis.

Geography

Many ERP systems run as a global single instance under various geographies. An organization may have manufacturing units in different continents or in different countries, for example; similarly, an organization may have the distribution system located across the globe. If the same OLTP system is accessed from different geographies, the sizing is impacted.

If the same application is running in different countries, local regulations and laws in the system must be considered; this is known as *localization*. Localization is normally implemented to account for the local taxes, financial statements, and government regulations. The more localization implementations, the greater the database overhead. Localization generally doesn't apply to custom applications. Only packaged application vendors care about deploying applications across different geographies.

If the organization is operative in more than one country, more than one language may be installed in the system. Local language is normally installed to facilitate the local users. Adding additional languages also adds overhead to the system.

Application Growth

The application growth factor must be taken into consideration when sizing the application. In any application, users can grow, the business can grow, and processing requirements can grow. Typically, an application is sized for next three or five years, and all aspects of the growth must be factored in during sizing.

Special Throughput Needs

Special throughput needs sometimes must be considered in addition to the regular OLTP activities. For example, there might be a special need to process 10,000 orders in an hour, to process 1 million lines of general ledger entries in a day, or to run the payroll biweekly.

Predictive Sizing Attributes to Consider

You can see that application predictive sizing is completely dependent on application characteristics. Since every application is different, it's impossible to cover the characteristics of each and every application. Following are some rough estimates for Exadata sizing for green field implementations. This information does not necessarily represent the entire picture.

E-Business Suite:

- Small to medium customers (500–1000 concurrent users): 1/8 to 1/4 rack Exadata

- Medium to large customers (1000–2000 concurrent users): 1/2 rack Exadata

- Very large customers (> 2000 concurrent users): 1/2 rack Exadata

PeopleSoft:

- Medium customers (2000 users): 1/4 rack Exadata

- Large customers (10,000 users): 1/2 rack Exadata

- Extra-large customers (20,000 users): 1 full rack Exadata

ATG:

- Small customers (100 peak page views per sec): 1/8 rack Exadata

- Medium customers (500 peak page views per sec): 1/8 rack Exadata

- Large customers (1000 peak page views per sec): 1/4 rack Exadata

- Extra-large customers (4000 peak page views per sec): 1/2 rack Exadata

Siebel:

- Small customers (up to 500 concurrent users): 1/8 rack Exadata

- Medium customers (500–2500 concurrent users): 1/8 to 1/4 rack Exadata

- Large customers (2500–10,000 concurrent users): 1/2 rack Exadata

JD Edwards:

- Small customers (500 concurrent users plus 500–1000 UBE [Universal Batch Engine]): 1/8 rack Exadata

- Medium customers (500–2500 concurrent users plus 1000–2500 UBE): 1/4 rack Exadata

- Large customers (2500–30,000 concurrent users plus 2000–5000 UBE): 1/4 to 1/2 rack Exadata

NOTE
If you need help in performing predictive sizing for an application, contact the application vendor, who can provide an estimate of what sized hardware is needed to run the application. They will provide the CPU memory and I/O requirements that can be used as you determine Exadata sizing using comparative sizing.

Predictive Sizing Questionnaire Examples

The following examples show the inputs that are typically needed to size an E-Business Suite and a Demantra environment. These real-life examples will help you understand what kind of information you need to perform predictive sizing for an application.

E-Business Suite Sizing Questionnaire

1. Provide the list of modules that will be implemented in the system (for example, Financials AP, AR, GL, FA; Manufacturing BOM, INV).

2. Provide the total and active users based on the modules. Use the following table as a reference.

	Total Users	Active Users Light	Medium	Heavy
Type of Client				
Forms Users – Fin (e.g., GL, AP, AR, FA, PO)				
– ERP (e.g., INV, MFG, BOM, WIP, OM)				
– Configurator				
– Core CRM (e.g., Sales, Mktg, Service)				
– Other Forms Modules				
Self-Service Users – SSHR, i(modules) (e.g., iProc, iTime, iExpenses)				
– CRM (e.g., Sales Mktg, Service)				

	Total Users	Active Users Light	Medium	Heavy
– Other Self-Service/Web Modules				
APS (Advanced Planning & Scheduling) Users				
– ASCP (Advanced Supply Chain Planning)				
– ODP (Oracle Demand Planning)				
– IO (Inventory Optimization)				
– GOP (Global Order Promising)				
– Collaborative Planning				
– Manufacturing Scheduling				
	Count			

3. How many batch jobs will be running in a day, week, and month? Any special requirement for the month-end or quarter-end jobs?

4. What is the overall OLTP:Batch ratio? Also include the OLTP and batch throughput requirements in terms of business events/hour (e.g., 100 users × "Enter Sales Order" 10 times per hour, etc.)

5. Scalability: If you will be increasing the number of users, specify the rate and timeframe (e.g., 15 percent increase in active concurrent users for each of the next three years). If you will be increasing the transaction volumes, specify the rate and timeframe (e.g., 10 percent increase in transaction volumes for each of the next three years).

6. Describe other specific high-volume workloads (e.g., 20,000 × "FA depreciations" per hour, etc.).

7. How many custom interfaces would be used? Describe the nature of custom interfaces that will be developed (e.g., 1000 × "Online Customer Lookup via network" per hour, etc.).

8. How many custom modules will be developed? Describe the details of each custom module.

9. Describe your Oracle HR (payroll) processing requirements (if applicable).

10. Describe any additional processing requirements that may impact this configuration recommendation.

11. Provide the details of the geographies where the product will be implemented.

12. Describe the localization and languages requirements.

Demantra Sizing Questionnaire

1. In how many locations will the system be deployed?

2. What are the total finished goods SKU?

3. What is the average number of finished goods per location?

4. What is the time bucket definition in the system (days, weeks, or months)?

5. What is the expected new product growth in the next five years?

6. What is the expected new location growth in the next five years?

7. How many concurrent users use the system in the peak planning cycle?

8. How many years of shipment/booking history is used for statistical purposes?

9. How many years of forecast planning will you generate?

10. What is the target forecast engine runtime in hours?

11. What modules are being planned: Sales Promotions, Promotion Modeling, CTO Implementation, SPF Implementation?

Disaster Recovery Environment Sizing

The disaster recovery (DR) environment is created so that the business and system can continue operating in case of any unforeseen events such as fire, earthquake, storm, and so on. The primary purpose of the disaster recovery environment is to provide uninterrupted operation in the business.

A standby Exadata system is a replica of the primary system. In most cases, Oracle Data Guard is used to maintain synchronized standby databases that are exact physical replicas of production databases hosted on the primary system. This provides optimal data protection and high availability if an unplanned outage makes the primary system unavailable. Sometimes Golden Gate is also used to synchronize the primary and standby database.

A standby Exadata system is most often located in a different data center or geography to provide disaster recovery by isolating the standby from primary site failures.

Configuring the standby system with identical capacity as the primary also guarantees that performance service level agreements can be met after a switchover or failover. Typically, the business SLA decides the sizing of the DR environment. If the business must operate with the same SLA used by production, DR Exadata is sized exactly to the production system. For example, if the production system is running on a half-rack Exadata, the DR must also be a half-rack Exadata. If the business can run with reduced capacity when the actual DR happens, then the

DR system can be undersized as per the SLA—in that case, you can run the production system on a half-rack Exadata and the DR on a quarter-rack Exadata.

TIP & TECHNIQUE
Oracle recommends that you size DR equal to production. It's not always clear what "degraded" performance might look like. A slightly undersized system can have a very large impact on performance.

Nonproduction Environment Sizing

In some cases, the nonproduction environment needs to be sized exactly like the production environment, whereas in other cases, it needs to be sized differently. In the following section, we will evaluate all the scenarios for nonproduction sizing.

Production Support/QA Environment

In the production support or quality assurance (QA) environment, any patch is tested before being moved into the production system. If new functionalities are being deployed in the production system, final validation happens in this environment before moving the changes in the production environment. Let's discuss the various options available for sizing this environment:

- **QA environment equally sized with production** In ideal cases, the production support/QA environment is the exact replica of the production environment. Having an exact replica of the production support ensures full performance validation at production scale.

- **QA environment running in the DR machine** In some cases, the production support/QA environment is run on the standby Exadata Machine. In this case, all the patches, software changes, and functional tests can be validated. Full performance validation can be done if using Data Guard Snapshot Standby, but this can extend recovery time if a failover is required.

- **QA environment running on a shared Exadata Machine** In many cases, the QA environment can be shared with different databases in Exadata Machine. In this case, the functional validation and patch validation can be done. This environment may be suitable for performance testing if enough system resources can be allocated to mimic production.

- **QA running on a smaller Exadata Machine** If the QA machine is sized to run a smaller machine than the production system, then all the patch and functional validation is possible, but it will not be possible to run the performance testing at production scale.

- **Using an older generation of Exadata for QA environment**   In this case, the functional validation and patch validation can be easily done. If the production system uses the new hardware features, those features can't be tested on this machine. The performance test will be limited to the old hardware features, and new features can't be compared with production during stress testing. If you have an older generation of Exadata Machine, it's not recommended to use it for the production support/QA environment. It can be used for a unit test or development environment.

- **Using a non-Exadata Machine for QA environment**   In this configuration, database and grid infrastructure software and patches can be validated. The database generic functional tests can be validated. Testing of Exadata-specific software features (such as EHCC, IORM, Storage Index, and so on) cannot be validated. The performance testing compared to production is not possible. This configuration is not recommended for the production support/ QA environment.

Development, Unit Test Environment

The development environment is where the developers create the new features in the OLTP system. This environment can be run with a reduced capacity and doesn't necessarily have to be sized equal to the production or QA environment. If the Exadata-specific features are not used to develop the new product functionality, the non-Exadata hardware can also be used to host this environment—with the caveat being that when the development environment is cloned from the production system, all the Exadata-specific features will be disabled in this environment such as HCC, storage indexes, and so on.

In the unit test environment, application functionality is tested. This environment can also be run with a reduced capacity, just like the development environment. If the Exadata-specific features are not used to develop the new product functionality, the non-Exadata hardware can also be used to host this environment. However, it is generally recommended to run the unit test machine in an Exadata Machine because the application code would provide a different result in an Exadata versus a non-Exadata environment since the database optimizer behaves in different ways.

Comparative Sizing Case Study

Let's do a real-life case study that will help you understand the concept of sizing. The comparative sizing questionnaire was sent to the customer who provided the following details. We will use this information and will do the sizing of Exadata.

Server

- Server make and model: IBM Power 595 (4.2 GHz)

- Chip count: 24

- Cores per chip: 2

- Peak CPU utilization: 70%

- Planned CPU growth: 10%

- System memory (RAM): 207GB

- Memory utilization: 100%

- Planned memory growth: NA

Database

- Database name: PROD

- Database version: 11.2.0.3

- RAC or non-RAC: non-RAC

- Database size: 6000GB

- Data growth rate: 10%

- ASM redundancy (normal, high): Normal

- Landing space: NA

- Number of disk backups: 1

- Backup mechanism (full/incremental) (compressed or uncompressed): Full/uncompressed

- Flashback enabled (if yes, then for how many days): NA

- Compression ratio: NA

- SGA size: 80GB

- PGA size: 80GB

- Physical read total I/O requests per second from AWR: 8627

- Physical write total I/O requests per second from AWR: 1963

From this information, let's calculate the four components, one by one:

- **CPU/core** The total number of cores of the existing system is $24 \times 2 = 48$ cores. Since the CPU utilization is 70 percent, effective CPU is 70 percent of 48, or 33.6. We need to add this number to CPU growth, so total required core becomes $33.6 \times 10\%$ of $33.6 = 37.2$. The clock speed of the CPU is 4.2 GHz. We can use any of the standard benchmarks to find which size of Exadata can handle a similar core requirement. An Exadata quarter rack has 48 cores of 2.7 GHz. After comparing the benchmark results, we found that a quarter rack can handle the CPU requirement.

- **Memory** The system memory is 207GB. A quarter rack has 512GB of RAM. The memory requirements will easily fit into a quarter rack. (We could have also added SGA + PGA for comparing memory, but in this case, memory is not at all a constraint.)

- **Storage** The database size is 6000TB. By adding 20 percent space for archive log files, it becomes 7200GB. Assuming one copy of backup will be stored in the disk, we need to add another 6000GB, so the total size becomes 13200GB. A quarter rack has 63TB of space with ASM double redundancy. The storage requirement easily fits into a quarter rack.

- **I/O** The read IOPS is 8627 and write IOPS is 1963; read IOPS + write IOPS = 10590. Assuming 50 percent of IOPS will be handled by Exadata Smart Flash Cache, the IOPS becomes 5295. The remaining 5295 IOPS needs to be handled by disks. As per the data sheet, a quarter rack (HC) has 7000 disk IOPS, which can easily handle the requirement of 5295 disk IOPS. In case of ASM double-redundancy, all the writes happen at two places, but that does not impact the write IOPS since with Write-Back Flash Cache, all the writes go to flash. A quarter rack can easily handle the I/O requirements.

By comparing all four aspects, we come to the conclusion that a quarter-rack Exadata is the correct fit.

Summary

Two main Exadata Machine sizing methodologies can be used: comparative and predictive. In the comparative sizing methodology, the existing hardware is compared against Exadata. Predictive sizing is done on the basis of the application's characteristics. In some cases, a combination of predictive and comparative sizing is required.

Business SLA typically derives the sizing of the DR environment. If the business needs to run with full capacity during the DR, then an equal-sized environment is needed for the DR system. If the business can operate with reduced capacity during an actual disaster, the DR environment can be sized less than the production environment. Ideally, you should have a full-sized DR system, but businesses often don't want to invest in a full-sized DR system.

It is recommended that you also have a performance testing environment that is equal to the size of the production environment for the production support/QA environment.

Development/unit test environments can run with much fewer cores and less memory than the production environment.

CHAPTER
6

Migrating Applications
to Exadata

Applications can be migrated to an Exadata Machine in several ways. The key is identifying the correct mechanism, which depends on factors that are influenced either by business or IT requirements. Some examples of important factors that govern the migration mechanism follow:

- **Downtime**   Downtime is a critical issue for businesses and can severely impact revenue. Depending on the criticality of the application, the business governs how much downtime is allowed for a particular application. Downtime is also a critical factor in deciding the migration path. Some migration paths needs lots of downtime, while others need zero or near-zero downtime. If the business can't afford large downtimes, you must plan for a proper migration plan with minimum downtime.

- **Database version**   The database version is a governing factor in deciding the optimum migration path. Exadata supports Oracle Database 11.2.0.3 and onward. An application running on a 10g database, for example, makes a big impact as you choose the appropriate migration path.

- **Operating system**   Exadata runs on Oracle Enterprise Linux, which is a little-endian platform (versus a big-endian platform). The terms "little-endian" and "big-endian" are derived from the phrases "little end in" and "big end in," respectively, and refer to the way in which memory is stored. In a little-endian architecture, the hexadecimal word 0x1234 is stored in memory as (0x34 0x12)—that is, the little end, or lower end, is stored first. In a big-endian architecture, the 0x1234 is stored in reverse fashion—(0x12 0x34)—in memory. The endian differs according to the OS and is another governing factor in deciding the migration path. If the application is running on a platform that is little-endian, the migration plan will be different from that of a platform that is big-endian.

- **Nature of the application**   The migration plan differs depending on the nature of the application. Every application is unique and may or may not support certain capabilities, and several compatibilities and incompatibilities may affect the migration methods. For example, some applications do not support logical Data Guard, and some applications do not work well with GoldenGate.

- **Automatic Storage Management (ASM) versus non-ASM**   Exadata requires ASM. If the application is currently running on non-ASM–based storage, you need to factor in ASM while preparing for migration.

Other factors influence the migration in an indirect way and must also be considered:

- **RAC versus non-RAC**   If the source application is running on a non-RAC single-instance database and migration to RAC is being planned after moving to Exadata, some additional preparation is required. Implementing RAC might be "optional" if a database and its workload easily fit into a single node of Exadata, but RAC is highly recommended because it provides high availability, scalability, and fault tolerance.

- **Partitioning**   Many customers implement partitioning during migration. Because migration involves moving the data from an old server to a new server, partitioning can be done along with the migration in a single downtime. Partitioning needs a partitioning strategy and application knowledge and must be planned ahead.

- **Compression**   Similar to partitioning, compression methodologies such as Advanced Compression or Hybrid Columnar Compression (HCC) can be implemented during migration to Exadata. If you plan to implement compression during migration, it must be factored in.

- **Cleanup**   Additional tasks can be planned during migration to Exadata, including tasks such as fixing the low-level allocation units, reorganizing tables or indexes, changing from locally managed tablespaces to dictionary managed tablespaces, and so on.

Planning and Preparing for Migration

Planning and preparing for migration are as important as the actual migration. You'll spend a lot of time preparing. Following are the critical activities that occur during the preparation stage:

- **Contingency or fallback plans**   More than one migration path could be available. A proper plan that aligns with business goals needs to be identified. It is always recommended that you include a contingency, or fallback, plan with the migration. The contingency plan should be executed automatically if the migration doesn't meet specific checkpoints in the required time. For example, you might have a downtime window of ten hours for the migration, but if the migration fails, you will need two hours to execute the fallback plan. That means the migration must be completed in eight hours or less to meet the ten-hour outage window. If the migration isn't complete after eight hours, the fallback plan needs to be executed.

■ **Personnel resources**   Identify who will be doing the actual migration, data validation, and testing. Personnel who perform the migration will need particular skill set; if no one on the team is skilled or if the person is not available in the require timeframe, partners and/or contractors must be scheduled.

■ **Project plans**   You should create a project plan documenting all the steps of the actual migration. Ideally, the project plan should include the micro-level details of the tasks that will be undertaken during the migration.

■ **Migration test iterations**   Run through at least two or three "dry runs" of the migration to streamline the process before the actual production migration. After the first iteration, analyze the process to find gaps and streamline the upcoming migration process. Any issues identified during the first migration iteration must be fixed and documented. Consequently, the project plan also needs to be updated. Repeat this process until it is completely streamlined and all outstanding issues arising due to migration are fixed.

■ **Validation after iteration**   Make sure the data is validated after every iteration process. The validation can be done using various methods—for example, with a simple count of database objects or a check for the validity of PL/SQL objects and so on. Depending on the method you use for moving data, you might want to take a count of rows in some of the tables.

■ **Environment/hardware**   Mock iterations should not be done in the production environment/hardware. A test environment with the most recent copy of the production data and a specification similar to the production environment should be used for mock iterations. For example, data in the test environment should be as identical as possible to that in the production environment, and the test environment should be using the same architecture that runs on the production environment.

■ **Functional and performance testing**   The mock iterations should be followed by a full round of functional and performance testing. Functional testing is needed to make sure that all the functionalities of the application are working as expected. Any functionality problems need to be identified, fixed, and documented. Performance testing ensures that the system is able to handle the production workload. Lots of testing tools are available to replicate the production workload, such as Oracle Real Application Testing, SQL Performance Analyzer, the Oracle Applications Testing Suite (OATS), and the third-party application LoadRunner. Before choosing any performance-testing tool, make sure that the application is certified with that testing tool.

- **Integrations** Very often, an OLTP environment is integrated with a number of other systems. The migration plan must include placeholders for all integration points. If a service-oriented architecture (SOA) or third-party tool such as TIBCO is being used for integrations, the migration plan must take all of them into account.

- **Single sign-on** If the application is integrated with a single sign-on (SSO) system, the migration plan must account for remapping the SSO on the new system.

Migration Paths

As discussed previously, more than one migration path may be available for a particular application. Let's evaluate each available migration option.

Migration Using RMAN

RMAN provides a couple of choices for migrating the database to Exadata. RMAN is a simple and powerful tool and is the easiest way to migrate to Exadata. To use RMAN for the migration, the following conditions must be met:

- The source and target database version must be same.

- The source and target OS platform must be same (except when running 12*c* database—12*c* provides RMAN-endian conversion).

These are the options RMAN provides for migration to Exadata. It is assumed that you are aware of the basic backup and recovery concept, as it is not covered in this book.

RMAN Backup and Restore

Backup and restore is the simplest way of migrating a database to Exadata. Both cold backup and hot backup can be used. If hot backup will be used, you need to establish a time when the existing production should be shut down (mounted). All archive log files should be captured and applied in the Exadata to ensure data integrity.

When migrating to Exadata using the backup and restore method, you can restore to Exadata from the normal backup location. If you normally back up to tape, the restore to Exadata will be from tape; however, the restore from tape is bit slow for migration and should be avoided to minimize downtime. If you normally back up to a local file system or NFS mount, the restore can come from that location if it's able to be mapped to Exadata.

Following are the steps for backup and restore:

1. Check the number of parallel channels allocated to RMAN. Use the command **show all** at the RMAN prompt to display that information. Adjust the number of parallel channels as per the hardware. The following example shows how to change the number of channels from 10 to 12:

```
RMAN> CONFIGURE DEVICE TYPE DISK PARALLELISM 12;
old RMAN configuration parameters:
CONFIGURE DEVICE TYPE DISK PARALLELISM 10 BACKUP TYPE TO
BACKUPSET;
new RMAN configuration parameters:
CONFIGURE DEVICE TYPE DISK PARALLELISM 12 BACKUP TYPE TO
BACKUPSET;
new RMAN configuration parameters are successfully stored
```

2. If a cold backup is being planned, put the database in a mounted state. If a hot backup is being planned, the database can remain open.

3. Back up the whole database using RMAN. A sample command is shown next. The command takes the backup of data files, control files, and ARCHIVELOG files in a location other than FRA:

```
RMAN target /
Recovery Manager: Release 11.2.0.3.0 - Production on Sat Mar 8
22:04:06 2014
Copyright (c) 1982, 2011, Oracle and/or its affiliates.  All
rights reserved.
connected to target database: VISOW (DBID=220594996)
RMAN> backup full database plus archivelog include current
controlfile format '/dbfsmnt/staging_area/exadatarman/
VISOW_%d_%s_%p_%t';
```

4. Store the backup files at /dbfsmnt/staging_area/exadatarman. Copy/scp the files from the source server to the Exadata. The RMAN backup files can be kept in the /dbfs file system depending on the size of the database. The database file system (DBFS) space is normally quite small, so if the database is very large, DBFS is likely not large enough for a full database backup. In that case, you can mount the external file system to keep the backup files.

   If a hot backup is being planned, before the intended downtime, back up all the archive log files and copy/scp the same in the Exadata.

5. In Exadata, create/edit the spfile and start the database in nomount mode. Restore the control file first using RMAN. A sample command is shown here:

```
RMAN > restore controlfile from '/dbfs/stage/rmanbackup/
kqntc0ifo_1_1';
```

6. After the control file is restored, mount the database and catalog the backup files:

```
RMAN > alter database mount;
RMAN > catalog start with '/dbfs/stage/rmanbackup';
```

7. Once the catalog is done, restore the database using the command **restore database**. In some cases, setting up the new name and switching data files before and after the database restore may be needed, depending on your source and target file system layout.

8. After the database restore, recover and open the database:

```
RMAN> restore database;
RMAN> recover database;
RMAN> alter database open resetlogs;
```

TIP & TECHNIQUE
Having too many RMAN channels impacts performance. Run a few iterations with different numbers of channels to determine the optimal number of channels for your system.

RMAN Database Duplication

The steps for RMAN database duplication are similar to the steps for RMAN backup and restore. The difference in this case is that RMAN makes a connection with the source database, gets all the information from the source, and then configures the target database.

Two methods are used for database duplication:

- **Backup-based duplication**   Requires a backup of the source database for the duplication

- **Active database duplication**   Doesn't need any backup and can transfer the data files directly from the source database during the duplication process

Backup-based Duplication   The backup-based duplication process requires that you back up the source database. Hot backup or cold backup can be used for the backup-based duplication. If hot backup is being planned, before the intended downtime, back up all the archive log files and copy/scp the same in the Exadata.

The backup can be invoked from the RMAN prompt. Here's a sample command:

```
RMAN> backup full database plus archivelog include current controlfile
```

Copy/scp the backup files from the source server to the Exadata Machine. The following tasks are required for database duplication:

1. Create the password file. The password file needs to be created at the Exadata Machine to establish connectivity.

```
orapwd file=/u01/app/oracle/product/11.2.0.3/dbhome_1/dbs/
password=manager
```

2. Edit the pfile/spfile and change the relevant parameters. All the parameters that reflect the file system of the source database server should be changed to reflect the target database server path names. If the path name for the data file and log file changes, the same path name must be reflected in the pfile/spfile. The following parameter takes care of copying the data files and log files from the old path name to the new path name:

```
DB_FILE_NAME_CONVERT='old_path_name_of_data_files','new_path_
name_of_data_files'
LOG_FILE_NAME_CONVERT='old_path_name_of_log_files','new_path_
name_of_log_files'
```

3. For running the database duplicate, the TNS connectivity must be established between the source and Exadata server. Edit the tnsnames.ora in $ORACLE_HOME/network/admin and put the proper entries so that the source database can be connected from the Exadata Machine. A sample entry is shown here:

```
VISOW =
  (DESCRIPTION =
    (ADDRESS = (PROTOCOL = TCP)(HOST = sca10linux-scan
.us.oracle.com)(PORT = 1521))
    (CONNECT_DATA =
      (SERVER = DEDICATED)
      (SERVICE_NAME = VISOW)
    )
  )
```

4. Once the TNS is configured correctly and you are able to connect the source machine from Exadata, run the duplicate database command. Start the database in nomount mode:

```
SQL> STARTUP NOMOUNT;
```

5. For database duplication, RMAN needs to be connected both to the Exadata and the source database. In the context of running the **RMAN** command, Exadata will be the AUXILIARY and the source database will be TARGET. The **RMAN** command can be run both in catalog or non-catalog mode. A sample command for running the duplicate database using non-catalog mode is

shown next; make sure RMAN has enough parallel channels before starting the database duplication.

```
RMAN
Recovery Manager: Release 11.2.0.3.0 - Production on Sun Mar 16
17:21:05 2014
Copyright (c) 1982, 2011, Oracle and/or its affiliates.  All
rights reserved.
RMAN> connect AUXILIARY /
connected to auxiliary database: VISOW (DBID=2105982882)
RMAN> connect target sys/manager@VISOW /
connected to target database: VISOW (DBID=220594996)
RMAN> DUPLICATE TARGET DATABASE TO VISOW NOFILENAMECHECK;
```

6. The duplicate database can be run against a particular log sequence—for example, **set until logseq 2200 thread 1**—until a particular time (when the database was shut down before the downtime) **set until time "to_date('16-MAR-2014 14:00:00','DD-MON-YYYY HH24:MI:SS')"**. An example is shown next using a particular time. For mock iterations to Exadata, **until logseq** or **until time** can be used, but for final cutover to Exadata, you should take a full backup and copy/scp the backup files to Exadata. Then put the database in mount state, back up the ARCHIVELOG files, copy/scp them to Exadata, and then start the database duplication from Exadata.

```
RMAN> connect AUXILIARY /
connected to auxiliary database: VISOW (DBID=2105982882)
RMAN> connect target sys/manager@VISOW /
connected to target database: VISOW (DBID=220594996)
RMAN> run {
2> set until time "to_date('16-MAR-2014 14:00:00','DD-MON-YYYY
HH24:MI:SS')"
3> DUPLICATE TARGET DATABASE TO VISOW NOFILENAMECHECK
4> };
```

7. Once the database duplication is complete, recover and open the database:

```
RMAN> restore database;
RMAN> recover database;
RMAN> alter database open resetlogs;
```

Active Database Duplication   Active database duplication is similar to backup-based duplication, except active database duplication doesn't require a database backup. This eliminates the need to back up the source database and copy the backup files into the Exadata Machine. You can choose this method instead of backup-based duplication if you have very strong network connectivity between the source machine and Exadata system.

RMAN must be connected as TARGET to the source database, which is the database that is being copied. The source database must be mounted or open. The source database must not be a standby database.

While performing the active database duplication, you cannot use the UNTIL clause. RMAN chooses a time based on when the online data files have been completely copied so that the data files can be recovered to a consistent point in time. When you are migrating to Exadata, it is recommended that the source database remain in mount state during the final migration to ensure that all data is migrated into Exadata.

RMAN must be connected as AUXILIARY to the instance of the duplicate database, which is the Exadata Machine. The instance of the duplicate database is called the *auxiliary instance* and must be started with the nomount option.

The source database and auxiliary instances must use the same SYSDBA password, which means that both instances must already have password files. You can create the password file with the orapwd utility. An example was shown in the previous section.

The source machine and Exadata Machine must have the tnsnames.ora file with proper entries. A sample entry from the tnsnames.ora file was shown in the previous section.

The Exadata machine must also have a listener running. By default, the listener is already configured with OneCommand (OneCommand is the utility used by Oracle Advanced Customer Services to install/configure the Exadata Machine for the first time), so the same can be leveraged for the active database duplicate.

Follow these steps:

1. Modify the parameter file (pfile/spfile) in the Exadata Machine to reflect the new path name of the data files, log files, and other important directories.

2. Put the database in nomount state to start the active database duplication. Make sure RMAN has enough parallel channels before starting the database duplication.

```
RMAN
Recovery Manager: Release 11.2.0.3.0 - Production on Sun Mar 16
17:21:05 2014
Copyright (c) 1982, 2011, Oracle and/or its affiliates.  All
rights reserved.
RMAN> connect AUXILIARY /
connected to auxiliary database: VISOW (DBID=2105982882)
RMAN> connect target sys/manager@VISOW /
connected to target database: VISOW (DBID=220594996)
RMAN> run
1 {
2 DUPLICATE TARGET DATABASE TO VISOW NOFILENAMECHECK
```

```
3 FROM ACTIVE DATABASE
4 };
```

TIP & TECHNIQUE
If you have good network connectivity between the source and target machines, you may prefer active database duplication over backup-based duplication, because active duplication eliminates the need to have a staging area.

Migration Using Data Pump Export and Import

Data Pump Export and Import can be leveraged to migrate the applications database into the Exadata Machine in the following scenarios:

- *When the source operating system uses a platform other than Exadata.* Exadata runs on the Linux operating system, which is little-endian. Data Pump Export and Import can be used for migrating the database running on a big-endian OS as well as a little-endian OS. Solaris, HP-UX, and AIX are big-endian operating systems. Data Pump solves the cross-platform migration issue and is especially helpful for cross-endian migration.

- *When the version of the database in the source is different from that of Exadata.* Exadata supports Oracle Database 11.2.0.3 and later. If the source database version is lower than supported by Exadata (such as 10g or 11gR1 or 11.2.0.1, 11.2.0.2), then Data Pump Export and Import can be used to migrate the database to Exadata.

Steps for the Database Export

Irrespective of the application, the steps for migrating a database to Exadata using Data Pump Export and Import are usually the same. There might be a few application-specific steps, which would be different from application to application—for example, you may need to apply a few application-specific performance patches before kicking off the export. But the overall process is same irrespective of the application.

The first step for the export/import process is to prepare the source system. The following tasks are usually undertaken during the preparation phase:

1. Apply application-specific DB patches. These patches could be performance patches or patches with export-specific scripts, or they may be interoperability patches. This step may or may not be applicable depending on the application.

2. Identify the list of the tablespaces. It is very important that the target database have the same set of tablespaces as the source database before the import is kicked off. Export can take care of identifying the tablespace definitions and the import can re-create the tablespaces, but the path name of the target data must match the path name of the source system. In most cases, the path name of the data file in Exadata will not match the source system, so manual creation of tablespaces is required. Also, if the source data files are not using ASM, tablespace creation as a part of export/import can't be leveraged because Exadata uses ASM.

3. Identify a mount point that will be used to keep the export dump files. The ideal scenario would be a mount point available from both the source machine and the Exadata Machine. This will save a lot of time transferring the dump file from the source to the target system. If an NFS mount point is used, make sure the file system is mounted with the correct mount options. For example, as the root user, you'd execute the following:

```
mkdir /datapump
chown oracle:dba /datapump
mount scadb01:/export/datapump -o rsize=32768,wsize=32768,
hard,actimeo=0,nolock
```

As the Oracle user:

```
mkdir /datapump/expimp
```

4. Create a database directory that will be used for export:

```
$ sqlplus '/ as sysdba '
SQL> create directory dmpdir_expimp as '/datapump/expimp';
```

You might also be required to take some application-specific steps with advanced queues and tables with long columns. Record advanced queues before the export or import, and enable them in the target database instance afterward. The patch 10396457 contains the auque1.sql file, which generates the auque2.sql script that can be used to enable the settings in the target database instance after the import is complete.

Long columns can be exported using Data Pump Export (not the old exp/imp); however, there are restrictions on Data Pump Export of long columns: you must use the DIRECT driver, but certain conditions prevent use of the DIRECT driver.

Once the source system is prepared, your next step is to export the database. Data Pump Export/Import should be used rather than the traditional export/import.

5. Export the database using the following command. If possible, the export should be run in a **nohup** command so that the process can run even if the session is lost.

```
nohup expdp "'/ as sysdba'" parfile='name of parameter file' &
```

The following shows a sample export parameter file:

```
directory=dmpdir_expimp
dumpfile= dumpfile=aexp01%U.dmp, aexp02%U.dmp, aexp03%U
.dmp, aexp04%U.dmp, aexp05%U.dmp, aexp06%U.dmp, aexp07%U.dmp,
aexp08%U.dmp,
# 1 Gb dump file size
filesize=1048576000
full=y
logfile=expdp.log
PARALLEL=16
METRICS=Y
```

The degree of parallelism depends on the number of CPUs and cores. You can change the number depending on the hardware specification. There might be some other application-specific parameters as well. For example, some applications may have only one schema in the database. In that case, the export of the whole database is not needed, and the export of that schema would be good enough.

6. Once the export is done, copy the dump file to Exadata. DBFS can be leveraged for storing the export dump file. External storage or ZFS can also be mounted with Exadata for keeping the dump files.

Steps for the Database Import

The Exadata Machine needs to be prepared before the import can be started. For example, you should make sure there are no issues with the network before the import takes place. Lots of activities during the preparation phase can occur in parallel. For example, during the import of the database, Exadata can be prepared in parallel.

The following steps typically occur when you're preparing the Exadata Machine for an import:

1. Create the database before the import starts. The Database Configuration Assistant (DBCA) can be used to create the database. Make sure the Exadata database template is chosen when running the DBCA. You should also note the character set of the source database. Problems can result if you change the character set during the migration, so the simplest solution is to match whatever character set was used on the source DB. DBCA can take care of creating the desired RAC nodes. If a single instance is planned initially, it can be converted to an RAC database later using the rconfig tool.

2. Create all the tablespaces that are used in the source database.

3. Apply all the interoperability patches and application-specific patches. These might be needed if the version of the database or the platform of the OS changes.

4. Perform the application-specific steps. Depending on the application, some special steps may be required, such as creation of certain objects in the system or sys schema, and so on.

5. Make sure all the data files are sized adequately. Also set the auto-extend on to all the data files. This will ensure that the import won't fail due to lack of space.

6. Create a database directory that will be used for import:

```
$ sqlplus system/
SQL> create directory dmpdir_mig as '/ebs/expimp';
```

7. Import the database.

Once the pre-import steps are done, create the import parameter file and kick off the import. If possible, the import should use the **nohup** command so that the process can continue in the background. Use the following command for the import:

```
impdp "'/ as sysdba'" parfile=impdp.par
```

A sample parameter file is shown here:

```
directory=dmpdir_mig
dumpfile=aexp%U.dmp
full=y
transform=oid:n
exclude=tablespace
logfile=impdp.log
parallel=16
metrics=Y
```

When the import is finished, perform a complete analysis of the log files to make sure everything is normal. If errors are present in the log files, they need to be fixed before the final production migration. If fixes can't be found easily, open a service request for each issue and follow up with Oracle Support.

A database import is usually followed by the post-import steps such as compilations of the invalid objects in the database, re-creating the advanced queues, data validation, configuration of the application tiers, and so on.

Migration Using Transportable Database (TDB)

Transportable database (TDB) can be used to convert and migrate a full database from a source platform to a target format. TDB requires that data files be converted to the target platform format. Following are the prerequisites for using the transportable database:

- The endian format of the source and target should be same. If the endian format between the source system is different from that of the target, in this case Exadata, the transportable database can't be used; in that case, a transportable tablespace needs to be used. Since Exadata is little-endian, if the source system is also little-endian, then the transportable database can be used for migrating to Exadata.

- The source system and the target system should be using the same version of Oracle Database. Since Exadata supports Oracle Database 11.2.0.3 and later, if the source platform is earlier than 11.2.0.3, this method can't be used for migration to Exadata and an upgrade to 11.2.0.3 would be required.

Following are the steps for migrating a database to Exadata using TDB.

1. Identify external tables, directories, and external binary files (BFILEs) that exist in the source database that need to be created on the Exadata Machine. The PL/SQL function CHECK_EXTERNAL identifies external tables, directories, and BFILEs that need to be moved during the migration so the target database is complete when the process is finished. An example is shown here:

```
SQL> set serveroutput on
SQL> declare x boolean;
 begin x := dbms_tdb.check_external; end;

The following external tables exist in the database:
INV.MATERIAL_TRANSACTIONS_EXT
The following directories exist in the database:
SYS.DATA_FILE_DIR, SYS.LOG_FILE_DIR, SYS.TTSDIR
The following BFILEs exist in the database:
PM.PRINT_MEDIA
PL/SQL procedure successfully completed.
```

The output of the CHECK_EXTERNAL function shows that an external table, database directories, and BFILEs exist in the database. Use the following queries to get detailed information about them.

To identify external table files, run this query:

```
SQL> select directory_path||'/'||location External_file_
path from dba_directories a, dba_external_locations b where
a.directory_name=b.directory_name;
EXTERNAL_FILE_PATH-------------------------
/dbfs/exa/inv2.dat
```

To identify the directories, run the following query. Create all the directories that exist in the source system using the **create directory** command.

```
SQL> select directory_path from dba_directories;
```

To identify the BFILEs and their corresponding directories, run the get_bfile .sql and get_bfile_dir.sql scripts. The scripts are included in Addendums 6.1 and 6.2 at the end of this chapter.

```
SQL> @get_bfile_dir.sql
```

The following directories contain external files for BFILE columns. Copy the files within these directories to the same path on the target system:

```
/dbfs/exa/cabo/
/dbfs/exa/images/
```

There are two directories with 181 total BFILEs.

2. If your source system uses OLAP analytic workspaces (AWs), it must be exported from the source database before the TDB process begins and imported into the target database after the TDB process is complete. AWs are exported and imported using the DBMS_AW.EXECUTE PL/SQL procedure. (Covering this is beyond the scope of this book; see MOS note 352306.1 for an example of export/import of AWs.)

3. TDB requires that the entire database be open in read-only mode. So whenever the source database becomes read-only, it remains unavailable to the users. If there is a Data Guard Standby environment, that can also be used as a source database to do the migration. Start the database in read-only mode by running the following command:

```
SQL> shutdown immediate;
SQL> startup mount;
SQL> alter database open read only;
```

If the standby database is running in read-only mode, this step is not needed.

4. Run the DBMS_TDB.CHECK_DB function to verify that the database can be migrated to the target platform and that the database is in the proper state to be migrated. If you're using a physical standby database, this function is run on the standby database instead of on the primary.

```
SQL> set serveroutput on
SQL> declare
 retcode boolean;
 begin
 retcode := dbms_tdb.check_db('Linux x86 64-bit)',
 dbms_tdb.skip_none);
 end;
```

Any condition reported by CHECK_DB must be resolved before TDB can proceed.

5. Run the **CONVERT DATABASE** command. If there are no issues reported, then the **CONVERT DATABASE** command can be run using **RMAN**. The **CONVERT DATABASE** can be run either from the source system or from the Exadata Machine. When performing a source system conversion, TDB creates a second copy of all data files on the source system in the format of the target system. The converted data files must then be transferred to the proper location on the Exadata Machine. When performing TDB on an Exadata system conversion, the original data files on the source system are first transferred to the Exadata system and placed in a staging area. Please note that the staging area should have enough space to accommodate all the data files of the source database. **RMAN** is then run to convert the data files to the Exadata system format and place them in their final location.

    Here's a sample script for running **CONVERT DATABASE** when the conversion is planned from the source system:

```
RMAN
RMAN> connect target /
RMAN> convert database
 transport script '/stage/transport_prod.sql'
 new database 'PROD'
 to platform 'Linux x86 64-bit'
 parallelism 12
 format '/stage/PROD'
 db_file_name_convert '/u01/oradata/PROD/datafile/','/stage
/datafiles'
```

The **CONVERT DATABASE** command will create a transport script named transport_prod.sql and a copy of the parameter file named init_prod.ora in the /stage directory. We will need those files later. The **RMAN** process converts the data files into the target platform format and dumps them into the /stage/datafiles directory. In this example, because the name of the database is prod, that's why running the command is going to create the init_prod.ora file. In the db_file_name_convert, the source database file locations and the target database file locations after the conversion are given. Thus, /u01/oradata/PROD/datafile/ is the location of the data files of the existing database, and /stage/datafiles is the location of the converted data files in the format of the target platform (Linux).

When the conversion is run from the Exadata Machine, **RMAN** first creates a script to be used in Exadata to convert all the data files. Here is a sample script for running the **CONVERT DATABASE** command when the conversion process is planned from Exadata. Please note that even in this case the **CONVERT DATABASE** command needs to be run from the source system, which creates the required files:

```
RMAN
RMAN> connect target /
RMAN> convert database on target platform
 convert script '/stage/convert_prod.rman'
 transport script '/tmp/transport_prod.sql'
 new database 'prod'
 format '/stage/prod%U'
 db_file_name_convert '/u01/oradata/PROD/datafile','/stage
/datafiles;
```

This command creates a script called convert_prod.rman, which, when run from Exadata Machine, will do the actual conversion. Similar to the conversion at the source, this command will also create a transport script and a parameter file, initprod.ora.

Copy the relevant files from the source to the Exadata Machine. Once the **CONVERT DATABASE** command is complete, transfer the parameter file, transport SQL script, and converted data files (if the conversion is done at the source system; if the conversion is planned in Exadata, the unconverted data files should already be copied), converted RMAN script, external table files, and BFILEs to the Exadata system using FTP, SCP, and so on. Both external table files and BFILEs should be placed in the file system that corresponds to the same directory object.

6. Perform the migration. Depending on the type of conversion chosen, source system or target system (Exadata), the process will vary:

- If the conversion is done at the source system, review the PFILE in the Exadata Machine to make sure that the path names of the data files are accurate. If the conversion is planned on the Exadata Machine, you can skip this step, but there is no harm in reviewing the PFILE.

- If the conversion is planned from Exadata, review the convert RMAN script. (Note that you should skip this step when conversion is done at the source system, since no convert RMAN script is generated.)

- The filename specified for **CONVERT DATAFILE** should be the unconverted data file that was transferred from the source system. The FORMAT specification should indicate the final location of the converted data file. This final location must match the location specified in the transport SQL script. (We will cover this shortly.)

■ In Exadata, ensure that the PFILE clause in the **STARTUP NOMOUNT** command refers to the location where the PFILE was copied to the target system.

■ Run the convert RMAN script. (Note that you should skip this step when conversion is done at the source system, since no convert RMAN script is generated.) After you review and edit the convert script as necessary, start the Exadata instance in nomount mode using the PFILE transferred from the source system, and then run the script. After running the convert script, shut down the target instance.

```
RMAN> connect target/
RMAN> @convert_prod.rman
RMAN> shutdown
```

■ Run the transport SQL script. The final step is to run the transport SQL script that was created by the **CONVERT DATABASE** command. This script needs to be run irrespective of the location where **CONVERT DATABASE** was run. Before running the script, edit the script on the target system to ensure that locations for all referenced files are correct. Ensure that the PFILE referenced in the **STARTUP** command in the transport script points to the location where the PFILE was placed when it was transferred from the source system. Ensure that the data file locations in the **CREATE CONTROLFILE** statement refer to the final location of the converted data files on the target system. If it is a target system conversion, then the data file locations should match where the **CONVERT DATAFILE** command placed its output. Ensure that the log file locations in the **CREATE CONTROLFILE** statement refer to the desired location of the online redo log files on the target system. If a location is not specified, Oracle-managed files are used to name and place the files. Ensure that the tempfile locations, if specified, are accurate for new tempfiles being created for temporary tablespaces. After you review and edit the transport script (as necessary), run this script. Once the script is complete, review the output for errors.

```
SQL> connect / as sysdba;
SQL> @transport_prod.sql
```

7. Import the OLAP analytic workspaces (AWs) if exported.

8. After the OLAP analytic import is complete, start the database and configure the applications with Exadata.

TIP & TECHNIQUE
*It is recommended that you run the conversion from
Exadata because Exadata features kick in during the
conversion process. Also, Exadata has a much greater
I/O, resulting in overall time reductions.*

Migration Using TTS or XTTS

A transportable tablespace (TTS) can be used to migrate the application's database
into the Exadata Machine. Moving data using TTSs is much faster than performing
either an export or import, because the data files containing all of the actual data
are copied to the destination location, and you use Data Pump to transfer only
the metadata of the tablespace objects to the new database. The application must be
certified to use cross-platform transportable tablespaces (XTTS) for doing the
migration.

The TTS can be used in the following scenarios:

- When the intended migration is across different platforms. All platforms do
  not support XTTS. The V$TRANSPORTABLE_PLATFORM lists the platforms
  that are supported. If the endian format for the source and target are
  different, then XTTS should be used to migrate the database; if they are the
  same, regular TTS should be used to migrate the database. Oracle Exadata
  Database Machine uses the Linux x86 64-bit operating system, which is in
  little-endian format.

  ```
  SQL> select platform_name , endian_format from  v$transportable_
  platform;
  PLATFORM_NAME                              ENDIAN_FORMAT
  Solaris[tm] OE (32-bit)                    Big
  Solaris[tm] OE (64-bit)                    Big
  Microsoft Windows IA (32-bit)              Little
  Linux IA (32-bit)                          Little
  AIX-Based Systems (64-bit)                 Big
  HP-UX (64-bit)                             Big
  HP Tru64 UNIX                              Little
  HP-UX IA (64-bit)                          Big
  Linux IA (64-bit)                          Little
  HP Open VMS                                Little
  Microsoft Windows IA (64-bit)              Little
  IBM zSeries Based Linux                    Big
  Linux x86 64-bit                           Little
  Apple Mac OS                               Big
  Microsoft Windows x86 64-bit               Little
  Solaris Operating System (x86)             Little
  ```

```
IBM Power Based Linux                         Big
HP IA Open VMS                                Little
Solaris Operating System (x86-64)            Little
Apple Mac OS (x86-64)                         Little
```

- When the version of Oracle Database in the source is different from Exadata. Exadata supports versions 11.2.0.3 and later. If the source database version is lower than that supported by Exadata (10g or 11gR1 or 11.2.0.1 or 11.2.0.2), then TTS cannot be used to migrate to Exadata.

- The source database and the target database must have the same character set and national character set.

Steps for the Database Migration Using XTTS and TTS

The steps for database migration using TTS are the same as those for using XTTS. XTTS has a few extra steps, however, since it involves conversion from one platform to another. The steps that involve the conversion from one platform to the other can be skipped for TTS.

As with Data Pump migration, some prep work is needed before you begin the migration using XTTS. The following tasks are typically done during the preparation phase:

- Make sure your platform is supported for the XTTS or TTS operation. If the platform you are running the Oracle Database on is not listed in the V$TRANSPORTABLE_PLATFORM view, then you can't use this method.

- XTTS does not move objects that reside in the SYSTEM or SYSAUX tablespaces of the source database. You must move the identified objects to a user tablespace prior to beginning the transport process so the objects can be transported by XTTS. Alternatively, you can move the objects separately with Data Pump, or you can manually re-create the objects after performing the platform migration. Run the following script to identify those objects:

```
select owner, segment_name, segment_type
from dba_segments
where tablespace_name in ('SYSTEM', 'SYSAUX')
and owner not in (select name
from system.logstdby$skip_support
where action=0);
```

- TTS migration is not supported for tables that have columns encrypted using Transparent Data Encryption (TDE). Tables that have encrypted columns must be decrypted prior to following the TTS migration and then encrypted in the target database after migration. If TDE is not used and another mechanism of encryption is implemented, then before transporting an encrypted tablespace, you must copy the Oracle wallet manually to the destination database, unless the master encryption key is stored in a Hardware Security Module (HSM) device instead of an Oracle wallet. When copying the wallet, the wallet password remains the same in the destination database. However, it is recommended that you change the password on the destination database so that each database has its own wallet password. You cannot transport an encrypted tablespace to a database that already has an Oracle wallet for Transparent Data Encryption. In this case, you must use Oracle Data Pump to export the tablespace's schema objects and then import them to the destination database. Also, you cannot transport an encrypted tablespace to a platform with different endian formats; they must be decrypted prior to XTTS and then can be encrypted after the migration.

■ Apply any database patches required by the application. These patches could be required for application performance reasons, for exporting objects of a particular application, or for interoperability with a specific application version. This step may or may not be applicable depending on the application.

■ Convert all the non-system dictionary-managed tablespaces to locally managed tablespaces. Check the dictionary-managed tablespace using the following query:

```
SELECT tablespace_name
FROM dba_tablespaces
where extent_management='DICTIONARY' and TABLESPACE_NAME <>
'SYSTEM';
```

If the query returns any row, those tablespaces need to be converted into locally managed tablespaces.

■ TTS and XTTS have some limitations with respect to XML types. Beginning with Oracle Database 11*g* R1, you must use only Data Pump to export and import the tablespace metadata for tablespaces that contain XMLTypes. The following query returns a list of tablespaces that contain XMLTypes:

```
select distinct p.tablespace_name from dba_tablespaces p,
dba_xml_tables x, dba_users u, all_all_tables t where
t.table_name=x.table_name and t.tablespace_name=p.tablespace_
name
and x.owner=u.username
```

If the query returns rows, then at the target database (Exadata), XML DB must be installed. If the schema for a transported XMLType table is not present in the target database, it is imported and registered. If the schema already exists in the target database, an error is returned unless the ignore=y option is set. If an XMLType table uses a schema that is dependent on another schema, the schema that is depended on is not exported. The import succeeds only if that schema is already in the target database.

■ Advanced queue settings are not propagated in the target database during the export/import process. Therefore, you must record them beforehand and enable them in the target database instance afterward. The patch 10396457 contains auque1.sql, which generates a script called auque2.sql that can be used to enable the settings in the target database instance after the import is complete.

■ Identify a mount point that will be used to keep the export dump files. In the ideal scenario, the mount point would be available from both the source machine and the Exadata Machine. This will save lot of time transferring the dump file from the source to the target system. If it is an NFS mount point, make sure the file system is mounted with the correct mount options. For example, as root user, execute the following:

```
mkdir //datapump
chown oracle:dba //datapump
mount scadb01:/export /datapump -o rsize=32768,wsize=32768,
hard,actimeo=0,nolock
```

As an Oracle user, execute the following:

```
mkdir //datapump/expimp
```

■ Create a database directory that will be used for export:

```
$ sqlplus '/ as sysdba '
SQL> create directory dmpdir_expimp as '//datapump/expimp';
```

■ It is very important that the tablespaces are self-contained when migrating using the TTS or XTTS method. In a self-contained tablespace, there is no reference to any other tablespace. Following are examples of violations of self-contained tablespaces:

   ■ An index inside the set of tablespaces is for a table outside of the set of tablespaces. It is not a violation if a corresponding index for a table is outside of the set of tablespaces—for example, if table ITEM_MASTER is created on tablespace DATA and has an index called ITEM_MASTER_IDX created on the tablespace.

   ■ A partitioned table is partially contained in the set of tablespaces. The tablespace set you want to copy must contain either all or none of the partitions of a partitioned table. If you want to transport a subset of a partitioned table, you must exchange the partitions for tables.

■ A referential integrity constraint points to a table across a set boundary. When transporting a set of tablespaces, you can choose to include referential integrity constraints. However, doing so can affect whether or not a set of tablespaces is self-contained. If you decide not to transport constraints, the constraints are not considered pointers.

■ A table inside the set of tablespaces contains an LOB column that points to LOBs outside the set of tablespaces.

■ An XML DB schema (*.xsd) that was registered by user A imports a global schema that was registered by user B, and the following is true: the default tablespace for user A is tablespace A, the default tablespace for user B is tablespace B, and only tablespace A is included in the set of tablespaces.

■ Check for the self-contained tablespace violations. Oracle provides a package called DBMS_TTS that has a procedure called TRANSPORT_SET_CHECK, which can be executed to determine if there is violation. Execute the procedure as shown in this example:

```
SQL> EXECUTE DBMS_TTS.TRANSPORT_SET_CHECK('APPS_TS_TX_DATA',
TRUE);
  PL/SQL procedure successfully completed.
```

After invoking this PL/SQL package, you can see all violations by selecting from the TRANSPORT_SET_VIOLATIONS view. If the set of tablespaces is self-contained, this view is empty. A sample of the violation is shown here:

```
SQL>SELECT * FROM TRANSPORT_SET_VIOLATIONS;
VIOLATIONS
----------------------------------------------------------------
ORA-39908: Index SYSTEM.MVIEW$_ADV_AJG_PK in tablespace APPS_TS_
TX_IDX enforces primary constraints  of table SYSTEM.MVIEW$_ADV_
AJG in tablespace APPS_TS_TX_DATA.

ORA-39908: Index SYSTEM.MVIEW$_ADV_FJG_PK in tablespace APPS_TS_
TX_IDX enforces primary constraints  of table SYSTEM.MVIEW$_ADV_
FJG in tablespace APPS_TS_TX_DATA.

ORA-39908: Index SYSTEM.MVIEW$_ADV_GC_PK in tablespace APPS_TS_
TX_IDX enforces primary constraints  of table SYSTEM.MVIEW$_ADV_
GC in tablespace APPS_TS_TX_DATA.
```

All violations need to be fixed before the transportable tablespace migration can take place. If you are unsure of how to fix the violations, log a service request with Oracle Support.

Once all the tablespaces are self-contained, the next step is to generate a transportable tablespace set. The following steps are involved in generating a transportable tablespace set.

1. Identify the tablespaces you want to migrate and make them read-only:

```
SQL> alter tablespace APPS_TS_TX_DATA read only;
Tablespace altered.
SQL> alter tablespace DEMANTRA read only;
Tablespace altered
```

2. Run **expdp** on the source machine and specify the tablespaces that are part of the transportable tablespace set. A sample command is shown here:

```
expdp system/manager DUMPFILE=xtts.dmp DIRECTORY= dmpdir_expimp
TRANSPORT_TABLESPACES = APPS_TS_TX_DATA,TS_SALES_DATA
Export: Release 11.2.0.3.0 - Production on Wed Mar 12 17:52:37
2014
Copyright (c) 1982, 2011, Oracle and/or its affiliates.  All
rights reserved.
Connected to: Oracle Database 11g Enterprise Edition Release
11.2.0.3.0 - 64bit Production
With the Partitioning, Real Application Clusters, Automatic
Storage Management, OLAP,
Data Mining and Real Application Testing options
Starting "SYSTEM"."SYS_EXPORT_TRANSPORTABLE_01":
system/******** DUMPFILE=xtts.dmp directory= transport_
tablespaces=APPS_TS_TX_DATA,TS_SALES_DATA
Processing object type TRANSPORTABLE_EXPORT/PLUGTS_BLK
Processing object type TRANSPORTABLE_EXPORT/TABLE
Processing object type TRANSPORTABLE_EXPORT/INDEX/INDEX
Processing object type TRANSPORTABLE_EXPORT/CONSTRAINT
/CONSTRAINT
```

If the tablespaces are not self-contained, then the export process will error out. Here is another way of validating whether the tablespaces are self-contained or not:

```
[oracle@exa10db01 tmp]$ expdp system/manager dumpfile=xttr.dmp
DIRECTORY= dmpdir_expimp TRANSPORT_TABLESPACES=DEMANTRA
Export: Release 11.2.0.3.0 - Production on Wed Mar 12 16:36:06
2014
Copyright (c) 1982, 2011, Oracle and/or its affiliates.  All
rights reserved.
Connected to: Oracle Database 11g Enterprise Edition Release
11.2.0.3.0 - 64bit Production
With the Partitioning, Real Application Clusters, Automatic
Storage Management, OLAP,
```

```
Data Mining and Real Application Testing options
Starting "SYSTEM"."SYS_EXPORT_TRANSPORTABLE_01":
system/******** dumpfile=xttr.dmp directory= TRANSPORT_
TABLESPACES=DEMANTRA
ORA-39123: Data Pump transportable tablespace job aborted
ORA-39187: The transportable set is not self-contained,
violation list is

ORA-39907: Index DEMANTRA.MDP_1_0_510_1531 in tablespace
DEMANTRA points to table DEMANTRA.MDP_1531_510_SMALL in
tablespace SYSTEM.
ORA-39907: Index DEMANTRA.MDP_1_1_510_1531 in tablespace
DEMANTRA points to table DEMANTRA.MDP_1531_510_SMALL in
tablespace SYSTEM.
ORA-39907: Index DEMANTRA.MDP_1_24_510_1545 in tablespace
DEMANTRA points to table DEMANTRA.MDP_1545_510_SMALL in
tablespace SYSTEM.
ORA-39907: Index DEMANTRA.MDP_1_24_510_1575 in tablespace
DEMANTRA points to table DEMANTRA.MDP_1575_510_SMALL in
tablespace SYSTEM.
ORA-39907: Index DEMANTRA.MDP_1_25_510_1545 in tablespace
DEMANTRA points to table DEMANTRA.MDP_1545_510_SMALL in
tablespace SYSTEM.
ORA-39907: Index DEMANTRA.MDP_1_25_510_1575 in tablespace
DEMANTRA points to table DEMANTRA.MDP_1575_510_SMALL in
tablespace SYSTEM.
```

3. If the platform of the source system is different from that of the Exadata Machine, then RMAN endian conversion also needs to be done. During this process, RMAN converts the data files of the tablespaces to make them compatible with the new platform. RMAN automatically identifies the data files of the tablespace and converts and stores them in the location specified in the command. In the following example, the data files for the Demantra tablespace are converted to Linux:

```
$ RMAN target /
Recovery Manager: Release 11.2.0.3.0 - Production on Wed Mar 12
16:21:11 2014
Copyright (c) 1982, 2011, Oracle and/or its affiliates.  All
rights reserved.
connected to target database: VISOW (DBID=220594996)
RMAN> CONVERT TABLESPACE DEMANTRA TO PLATFORM 'Linux x86 64-bit'
Format '/tmp/%U';
Starting conversion at source at 12-MAR-14
using target database control file instead of recovery catalog
```

```
allocated channel: ORA_DISK_1
channel ORA_DISK_1: SID=11706 instance=VISOW1 device type=DISK
channel ORA_DISK_1: starting datafile conversion
input datafile file number=00349 name=+Q1DATA/visow/datafile
/demantra.1377.826041183
converted datafile=/tmp/data_D-VISOW_I-220594996_TS-DEMANTRA_
FNO-349_s2p30js5
channel ORA_DISK_1: datafile conversion complete, elapsed time:
00:00:25
Finished conversion at source at 12-MAR-14

Starting Control File Autobackup at 12-MAR-14
piece handle=+Q1DATA/visow/autobackup/2014_03_12
/n_842026910.705.842026911 comment=NONE
Finished Control File Autobackup at 12-MAR-14
```

In this example, the converted data file is stored in /tmp directory.

1. Change the tablespaces back into read-write mode:

```
SQL> alter tablespace demantra read write ;
Tablespace altered
```

■ Transfer the transportable tablespace set (the export files and the converted data files of the tablespaces) into the Exadata Machine. You can use the DBFS file system as a placeholder to keep these files.

■ Create the database in Exadata. You can use DBCA to create the database or use the database that was installed by Oracle ACS as a part of Exadata installation. You can also import any existing database running in the Exadata Machine. All the users need to be created in the database before running the import.

■ Import the tablespace metadata into the database. When running the import, the data file and dump file details are given as an input. In the next example, we are using the converted data files:

```
impdp system/password DUMPFILE= xttr.dmp DIRECTORY= dmpdir_
expimp
TRANSPORT_DATAFILES=/dbfs/stage/data_D-VISOW_I-220594996_TS-
DEMANTRA_FNO-349_s2p30js5/salesdb/sales_201.dbf
```

When there is a large number of data files, running **impdp** using a parameter file is preferred. After the import, if needed, put the tablespaces back into read-write mode.

TIP & TECHNIQUE
When you are migrating your application, if you have
to choose between TTS and Data Pump Export/Import,
choose TTS because it is much less time-consuming.

Cross-Platform Incremental Backup

The XTTS can be combined with RMAN's ability to roll forward data file copies using incremental backup. By using a series of incremental backups, each smaller than the last, the data at the destination system can be brought close to current with the source system, before any downtime is required. The downtime required for data file transfer and convert when combining XTTS with cross-platform incremental backup is now proportional to the rate of data block changes in the source system.

Following are the steps involved in a migration using XTTS and cross-platform incremental backup. The scripts described in this method can be downloaded from MOS note 1389592.1. The process involved for this method can be divided into four steps:

1. Initial setup phase

2. Prepare phase

3. Roll-forward phase

4. Transport phase

Initial Setup Phase   A starter database is created during Exadata installation; the same database can be used for migration. If the Exadata comes with Oracle Database 11.2.0.3, an additional separate incremental convert instance needs to be configured. To do this, install a new 11.2.0.4 database home on the Exadata machine—this is the incremental convert home. We can call this xtt_home (/u01/app/oracle/product/11.2.0.4/dbhome_1). If the Exadata shipped with version 11.2.0.4 or if you are planning to migrate to 11.2.0.4, a convert instance is not needed.

1. From the incremental convert home, start an instance in the nomount state. This is the incremental convert instance. A database does not need to be created for the incremental convert instance—only a running instance is required.

   Once the instance is running, the tablespaces need to be identified; they will be converted and transported into Exadata. The steps in this preparation phase are very similar to the steps in the XTTS migration method. In this phase, the tablespaces that need to be migrated are identified and their data files are converted to little-endian.

2. Create the staging areas on the source and destinations systems as defined by the following xtt.properties parameters: backupformat, backupondest, dfcopydir, and stageondest.

3. On the source system, as the Oracle software owner, extract the scripts (rman-xttconvert.zip) downloaded from MOS: 1389592.1

```
[oracle@adc201fam]$ pwd :/home/oracle/xtt
[oracle@adc201fam]$ unzip rman-xttconvert.zip
Archive: rman-xttconvert.zip
  inflating: xtt.properties
  inflating: xttcnvrtbkupdest.sql
  inflating: xttdbopen.sql
  inflating: xttdriver.pl
  inflating: xttprep.tmpl
  inflating: xttstartupnomount.sql
```

4. Configure xtt.properties on the source system.

5. Edit the xtt.properties file on the source system with your site-specific configuration. The details of the parameter are shown in Table 6-1. Copy xttconvert scripts and xtt.properties to the destination system.

6. In both source and Exadata systems, set the environment variable TMPDIR to the location where the supporting scripts exist:

```
[oracle@adc201fam]$ export TMPDIR=/home/oracle/xtt
```

Prepare Phase   Once the initial preparation is done during this phase, data files of the tablespaces to be transported are transferred to the destination system and converted by the xttdriver.pl script.

During this phase, data file copies of the tablespaces to be transported are created on the source system, transferred to the destination system, converted, and placed in their final location to be used by the destination database. The steps in this phase are run only once. The data being transported is fully accessible in the source database during this phase.

1. As the Oracle owner, and after sourcing the environment, run this script:

```
[oracle@adc201fam]$ $ORACLE_HOME/perl/bin/perl xttdriver.pl -p
```

The script performs the following actions on the source system:

- Creates data file copies of the tablespaces that will be transported in the location specified by the xtt.properties parameter dfcopydir.

Parameter	Description	Example Setting
tablespaces	Comma-separated list of tablespaces to transport from source database to destination database.	tablespaces=TS1,TS2
platformid	Source database platform ID, obtained from V$DATABASE.PLATFORM_ID.	platformid=2
dfcopydir	Location on the source system where data file copies are created during the "-p prepare" step.	dfcopydir=/stage_source
backupformat	Location on the source system where incremental backups are created.	backupformat=/stage_source
stageondest	Location on the destination system where data file copies are placed by the user when they are transferred manually from the source system. This is also the location from where data file copies and incremental backups are read when they are converted in the "-c conversion of data files" and "-r roll forward data files" steps. This location may be a DBFS-mounted file system.	stageondest=/stage_dest
storageondest	Location on the destination system where the converted data file copies will be written during the "-c conversion of data files" step.	storageondest=+DATA
backupondest	Location on the destination system where converted incremental backups on the destination system will be written during the "-r roll forward data files" step.	backupondest=+RECO
cnvinst_home	Set this parameter only if a separate incremental convert home is in use. ORACLE_HOME of the incremental convert instance that runs on the destination system.	cnvinst_home=/u01/app/oracle/ product/11.2.0.4/xtt_home
cnvinst_sid	Set this parameter only if a separate incremental convert home is in use. ORACLE_SID of the incremental convert instance that runs on the destination system.	cnvinst_sid=xtt
asm_home	ORACLE_HOME for the ASM instance that runs on the destination system.	asm_home=/u01/app/11.2.0.4/grid
asm_sid	ORACLE_SID for the ASM instance that runs on the destination system.	asm_sid=+ASM1
parallel	Defines the degree of parallelism set in the RMAN CONVERT command file rmanconvert.cmd. This file is created during the prepare step and used by RMAN in the "convert data files" step to convert the data file copies on the destination system. If this parameter is unset, xttdriver.pl uses parallel=8.	parallel=8
rollparallel	Defines the level of parallelism for the "-r roll forward" operation.	rollparallel=8

TABLE 6-1. *Parameters for xtt.properties File*

- Verifies that tablespaces are online, in read-write mode, and do not contain offline data files.

- Creates the files xttplan.txt and rmanconvert.cmd used later in this procedure.

The set of tablespaces being transported must all be online, must contain no offline data files, and must be read-write. The script will signal an error if one or more data files or tablespaces in your source database are offline or read-only. If a tablespace is read-only and will remain so throughout the procedure, simply transport the tablespace using the traditional XTTS process. No incremental apply is needed for those files.

2. On the Exadata Machine, logged in as the Oracle user, transfer the data file copies created in the previous step from the source system. Data file copies on the source system are created in the location defined in the xtt.properties parameter dfcopydir. The data file copies must be placed in the location defined by the xtt.properties parameter stageondest.

   If a shared storage is mounted across the source system and Exadata—that is, if the dfcopydir location on the source system and the stageondest location on the destination system refer to the same NFS storage location—then this step can be skipped since the data file copies are already mounted in the Exadata.

3. Once the data files are copied, the next step is to convert them. To do this, copy the rmanconvert.cmd file created previously from the source system and run the convert data files step as follows:

```
[oracle@exa10db01]$ scp oracle@source:/home/oracle/xtt/
rmanconvert.cmd/home/oracle/xtt
[oracle@exa10db01]$ $ORACLE_HOME/perl/bin/perl xttdriver.pl -c
```

The convert data files step converts the data file copies in the stageondest location to the endian format of the Exadata system. The converted data file copies are written in the location specified by the xtt.properties parameter storageondest. This is the final location where data files will be accessed when they are used by the destination database. When this step is complete, the data file copies in the stageondest location are no longer needed and may be removed.

Roll-Forward Phase   During this phase, an incremental backup is created from the source database, transferred to the destination system, converted to the destination system endian format, and then applied to the converted destination data file copies to roll them forward. This phase may be run multiple times. Each successive incremental backup should take less time than the prior incremental backup (you need to have block change tracking enabled, or it will scan every block and the time almost certainly won't be less), and will bring the destination data file copies more current with the source database. The data being transported is fully accessible during this phase.

1. Create the incremental backup of the tablespaces being transported on the source system as follows:

   ```
   [oracle@adc201fam]$ $ORACLE_HOME/perl/bin/perl xttdriver.pl -i
   ```

   The create incremental step executes RMAN commands to generate incremental backups for all tablespaces listed in xtt.properties. It creates the following files used later in this procedure:

   - tsbkupmap.txt

   - incrbackups.txr

2. Transfer the incremental backups created during the previous step to the stageondest location on the destination system. The list of incremental backup files to copy are found in the incrbackups.txt file on the source system.

   ```
   [oracle@adc201fam]$ scp 'cat incrbackups.txt' oracle@exa10db01:/
   stage_dest
   ```

   If the backupformat location on the source system and the stageondest location on the destination system refer to the same NFS storage location, then this step can be skipped since the incremental backups are already available in the expected location on the destination system.

3. Once the incremental backup is taken, convert the incremental backups and apply them to the data file copies on the Exadata system. To do this, copy the xttplan.txt and tsbkupmap.txt files created previously from the source system and run the roll-forward data files step as follows:

   ```
   [oracle@exa10db01]$ scp oracle@source:/home/oracle/xtt/xttplan
   .txt /home/oracle/xtt
   [oracle@exa10db01]$ scp oracle@source:/home/oracle/xtt/
   tsbkupmap.txt /home/oracle/xtt
   [oracle@exa10db01]$ $ORACLE_HOME/perl/bin/perl xttdriver.pl -r
   ```

   The roll-forward data files step connects to the incremental convert instance as SYS, converts the incremental backups, and then connects to the destination database and applies the incremental backups for each tablespace being transported. You must copy the xttplan.txt and tsbkupmap.txt files each time this step is executed, because their content is different for each iteration.

4. Determine the FROM_SCN for the next incremental backup. Run the following script in the source system to find out the FROM_SCN.

   ```
   [oracle@adc201fam]$ $ORACLE_HOME/perl/bin/perl xttdriver.pl -s
   ```

The new FROM_SCN step calculates the next FROM_SCN, records it in the file xttplan.txt, and then uses that SCN when the next incremental backup is created. If you need to bring the files at the destination database closer in sync with the production system, repeat the roll-forward phase until the database is as close as desired to the source database; then proceed to the transport phase. Before doing the actual cutover, you need to schedule a downtime so that all the data can be migrated from the source to the Exadata Machine.

Transport Phase   During this phase, the source data is made read-only and the destination data files are made consistent with the source database by creating and applying a final incremental backup. After the destination data files are made consistent, the normal transportable tablespace steps are performed to export object metadata from the source database and import it into the destination database. The data being transported is accessible only in read-only mode until the end of this phase.

1. Run the following command for making the tablespace read-only:

    ```
    system@adc201fam/prod SQL> alter tablespace TS1 read only;
    Tablespace altered.
    ```

2. Create the final incremental backup, and then transfer, convert, and apply it to the destination data files:

    ```
    [oracle@adc201fam]$ $ORACLE_HOME/perl/bin/perl xttdriver.pl -i
    [oracle@adc201fam]$ scp 'cat incrbackups.txt' oracle@dest:/
    stage_dest
    [oracle@exa10db01]$ scp oracle@source:/home/oracle/xtt/xttplan
    .txt /home/oracle/xtt
    [oracle@exa10db01]$ scp oracle@source:/home/oracle/xtt/
    tsbkupmap.txt /home/oracle/xtt
    [oracle@exa10db01]$ $ORACLE_HOME/perl/bin/perl xttdriver.pl -r
    ```

3. Once the incremental backup is applied in the Exadata system, import the object metadata into the database running on Exadata. To do this, run the generate Data Pump TTS command as follows:

    ```
    [oracle@exa10db01]$ $ORACLE_HOME/perl/bin/perl xttdriver.pl -e
    ```

    The generate Data Pump TTS command step creates a sample Data Pump network_link transportable import command in the file xttplugin.txt with the transportable tablespaces parameters TRANSPORT_TABLESPACES and TRANSPORT_DATAFILES correctly set. Note that network_link mode initiates an import over a database link that refers to the source database. A separate export or dump file is not required. If you choose to perform the tablespace transport with this command, you must edit the import command to replace import parameters DIRECTORY, LOGFILE, and NETWORK_LINK with site-specific values.

The following is an example of a network mode transportable import command:

```
[oracle@exa10db01]$ impdp directory=DATA_PUMP_DIR logfile=tts_
imp.log network_link=ttslink \
transport_full_check=no \
transport_tablespaces=TS1 \
transport_datafiles='+DATA/prod/datafile/ts1.285.771686721', \
'+DATA/prod/datafile/ts1.286.771686723', \
'+DATA/prod/datafile/ts1.287.771686743'
```

After the object metadata being transported has been extracted from the source database, the tablespaces in the source database may be made read-write again, if desired.

Database users that own objects being transported must exist in the destination database before you perform the transportable import. If you do not use network_link import, then perform the tablespace transport by running transportable mode Data Pump Export on the source database to export the object metadata being transported into a dump file, transfer the dump file to the destination system, and then run transportable mode Data Pump Import to import the object metadata into the destination database.

4. At this step, the transported data is read only in the destination database. Perform application-specific validation to verify the transported data.

5. Also, run rman to check for physical and logical block corruption by running VALIDATE TABLESPACE as follows:

```
RMAN> validate tablespace TS1, TS2 check logical;
```

6. The final step is to make the destination tablespace(s) read-write in the destination database:

```
system@dest/prod SQL> alter tablespace TS1 read write;
Tablespace altered.
```

Migration Using Oracle Data Guard

If the source system is running on a Linux platform and running on database version 11.2.0.3 or later, Data Guard can be leveraged to migrate the database from existing servers to the Exadata Machine. The idea is to create a standby database in the Exadata Machine and then switch over to Exadata, thereby making it primary and repointing all the applications to the Exadata database.

Data Guard is very simple and easy to set up and can be configured between the source and the Exadata machines without much hassle. Data Guard can be used for migration to Exadata even if the source database is running on a single instance or is not using ASM.

Steps for Migrating to Exadata Using Data Guard

The source database should be running on ARCHIVELOG mode. If the source system is not running on ARCHIVELOG mode, the first step is to enable ARCHIVELOG in the source database. The FRA can also be set at the same time so that all the archive log files go to FRA.

1. To enable FRA, the initialization parameters db_recovery_file_dest and db_recovery_file_dest_size need to be set. An example is shown here:

   ```
   SQL> alter system set db_recovery_file_dest='+FRA scope=SPFILE
   sid='*';
   SQL> alter system set db_recovery_file_dest_size=4000G
   scope=SPFILE  sid='*';
   ```

2. Cross-check the parameters by running this query:

   ```
   SQL> show parameter db_recovery
   ```

3. Enable the ARCHIVELOG in the source database by running the following commands:

   ```
   SQL> shutdown immediate
   SQL> startup mount
   SQL> alter database archivelog;
   SQL> alter database open;
   ```

4. Verify by running this command:

   ```
   SQL> select log_mode from v$database;
   LOG_MODE
   ------------
   ARCHIVELOG
   ```

5. Force logging must be turned on in the source database. This ensures that redo is logged irrespective of table definition. Even if the tables are created with the NOLOGGING clause, force logging will override the NOLOGGING clause and will start generating redo at the database level. Set force logging by running the following SQL command:

   ```
   SQL> alter database force logging;
   ```

   The primary database must have a db_unique_name value defined. The db_unique_name should be different between the primary and standby databases. The db_name, however, must be the same between the primary and standby databases.

   ```
   SQL> show parameter db_unique_name
   NAME                                TYPE        VALUE
   ----------------------------------- ----------- --------------
   db_unique_name                      string      VISOW
   ```

In this case, the db_uniqiue_name on the primary is VISOW, so for the standby database, it should be different from VISOW. For example, you can set VISOW_DG as the db_unique_name on the standby side.

6. The db_unique_name values of the primary and standby databases need to be set in the DG_CONFIG part of the LOG_ARCHIVE_CONFIG parameter:

```
SQL> ALTER SYSTEM SET LOG_ARCHIVE_CONFIG='DG_
CONFIG=(VISOW,VISOW_DG)';
```

7. The FRA is used to keep the archive redo log in a local location; you can alternatively specify a different location:

```
SQL> alter system set log_archive_dest_1 = 'location=use_db_
recovery_file_dest valid_for=(all_logfiles, all_roles) db_
unique_name=VISOW';
```

8. Set the remote archive log destination for the standby, which will be in the Exadata:

```
ALTER SYSTEM SET LOG_ARCHIVE_DEST_2='SERVICE=VISOW_DG NOAFFIRM
ASYNC VALID_FOR=(ONLINE_LOGFILES,PRIMARY_ROLE) DB_UNIQUE_
NAME=VISOW_DG';
ALTER SYSTEM SET LOG_ARCHIVE_DEST_STATE_2=ENABLE;
```

9. The FAL_SERVER parameter specifies the location where the database should look for the ARCHIVELOG files if there is a gap. If there is an interruption in the redo transport service, gaps may arise.

```
ALTER SYSTEM SET FAL_SERVER=VISOW_DG;
```

10. Set the LOG_ARCHIVE_FORMAT, LOG_ARCHIVE_MAX_PROCESSES, and REMOTE_LOGIN_PASSWORDFILE parameters:

```
ALTER SYSTEM SET LOG_ARCHIVE_FORMAT='%t_%s_%r.arc' SCOPE=SPFILE
sid='*';
ALTER SYSTEM SET LOG_ARCHIVE_MAX_PROCESSES=20 sid='*';
ALTER SYSTEM SET REMOTE_LOGIN_PASSWORDFILE=EXCLUSIVE
SCOPE=SPFILE sid='*';
```

11. Create standby redo logs on the primary and standby database. The size of the redo log files should be the same as that of the online redo logs. Oracle recommends having the same number plus one additional standby redo log for each thread:

```
SQL> alter database add standby logfile thread 1
group 4 size 2G, group 5 size 2G;

SQL> alter database add standby logfile thread 2
group 6 size 2G, group 7 size 2G;
```

12. From the Exadata Machine, start the database listener. The database listener must offer a static SID, which is the same ORACLE_SID as the source. The listener.ora must have an entry for the SID_NAME. An entry from the listener .ora from the Exadata Machine is shown next. In this case, VISOW1 is the SID of the database both at the source and the target (Exadata).

```
SID_LIST_VISOW =
  (SID_LIST =
    (SID_DESC =
      (ORACLE_HOME= /u01/app/oracle/product/11.2.0.3/dbhome_1)
      (SID_NAME = VISOW1)
    )
  )
```

13. Similarly on the source node, create an Oracle Net alias to connect to the listener created in the previous step.

14. Create a password file on the Exadata Machine. This needs to be created in each RAC node of the Exadata.

```
orapwd file=orapwvisow1 password=<source database sys password>
```

15. On all Exadata Machines, create the audit directory for the primary database:

```
mkdir -p /u01/app/oracle/admin/SID/adump
```

16. TNS connectivity must be established between the source and Exadata server so that the databases can locate each other using the service names configured. Edit the tnsnames.ora in $ORACLE_HOME/network/admin and add the proper entries so that the source database can be connected from the Exadata Machine. A sample entry is shown in the "Backup-based Duplication" section earlier in this chapter.

17. In Exadata, set the ORACLE_SID same as the primary database SID and startup nomount the standby instance.

You need to create the standby database before the Data Guard application is created. The simplest method to create a standby database is to use Oracle Recovery Manager (RMAN).

You have two options. The first option uses the active database duplicate methodology. The second option uses backup-based duplication from auxiliary instance.

The advantage of active database duplication is that it does not require source database backups or additional disk space for a staging area on the target system. Active duplication copies mounted or online data files over a network directly to an auxiliary instance. There are, however, tradeoffs to this approach. It will impact network and primary host performance because the source database will run processes required to transfer the files to the target host. Here is a sample script for creating a standby database using the active database duplication:

```
RMAN <<EOF
connect target sys/manager;
connect auxiliary sys/manager@visow1;
run {
duplicate target database for standby from active database
spfile
set db_unique_name='visow_'dg
set db_create_online_log_dest_1='+DATA'
set db_create_file_dest='+DATA'
set db_recovery_file_dest='+RECO'
set control_files='+DATA/visow/standby.ctl'
set local_listener='visow_local_listener'
set remote_listener='exa10-scan:1521';
} EOF
```

If the source data file location is different from the Exadata location, then the parameters db_file_name_convert and log_file_name_convert need to be added to the script. An example is shown next:

```
db_file_name_convert '/u01/data','+DATA'
log_file_name_convert '/u01/data','+DATA','/u01/reco','+RECO'
```

For backup-based duplication, you can use the same script, except you must remove the clause "from active database." Therefore, the command line will say, "duplicate target database for standby." The step for making the RMAN backup was discussed previously in this chapter.

Once the duplication is done, you may need to undertake some additional steps in configuring each RAC node, which can be done after the migration.

Next, you need to start the redo apply process in the standby instance. To start the process, run this command:

```
SQL> ALTER DATABASE RECOVER MANAGED STANDBY DATABASE USING CURRENT
LOGFILE DISCONNECT FROM SESSION;
```

This command will start the redo application process from the primary side using the standby log files.

Once you create the physical standby database and set up redo transport services, you may want to verify that database modifications are being successfully transmitted from the primary database to the standby database. To check that redo data is being received on the standby database, first identify the existing archived redo log files on the standby database, force a log switch and archive a few online redo log files on the primary database, and then check the standby database again.

Check the archived log file using this command:

```
SQL> SELECT SEQUENCE#, FIRST_TIME, NEXT_TIME FROM V$ARCHIVED_LOG ORDER
BY SEQUENCE#;
```

Switch the log file a couple of times in the primary by running this command:

```
SQL> ALTER SYSTEM SWITCH LOGFILE;
```

Run this command again on the standby side to make sure new logs are getting applied. This will validate that the Data Guard setup is configured correctly.

Once the Data Guard setup is done, you can plan for downtime to flip over to Exadata. As soon as the switchover to Exadata happens, you need to point the application to the Exadata servers. You might need to complete some application-related steps at this point.

During the planned downtime, shut down the primary database, and on the Exadata Machine, run the following command:

```
SQL>ALTER DATABASE COMMIT TO SWITCHOVER TO PRIMARY WITH SESSION
SHUTDOWN
```

Open the database in Exadata:

```
SQL> ALTER DATABASE OPEN;
```

Migration Using GoldenGate

Oracle GoldenGate is often used in conjunction with other migration methods for zero-downtime migration to Exadata. Oracle GoldenGate provides real-time, log-based change data capture and delivery between heterogeneous systems and synchronizes the new Exadata environment with the production environment to enable continuous business operations on the production environment while the migration is in progress. It can also be used for immediate switchover to the Exadata system without database downtime.

GoldenGate works by capturing changed data operations committed in the database transaction logs; then it routes those operations using a variety of transport protocols, and it can compress and encrypt changed data prior to routing. Transactional data can be delivered via Open Database Connectivity (ODBC). It also transforms the data before applying the data to the target system—for example, GoldenGate can be used to execute a number of built-in functions, such as filtering and transformations. Then it applies the changed transactional data to one or more targets with only subsecond latency, preserving transactional integrity.

GoldenGate Modules and Components

GoldenGate has four important modules and components:

- **GoldenGate Capture module**   The Capture module grabs the result of DML (insert, update, and delete operations) and Data Dictionary Language (DDL) statements executed against a database as they occur, and then routes them for distribution. GoldenGate Capture is a log-based mechanism that extracts change data from the live transaction logs of the source database. This means high performance with minimal impact to the source database. GoldenGate can capture the data from archive logs as well.

- **Trail file**   The Capture module captures the data and stores it in files known as trail files. The trail file contains the most recently changed data in a transportable, platform-independent format called the Oracle GoldenGate Universal Data Format, and can be converted to XML and other popular formats for consumption by different applications.

- **GoldenGate Delivery module**   The Delivery module takes any changed transactional data that has been placed in a trail file and immediately applies it to the target database. The Delivery module applies each database change in the same order as it was committed in the source database to provide data and referential integrity. In addition, it applies changes within the same transaction context as they were on the source system for consistency on the target.

- **GoldenGate Manager module**   The GoldenGate Manager module provides a command-line interface to perform a variety of administrative, housekeeping, and reporting activities, including setting parameters to configure and fine-tune Oracle GoldenGate processes; starting, stopping, and monitoring the Capture and Delivery modules; critical, informational event and threshold reporting; resource management; and trail file management. The Manager module can be used to restart Oracle GoldenGate components, monitor latency, and perform a variety of administrative, housekeeping, and reporting tasks.

GoldenGate is used in conjunction with other migration methods, so when the Exadata Machine is ready and the preliminary data load is already done through some other method (for example, perhaps the data load is done using RMAN backup and now GoldenGate will be used to capture the delta between the existing production and the Exadata system), GoldenGate starts capturing the new transactions (only changed data) in the source system or the existing production system. Once the Exadata Machine is ready to be synchronized after the initial data load, GoldenGate delivers change data to Exadata and continues to keep the systems in synch with the source system. While the migration is taking place, the old system stays open for transactions, and GoldenGate moves new transactions to the target system in real time. This is fundamentally different from the traditional migration methods that require you to stop the production database to keep the target environment in synch after the initial copy. This approach minimizes the downtime required for the migration/upgrade to a duration that is needed for application switchover only.

For failback, Oracle GoldenGate can be set up to capture the transactions that take place in the new Exadata environment and deliver them to the old production environment to keep the old system in synch. This allows you to switch back to the old system with minimal or no data loss in the event that the new production system has any issues.

Steps to Migrate to Exadata Using GoldenGate

The following steps are involved in migrating to Exadata using GoldenGate:

1. *Install Oracle GoldenGate in the source system.* Before staring the migration, install GoldenGate in the source system, including GoldenGate binaries, capture process, trail files, and so on. (The details of the installation/configuration of GoldenGate is beyond the scope of this book.)

2. *Start the GoldenGate Capture system on the source.* Install the Oracle GoldenGate Capture process and start capturing new transactions before the production database copy is made for setting up the target system. Any open transactions that were ongoing when GoldenGate Capture started should be closed before starting a production database backup. GoldenGate trail files store change data until the target system is ready for synchronization.

3. *Set up Exadata and the initial data load.* In Exadata Machine, create the database before the initial data load starts. You can create the database structure in multiple ways using DBCA or by using the **create database** command. Or you can use the default template database configured by ACS for loading data. Once the database is created, do the preliminary data load via RMAN backup and restore, RMAN database duplication, Data Pump Export/Import, or another mechanism. GoldenGate uses Commit Sequence Number (CSN) to apply the change data to the Exadata Machine, which handles applying data that has been already been "applied" by virtue of copying data after the same change data has been captured.

4. *Configure GoldenGate on Exadata.* To enable incremental data load to Exadata, you need to configure GoldenGate at the Exadata Machine. The following steps are involved in setting up the GoldenGate process on Exadata.

a. *Set up DBFS on Exadata.* When setting up the configuration, the best practice is to store the Oracle GoldenGate trail files, checkpoint files, and bounded recovery and configuration files in DBFS to provide the best performance, scalability, recoverability, and failover capabilities in the event of a system failure. Because DBFS is mounted across all the nodes in an Exadata Machine, in the event of node failure, trail files are available from other nodes. This ensures that the extract process can continue mining from the last known archived redo log file position, and Replicat processes can start applying from the same trail file position before a failure occurred. On Exadata, it is recommended that you run the DBFS database in ARCHIVELOG mode so that recoverability is not compromised in the event of media failures or corruptions. It is also recommended that you allocate enough trail file disk space to permit storage of up to 12 hours of trail files.

     The DBFS can be installed by Oracle ACS. If ACS is not installing the DBFS, follow the MOS note 1054431.1 to install it. The steps for creating the DBFS are beyond the scope of this book.

     On Exadata, where the Replicat processes read the trail files and apply the data to the target database, two separate DBFS file systems are necessary to separate the different I/O requirements of the trail and checkpoint files.

b. *Install GoldenGate.* Download the GoldenGate software from Oracle Technology Network. Install GoldenGate locally on the source and target. It is important that the installation directory be the same on all nodes.

c. *Configure GoldenGate and database parameters.* GoldenGate can be configured in Integrated Capture mode or Classic Capture mode. After you have configured it, you need to configure Data Pump with the PASSTHRU parameter if the process is not carrying out any mappings or conversions. Using PASSTHRU reduces CPU by the Data Pump because it does not require table definition lookups, either from the database or from a data definitions file.

d. *Set up checkpoint files and trail files in DBFS.* Checkpoint files contain the current read and write positions of the Extract and Replicat processes. Checkpoints provide fault tolerance by preventing the loss of data should the system, the network, or an Oracle GoldenGate process need to be restarted. Place the checkpoint files needed on DBFS; the best practice is to create a symbolic link from the Oracle GoldenGate home directory to a directory in DBFS.

Trail files contain the data extracted from the archived redo log files. The trail files are automatically generated by the Extract process. Store the trail files on DBFS. By mounting the same DBFS directory on both the source and target databases, much like an NFS mount, the Replicat process can read from the same trails created by the Extract process.

e. *Set up the discard file on the local file system.* The discard file is used to capture information about GoldenGate operations that failed. This information helps to resolve data errors, such as those that involve invalid column mapping. The discard file reports such information as the database error message, the sequence number of the data source or trail file, the relative byte address of the record in the data source or trail file, and the details of the discarded operation (such as column values of a DML statement or the text of a DDL statement). A discard file can be used for Extract or Replicat, but it is most useful for Replicat to log operations that could not be reconstructed or applied.

f. *Configure Replicat commit behavior.* With Oracle GoldenGate versions 11.2.1 and later, if a checkpoint table is configured, Replicat will automatically operate using COMMIT NOWAIT. The Replicat processes will no longer wait at each commit when applying transactions, increasing throughput performance. If you are using Oracle GoldenGate version 11.1.1 or earlier, setting the Replicat commit behavior to COMMIT NOWAIT is configured separately from creating a checkpoint table. Consider this only when using a checkpoint table due to protection of recovery data during a checkpoint.

   Set the Replicat parameter file to COMMIT NOWAIT as follows:

   ```
   "ALTER SESSION SET COMMIT_WRITE='NOWAIT'";
   ```

g. *Configure autostart of Extract, Data Pump, and Replicat processes.* Configure the Extract, Data Pump (if used), and Replicat processes to start automatically when the Manager process is started. Add the following parameter to the Manager parameter file:

   ```
   AUTOSTART ER * AUTORESTART ER *
   ```

h. *Configure Oracle Clusterware.* GoldenGate needs to be configured with Oracle Clusterware so that Clusterware can start/manage the GoldenGate process.

5. *Synchronize with GoldenGate.* Oracle GoldenGate's main benefit is to provide incremental data synchronization for the new Exadata environment in real time to eliminate downtime during migration. For this purpose, it needs to be configured to capture changed data from the active production

database. The Capture module can be set to start propagating transactions against an existing target database from a given point. DML and, optionally, DDL changes are captured from the transaction logs. GoldenGate Capture module should be set to capture all transactions that have a commit time stamp higher than the quiesce point where the production database was cloned.

The Oracle GoldenGate trail files describe DML operations (inserts, updates, and deletes) along with transactional context as captured from the source database. Trail files are persisted to disk and minimize the risk of data loss or corruption in the event of an outage at the source or target site.

The Oracle GoldenGate Delivery process runs on the target system, reads the captured data from the trail files, and applies the new transactions that were committed at the source since the initial load started. The Capture and Delivery modules continue to run, ensuring that all ongoing data changes at the source move in real time to the target.

6. *Test the system.* GoldenGate allows the production system to be operational throughout the migration period and feeds new transactions to the target system when it is ready. Functional teams and businesses have the full flexibility to test the target environment with production data until they are absolutely comfortable with the switchover. Tools such as GoldenGate Veridata can be used for live database comparison to make sure data is completely in synch to provide an additional level of validation before switchover.

7. *Switch over to the new system.* Once the target Exadata system has been tested thoroughly to handle production workload and data is synchronized with the existing operational systems, applications can be pointed to the new Exadata environment.

Summary

Various options are available for migrating to Exadata, whether your source database is running on a platform other than Linux, you are running a version of Oracle Database earlier than 11.2.0.3, or you are running your existing database in a non-RAC environment without ASM. With so many options on the table, you'll find migrating to Exadata to be a simple and straightforward process.

Planning for the migration is the most crucial step. A proper plan needs to be identified after you evaluate the pros and cons of all the available approaches. Since most of the OLTP systems are integrated with lots of other systems, integration needs to be planned as well. It's recommended that you test at least three or four iterations of the migration before production system migration to ensure that there are no surprises after migrating to Exadata.

Addendum 6.1: get_bfile.sql

```
REM
REM List all BFILE external files in database
REM
set serveroutput on;
set feedback off;
declare
 type cur_type is REF CURSOR;
 v_cur cur_type;
 v_sqlstmt varchar2(100);
 v_bfile_loc bfile;
 v_bfile_dir_name varchar2(30);
 v_bfile_filename varchar2(250);
 v_bfile_realpath varchar2(4000);
begin
 -- loop through all columns that are BFILE type
 for bf in
 (select owner,table_name,column_name
 from dba_tab_cols
 where data_type='BFILE')
 loop
 dbms_output.put_line('External files for BFILE column'
 || bf.column_name || ' in table '
 || bf.owner || '.' || bf.table_name);
 v_sqlstmt:='select ' || bf.column_name || ' from '
 || bf.owner || '.' || bf.table_name;
 open v_cur for v_sqlstmt;
 loop
 fetch v_cur into v_bfile_loc;
 exit when v_cur%notfound;
 -- get BFILE directory alias and filename
 dbms_lob.filegetname(v_bfile_loc, v_bfile_dir_name,
 v_bfile_filename);
 -- resolve the directory alias to a full path
 select directory_path
 into v_bfile_realpath
 from all_directories
 where directory_name = v_bfile_dir_name;
dbms_output.put_line(v_bfile_realpath || '/'
 || v_bfile_filename);
 end loop;
 close v_cur;
 end loop;
end;
 /
```

Addendum 6.2: get_bfile_dir.sql

```
REM
REM List all directories that contain BFILEs
REM
set serveroutput on format wrap;
set feedback off;
declare
 type cur_type is REF CURSOR;
 v_cur cur_type;
 v_sqlstmt varchar2(100);
 v_bfile_loc bfile;
 v_bfile_dir_name varchar2(30);
 v_bfile_filename varchar2(250);
 v_bfile_realpath varchar2(4000);
 type array_type is table of number index by varchar2(512);
 bfile_dirs array_type;
 mydir varchar2(512);
 total_bfiles number := 0;
begin
 -- loop through all columns that are BFILE type
 for bf in
 (select owner,table_name,column_name
 from dba_tab_cols
 where data_type='BFILE')
 loop
 v_sqlstmt:='select '||bf.column_name||' from '
 ||bf.owner||'.'||bf.table_name;
 open v_cur for v_sqlstmt;
 loop
 fetch v_cur into v_bfile_loc;
 exit when v_cur%notfound;
 -- get BFILE directory alias and filename
 dbms_lob.filegetname(v_bfile_loc, v_bfile_dir_name,
 v_bfile_filename);
 if bfile_dirs.exists(v_bfile_dir_name) then
 bfile_dirs(v_bfile_dir_name) := bfile_dirs(v_bfile_dir_name) +
1;
 else
 bfile_dirs(v_bfile_dir_name) := 1;
 end if;
 end loop;
 close v_cur;
 end loop;
 dbms_output.put_line(' ');
 dbms_output.put_line('The following directories contain external
files for BFILE columns');
```

```
 dbms_output.put_line('Copy the files within these directories to the
same path on the target system');
 dbms_output.put_line(' ');
 -- loop through array of all directories
 mydir := bfile_dirs.first;
 while mydir is not null loop
-- resolve the directory alias to a full path
 select directory_path
 into v_bfile_realpath
 from all_directories
 where directory_name = mydir;
 dbms_output.put_line(v_bfile_realpath);
 total_bfiles := total_bfiles + bfile_dirs(mydir);
 mydir := bfile_dirs.next(mydir);
 end loop;
 dbms_output.put_line(' ');
 dbms_output.put_line('There are ' || bfile_dirs.count
 || ' directories, ' || total_bfiles
 || ' total BFILEs');
 dbms_output.put_line(' ');
end;
 /
```

CHAPTER
7

Application
Consolidation in Exadata

The data center has evolved considerably since the mainframe era. In those days, dedicated silos of hardware and software were built for each application, which made it easy to provide predictable levels of service—unless, of course, there were wild peaks in load. However, it also meant that hardware and software had to be overprovisioned to meet peak demands. It was difficult to scale as the application's, demand grew, often requiring forklift updates and the associated downtime. Because customers tended to overprovision, they paid more than they needed to for hardware, software, and maintenance. And because each silo was independently managed, costs increased even more. As customers started realizing that there were too many moving parts with this approach—in capital expenditure and operational expenditure costs, issues with manageability, paying for unused hardware—they started looking at consolidation.

Today, Exadata is a great and often-chosen candidate for consolidation. Application consolidation on Exadata helps in using resources more effectively; it can significantly save IT costs, lower administration and operational costs, and reduce the excess system capacity per server from traditional servers. Exadata has all the characteristics that a consolidated platform should have, making it a universal choice for consolidation.

Following are some benefits of consolidating applications on Exadata:

- **Highly scalable** Eight racks of Exadata can be cabled together without requiring additional switches. Additional racks can be connected by adding an InfiniBand switch, and there is no limit to how many machines can be connected together. Thus, Exadata can handle any volume of application growth.

- **Resource control** Exadata provides a mechanism to control resources at each and every level. Depending on the criticality of the application, the CPU, memory, I/O, and flash can be increased or decreased. Resources can be controlled at all levels of the hardware, so even during peak usage, no resource will create a bottleneck that affects other applications. Exadata also provides the flexibility to increase or decrease the resources on demand, which helps critical applications get more resources during important activities.

- **High availability** Exadata provides high availability at all levels, from the database server, to the Exadata Smart Flash Cache, to storage, which helps mission-critical applications run without interruption.

- **Manageability** Oracle Enterprise Manager (OEM) provides a simple and intuitive graphical interface for managing the Exadata. Using OEM, you can control resources at all the layers in a simplified way. OEM simplifies application consolidation and management.

■ **Segregation of roles, responsibilities, and resources**   In any consolidation platform, application owners should be able to segregate the roles, responsibilities, and resources to a specific application. Certain applications need to comply with the Payment Card Industry data security standards (PCI DSS), and others must comply with the Sarbanes-Oxley Act (SOX). In an Exadata Machine, you can easily segregate roles, responsibilities, and resources, and it adheres to all security standards and compliances, including PCI and SOX.

Advantages of Server Consolidation

The main advantages of consolidation are provided here:

■ **Fewer number of servers**   Consolidation helps in cutting down the number of servers in use, and that saves data center space, reduces power requirements, and generates less heat, which in turn saves money in cooling systems and helps an organization lower its carbon footprint.

■ **Less maintenance**   Maintenance overhead is reduced. Instead of your organization paying annual maintenance contracts for multiple servers, only one server will require service.

■ **Manageability**   System administrators have fewer servers to manage. Less hardware means fewer updates and less troubleshooting, and administrators won't need to use different management tools on different servers.

■ **Maximum resource utilization**   In standalone servers, the capacity of the server is often underutilized, yet organizations must pay for the unused server capacity. With server consolidation, servers are always utilized properly, providing a greater return on investment (ROI) and total cost of ownership (TCO). It also helps contain IT spending.

■ **Guaranteed service level agreements**   Even after consolidating multiple servers into one server, you can use the system resources optimally without compromising the SLAs. Various tools can be used to help you achieve this objective.

■ **On-demand resource provisioning**   In consolidated environments, you can quickly allocate more resources such as CPU, memory, and I/O as and when the business demands.

■ **Fewer software licensing costs**   Oracle is always licensed on a per-core basis. In a consolidated environment, you can include more databases compared to standalone hardware, saving licensing fees.

How to Consolidate in Exadata

For consolidation, you must ensure that all the application databases you want to include will fit in the Exadata Machine. For production environments, the sum total of resources required for each database should be less than or equal to the resources available in Exadata:

Total capacity of Exadata >= (Resource needed for database 1 + Resource needed for database 2 + Resource needed for database *n*)

For nonproduction, noncritical test and development environments, you can overprovision the total number of resources required in each database to be greater than the total capacity of available resources in an Exadata Machine. If you want to overprovision for a production environment, however, you can overprovision only CPU and I/O. Be very careful with memory, because the capacity of the memory is fixed. In addition, regarding storage, you can't overprovision the disk in Exadata.

TIP & TECHNIQUE
Never consolidate production and nonproduction environments on the same Exadata Machine. Production systems always have an associated SLA, whereas nonproduction systems are not mission-critical.

Before you consolidate, you need to size each database individually in terms of CPU, memory, I/O, and storage requirements. Then all the parameters (CPU, memory, I/O, and storage) should be aggregated and compared against the total resources available in the Exadata Machine. Sizing individual databases for these parameters was discussed in Chapter 5. The same methodology can be applied when you're sizing the database for consolidation.

When sizing multiple applications into Exadata, you also need to factor in the recovery time objectives (RTOs) and recovery point objectives (RPOs). If you are planning for high availability (HA) at all levels, you must consider the following as well: What happens if one of the nodes goes down? How much of a performance hit can the application take? An ideal consolidation sizing scenario covers all the scenarios.

Using Consolidation Planner

If your organization uses Oracle Enterprise Manager 12*c*, the Consolidation Planner utility can help you with consolidation planning. To start the Consolidation Planner from the main page of Enterprise Manager, choose Enterprise | Consolidation Planner, as shown in Figure 7-1.

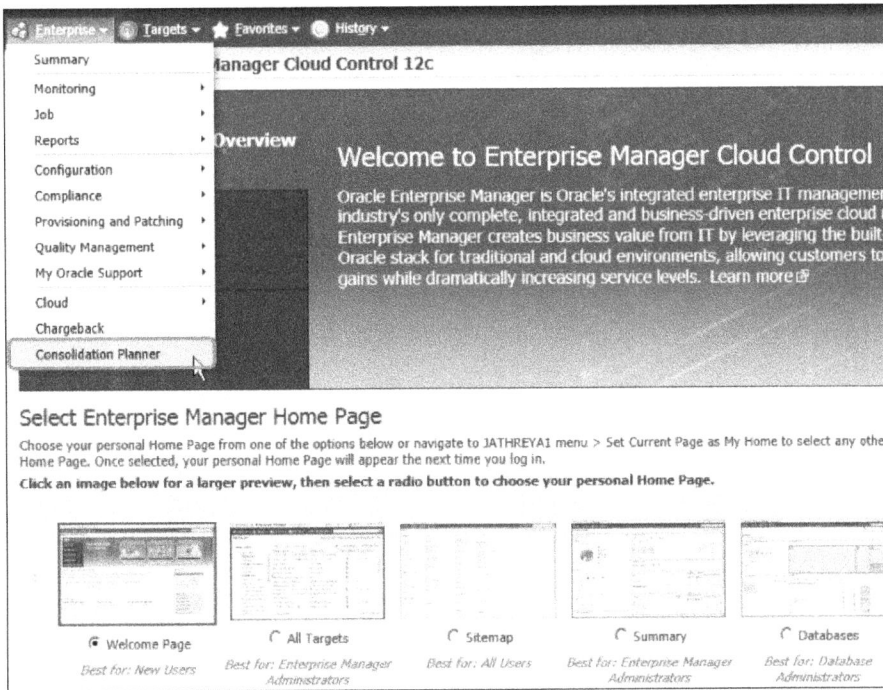

FIGURE 7-1. *Opening Consolidation Planner*

After you open Consolidation Planner, follow these steps to plan your consolidation:

1. Start a new project for the consolidation and assign a unique name for the project, as shown in the next illustration.

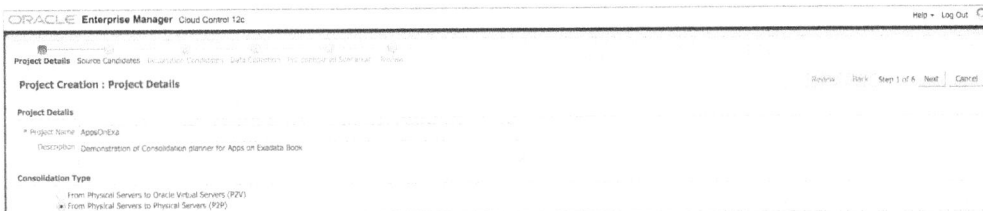

2. Select the From Physical Servers To Physical Servers (P2P) option; Exadata is a physical server, not a virtual server. Then click Next.

3. In the Servers To Be Involved In Consolidation screen, click the Add Servers link, shown next. In this screen, you can add all the databases you want to consolidate to Exadata.

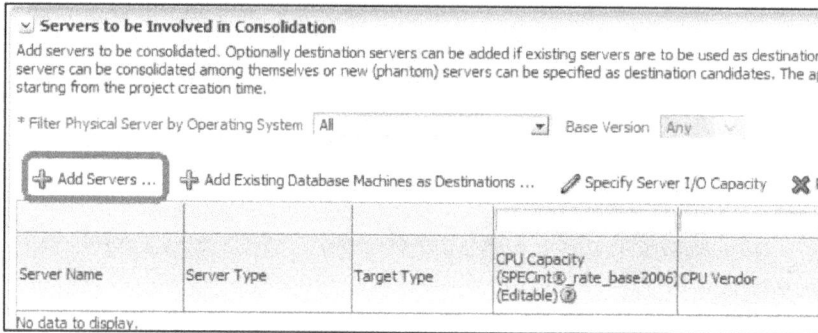

4. The Search And Select: Targets screen lists values for all the targets that are integrated with the OEM infrastructure. From the Lifecycle Status drop-down list, shown next, filter the values for the Cluster Database or Database Instance, and then add all servers running databases that you want to consolidate on Exadata by highlighting the database in the list and clicking Select. When you are finished adding targets, you are taken to the Source Candidate Screen.

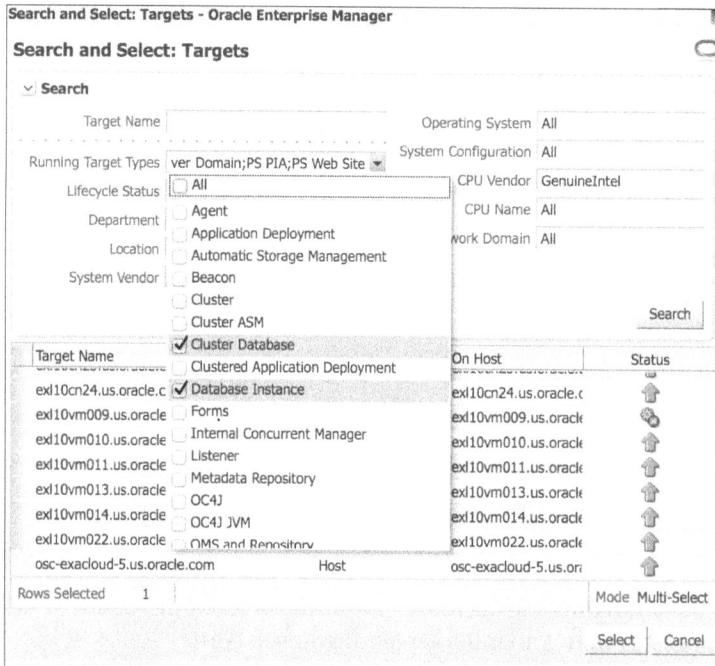

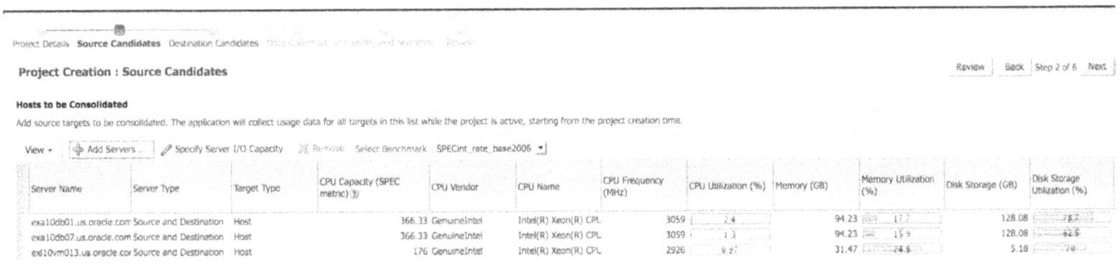

FIGURE 7-2. *Servers added for consolidation*

5. Figure 7-2, the Source Candidates screen, shows that three servers were added to the project for consolidation. Consolidation Planner gathers all the metrics of the servers in terms of CPU, memory, I/O, disk storage, network I/O, and other factors.

6. With Consolidation Planner, you can use either the SPECint_rate_base2006 or SPECjbb2005 benchmark. Because we are consolidating the databases, from the Select Benchmark list, choose SPECint_rate_base2006. Click Next.

7. If your Exadata consolidated system is already integrated with the OEM infrastructure, you can choose it from the Destination Candidates screen by clicking the Add Existing Engineered Systems As Destinations link. If Exadata is not yet integrated, as shown in the following screen, click Next without making a choice.

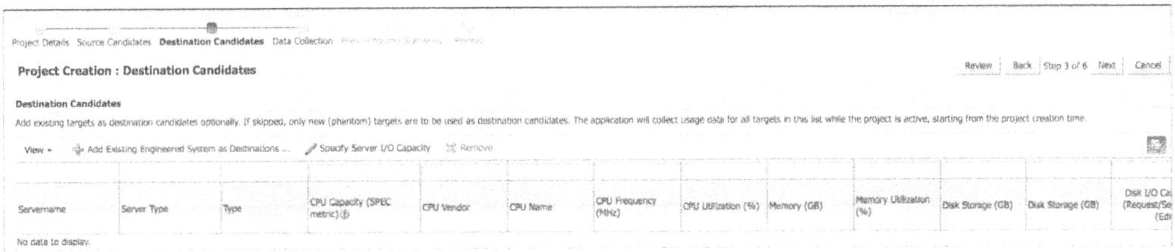

8. The Data Collection screen prompts for the minimum and maximum number of days for data collection metrics for all the components (CPU, memory, disk storage, disk and network I/O, and so on). Consolidation Planner extracts the resource utilization data from the Enterprise Manager metric tables. Figure 7-3 shows the prompts for the minimum and maximum number of days. You can start the data capture immediately or schedule it for a later period of time. Click Next after you have made your selections.

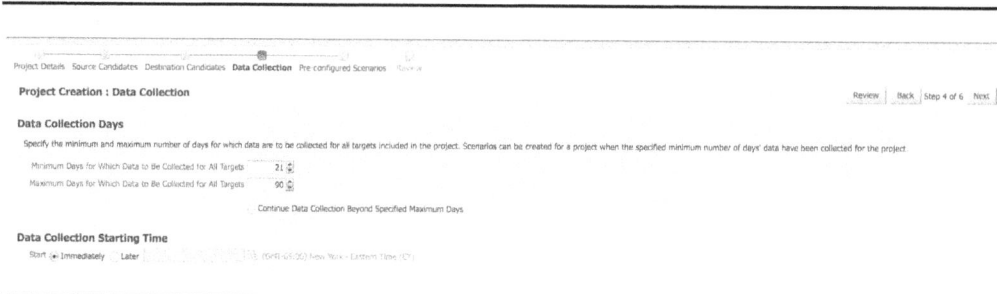

FIGURE 7-3. *Number of days to capture data*

9. The Pre-configured Scenarios screen provides two ways of sizing the Exadata system, with or without a preconfigured scenario. The preconfigured scenario provides three options for sizing the Exadata:

- **Conservative Scenario** Resource use in Exadata is limited to 70 percent

- **Medium Scenario** Resource use in Exadata is limited to 80 percent

- **Aggressive Scenario** Resource use in Exadata is limited to 90 percent

   Select the options Use New (Phantom) Servers and Use Oracle Engineered System, and then click Next. In the example, we have chosen all three scenarios. Figure 7-4 shows the details of the preconfigured scenarios.

10. The Review screen (Figure 7-5) shows all the details that you have chosen in the previous screens. If you find anything wrong, you can go back to a previous screen and rectify the error.

11. After reviewing the scenario, if everything looks good, click Submit to submit the consolidation. The confirmation screen is shown in Figure 7-6.

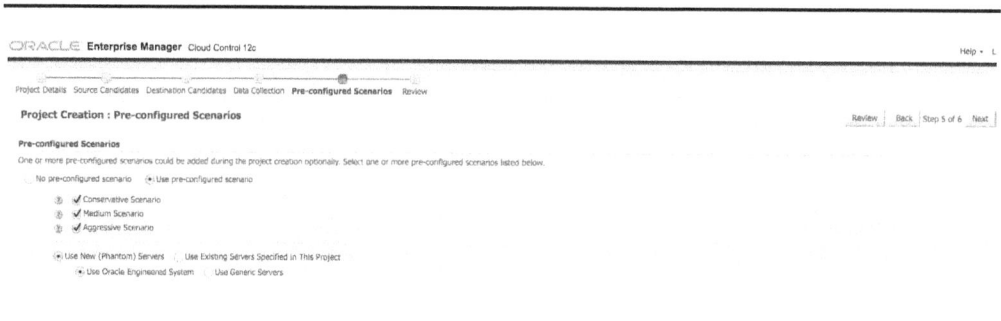

FIGURE 7-4. *Preconfigured scenarios*

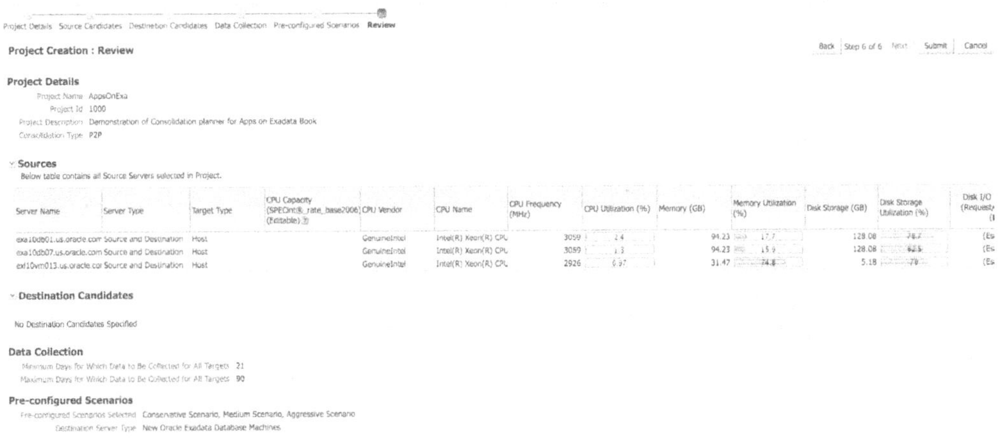

FIGURE 7-5. *Review screen*

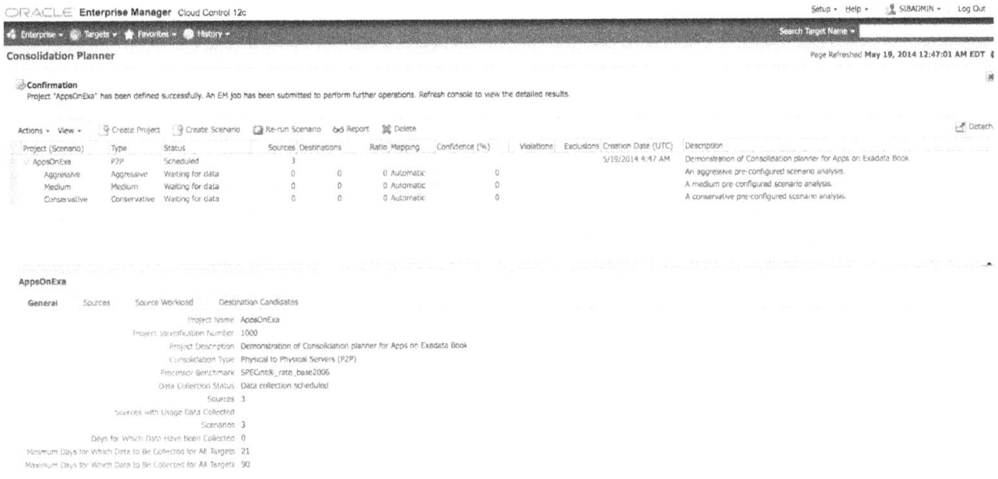

FIGURE 7-6. *Confirmation screen*

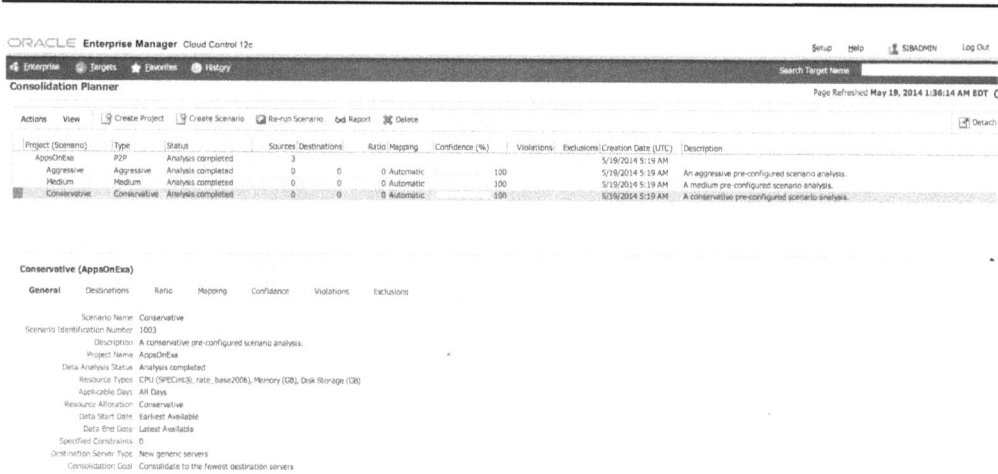

FIGURE 7-7. *Sample report screen*

When the job is finished, click the Report icon from the confirmation screen. A comprehensive report with various tabs will be displayed. Click the Aggressive, Medium, and Conservative options to see the details of each report. On each report are several tabs: General, Destinations, Ratio, Mapping, Confidence, Violations, and Exclusion. Figure 7-7 shows the sample report screen.

Click each tab to see details. The next illustration shows the target server's CPU and memory details.

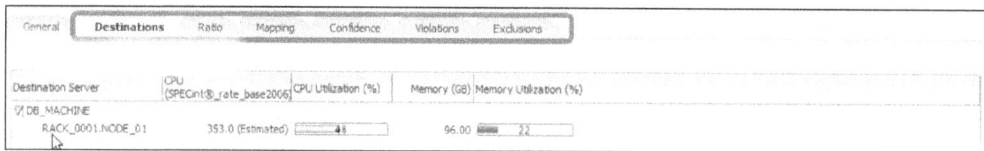

The Consolidation Planner gives you lots of flexibility and options. You can choose an existing engineered system or add a new engineered system. You can choose different models of systems (X4-2, X3-2, and so on) and disk types. You can even plan the consolidation for the middle-tier workload. (The tool is so comprehensive that a whole chapter could be written about its features. Covering Consolidation Planner in depth, however, is outside the scope of this book.)

Managing Resources in Exadata After Consolidation

In a consolidated environment, it becomes very important to manage the resources across and within the database efficiently and appropriately. Improper use of resources can cause performance delays, noncompliance with the SLA, and severely impact the business. You can manage resources in an Exadata Machine in a number of ways:

- Instance caging helps you manage the CPU resources.

- Database Resource Manager (DBRM) can be leveraged at the database server level to manage the server resources.

- I/O Resource Manager (IORM) works with DBRM at the storage cell level to manage I/O utilization, Flash Cache, and so on.

Instance Caging

After you consolidate multiple applications into Exadata, all the applications share the same resources within the Exadata Machine—CPU, memory, and I/O bandwidth. Instance caging enables you to manage the CPU by limiting the CPU usage according to the database instance.

Instance caging can be done in two ways: using the partitioning approach or the overprovisioning approach.

Partitioning Approach

This approach is the simplest way to allocate CPU resources across a number of running database instances. In this method, the total number of CPUs used for all the database instances is equal to the total number of CPUs of the server. So, for example, if a node of Exadata has 24 CPUs and four database instances are running in the node, you could divide the CPUs equally by allocating six CPUs per database instance (6 + 6 + 6 + 6), or you could divide the 24 CPUs according to database usage (8 + 4 + 10 + 2).

This method guarantees an allocated CPU for each database instance; a fixed number of CPUs allows for predictable performance. This method also makes sure that one database instance's CPU workload doesn't affect another.

This method is useful in deploying mission-critical OLTP applications, where SLAs and performance are key and can't be compromised. Note that this approach is non-adaptive, so you need to make sure it's done correctly the first time!

Overprovisioning Approach

In most systems, all databases aren't equally busy at the same time, and sometimes a database may be totally idle. By overprovisioning available CPUs, you can take advantage of the slack time in one database to accommodate the busy times in others. So you can allocate more CPUs for each database by overprovisioning the available CPUs, essentially providing more CPU resources to your databases than you would by partitioning the CPUs. If one or two database instances are idle, then the overprovisioning method is of great use because it minimizes the number of unutilized CPUs.

As discussed, with partitioning, if 24 CPUs are divided across four database instances, you could assign the CPUs accordingly up to a total of 24 (6 + 6 + 6 + 6 or 10 + 4 + 3 + 7, for example). With overprovisioning, you could arrange the CPUs in a way that can actually equal more than 24 (8 + 8 + 8 + 8 or 10 + 10 + 10 + 10, for example).

In general, if all database instances use instance caging, the maximum percentage of CPU resources that a database instance can consume at any point in time is its own limit divided by the sum of the usage for all active databases: This is because instance caging limits the number of runnable processes for each instance, and the operating system allocates the CPU in proportion to the runnable processes for that instance.

Consider our overprovisioning scenario of 8 + 8 + 8 + 8: If all four database instances are active and CPU-bound, then one instance will be able to consume $8 / (8 + 8 + 8 + 8) = 25$ percent of the CPU. If only two instances are active and CPU-bound, then one instance will be able to consume $8 / (8 + 8) = 50$ percent of the CPU.

With overprovisioning, a DBA can predict the worst-case scenario—what is the minimum CPU a database instance will get when all the databases are aggressively being used?

This method is especially useful for nonproduction environments such as test and development environments and low-load, noncritical environments where performance and guaranteed SLAs are not required. This method can also be used in the disaster recovery (DR) Exadata system, where the DR hardware is shared between the test and development environments. Since the DR environment stays in a mounted state most of the time, overprovisioning allows other databases running on the Exadata Machine to use some of the resources from the DR database.

Steps for Enabling Instance Caging

Instance caging is simple to set up. You basically add an entry, cpu_count, in the initialization parameter file of the database. It also needs a resource plan and Resource Manager to manage the CPU.

The initialization parameter cpu_count is not set by default in any database instance. To set up instance caging, you must set this parameter at the instance level to the maximum number of CPUs that the database instance should use at any time. For example, to limit the database instance to six CPUs, you would add the following:

```
alter system set cpu_count = 4 scope=SPFILE sid='INSTANCE1';
```

Although cpu_count is a dynamic parameter, Oracle does not recommend frequent or large modifications. As a best practice, Oracle recommends using a minimum value of 2. Note that changes to cpu_count also affect other settings, such as parallel execution.

Next, you must enable a resource plan that manages the CPU. The resource plan describes how CPU resources should be allocated to processes within the database instance. You can enable Resource Manager by setting the resource_manager_plan parameter as follows:

```
alter system set resource_manager_plan = 'name_of_resource_plan';
```

Enabling a resource plan and setting the cpu_count parameter turns on instance caging. (Resource Manager is covered in more detail in later sections of this chapter.)

Because setting up instance caging will adjust the speed of the CPUs, you should regularly monitor the Automatic Workload Repository (AWR) report to see if any wait events are occurring on the CPU. The AWR report will show a resmgr:cpu quantum wait event if there is a CPU wait. If waits on the CPU are happening too frequently, more CPUs should be allocated to that database instance.

You can also monitor the v$rsrcmgrmetric_history view to see details on CPU throttling. The v$rsrcmgrmetric_history view shows the amount of CPU consumption and throttling for each minute in the past hour. For each consumer group, cpu_consumed_time specifies the number of milliseconds of CPU consumed, and cpu_wait_time specifies the number of milliseconds that processes were throttled.

```
select begin_time, consumer_group_name, cpu_consumed_time, cpu_wait_time
from v$rsrcmgrmetric_history order by begin_time;
```

The v$rsrc_consumer_group view shows the amount of CPU consumption and throttling since CPU resource management was enabled. The consumed_cpu_time and cpu_wait_time parameters measure time in milliseconds.

```
select name, consumed_cpu_time, cpu_wait_time from v$rsrc_consumer_group;
```

TIP & TECHNIQUE
Instance caging can also be set up using Enterprise Manager.

Database Resource Manager (DBRM)

DBRM is used to manage resources within a database. It is not used to manage the resources across multiple databases, so we can say that DBRM is used for intra-database and not inter-database management. In any application system, various types of activities occur on a day-to-day basis—online transactions, batch jobs, system activities, reporting, ad hoc queries, maintenance activities, user queries, and so on. DBRM helps in prioritizing these various activities. For example, you can prioritize any activity being run by a system user over any reporting activity, or you can prioritize online transactions over the running of ad hoc queries.

The first step in creating the DBRM is to identify the workload and create a consumer group for each type of workload. For example, you can create a consumer group called OLTP, a consumer group called DBA activities, and so on. You can even create a consumer group for each type of application if more than one application shares the same database. For example, if Demantra is a separate schema in the E-Business Suite Database, you can create a separate consumer group called Demantra that can handle all the requests coming from the Demantra application.

If you are creating consumer groups manually, you need to do some preparation work that involves assigning proper permissions and creating a pending area. If OEM is performing all the steps, however, preparation work is not needed because OEM takes care of it.

Start by assigning proper permissions so that the Resource Manager can be administered. Administering Resource Manager requires the ADMINISTER_RESOURCE_MANAGER privilege, which is automatically granted to SYS. If you want to grant this privilege to any other user, run the following PL/SQL command. In this example, the privilege is given to the Demantra user:

```
SQL> exec dbms_resource_manager_privs.grant_system_privilege
(grantee_name => 'demantra',  admin_option => true);
```

Once the privilege is granted, your next step is to create a pending area that is used as a temporary work area for Resource Manager configuration. The changes in the pending area are not visible until the pending area is submitted. Create the pending area as follows:

```
SQL> exec dbms_resource_manager.create_pending_area();
```

At any time, you can abandon the changes in the pending area as follows:

```
SQL> exec dbms_resource_manager.clear_pending_area();
```

After you have granted permission to administer Resource Manager and have created a pending area, you can create consumer groups. Oracle Database comes with a lot of built-in consumer groups that you can leverage instead of creating new groups. The list of default consumer groups is shown in Figure 7-8.

Select	Consumer Group ▲	Mandatory	Description
	AUTO_TASK_CONSUMER_GROUP	NO	System maintenance task consumer group
	BATCH_GROUP	NO	Consumer group for batch operations
	DEFAULT_CONSUMER_GROUP	YES	Consumer group for users not assigned to any consumer group
	DSS_CRITICAL_GROUP	NO	Consumer group for critical DSS queries
	DSS_GROUP	NO	Consumer group for DSS queries
	ETL_GROUP	NO	Consumer group for ETL
	INTERACTIVE_GROUP	NO	Consumer group for interactive, OLTP operations
	LOW_GROUP	NO	Group of low priority sessions
	ORA$APPQOS_0	YES	Consumer group for Application QOS
	ORA$APPQOS_1	YES	Consumer group for Application QOS
	ORA$APPQOS_2	YES	Consumer group for Application QOS
	ORA$APPQOS_3	YES	Consumer group for Application QOS
	ORA$APPQOS_4	YES	Consumer group for Application QOS
	ORA$APPQOS_5	YES	Consumer group for Application QOS
	ORA$APPQOS_6	YES	Consumer group for Application QOS
	ORA$APPQOS_7	YES	Consumer group for Application QOS
	ORA$AUTOTASK_HEALTH_GROUP	YES	Consumer group for health checks
	ORA$AUTOTASK_MEDIUM_GROUP	YES	Consumer group for medium-priority maintenance tasks
	ORA$AUTOTASK_SPACE_GROUP	YES	Consumer group for space management advisors
	ORA$AUTOTASK_SQL_GROUP	YES	Consumer group for SQL tuning
	ORA$AUTOTASK_STATS_GROUP	YES	Consumer group for gathering optimizer statistics
	ORA$AUTOTASK_URGENT_GROUP	YES	Consumer group for urgent maintenance tasks
	ORA$DIAGNOSTICS	YES	Consumer group for diagnostics
	SYS_GROUP	YES	Consumer group for system administrators

FIGURE 7-8. *Default consumer groups*

If the existing consumer groups can't be leveraged, you can create a new consumer group using the following PL/SQL command:

```
SQL> exec dbms_resource_manager.create_consumer_group(
'DEM', 'Consumer group for managing Demantra Application');
```

If OEM is integrated with Exadata, you can create consumer groups from the EM console. In fact, OEM should be preferred over using the command line.

To add a consumer group from OEM, do the following:

1. From the EM console, choose Administration | Resource Manager | Consumer Groups.

2. Click Create to create a new consumer group.

3. Type a name and description, and then choose a scheduling policy for the new group, as shown in Figure 7-9. Then click OK.

After you have created the consumer group, you can map sessions to the group. Sessions can be automatically mapped to a consumer group by defining consumer group mapping rules. You can create various rules according to the session attributes shown in Table 7-1.

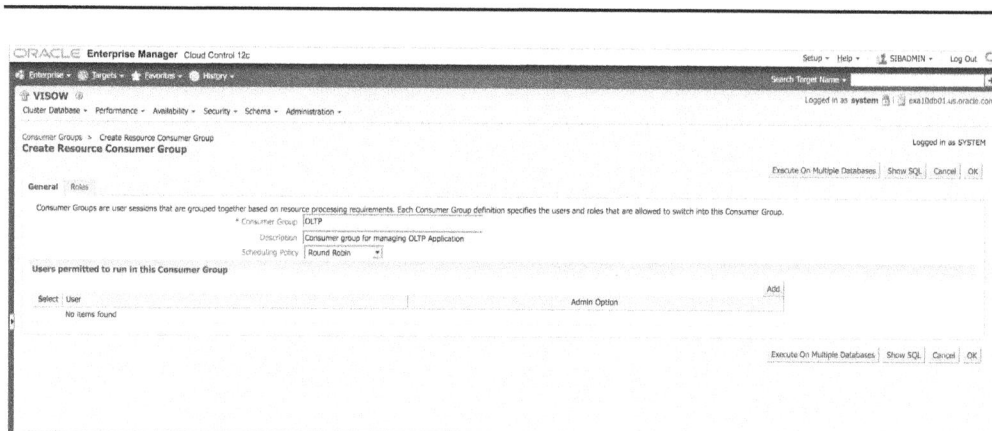

FIGURE 7-9. *Create a consumer group*

Session Attribute	Description
Service module and action	A combination of service name, module name, and action name, in this format: service_name.module_name.action_name
Service and module	A combination of service and module names in this format: service_name.module_name
Module and action	A combination of module and action names in this format: module_name.action_name
Module	The module name in the currently running application
Service	The service name used by the client to establish a connection
Oracle user	The Oracle Database username
Client program	The name of the client program used to log on to the server
Client OS user	The operating system username of the client
Client machine	The name of the computer from which the client is making the connection
Client ID	The client identifier

TABLE 7-1. *Session Attributes and Description*

Following are some examples of how the consumer group mappings can be done:

- Service = 'DEMANTRA' can be mapped to the consumer group OLTP.

- Client program = 'Discoverer' can be mapped to the consumer group Reports.

- A consumer group with low priority can be created and the following mappings can be a part of it:

    - client program = 'DISCOVERER' && module = 'AdHoc'

    - query has been running > 1 hour

    - estimated execution time of query > 12 hours

As you can see, query attributes can also be used as a part of consumer group mapping (for example, the query is running for more than an hour). The following query attributes can be a part of the consumer group mapping:

- Estimated execution time

- CPU time used so far

- I/O requests issued so far

- Amount of I/O issued so far

- Function being performed

- Backup (RMAN)

- Data load (Data Pump)

You can map consumer groups by running the following command. In the example, the following rule maps sessions in the DEMANTRA service to the DEM consumer group:

```
SQL> exec dbms_resource_manager.set_consumer_group_mapping(
attribute => dbms_resource_manager.service_name, value => 'DEMANTRA',
consumer_group => 'DEM');
```

Sessions can be automatically mapped to a consumer group using the **dbms_resource_manager.set_consumer_group_mapping()** procedure. Sessions can also be manually switched into a consumer group using the **dbms_session.switch_consumer_group()** procedure.

You can also map consumer groups using OEM:

1. From the EM console, choose Administration | Resource Manager | Consumer Group Mappings.

2. Select the Service radio button, and then click Add Rule For Selected Type. In the example shown in Figure 7-10, the Module and Action session attribute is selected to assign sessions to the consumer group.

3. For this example, we used Inventory as a module and Concurrent Request as the action to map to the consumer group OLTP. From the Select Consumer Group drop-down list, select the consumer group. In this case, we chose OLTP. You can add even more actions in the text boxes. In this example, we manually typed the action Concurrent Request in the text box under Module and Action. Click OK when you're done. Figure 7-11 shows the details of creating the consumer group mapping.

Once mapping is created, an update message is displayed at the top of the OEM window, as shown in Figure 7-12. It also shows how the consumer group is mapped with the attribute. Click Apply to save the modification.

Once the consumer group is done, your next step is to create the resource plan. Oracle Database comes preconfigured with multiple resource plans. You can use an

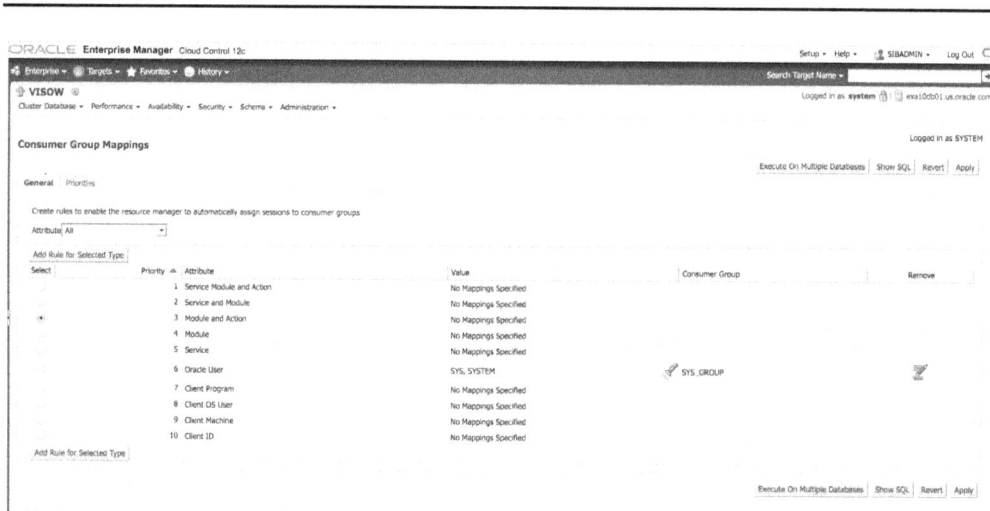

FIGURE 7-10. *Consumer group mapping*

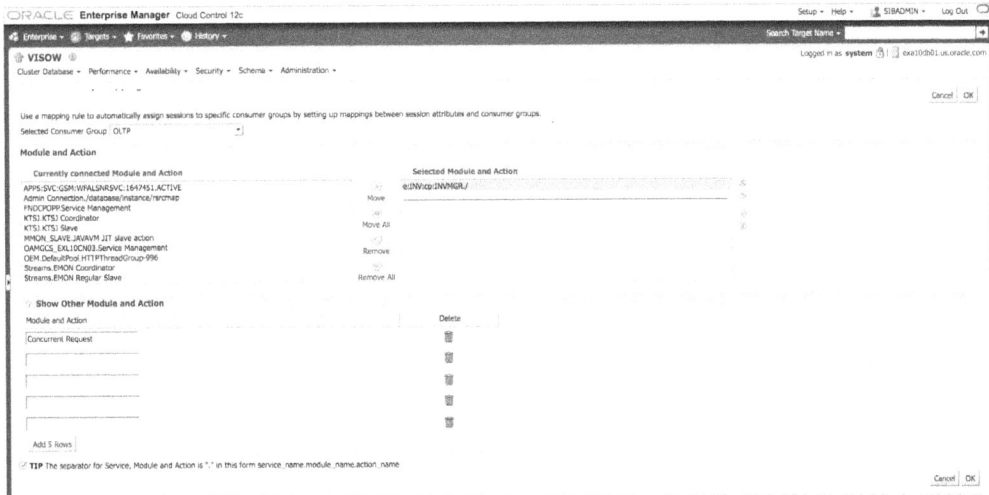

FIGURE 7-11.   *Creating a consumer group mapping*

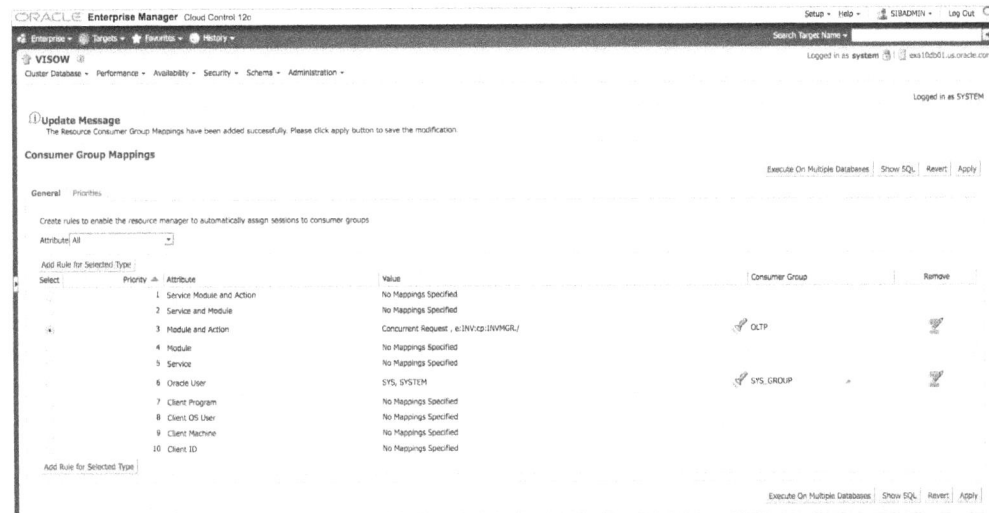

FIGURE 7-12.   *Successful creation of consumer group mapping*

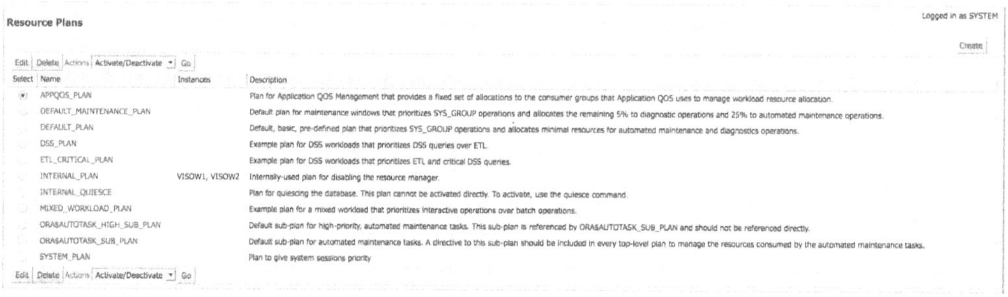

FIGURE 7-13. *Preconfigured resource plans*

existing resource plan, or, if none meets your requirements, you can create your own resource plan. Figure 7-13 shows the preconfigured resource plans.

The consumer group created previously needs to be added to the resource plan that we will create now. You can add multiple consumer groups in one resource plan. In the following example, we will create a resource plan called AppsOnExa and will add the consumer groups DEM and OLTP, which we have created previously.

Managing CPU Resources with the Resource Plan

As you know, multiple consumer groups can be a part of a resource plan. DBRM enables you to control the CPU resources for each consumer group; you can define the priority of a consumer group and allocate the CPU accordingly. DBRM uses plan directives to allocate the database resources to the consumer groups. The plan directive uses various levels (level 1 to 8) internally to define the priority of the consumer group and allocate CPU resources. It also uses the parameter Max Utilization Level to allocate the maximum CPU for a particular consumer group. The following example will explain this in more detail.

This example is part of the Create Resource Plan screen, which you can access from OEM by choosing Administration | Resource Manager | Create Resource Plan. In the example, we have added three consumer groups, with three different levels defined in the AppsOnExa Resource Plan. Click OK to create the resource plan.

As shown in Figure 7-14, we have set the DEM consumer group at Level 1, which means the DEM will be top priority, 80 percent, in terms of CPU resources. The Max Utilization Limit for DEM shows as 85 percent, which means DEM can take up to 85 percent of the total CPU if needed.

OLTP is at Level 2, the second priority in terms of resource allocation. DEM is already allocated 80 percent of the CPU, which means 20 percent of the CPU remains free for OLTP. Of the available 20 percent, OLTP will get 70 percent, since we have capped OLTP at 70 percent, which translates to 14 percent of the total system CPU.

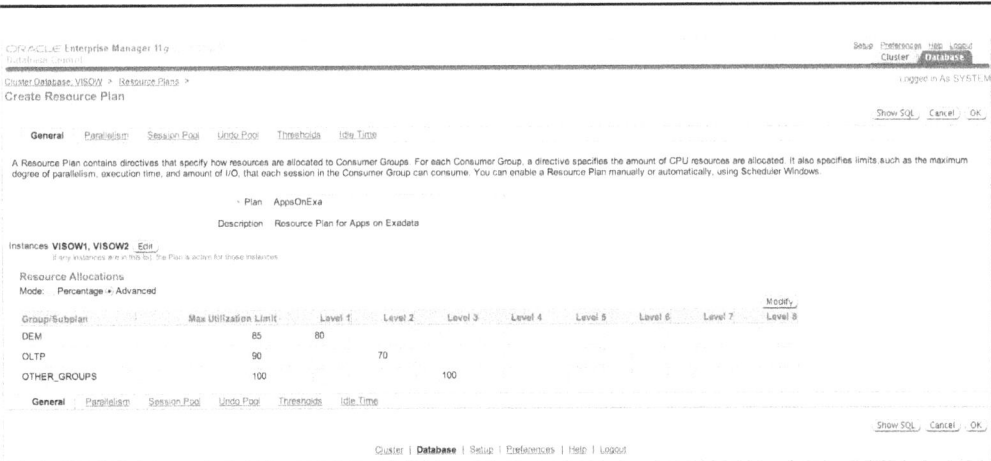

FIGURE 7-14. *Create Resource Plan screen, allocating resources*

OTHER_GROUPS is at Level 3, so it will use the leftover CPU resources remaining after allocating to DEM and OLTP. DEM is using 80 percent CPU and OLTP has 14 percent, so OTHER_GROUPS will get only 6 percent of the total CPU resources. You can see in the figure that OTHER_GROUPS is allocated at 100 percent CPU, which means it can use the entire 6 percent of the leftover CPU resources.

Now, assuming DEM takes the maximum allocated CPU—85 percent—the CPU available for OLTP would be 70 percent of 15 percent. Thus, OLTP will get 10.5 percent of the system CPU. So OTHERS_GROUP will get 100 – (85 + 10.5) = 4.5 percent of the system CPU. If DEM also takes the maximum allocated CPU, then DEM gets 90 percent of 15 percent, which would be 13.5 percent of the system CPU. In that case, OTHERS_GROUP will get only 100 – (85 + 13.5), or 1.5 percent of the system CPU.

Note that you can also create a resource plan from the command line:

```
SQL> exec dbms_resource_manager.create_plan(
'AppsOnExa', Resource Plan for Apps on Exadata');
```

Once the plan is created, you can add the resource plan directives that specify how much CPU resources should be allocated to the consumer group. You can create a new directive by calling dbms_resource_manager.create_plan_directive(). You can update or delete a directive by calling update_plan_directive or delete_plan_directive(). The parameter mgmt_p1 specifies the percentage of CPU to allocate for the consumer group. The parameter mgmt_p1 also specifies the first level of priority, mgmt_p2 is the second level, mgmt_p3 is the third level, and so on.

```
SQL> exec DBMS_RESOURCE_MANAGER.CREATE_PLAN_DIRECTIVE(
PLAN => 'AppsOnExa',
GROUP_OR_SUBPLAN => 'DEM',
COMMENT => 'CPU for Demantra',
MGMT_P1 => 80,
MAX_UTILIZATION_LIMIT => 85,
);

SQL> exec DBMS_RESOURCE_MANAGER.CREATE_PLAN_DIRECTIVE(
PLAN => 'AppsOnExa',
GROUP_OR_SUBPLAN => 'OLTP',
COMMENT => 'CPU for OLTP Con group',
MGMT_P2 => 70,
MAX_UTILIZATION_LIMIT => 90,
);

SQL> exec DBMS_RESOURCE_MANAGER.CREATE_PLAN_DIRECTIVE(
PLAN => 'AppsOnExa',
GROUP_OR_SUBPLAN => 'OTHER_GROUPS',
COMMENT => 'CPU for All Other',
MGMT_P3 => 100,
MAX_UTILIZATION_LIMIT => 100,
);
```

At any moment, if any CPU is not being used by one or more consumer groups, then Resource Manager redistributes it to the consumer groups that need it. In this example, the DEM consumer group is not running, so Resource Manager will allocate its CPU resources to OLTP and OTHER_GROUP. Therefore, mgmt_p2 specifies the amount of CPU that the OLTP consumer group is guaranteed to get. In this case, it will get 70–90 percent of the system CPU as compared to 14 percent or 10.5 percent previously.

Once you have configured the resource plan, you can use the following PL/SQL to persist your changes in the database. If you are editing a resource plan that is currently active, your changes will be immediately enabled.

```
SQL> exec dbms_resource_manager.submit_pending_area();
```

If your plan has any errors, this command will fail with an error that describes the problem.

After your resource plan is defined, you can enable it by setting the resource_manager_plan parameter with your resource plan name:

```
SQL> alter system set resource_manager_plan = 'AppsOnExa' sid='*';
```

If the resource plan is created using OEM and the instances are selected during that step, then OEM automatically takes care of enabling the resource plan. In Figure 7-14, you can see that instances VISOW1 and VISOW2 are selected for creating the resource plan.

In addition to managing the CPU, you can control other resources using DBRM, as discussed next.

Degree of Parallelism

Degree of parallelism can also be controlled using a resource plan. For every consumer group, you can allocate a higher or lower degree of parallelism depending on the criticality of the group. Defining the degree of parallelism (DOP) helps you run enough parallel statements to utilize system resources fully. You can reserve parallel servers for important queries and queue parallel statements that are noncritical.

You set the degree of parallelism at the Create Resource Plan screen's Parallelism tab. As shown in Figure 7-15, we have allocated 12 degrees of parallelism to the consumer group DEM, 4 to OLTP, and UNLIMITED for all other processes. You can also define what percentage of a parallel server target a particular consumer group should get. The Parallel Queue Timeout field shows after how much time the process should time out.

The DOPs are enabled at the database by setting the parameter shown next in the database initialization parameter file. This setting also enables a feature called Auto DOP, whereby the database determines the degree of parallelism of all operations automatically.

```
SQL>alter system set parallel_degree_policy = 'auto';
```

Because you need to understand how all of this works together, your first step is to have good statistics with histograms. You also need to "prime the pump" with

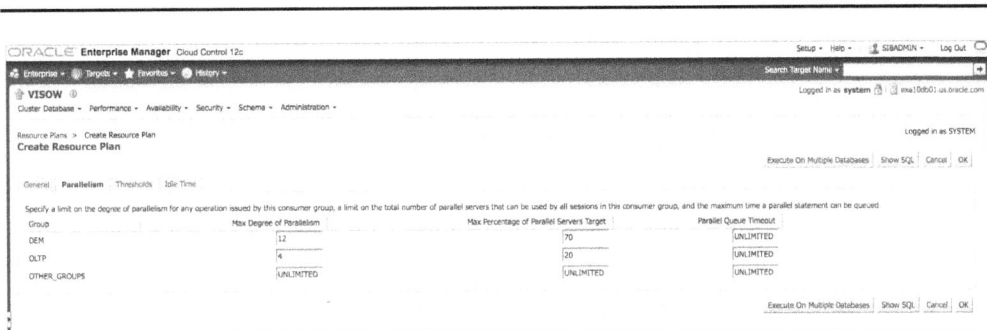

FIGURE 7-15.   *Create plan showing allocation of DOP*

SQL to get good histograms. Once that is done, you can set the parallel_degree_ policy to auto. We also recommend using this in conjunction with a resource plan to "cap" the DOP. Auto DOP has an ugly habit of overallocating DOP, so your resource plan provides a failsafe mechanism. This is also preferable to session-level settings, which experienced users can override. You really shouldn't give anyone unlimited DOP, except perhaps the DBA.

Managing I/O and Runaway Processes

A resource plan also provides the flexibility to configure I/O allocation within a database using the Database Resource Plan. DBRM enables you to control the I/O for each consumer group within a database.

For a particular consumer group, you can set the I/O request limit from the resource plan. As shown in Figure 7-16, a resource plan provides a lot of flexibility at the consumer group level. You also can specify the maximum I/O limit for the consumer group.

Managing the I/O from the DBRM requires that you enable the I/O resource plan. You will learn more about that in the later section, "I/O Resource Manager (IORM)."

You can also manage runaway queries from a resource plan. Runaway queries are often caused by missing indexes, unexpected inputs, and bad execution plans, which severely impact performance of well-behaved queries. It's very hard to control runaway queries. Using a resource plan, however, you can easily manage

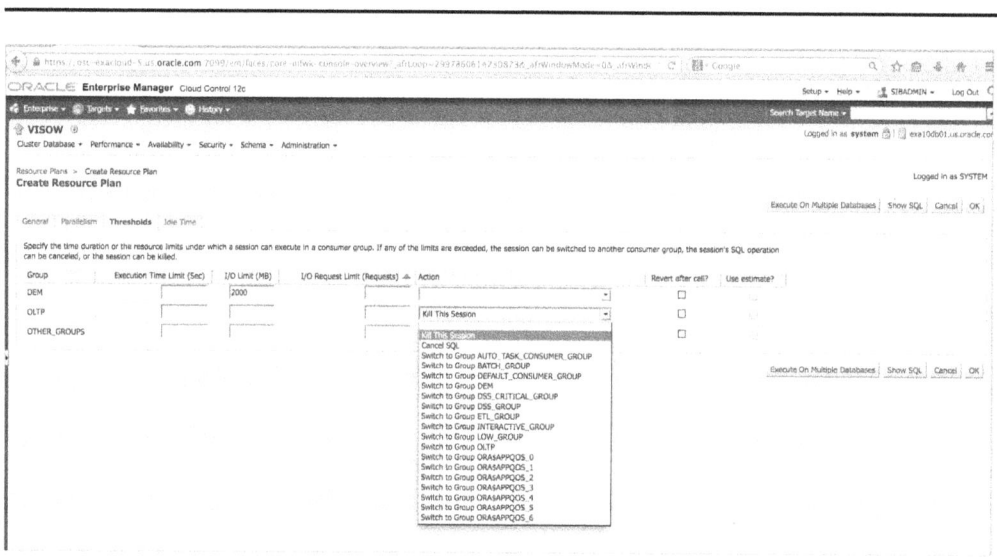

FIGURE 7-16. I/O limit setting in the Create Resource Plan screen

a runaway query by defining the runaway queries as per an estimated execution time, amount of CPU time used, number of I/Os issued, or bytes of I/O issued, and you can manage them by killing the session, aborting the call, or switching to a another consumer group.

Here are a few examples of runaway queries and how to manage them:

- For a DEM consumer group, runaway means more than 300 seconds of execution time. To manage the problem, switch to a "low priority" consumer group.

- For a reports consumer group, runaway means consuming over 32GB of I/Os. To manage the problem, abort the query.

- For the ad hoc consumer group, runaway means more than 24 hours of estimated execution time. To manage the problem, don't execute the query.

Monitoring DBRM

To determine whether Resource Manager is currently enabled, run the following query:

```
SQL> select name, cpu_managed from v$rsrc_plan where is_top_plan = 'TRUE';
```

This query returns the name of the current resource plan. If no rows are returned, Resource Manager is currently disabled. The column cpu_managed specifies whether Resource Manager is managing the CPU.

To determine the history of Resource Manager usage, run the following query:

```
SQL> select name, to_char(start_time, 'MON DD HH24:MI') start_time, to_
char(end_time, 'MON DD HH24:MI') end_time, window_name
from v$rsrc_plan_history order by start_time;
```

This query returns the name of the plan, the time that it was enabled and disabled, and the scheduler window that was used to enable it (if any). Each row corresponds to an occurrence of Resource Manager being enabled or disabled. A history of up to 16 occurrences is maintained.

Once a resource plan has been enabled, you should monitor the performance of the consumer groups and adjust the CPU allocations as necessary. It's important that you find out how much Resource Manager is throttling the consumer groups. The following query provides a minute-by-minute comparison for each consumer group with the following information:

- **total**   The amount of CPU time available on the server

- **db_total**   The amount of CPU time available for this database instance (lower if instance caging is enabled)

- **consumed**   The amount of CPU time this consumer group consumed

- **cpu_utilization**   The percentage of the CPU available to this database consumed by this consumer group

- **throttled**   The amount of time this consumer group was throttled

```
SQL> select to_char(begin_time, 'HH:MI') time,
consumer_group_name,
 60 * (select value from v$osstat where stat_name = 'NUM_CPUS') total,
 60 * (select value from v$parameter where name = 'cpu_count') db_total,
cpu_consumed_time / 1000 consumed,
cpu_consumed_time / (select value from v$parameter where name =
 'cpu_count') / 600 cpu_utilization,
cpu_wait_time / 1000 throttled
from v$rsrcmgrmetric_history
order by begin_time;
```

Monitoring Parallel Statements

The following query lists the current parallel statements by session ID, consumer group, active or queued state, active or queued time in milliseconds, and the parallel servers used or needed:

```
select s.inst_id, s.sid, s.resource_consumer_group, r.pq_active, decode(r.
pq_active, 'TRUE', r.current_pq_active_time, r.current_pq_queued_time) active_
or_queued_time, r.dop parallel_servers from gv$session s, gv$rsrc_session_info r
where s.inst_id = r.inst_id and s.sid = r.sid and r.dop > 0 order by s.resource_
consumer_group, r.pq_active;
```

(Note that the last field, dop, is the number of parallel servers used or needed, not the degree of parallelism.)

The following query lists the number of parallel statements that are currently running or queued per consumer group. It also lists the number of parallel servers currently used per consumer group:

```
select name, sum(current_pqs_active) pqs_active, sum(current_pq_servers_active)
pq_servers_active, sum(current_pqs_queued) pqs_queued from gv$rsrc_consumer_
group group by name;
```

The following query lists the number of parallel statements run, the average runtime, the number of parallel statements queued, and the average queue time by consumer group:

```
select name, sum(pqs_completed) pqs_completed, sum(decode(pqs_completed, 0, 0,
pq_active_time / pqs_completed)) avg_pq_run_time, sum(pqs_queued) pqs_queued,
sum(decode(pqs_queued, 0, 0, pq_queued_time / pqs_queued)) avg_pq_queue_time
from gv$rsrc_consumer_group group by name;
```

I/O Resource Manager (IORM)

DBRM allows you to manage I/O for consumer groups that are part of a single database—that is, it can be used to control intra-database I/O. DBRM doesn't have the flexibility to control the I/Os across multiple databases, however. If you're planning to use Exadata as a consolidated platform with multiple databases, you need the flexibility of allocating the I/O across the databases according to their priority. IORM provides the ability not only to allocate I/O across multiple databases running in a Exadata Machine, but also to manage I/O resources within a database across various consumer groups.

IORM works at the Exadata Storage Server level and works on per-cell basis. The moment I/O requests start to saturate the storage cell's capacity, IORM goes into action and starts scheduling all the incoming I/O requests. When the database server sends the I/O request to the Exadata Storage Cells, it is sent as an iDB message, which includes metadata information. This metadata information also indicates whether a consumer group and resource plan are associated with the I/O request. When the CELLSRV gets the request, it passes it on to IORM. At this point, a handshake occurs between the DBRM and the IORM. Oracle Exadata Storage Server software uses the IORM and database resource plans together to allocate I/O resources.

IORM schedules I/O by immediately issuing some I/O requests and queuing others. The I/O requests that are immediately issued are from workloads that have not exceeded their resource allocation according to the resource plans. The I/O requests that are queued are from workloads that have exceeded their resource allocation. They are issued when their workload no longer exceeds its resource allocation or when the cell is operating below capacity. When the cell is operating below capacity, IORM does not queue I/O requests.

For example, if in a production Exadata Machine, an OLTP database and a reporting database are sharing the same Oracle Exadata Storage Server, you can configure resource plans that give priority to the OLTP database. In this case, whenever the reporting database load would affect the OLTP database performance, IORM schedules the I/O requests such that the OLTP database I/O performance is not impacted. This means that the reporting database I/O requests are queued until they can be issued without disturbing the OLTP database I/O performance.

When consolidating multiple databases in an Exadata Machine, you can manage inter-database resources with an inter-database plan. An inter-database plan specifies how resources are allocated by percentage or shared among multiple databases for each cell. The directives in an inter-database plan specify allocations to databases rather than consumer groups, which is used in DBRM. The inter-database plan is configured and enabled with the CellCLI utility at each cell. The inter-database plans specify a resource allocation for each database.

The inter-database plan is very similar to a database resource plan, in that each directive consists of an allocation amount and a level from 1 to 8, with level 1 being the top priority and level 8 being the least priority. For a given plan, the total allocations at any level must be less than or equal to 100 percent. An inter-database plan differs from a database resource plan in that it cannot contain subplans and contains only I/O resource directives. Only one inter-database plan can be active on a cell at any given time.

The inter-database plan allocates the I/O resources to individual databases. Any unused resources are reallocated to other databases, as specified by the plan, similar to database resource plans. Next, the database resource plan for each database allocates the I/O resources to consumer groups. If a database does not have an active database resource plan, all user I/Os are treated the same. Background I/Os are automatically prioritized relative to the user I/Os based on their importance.

Database Resource Manager enables you to specify a category for every consumer group. While consumer groups represent collections of users within a database, categories represent collections of consumer groups across all databases. You can manage I/O resources based on categories by creating a category plan. You can add any number of categories or modify the predefined categories. You should map consumer groups to the appropriate category for all databases that use the same cell storage. Any consumer group without an explicitly specified category defaults to the OTHER category. When a category plan is enabled, the category plan is first used to allocate resources among the categories. For each category that is selected, the inter-database plan is used to select those databases that have consumer groups with the selected category. Finally, the database resource plan of the selected database is used to select one of its consumer groups. Category plans are configured and enabled using the CellCLI utility on the cell. Only one category plan can be enabled at a time.

An IORM plan can be created from the Exadata Storage Cells, as well as from OEM. The IORM plan needs to be created from each Exadata Storage Cell. An Exadata Storage Cell can have a different IORM plan than the other Exadata Storage Cells, but that is not recommended unless you have a very unique requirement. In an IORM plan, the **objective** option specifies the optimization mode for the IORM. Five **objective** options are provided by the IORM plan:

- **basic** This is the default objective option of an IORM plan. In basic mode, there is no degradation to the overall throughput, and IORM protects small I/Os against extreme latencies that may occur during heavy I/O loads. IORM ensures that throughput is not impacted by issuing just enough outstanding I/Os to maximize the disk throughput. If the objective has been set to something other than basic, then IORM prioritizes the I/O resources in one of two ways. First, it manages I/O if any database has set a database resource plan. Second, it manages I/O if an inter-database or category plan is configured. Use this setting to disable I/O prioritization and limit the maximum small I/O latency.

- **low_latency** Use this setting for critical OLTP workloads that require extremely good disk latency. This setting provides the lowest possible latency by significantly limiting disk utilization.

■ **balanced**   Use this setting for critical OLTP and DSS workloads. This setting balances low disk latency and high throughput. It limits disk utilization of large I/Os to a lesser extent than low_latency to achieve a balance between good latency and good throughput.

■ **high_throughput**   Use this setting for critical DSS workloads that require high throughput.

■ **auto**   Use this setting to have IORM determine the optimization objective. IORM continuously and dynamically determines the optimization objective, based on the workloads observed and resource plans enabled.

You can use IORM not only for managing the I/Os across the database, but also for managing Flash Cache and Smart Flash log usage for a particular database. For example, for noncritical databases, you can configure the IORM plan in such a way that Smart Flash Logging is set to off, saving it for critical databases. IORM is active by default. In the default state, IORM is used to manage Flash Cache, Flash Logging, and the latency for small I/Os.

Let's look at some examples to help you understand IORM and see its practical usage. As discussed previously, there can be two types of IORM plans: category plan (catPlan) and database plan (dbPlan). The catPlan plan is used to allocate the resources according to the category of the request, whereas the dbPlan is used mainly to allocate the resources across multiple databases.

TIP & TECHNIQUE
Remember that a category plan is used to manage I/O within a database, whereas a database plan is used to manage I/O across multiple databases.

You can create a category plan by defining workloads, which fall into various categories. An example plan is shown in Table 7-2.

The plan in this example prioritizes administrative activity across all databases. It also prioritizes OLTP activity over report, operation, and other activities. In the sample plan, the following are the resource allocations:

■ Level 1 is given 80 percent of the I/O resources. The DBA category is the only category in level 1.

■ Level 2 is given all resources that were unallocated or unused by level 1. In this example, level 2 is given 20 percent of the I/O resources and any resources unused by the DBA category. The OLTP category gets 70 percent of the level 2 amount.

Category Name	Category Description	Level 1 (%)	Level 2 (%)	Level 3 (%)
DBA	High-priority, urgent administrative work	80		
OLTP	For high-priority OLTP transactions		70	
REPORT	All batch jobs			70
OPERATION	All maintenance jobs			10
OTHER	All other consumer groups that don't fall under any category			20

TABLE 7-2. *Example Category Plan*

■ Level 3 categories are given the remaining resources, including those not used by the OLTP category. Of the remaining resources, the REPORT category gets 70 percent, the OTHER category gets 20 percent, and the OPERATION category gets 10 percent.

All important administrative consumer groups in all databases should be mapped to the DBA category. All high-priority activity, such as consumer groups for important online transactions and time-critical reports, should be mapped to the OLTP category. All low-priority user activity, such as reports, maintenance, and low-priority transactions, should be mapped to the REPORT, OPERATION, and OTHER categories.

You can create the IORM plan at the storage cell by running the **alter iormplan** command. Thus, for the previous example, here is the command for creating the IORM plan:

```
CellCLI> ALTER IORMPLAN
catPlan=( (name=dba, level=1, allocation=80),
(name=oltp, level=2, allocation=70),
(name=report, level=3, allocation=70),
(name=operation, level=3, allocation=10),
(name=other, level=3, allocation=20))
```

Let's look at another example to help you understand the database plan (dbPlan). Suppose we have four databases, E-Business Suite (ebs), PeopleSoft (psft), JD Edwards (jde), and Siebel (sbl), which we want to consolidate in an Exadata Machine. Let's say ebs and psft are more critical than jde and sbl, so we'd like to give them more disk bandwidth when there is disk contention. We therefore set the allocations in a 40-40-10-10 ratio. This means that when there is disk contention, ebs and psft will get equal disk bandwidth. They will each also get four times the bandwidth of jde and sbl:

```
CellCLI> ALTER IORMPLAN
dbplan = (
(name=ebs, level=1, allocation=40),
(name=psft, level=1, allocation=40),
(name=jde, level=1, allocation=10),
(name=sbl, level=1,allocation=10));
```

IORM provides the following directives for managing Exadata resources on a per-database basis. These directives can be set using the **alter iormplan** CellCLI command:

- **allocation**   Specifies the relative amount of disk resources for this database

- **limit**   Specifies a hard limit for this database's disk utilization

- **flashCache**   Enables or disables the use of Flash Cache for a particular database

- **flashLog**   Enables or disables the use of Flash Logging for a particular database

- **role**   Specifies whether the database is primary or standby

Let's use these features and edit our I/O resource plan. This time, we'll set a hard limit for ebs and psft of disk utilization to 50 percent, turn off Exadata Smart Flash Cache for the jde, and turn off Smart Flash Logging for the sbl database:

```
CellCLI> ALTER IORMPLAN
dbplan = (
(name=ebs, level=1, allocation=40 , limit=50),
(name=psft, level=1, allocation=40, limit=50),
(name=jde, level=1, allocation=10, flashCache=off ),
(name=sbl, level=1,allocation=10, flashLog=off ));
```

Thus, the directive for a database plan (dbPlan) is of the following format:

```
(name=db_or_category_name, [share=number] [,level=number,
allocation=number][,limit=number] [, role={ primary | standby }]
[, flashcache={on|off}][, flashLog={on|off}]
```

By default, the name of the IORM plan will be <name_of_cell>_IORMPLAN. The plan can be cross-checked from a cell by running the command shown here:

```
CellCLI> LIST IORMPLAN DETAIL
name: exa10db01_IORMPLAN
status: active
catPlan: name=dba,level=1,allocation=80
name=oltp,level=2,allocation=70
name=report,level=3,allocation=70
name=operation,level=3,allocation=10
name=other,level=3,allocation=20
dbPlan: name=ebs,level=1,allocation=40
name=psft,level=1,allocation=40
name=jde,level=1,allocation=10
name=sbl_test,level=1,allocation=10
objective: balanced
```

The IORM plan can be also created using the OEM 12*c*. Choose Targets | Exadata and expand the Exadata Machine where you want to create the I/O resource plan. From the Exadata Storage Server Grid menu, choose Administration | Manage IO Resource, as shown in Figure 7-17.

The next screen will show all the storage cells that are part of the Exadata Machine you chose. You'll see all the options for creating the IORM. From here, you can add databases to create plans within multiple databases, and choose Advance Plan to get more ability to control the various levels (1–8). Figure 7-18 shows the creation of the IORM plan using OEM. The page is very much self-explanatory. Click Update All to create the IORM resource plan.

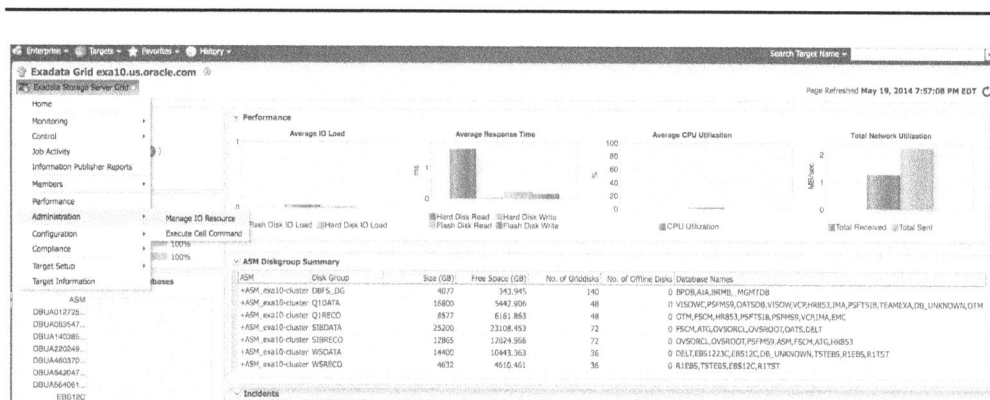

FIGURE 7-17. *Selecting to manage I/O resources from OEM*

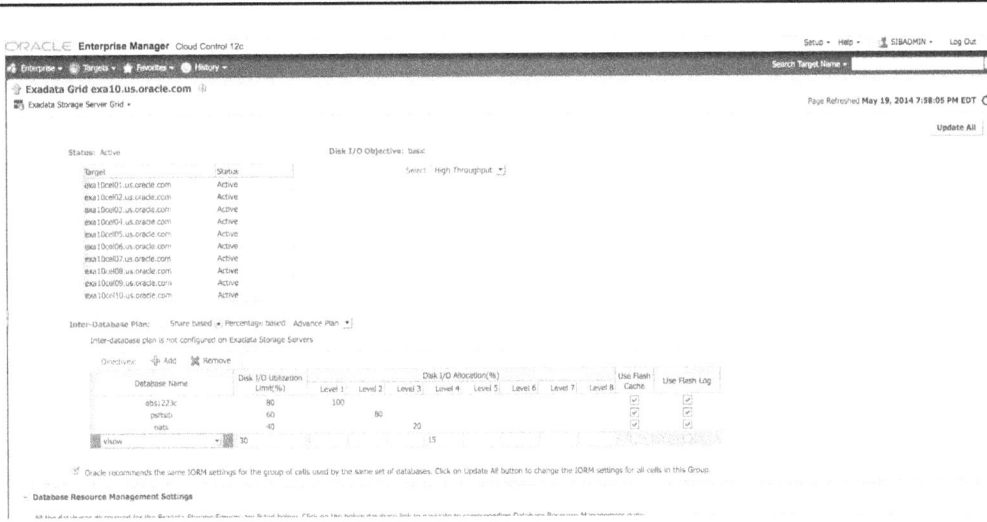

FIGURE 7-18.   *Creating an IORM plan using OEM*

Enabling IORM

As discussed previously, managing I/O from the DBRM requires that you create an
IORM plan; IORM needs to be enabled before DBRM or IORM can take advantage
of the plan. In Exadata Storage Cells beginning with version 11.2.3.2, IORM is
enabled by default. If you are running an older version, you need to take this step.

In versions 11.2.3.2 and later, IORM is enabled by default to guard against
excessively high latencies for small I/Os, using the **basic** objective. User-defined
Resource Manager plans are not enforced in this mode. To enable IORM for user-
defined Resource Manager plans, the objective must be set to **auto** (or any setting
other than **basic**). Use the following CellCLI command to change the objective:

```
CellCLI> ALTER IORMPLAN objective='auto';
```

To disable IORM, use the following CellCLI command to return IORM to the
basic objective. Note that **alter iormplan inactive** is deprecated in versions 11.2.3.2
and later because IORM is minimally always in **basic** mode. Running **alter iormplan
inactive** will result in the error message "IORMPLAN status cannot be set to
inactive."

```
CellCLI> ALTER IORMPLAN objective='basic';
```

On Exadata Storage Cells in versions 11.2.2.2 to 11.2.3.1, IORM is disabled by
default. To enable IORM, use the following CellCLI commands: **alter iormplan active**

which enforces any flash-related directives in the IORM plan, and **alter iormplan objective** enables IORM for disk I/Os and enforces any user-defined resource manager plans.

```
CellCLI>ALTER IORMPLAN active;
CellCLI>ALTER IORMPLAN objective='auto';
```

To disable IORM on Exadata Storage Cells in versions 11.2.2.2 to 11.2.3.1, run this command:

```
CellCLI> ALTER IORMPLAN objective='off';
```

To enable/disable IORM on Exadata Storage Cells in versions before 11.2.2.2, use the following CellCLI command:

```
CellCLI>ALTER IORMPLAN active|inactive;
```

Monitoring IORM

You can monitor the I/O metric from the Exadata Storage Cells from the CellCLI interface. The I/O request is mainly divided into two categories for the metric collection: large I/O requests and small I/O requests. Large I/O requests are greater than 128KB; they are mainly used by large queries, backups, and disk rebuilds, and they are throughput-sensitive workloads. Smaller I/O requests are less than or equal to 128KB; they are mainly used by OLTP workloads and are latency-sensitive workloads.

Use the following metrics to find the rate of I/Os that each database or consumer group is issuing:

- **db_io_rq_lg_sec**   Number of large I/O requests issued by a database per second

- **db_io_rq_sm_sec**   Number of small I/O requests issued by a database per second

- **cg_io_rq_lg_sec**   Number of large I/O requests issued by a consumer group per second

- **cg_io_rq_sm_sec**   Number of small I/O requests issued by a consumer group per second

Use the following metrics to determine how much each consumer group or database was throttled by IORM:

- **db_io_wt_lg_rq**   Average IORM wait time per large I/O request issued by a database

- **db_io_wt_sm_rq**   Average IORM wait time per small I/O request issued by a database

- **cg_io_wt_lg_rq**   Average IORM wait time per large I/O request issued by a consumer group

- **cg_io_wt_sm_rq**   Average IORM wait time per small I/O request issued by a consumer group

Use the following metrics to find the average disk latency:

- **cd_io_tm_r_sm_rq**   Average latency of reading small blocks per request to a cell disk

- **cd_io_tm_w_sm_rq**   Average latency of writing small blocks per request to a cell disk

An example of disk latency of reading small blocks is shown here:

```
CellCLI> list metriccurrent where name ='CD_IO_TM_R_SM_RQ';
         CD_IO_TM_R_SM_RQ     CD_00_exa10cel01      189 us/request
         CD_IO_TM_R_SM_RQ     CD_01_exa10cel01      0.0 us/request
         CD_IO_TM_R_SM_RQ     CD_02_exa10cel01      0.0 us/request
         CD_IO_TM_R_SM_RQ     CD_03_exa10cel01      0.0 us/request
         CD_IO_TM_R_SM_RQ     CD_04_exa10cel01      0.0 us/request
         CD_IO_TM_R_SM_RQ     CD_05_exa10cel01      0.0 us/request
         CD_IO_TM_R_SM_RQ     CD_06_exa10cel01      0.0 us/request
         CD_IO_TM_R_SM_RQ     CD_07_exa10cel01      0.0 us/request
         CD_IO_TM_R_SM_RQ     CD_08_exa10cel01      0.0 us/request
         CD_IO_TM_R_SM_RQ     CD_09_exa10cel01      0.0 us/request
         CD_IO_TM_R_SM_RQ     CD_10_exa10cel01      0.0 us/request
         CD_IO_TM_R_SM_RQ     CD_11_exa10cel01      0.0 us/request
         CD_IO_TM_R_SM_RQ     FD_00_exa10cel01      171 us/request
         CD_IO_TM_R_SM_RQ     FD_01_exa10cel01      133 us/request
         CD_IO_TM_R_SM_RQ     FD_02_exa10cel01      124 us/request
         CD_IO_TM_R_SM_RQ     FD_03_exa10cel01      100 us/request
         CD_IO_TM_R_SM_RQ     FD_04_exa10cel01      130 us/request
         CD_IO_TM_R_SM_RQ     FD_05_exa10cel01      131 us/request
         CD_IO_TM_R_SM_RQ     FD_06_exa10cel01      0.0 us/request
         CD_IO_TM_R_SM_RQ     FD_07_exa10cel01      134 us/request
         CD_IO_TM_R_SM_RQ     FD_08_exa10cel01      152 us/request
         CD_IO_TM_R_SM_RQ     FD_09_exa10cel01      131 us/request
         CD_IO_TM_R_SM_RQ     FD_10_exa10cel01      129 us/request
         CD_IO_TM_R_SM_RQ     FD_11_exa10cel01      136 us/request
         CD_IO_TM_R_SM_RQ     FD_12_exa10cel01      140 us/request
         CD_IO_TM_R_SM_RQ     FD_13_exa10cel01      129 us/request
         CD_IO_TM_R_SM_RQ     FD_14_exa10cel01      145 us/request
         CD_IO_TM_R_SM_RQ     FD_15_exa10cel01      138 us/request
```

Other Considerations/Recommendations for Consolidation

There are some additional considerations that need to be factored in when planning for consolidation. They include ORACLE_HOME, ASM Diskgroups, Users, and Memory. These are discussed in detail in the following sections.

ORACLE_HOME

When you consolidate multiple application databases in an Exadata Machine, each database should run independently without impacting the others. By default, only one ORACLE_HOME is installed. If the ORACLE_HOME is shared across many applications, patching or any other activities in the ORACLE_HOME will impact all the applications. Therefore, when you're consolidating multiple applications, each application should have its own ORACLE_HOME to minimize the impact and downtime. With 11g, you can have 50 to 60 active instances per node. That is probably more ORACLE_HOMEs than you want to have. Make sure you double-check the amount of space available, considering that you need to leave room for log files, dump files, and so on. Clone the ORACLE_HOME for each application. The steps for cloning the ORACLE_HOME are shown next.

> **NOTE**
> *The default location of the ORACLE_HOME is /u01/app/oracle/product/11.2.0/dbhome_1.*

To clone the ORACLE_HOME directories, use the **tar** command and run the clone locally on each node in the cluster via the **dcli** command. Run these commands as the Oracle user.

Copy the database home to its new location:

```
(oracle)$ export ORACLE_HOME=/u01/app/oracle/product/11.2.0/dbhome_2
(oracle)$ dcli -g ~/dbs_group -l oracle mkdir -p $ORACLE_HOME
(oracle)$ dcli -g ~/dbs_group -l oracle "cd /u01/app/oracle/
product/11.2.0/dbhome_1; \
tar cf - . | ( cd $ORACLE_HOME ; tar xf - )"
```

Once the binaries are copied to the new destination on each node, the clone.pl script will perform the necessary steps to update files in the ORACLE_HOME directory. Run the **clone.pl** command as the software owner on each cluster node in parallel. Run **clone.pl** for the RDBMS ORACLE_HOME. Run the **runInstaller -updateNodeList** command manually on each node to avoid locking conflicts.

```
(oracle)$ export ORACLE_HOME=/u01/app/oracle/product/11.2.0/dbhome_2
(oracle)$ dcli -g ~/dbs_group -l oracle "cd $ORACLE_HOME/clone/bin; \
```

```
./clone.pl ORACLE_HOME=$ORACLE_HOME \
ORACLE_HOME_NAME=OraDB_home2 ORACLE_BASE=/u01/app/oracle"
(oracle)$ $ORACLE_HOME/oui/bin/runInstaller \
-updateNodeList ORACLE_HOME=$ORACLE_HOME "CLUSTER_
NODES={exa10db01,exa10db02}"
```

As the software owner, relink the Oracle binary to use RDS. The cloning step causes the Oracle binary to be relinked with UDP instead of RDS:

```
(oracle)$ export ORACLE_HOME=/u01/app/oracle/product/11.2.0/dbhome_2
(oracle)$ dcli -g ~/dbs_group -l oracle "cd $ORACLE_HOME/rdbms/lib; \
ORACLE_HOME=$ORACLE_HOME make -f ins_rdbms.mk ipc_rds ioracle"
```

Run the root.sh steps for each of the cloned ORACLE_HOME directories as the root user on each node:

```
(root)# export ORACLE_HOME=/u01/app/oracle/product/11.2.0/dbhome_2
(root)# dcli -g ~/dbs_group -l root $ORACLE_HOME/root.sh
```

After you've finished cloning, verify that all nodes have the same version of OPatch. If the versions do not match, you may need to update OPatch on the nodes running older versions so that all nodes have the same version:

```
(oracle)$ export ORACLE_HOME=/u01/app/oracle/product/11.2.0/dbhome_2
(oracle)$ dcli -g ~/dbs_group -l oracle "$ORACLE_HOME/OPatch/opatch
version"
```

On all nodes, verify that "RAC system comprising of multiple nodes" is shown from the lsinventory by running the following commands as the Oracle user before running this step:

```
(oracle)$ export ORACLE_HOME=/u01/app/oracle/product/11.2.0/dbhome_2
(oracle)$ dcli -g ~/dbs_group -l oracle "$ORACLE_HOME/OPatch/opatch \
lsinventory -oh $ORACLE_HOME | grep node"
```

Now apply all patches to the new RDBMS ORACLE_HOME directory according to the patch README. Be sure to set the proper ORACLE_HOME environment variables (/u01/app/oracle/product/11.2.0/dbhome_2) to apply the patches to the proper ORACLE_HOME.

ASM Disk Groups

By default, in a Exadata Machine, two disk groups are created: one for the Data Area (+DATA) and other for the Fast Recovery Area (+RECO). Figure 7-19 shows the default ASM disk groups in Exadata. All the databases running in the Exadata Machine use these two ASM disk groups. This approach has several advantages: it's simple and easy to manage, it's a balanced configuration where applications have

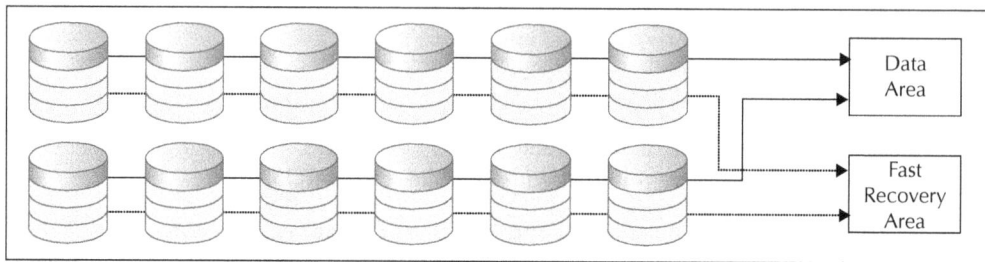

FIGURE 7-19. *Default ASM disk groups in Exadata*

full access to I/O bandwidth and storage, it provides tolerances for failures and rolling upgrades, and the free space available in the Exadata Machine can be allocated to any databases running in the machine.

In your security standard, for example, if you are required to match the Department of Defense (DOD) configuration, which needs a separate disk group for each application, you can create two separate disk groups for each application. If you have databases in e-Business Suite, PeopleSoft, and JD Edwards running, you would need to create two disk groups for e-Business Suite (+EBSDATA and +EBSRECO), two disk groups for PeopleSoft (+PSFTDATA and +PSFTRECO), and two disk groups for JD Edwards (+JDEDATA and +JDERECO). This approach creates more management tasks, restricts the application I/O bandwidth only to the disk group it uses, and sometimes means that a rolling upgrade may not be possible. Unless your security standard mandates such a requirement, you should go with the first option, which is having +DATA and +RECO disk group.

Users

For each application database running on an Exadata Machine, either one Oracle account (user) can own all the databases or you can create a separate user for each application database. The choice between one user or multiuser is mainly driven by compliance and policies.

Memory

HugePages should equal the sum of the shared memory segments used by all the database instances. When all the database instances are running, the amount of shared memory being used can be calculated by analyzing the output from the **ipcs -m** command. MOS note 401749.1 provides a script you can use to determine the amount of shared memory in use. Make sure you set the initialization parameter to use_large_pages=only to keep the SGA from residing outside the HugePages space.

When consolidating production environments into Exadata, the memory used by all the databases should not exceed 75 percent of the physical memory of the machine. For nonproduction environments, it can go up to 85 percent. Memory swapping should be avoided at all times.

Thus, for production consolidation to Exadata, use the following:

```
SUM of databases (SGA_TARGET + PGA_AGGREGATE_TARGET) + 4 MB * (Maximum
PROCESSES) <  75% of Physical Memory per Database Node
```

And for nonproduction environments, use the following:

```
SUM of databases (SGA_TARGET + PGA_AGGREGATE_TARGET) + 4 MB * (Maximum
PROCESSES) <  85% of Physical Memory per Database Node
```

Memory per process varies, but a 4MB allocation has been observed in Oracle's internal application benchmark on Exadata. You can readjust this value in your calculations after monitoring actual process memory utilization.

Set the number of shared memory segments (kernel.shmmni) greater than the number of databases. The number of shared memory identifiers should be set greater than the number of database instances running on the node. Check the setting for kernel.shmmni using the **sysctl** command (for example, **/sbin/sysctl -a | grep shmmni**). If necessary, you can make adjustments by setting kernel.shmmni in /etc/sysctl.conf on Linux systems. The SHMMNI default setting (4096) should accommodate all cases.

Set the maximum shared memory segment size (kernel.shmmax) to 85 percent of physical memory size, which is the default. The maximum shared memory segment size should be set to 85 percent of the database server physical memory size. Check the setting for kernel.shmmax using the **sysctl** command. If necessary, you can make adjustments by setting kernel.SHMMAX in /etc/sysctl.conf on Linux systems.

Set the maximum total number of system semaphores (SEMMNS) greater than the sum of all database processes. The maximum number of semaphores in the system must be greater than the sum of the processes, as specified by the database PROCESSES parameter, for all of the database instances running on the system. Check the setting for kernel.sem using the **sysctl** command. The setting for kernel .sem contains a list of four numeric values. The setting for the total number of semaphores on the system, also known as SEMMNS, is the second value in the list. If necessary, you can make adjustments by setting kernel.sem in /etc/sysctl.conf. The SEMMNS default setting (60000) should accommodate all cases.

Set the maximum number of semaphores in a semaphore set (SEMMSL) greater than the largest number of processes in any single database. The maximum number of semaphores in a semaphore set should be greater than the largest number of processes for any single database instance running on the database server. Check the setting for kernel.sem using the **sysctl** command. The setting for the maximum number of semaphores in a semaphore set, also known as SEMMSL, is the first value in the list. If necessary, you can make adjustments by setting kernel.sem in /etc/sysctl.conf on Linux systems.

Summary

Consolidation provides several advantages, and Exadata is an ideal choice for consolidating database applications. The computing requirements of all the databases to be consolidated in Exadata should never exceed the capacity of the machine. Use the Consolidation Planner in OEM12c to plan for consolidation.

Instance caging enables you to manage the CPU across multiple databases, DBRM enables you to manage resources with a database, and IORM enables you to manage I/Os, Exadata Smart Flash Cache, and Exadata Smart Flash Logging across multiple databases. Make sure you monitor resources—CPU, memory, and I/O—on a regular basis to find any anomalies.

CHAPTER

8

Monitoring Exadata

As with any other system, you need to monitor Exadata to ensure that the system is running optimally, that no hardware failures have occurred, and that the SLAs are being met. By proactively monitoring the system, you ensure that potential problems can be fixed before they become serious problems. When mission-critical applications are deployed in Exadata, good monitoring can significantly reduce the time you spend determining the root cause of performance or availability issues.

At the same time, it's equally important that you know what needs to be monitored. Not every situation needs to be monitored. You don't want your inbox to be cluttered with every possible alert, because this could result in your overlooking the more important alerts.

In this chapter we will cover the important metrics you need to monitor to achieve uninterrupted service. You can set up monitoring using custom scripts or using Oracle Enterprise Manager (OEM). Custom scripts can also be integrated with OEM. It is strongly recommended, however, that you use OEM as a single console for monitoring all the components in an Exadata Machine.

Monitoring Using Enterprise Manager

OEM enables you to monitor all the components of the Exadata Machine, including the following:

- Compute nodes

- Storage cells

- InfiniBand switches

- Integrated Lights Out Manager (ILOM)

- Keyboard video monitor (KVM)

- Power distribution unit (PDU)

- Cisco switch

And, of course, you can also use OEM to monitor all the databases running on your Exadata Machines. As soon as OEM discovers Exadata, you can navigate to the machine by choosing Targets | Exadata from the OEM Cloud Control (OEMCC) main page, as shown in Figure 8-1.

The next page shows the machines registered with OEM. If you have more than one Exadata Machine, all will be listed in this page. In Figure 8-2, you can see that only one Exadata Machine is integrated with OEM, DB Machine exa10.us.oracle.com.

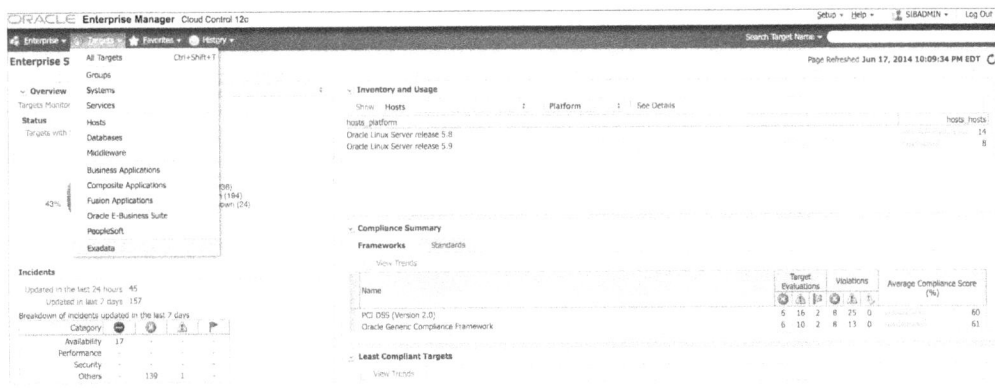

FIGURE 8-1. *Navigating to the Exadata Machine*

After you select an Exadata Machine, a schematic view of the machine is shown, which depicts the actual layout of the compute nodes and the storage cells as per the actual Exadata Machine. As you can see in Figure 8-3, the schema shows you live data of the machine at that point in time.

In Figure 8-3, the schematic view shows an overview of the machine. The status of each component is shown. A green up arrow key tells you that the component is up and running; a red down arrow indicates that the component is down. In Figure 8-3, all eight compute nodes, fourteen storage cells, three IB switches, one Cisco switch, two PDUs, and the keyboard video monitor (KVM) are up and running.

The green dot to the right of the component (compute node, storage cells, IB switches) in the schematic view shows that the particular component is up and running. Next to the green dot is the temperature of each component. If you hover the cursor over the name of the compute node or storage cell, CPU and memory utilization of that particular node are shown in a pop-up—in the figure, you can see

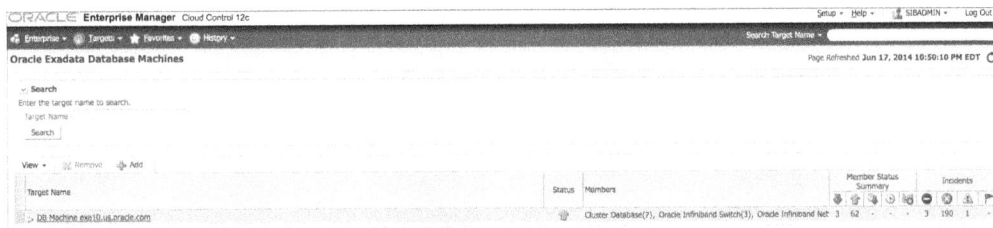

FIGURE 8-2. *Exadata Machine exa10.us.oracle.com*

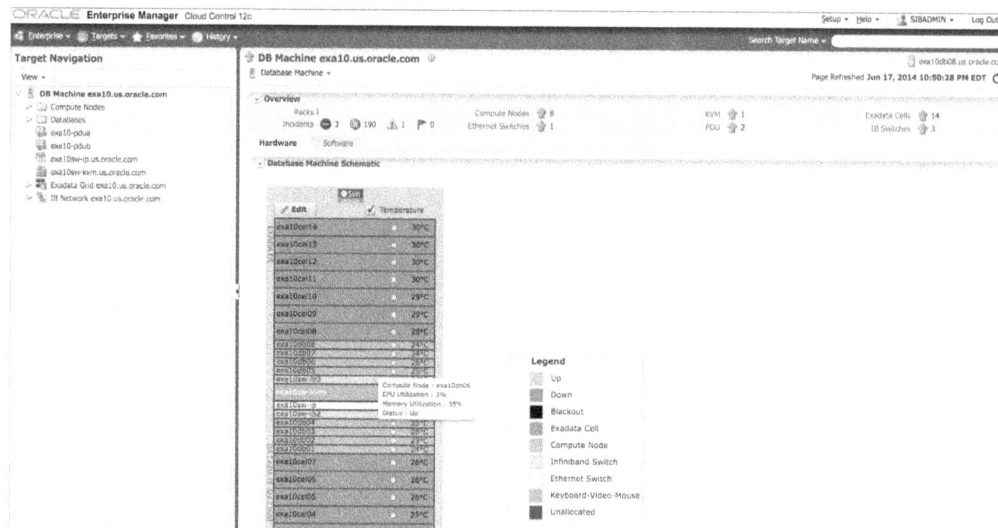

FIGURE 8-3. *Schematic view of an Exadata Machine*

that for DB node 6, the CPU utilization is 3 percent and memory utilization is 35 percent. The schematic view gives you a glimpse of CPU and memory utilization across all the nodes, without your needing to log in to any of the nodes to help you quickly determine whether anything is wrong in any of these nodes.

In the left side of the page, all the components of the machine are shown. Click to expand a node and move to an individual component from there.

In the next sections we'll use OEM to monitor the components.

Monitoring Compute Nodes

Expand the Compute Nodes folder to see all the compute nodes and the corresponding ILOM associated with each node, as shown in Figure 8-4.

Let's select one of the compute nodes and monitor all the metrics.

Click exa10db01.us.oracle.com. To the right, you'll see a summary of the compute node and metrics related to CPU, memory, file system, and network utilization, as shown in Figure 8-5. In the figure, you can see that the CPU is barely utilized in the machine, memory utilization ranges between 10 and 30 percent, and so on.

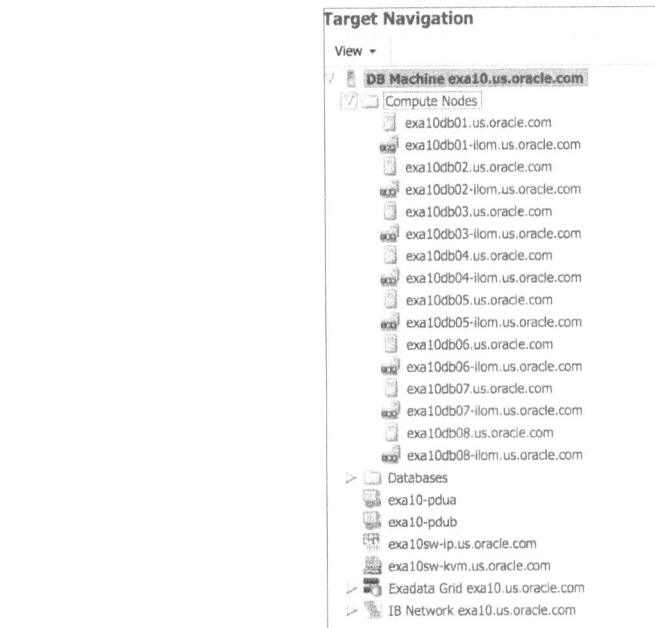

FIGURE 8-4. *Expanded DB compute nodes*

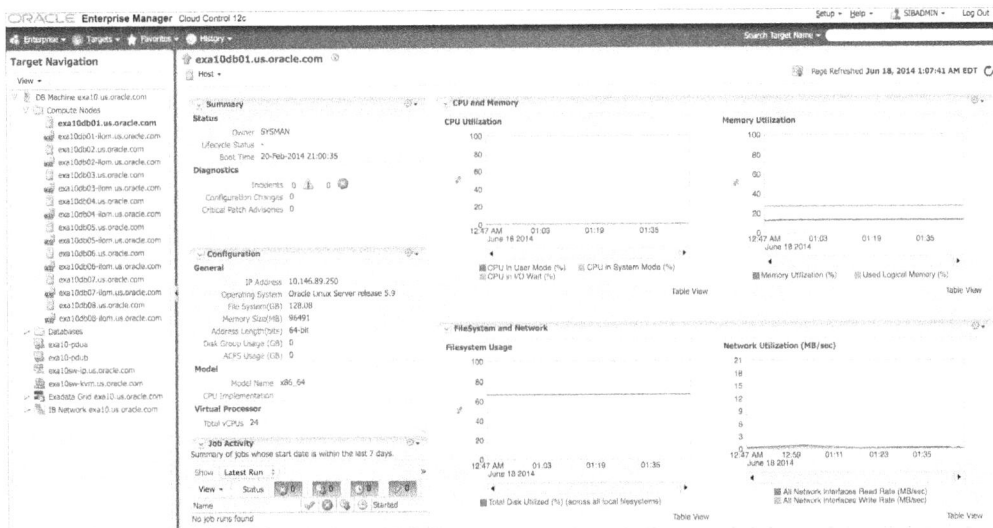

FIGURE 8-5. *Metrics related to the DB compute node*

Figure 8-6 shows the usage a bit later after we have clicked Table View under Memory Utilization. The table view shows the average memory utilization in the past month.

If you want to see more information about any metric, choose Host | Monitoring, and then choose the metric name from the list, as shown in Figure 8-7.

Let's look at the CPU for detailed monitoring; choose Host | Monitoring | CPU Details. Figure 8-8 shows the details of the various metrics related to the CPU, including CPU utilization, CPU I/O wait, CPU load, and top 10 processes ordered by the CPU.

Click CPU Utilization, CPU I/O Wait, or CPU Load below the respective graph to see detailed information about that metric. (Notice that in Figure 8-8, the navigation pane is not visible because we hid it by clicking the middle of the pane to get a full-page view.)

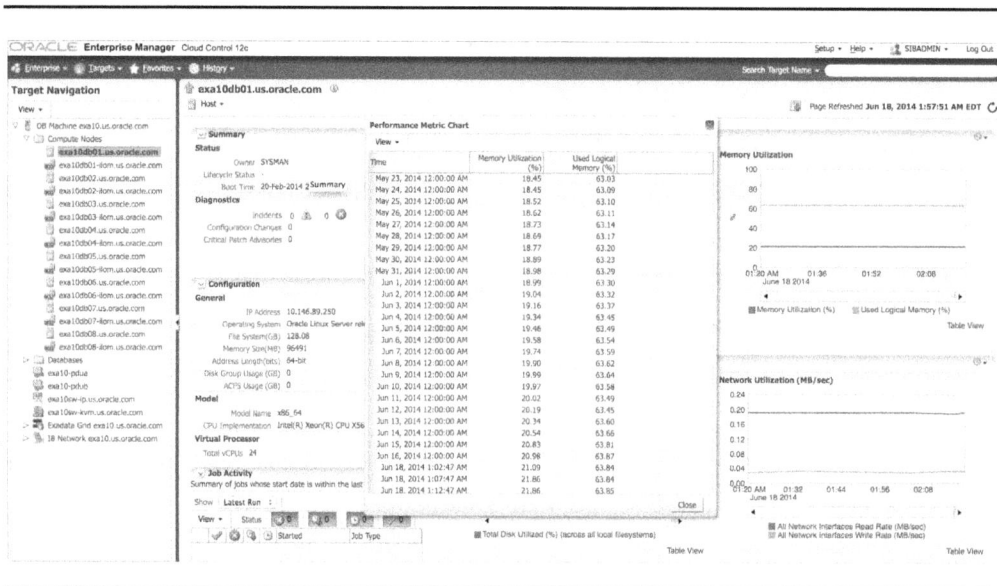

FIGURE 8-6. *Historical view of memory utilization*

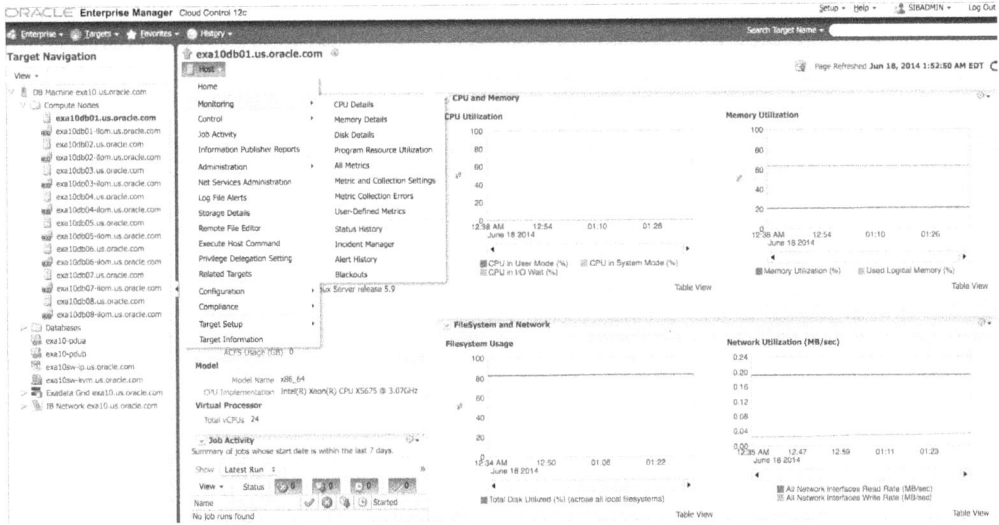

FIGURE 8-7. *Selecting the metric for monitoring*

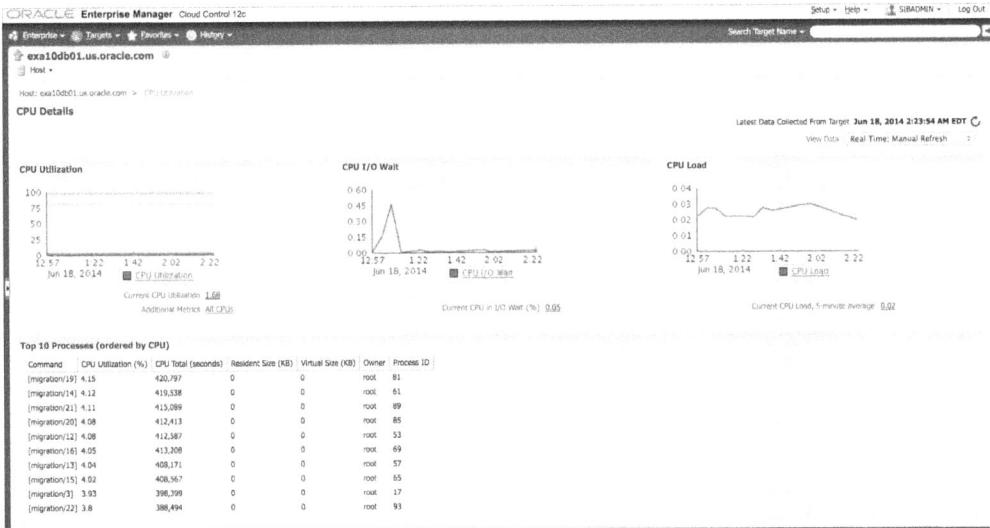

FIGURE 8-8. *Detailed CPU metrics*

To see more information about memory utilization on the compute node, choose Host | Monitoring | Memory Details. The Memory Details page is shown in Figure 8-9. This page shows the detailed view of the memory utilization, swap utilization, memory page scan, and top 10 processes ordered by memory. It also shows the commands that are consuming the highest memory. Click the metric name (Memory Scan Rate, Memory Utilization %, Swap Utilization, Paging Details, and so on) below the graph to open a new page with detailed information.

NOTE
Linux is essentially "lazy" in how it frees memory. It's common to see all memory being "used" in the page view, even though quite a bit is "freeable." This appears differently in different tools and is completely normal.

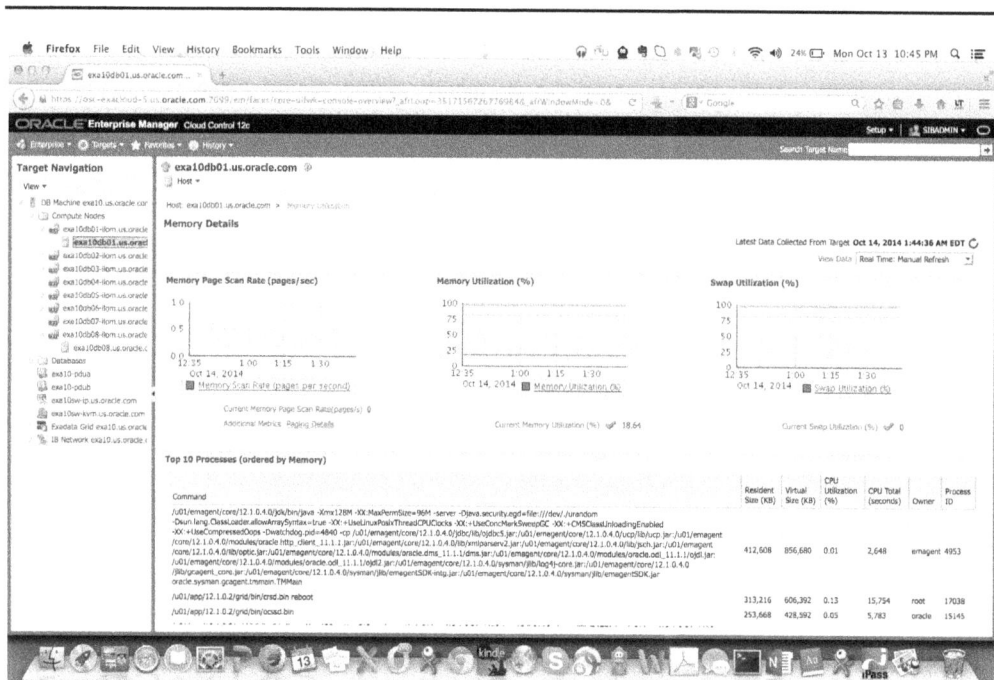

FIGURE 8-9. *Memory Details page*

Similarly, you can see the metrics related to disk utilization by choosing Host |
Monitoring | Disk Details. Figure 8-10 shows the metrics related to disks, including
Disk I/Os. OEM shows metrics related to each disk plus the total and average of
the Disk I/Os.

NOTE
*Figure 8-10 shows details of the local disks that are
compute nodes that host the ORACLE_HOME, root
file system, and u01 file system. Do not confuse
these disks with the disks that are inside the
storage cells.*

As with any Linux/UNIX system, you need to be careful about filling the disk to
100 percent, especially in the root partition. This situation can be quite difficult to
fix, and this is why the u01 file system is kept separate (it's more likely to become
full than any other disk on the system).

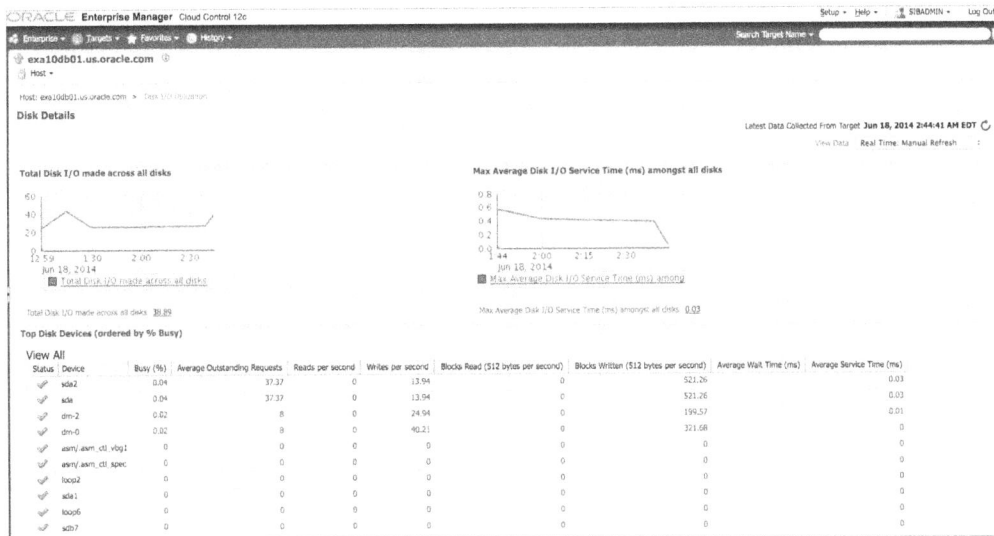

FIGURE 8-10. *Disk Details*

You can also monitor other metrics in the compute node of the database by choosing Host | Monitoring and then choosing the metric name, as was shown in Figure 8-7. If you choose All Metrics, you'll see all the available metrics that exist in a compute node, as shown in Figure 8-11. Click the metric in the left pane to see detailed information about that metric.

In addition to the metrics discussed so far, you can view the following metrics by choosing Host | Monitoring:

- **Metric and Collection Settings** Shows the time for which the metric is captured. You can also change the metric collection time here.

- **Metric Collection Errors** Shows all the errors related to metric collection.

- **User-Defined Metrics** Create custom metrics and integrate your own scripts to collect the custom metrics.

- **Status History** Shows the overall status history of the storage cell when it was up, when it was down, and if there was any blackout.

FIGURE 8-11. *All metrics in a compute node*

- **Incident Manager** Shows all the incidents that are open, assigned, unassigned, open problems, and so on.

- **Alert History** Shows all the alerts that were raised for the storage cells.

- **Blackouts** Create and view blackout windows.

Monitoring ILOM

As shown back in Figure 8-4, the link for the ILOM for a particular DB node is located immediately below the database compute node. Click the ILOM for a particular compute node to see the ILOM Summary page, shown in Figure 8-12. You can see an overview of the ILOM, including its status, any incidents, and a link to log in to the actual ILOM Web Interface at the bottom of the page.

To see more detail on ILOM metrics, choose ILOM | Monitoring | All Metrics, as shown in Figure 8-13.

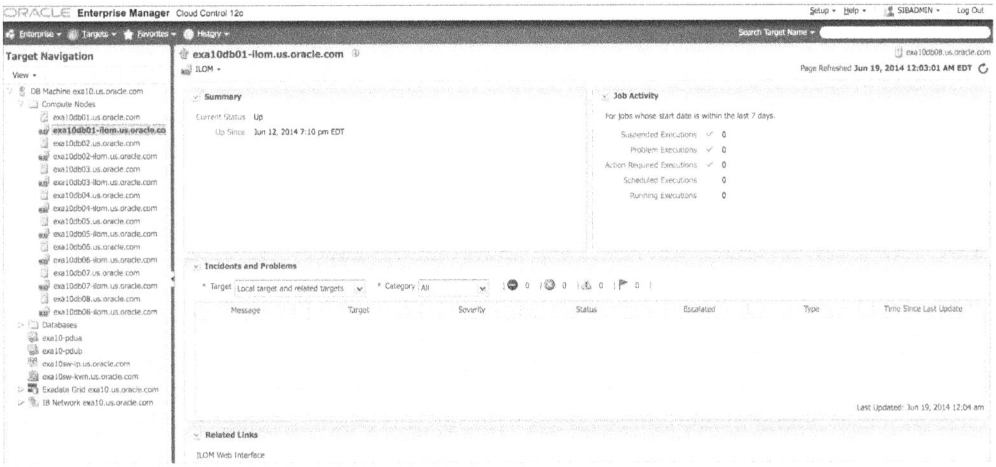

FIGURE 8-12. *Summary page of ILOM*

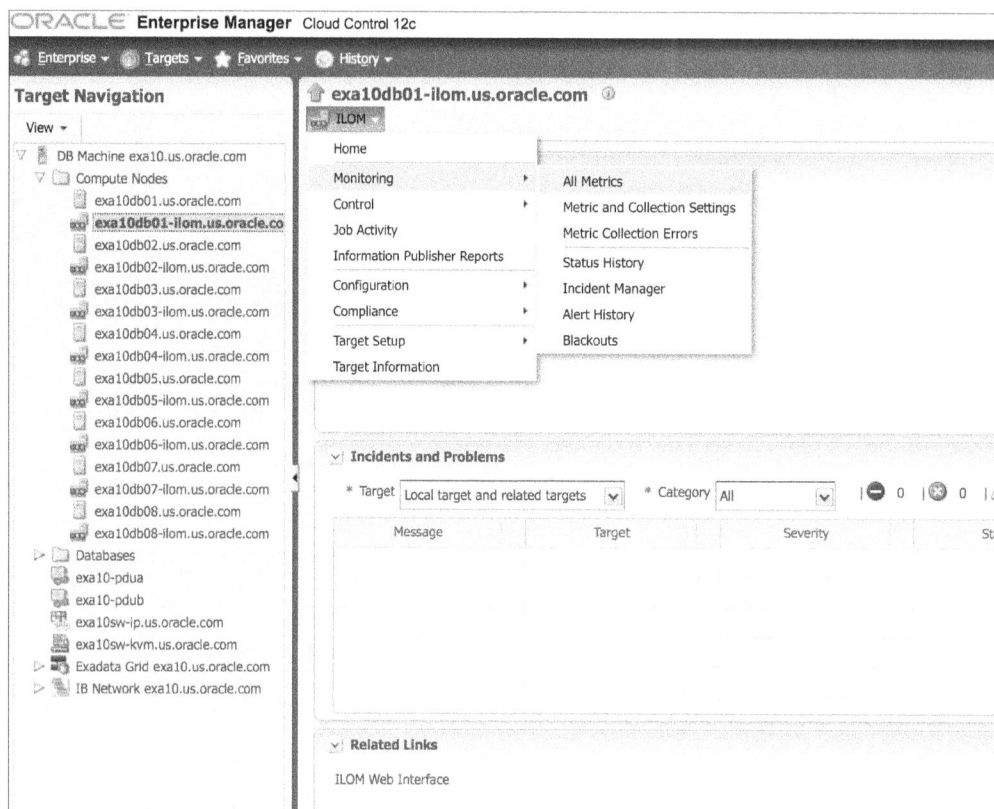

FIGURE 8-13. *Going to the All Metrics page*

Figure 8-14 shows all the metrics that can be queried for an ILOM.

ILOM need not be monitored as aggressively as you would monitor a DB node, but you can set up custom alerts from OEM that will tell you if ILOM goes down.

Monitoring Storage Cells

You can monitor the storage cells by expanding the Exadata Grid in the left side of the main navigation pane, as shown in Figure 8-15.

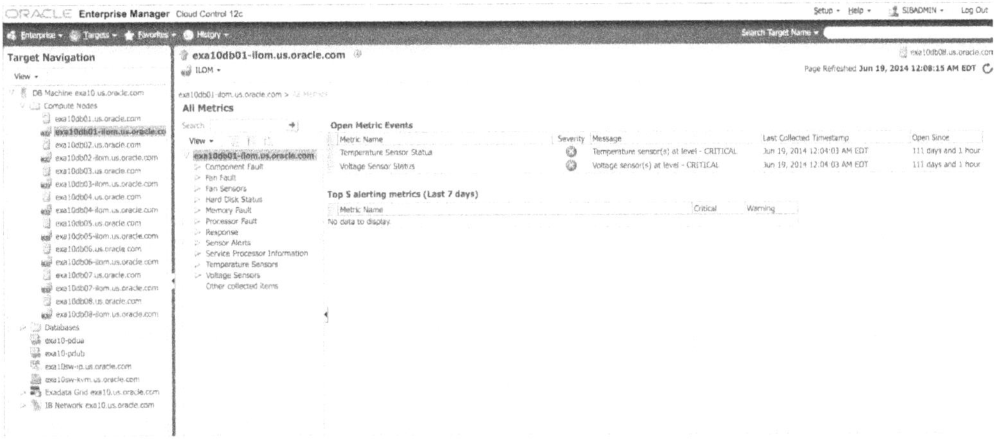

FIGURE 8-14. *All metrics for an ILOM*

FIGURE 8-15. *Navigation for storage cells*

Select a storage cell you want to monitor to see the Summary page for that cell, as shown in Figure 8-16. This page provides an overview of the I/O for both the physical disk and flash disk, the I/O response time for both read and write for flash and disk, CPU utilization, network utilization, ASM disk group space usage, workload distribution across databases, and any open incidents.

To see detailed metrics related to storage cells, choose Exadata Storage Server | Monitoring | All Metrics. You'll see all the metrics related to the cell disk, flash disk, Flash Cache, I/O operations per second (IOPS), response time, and so on, as shown in Figure 8-17.

Some of the important things that need to be watched are the metrics related to the Flash Cache usage, response time, disk latency and physical disks, I/O load, read and write throughput, capacity, alerts, cell load, and Host Channel Adapter (HCA) port state and alerts. If you have enabled IORM, you can monitor it from this page.

The metrics for all the alerts are collected at either 15 minutes or 5 minutes. You can customize this as per your system's requirement by choosing Exadata Storage Server | Monitoring | Metric And Collection Settings, as shown in Figure 8-18.

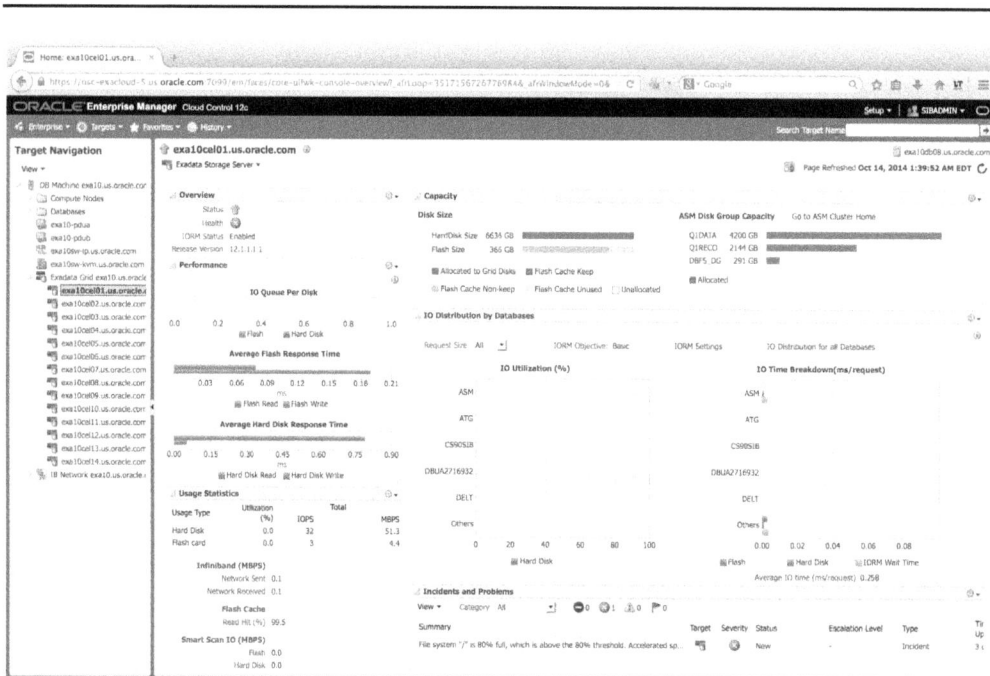

FIGURE 8-16. *The Summary page for the storage server*

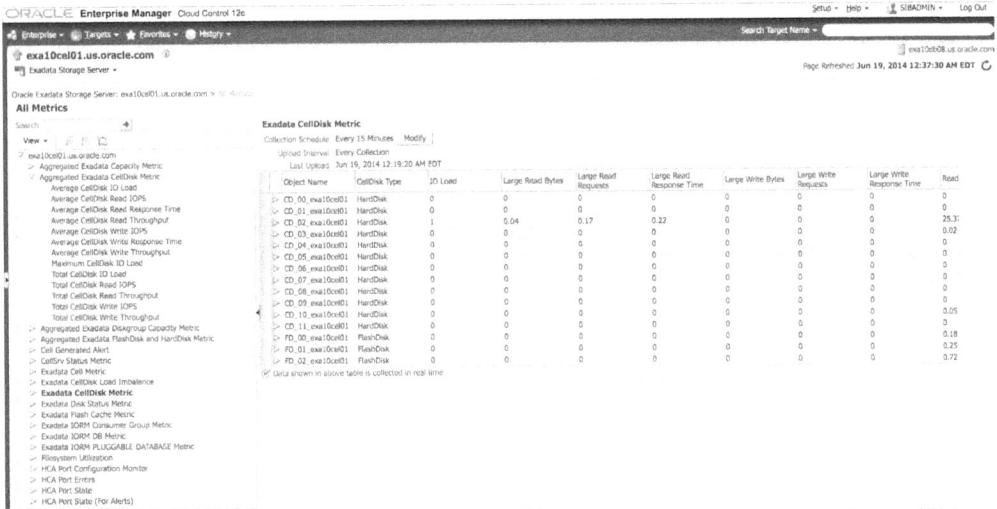

FIGURE 8-17. *Detailed metrics for the storage cell*

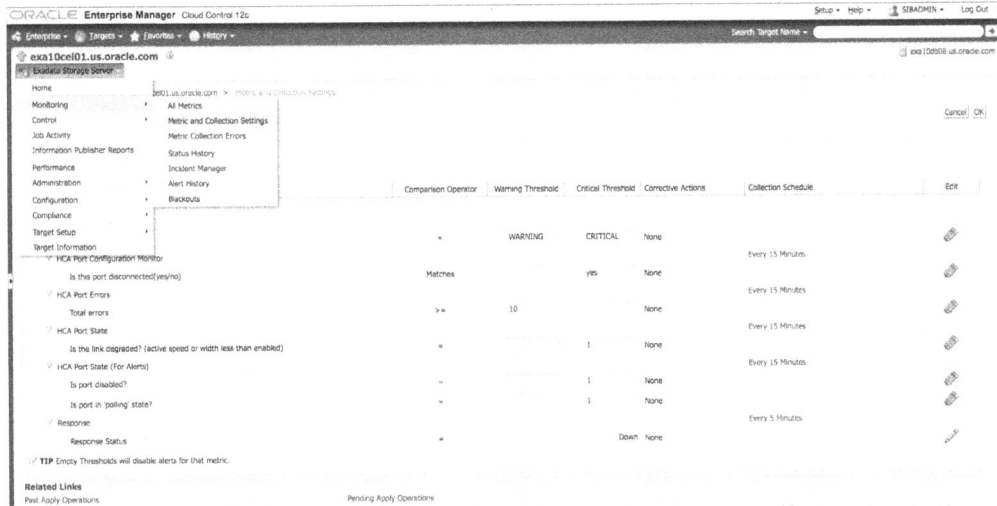

FIGURE 8-18. *Editing the metric and collection settings*

In Figure 8-18, you can see a few other metrics available for monitoring:

- **Metric Collection Errors**   Shows where all the errors related to metric collection can be obtained.

- **Status History**   Shows the overall status history of the storage cell when it was up, when it was down, and if there was any blackout.

- **Incident Manager**   Opens the main page of the Incident Manager, which shows all the incidents that are open, assigned, and unassigned; open problems; and other information.

- **Alert History**   Shows all the alerts raised for the storage cells.

- **Blackouts**   Create and view blackout windows.

Monitoring InfiniBand

To open the monitoring overview for the InfiniBand network, shown in Figure 8-19, click the IB Network listing in the left navigation pane. The overview page shows the aggregate view for all the InfiniBand switches in your Exadata Machine, including network usage, status of each switch, issues with any of the ports (errors are shown in red), information on the DB nodes, and information on storage cells with the mapping of InfiniBand switches.

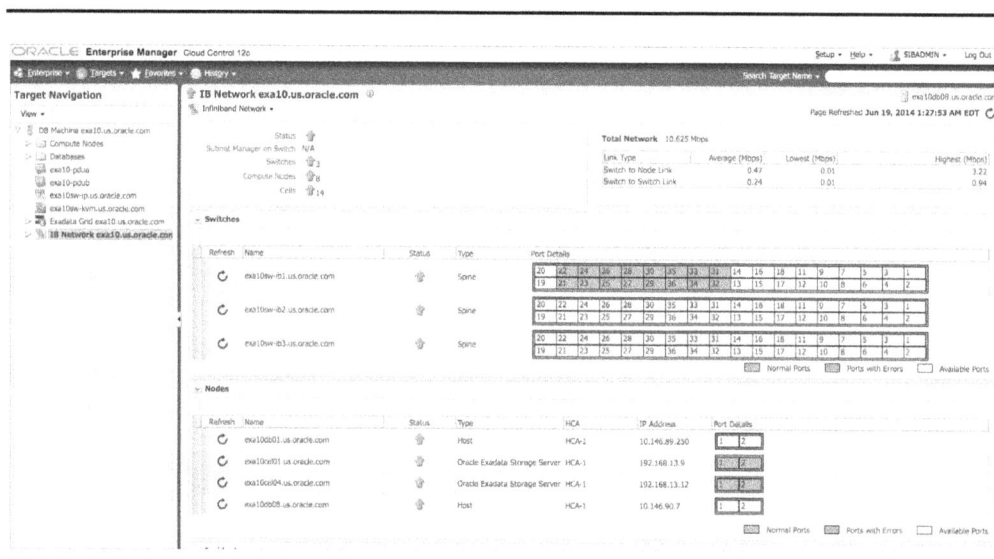

FIGURE 8-19.   *Monitoring overview page of IB switch*

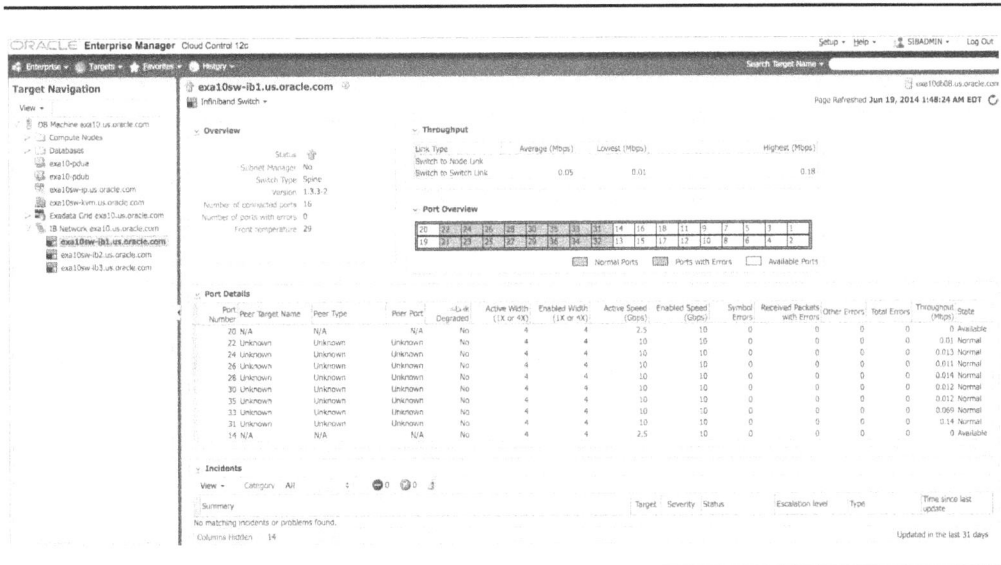

FIGURE 8-20. *Overview page for selected IB switch*

To get more information on a particular switch, expand the IB network listing in the left panel and click the IB switch. The overview page for that particular switch shows the status of the switch, the type of switch (leaf or spine), throughput, detailed information about data transfer for each port in use, and any open incidents, as shown in Figure 8-20.

Similar to compute nodes and storage cells, choose InfiniBand Switch | Monitoring to see all the metrics related to the InfiniBand switch. You can also edit the metric collection settings; view the status history, Incident Manager, and alert history; and create a blackout window.

Monitoring the Cisco Ethernet Switch, KVM, and PDUs

To see the overview page for the Cisco switch, KVM, and PDUs, select the appropriate tab in the left navigation pane. The overview page for the Cisco switch shows the status or any problems with the Cisco switch. Similarly, the KVM and PDUs overview page shows issues with the PDUs or KVM. Click the link at the bottom of the page to launch the KVM and PDU management console.

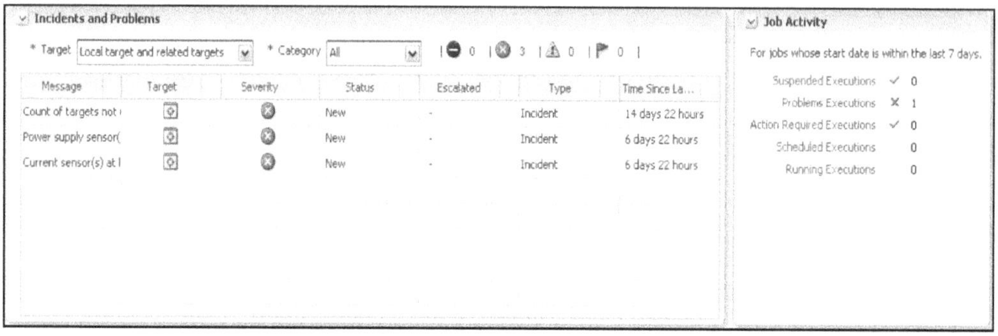

FIGURE 8-21. *Sample Incidents and Problems page*

The following metrics are measured:

- **PDU**   Power supply failure, fan failure, temperature out of range

- **Cisco Switch**   Configuration change tracking and reporting, unauthorized SNMP access

- **KVM**   Server connected to KVM added or removed, or powered on or off

A sample Incidents and Problems page is shown in Figure 8-21.

Monitoring the Databases

You can monitor the databases running on an Exadata Machine using the OEM exactly as you would to monitor hardware. All the OEM features for monitoring the database are available in Exadata. To open the main monitoring page for the databases, select the database name in the left navigation pane, as shown in Figure 8-22. Expanding the database will show the number of RAC instances running for that particular database.

Selecting the database takes you to the main monitoring page of the database. If you are using OEM, you should be familiar with the monitoring page shown in Figure 8-23.

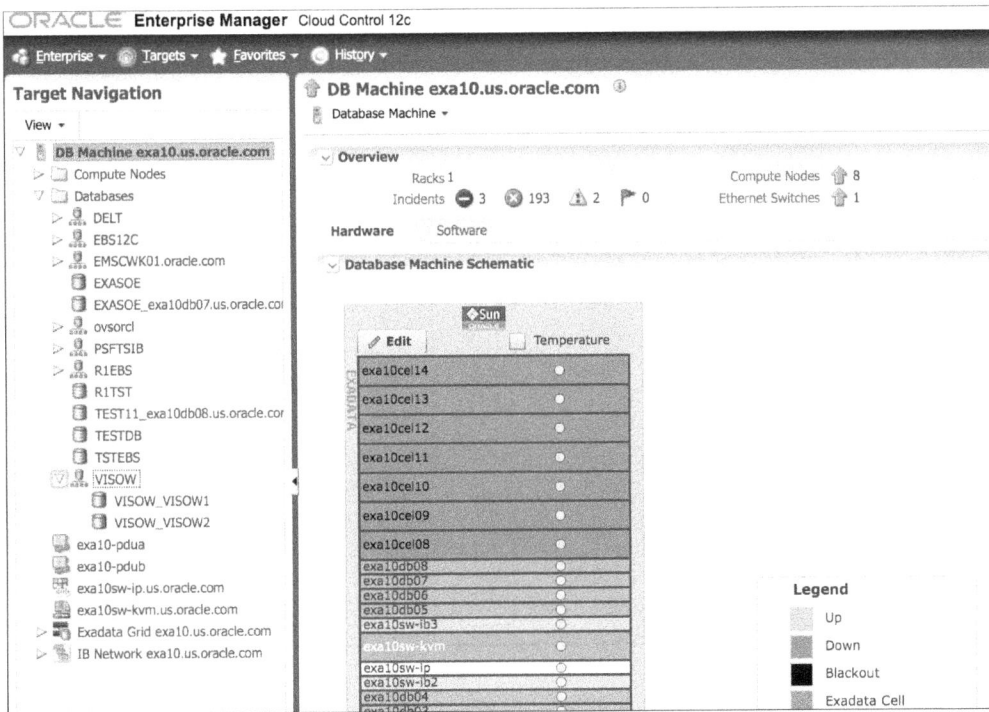

FIGURE 8-22. *Selecting the database for monitoring*

As you can see in Figure 8-23, this page shows all the database-related metrics—CPU and memory usage, active sessions, SQLs currently running, and so on. To get more details, choose Performance | Performance Home. When you are prompted, log in using your DBA credentials. The OEM Performance Home page is the one-stop page for monitoring all DBA-related activities in the database. You'll see metrics such as top sessions, top running SQLs, blocking sessions, instance activity, I/O statistics, CPU and memory-related statistics, and many other related metrics. Discussing this page in detail is beyond the scope of this book.

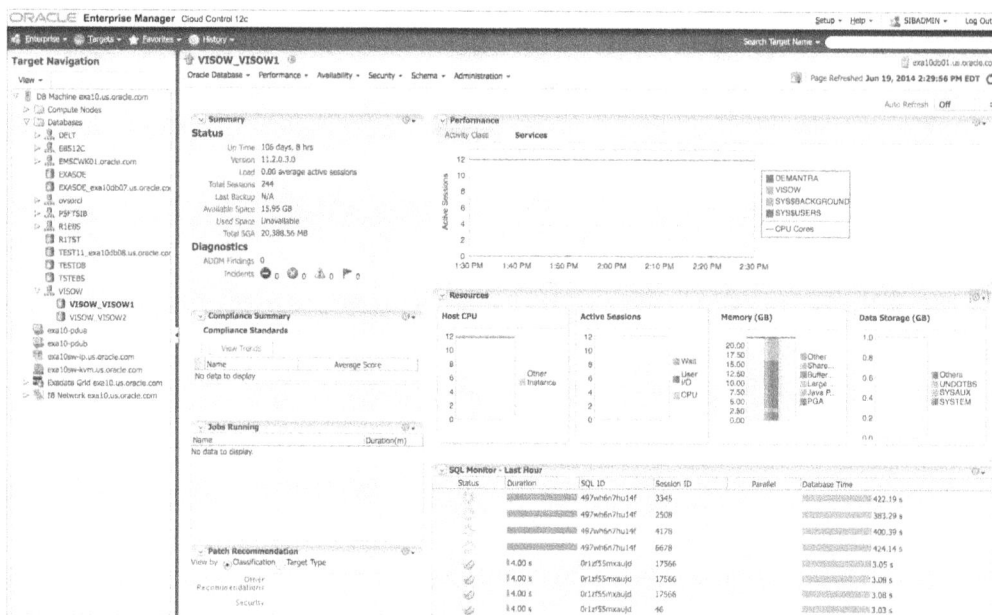

FIGURE 8-23. *Monitoring page for the database*

From the performance page, the DBA can look at the color of the Exadata System Health button to see quickly whether the machine is encountering some issues. When the tab color is green, the Exadata Machine is running fine, but when the color is red, the DBA knows there are some problems with the system (see Figure 8-24).

Clicking the red Exadata System Health button will take you directly to the list of issues the machine is experiencing, as shown in Figure 8-25.

Monitoring SQL

Another feature worth discussing is SQL monitoring. Although this OEM feature is not specific to databases running on Exadata, it is useful and something of which many DBAs are not aware. SQL monitoring shows runtime execution of the SQLs that are currently running. It shows any SQL statements that run longer than an established threshold, such as 1 second. Anything faster than the threshold won't be shown, which is fine because fast-running SQL doesn't need tuning.

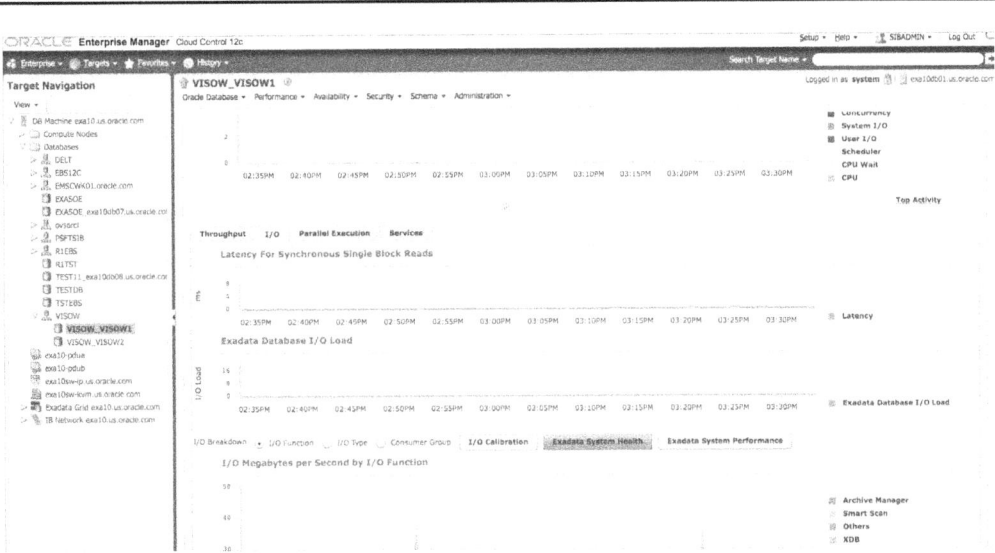

FIGURE 8-24. *Exadata system health*

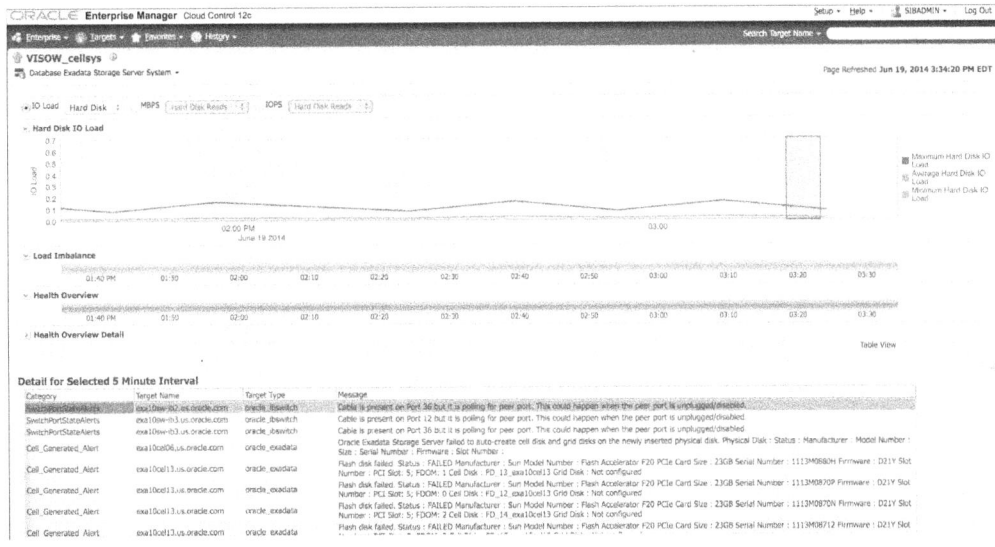

FIGURE 8-25. *Exadata system health issues*

To view the SQL monitoring tab, choose Performance | SQL Monitoring. Figure 8-26 shows the SQL monitoring page.

A spinning green circle appears to the left of any SQL that is currently being executed. Click the spinning green circle to see the details page for that SQL. From here you can capture all the metrics related to the SQL. You can see metrics related to I/O requests, CPU used, I/O throughput, cell offloads, PGA usage, temperature, and so on. The SQL monitoring page also shows the explain plan for the running query with the details of the phase that is currently executing, including how much data SQL is getting from the smart scans and storage cell offload. Figure 8-27 shows the detailed metrics for a running SQL.

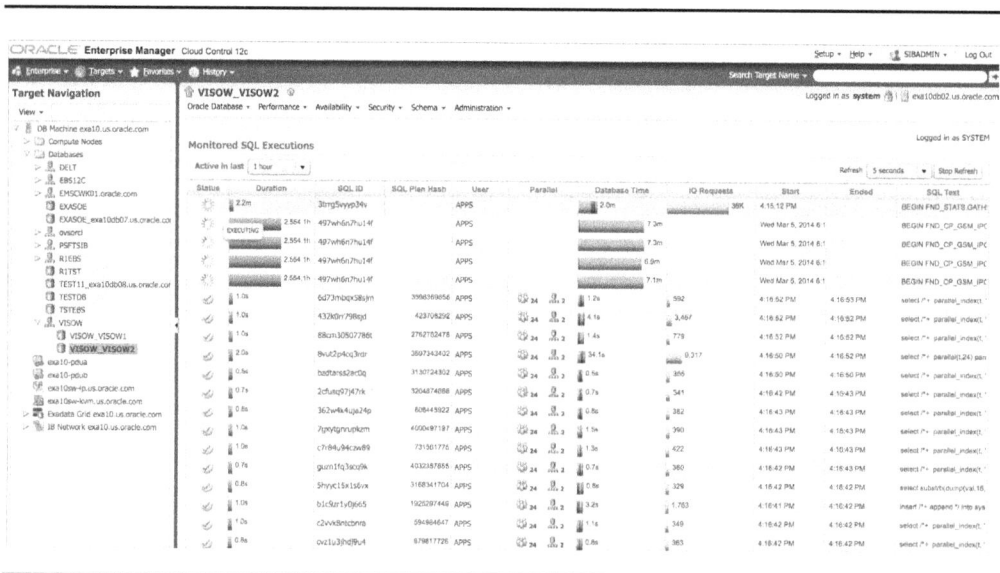

FIGURE 8-26. *SQL monitoring page*

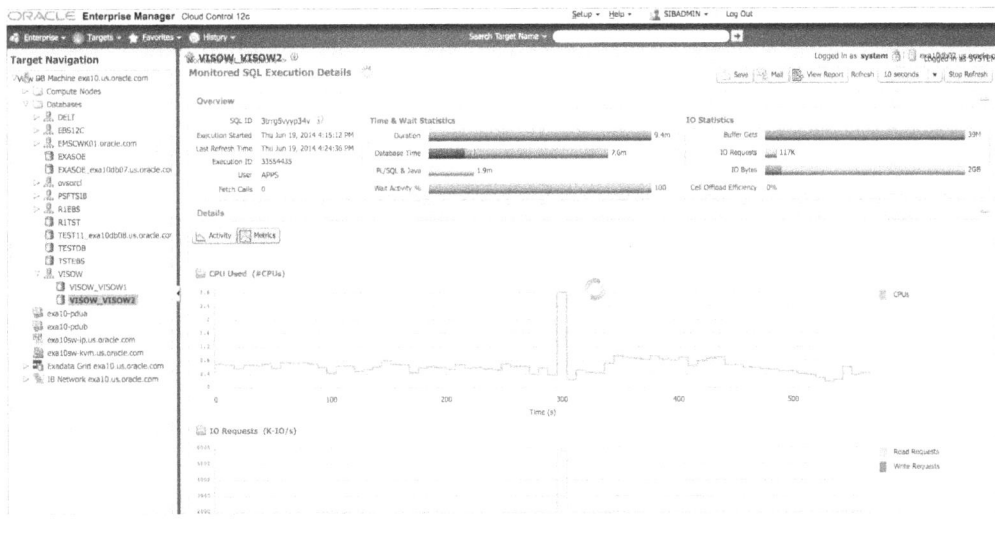

FIGURE 8-27. *SQL monitoring metric for a running SQL*

Monitoring from the Servers Directly

Although OEM enables you to perform end-to-end monitoring of the Exadata Machine, you can monitor the server without OEM by logging in to the servers directly and running various tools and scripts, as described in the following sections.

OS System Log

In the system log, most of the OS-related messages and errors are published. The standard location for this file on a Linux OS is /var/log/messages. The log file location can be configured to view this information reference, /etc/syslog.conf.

CPU Utilization

You can measure the CPU utilization of the database compute nodes using native OS tools or third-party tools. Some of the most popular tools are top, iostat, and vmstat. Remember that the Exadata compute node has Intel CPUs that allow hyper-threading, so you must consider hyper-threading when measuring the CPU utilization. We discussed the hyper-threading of Intel chipsets in Chapter 5.

```
[oracle@exa10db01 ~]$ top -c
top - 16:59:40 up 118 days, 18:59, 3 users, load average: 1.04, 1.07, 0.99
Tasks: 762 total, 2 running, 760 sleeping, 0 stopped, 0 zombie
Cpu(s): 24.0%us, 1.4%sy, 0.0%ni, 74.4%id, 0.0%wa, 0.0%hi, 0.2%si, 0.0%st
```

```
Mem: 98807256k total, 88865280k used, 9941976k free, 3514016k buffers
Swap: 25165820k total, 1804k used, 25164016k free, 22142128k cached

  PID USER      PR  NI  VIRT  RES  SHR S %CPU %MEM    TIME+  COMMAND
25250 root      20   0 13288 6896  432 R 99.5  0.0  0:09.65 bzip2 /opt
/oracle.ExaWatcher/archive/Top.ExaWatcher/2014_06_19_15_59_07_TopExaWatcher_
exa10db01.us.oracle.com.dat
27639 oracle    20   0 20.2g  33m  27m S 35.6  0.0 23:48.14 ora_p020_VISOW1
27625 oracle    20   0 20.2g  34m  28m S 34.9  0.0 10:57.75 ora_p014_VISOW1
27637 oracle    20   0 20.2g  34m  28m S 34.9  0.0 21:16.11 ora_p019_VISOW1
27629 oracle    20   0 20.2g  34m  28m S 34.6  0.0 21:13.50 ora_p016_VISOW1
27635 oracle    20   0 20.2g  34m  28m S 34.6  0.0 21:17.28 ora_p018_VISOW1
27621 oracle    20   0 20.2g  34m  28m S 33.9  0.0 11:03.56 ora_p012_VISOW1
27646 oracle    20   0 20.2g  33m  27m S 33.6  0.0 23:50.24 ora_p023_VISOW1
27627 oracle    20   0 20.2g  34m  28m S 32.3  0.0 11:04.66 ora_p015_VISOW1
27631 oracle    20   0 20.2g  34m  28m S 32.3  0.0 21:16.56 ora_p017_VISOW1
27643 oracle    20   0 20.2g  36m  30m S 32.3  0.0 23:48.54 ora_p022_VISOW1
```

> **TIP & TECHNIQUE**
> *Exadata runs on Oracle Enterprise Linux,*
> *so all the Linux commands for monitoring*
> *also work in Exadata.*

Memory Utilization

You can monitor memory utilization with the /proc/meminfo virtual file. Add up the MemFree: and Cached: metrics to get an indication of the total available free memory. Linux will free memory from cache when necessary, so this can be regarded as part of free memory. Exadata databases do not use the Linux page cache for database I/Os, so you need a relatively small Linux page cache. Here is an example:

```
[oracle@exa10db01 ~]$ cat /proc/meminfo | egrep
'MemTotal:|MemFree:|Cached:'
MemTotal:      98807256 kB
MemFree:       10248156 kB
Cached:        21868344 kB
SwapCached:          40 kB
```

ILOM Events

Integrated Lights Out Manager is a dedicated service processor that you can use to manage and monitor servers. Each storage server, compute node, and InfiniBand switch has a dedicated ILOM. Log in to the web management console of ILOM and select Fault Management to see the system overview shown in Figure 8-28.

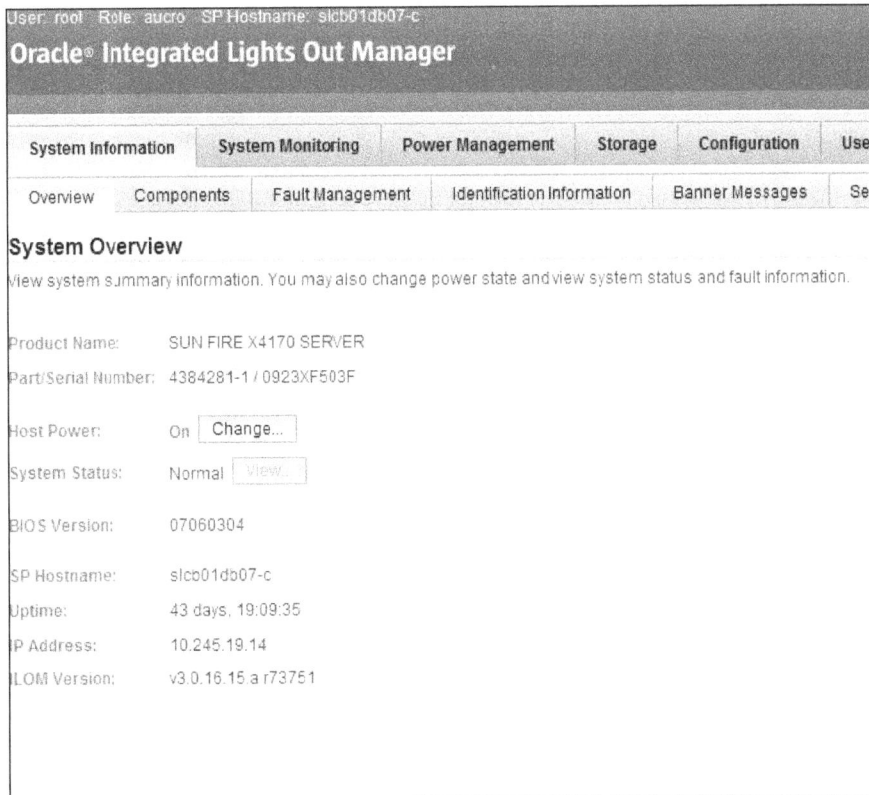

FIGURE 8-28. *ILOM console*

You can also view the System Event Log to get additional information that's not classified as a fault (such as fans over or under speed, temperature sensor warnings, and so on). Select the System Monitoring tab and then the Event Logs tab. Use the filter drop-down box to filter events by type.

Storage Cell Metric

You can run the same commands that you run in DB compute node for capturing CPU and memory information. You can obtain the disk-related metrics by using OSWatcher, which is installed by default in the storage cell. Every 5 seconds, OSWatcher captures snapshots for both the physical disks and flash disks. On a cell, go to /opt/oracle.oswatcher/osw/archive/oswiostat. The snapshots are stored in a separate file for each hour. Snapshots are retained for seven days.

Here's a sample output of oswiostat:

```
avg-cpu: %user    %nice %system %iowait  %steal   %idle
         10.72     0.00    0.34    5.50    0.00   83.44
Device:      rrqm/s wrqm/s   r/s   w/s   rsec/s   wsec/s avgrq-sz avgqu-
sz   await svctm %util
sda (system) 53.20  20.20 61.00 12.20 119305.60   275.20  1633.62
50.51  704.65 12.94  94.74
sdb (system) 63.00  21.60 67.40  9.60 134588.80   278.40  1751.52
185.82 2424.44 12.99 100.02
sdc          77.80   0.00 80.00  2.60 154174.40    11.60  1866.66
15.03  158.55  9.59  79.24
sdd          77.40   0.00 78.60  0.40 156766.40    12.80  1984.55
13.10  163.34  9.46  74.70
sde          53.00   0.00 64.80  0.20 129342.40     1.60  1989.91
28.14  506.29  9.95  64.68
sdf          67.60   0.00 70.00  0.40 138744.00    32.00  1971.25
9.12   130.45 10.51  73.96
sdg          88.40   0.00 83.00  0.80 159870.40    57.60  1908.45
15.11  148.26  9.76  81.76
sdh          86.80   0.00 83.00  4.60 165675.20  1640.00  1909.99
14.57  139.70  9.28  81.26
sdi          93.60   0.00 94.20  0.00 188516.80     0.00  2001.24
18.27  183.00  9.34  87.96
sdj          83.40   0.00 89.80  3.20 178910.40  1235.20  1937.05
12.79  140.77  8.79  81.76
```

The results of oswiostat can be interpreted as follows:

- **Device**   Device name (map device back to cell disk)
- **r/s**   Number of read I/Os per second
- **w/s**   Number of write I/Os per second
- **rsec/s**   Number of sectors (half KB) read per second
- **wsec/s**   Number of sectors (half KB) written per second
- **avgrq-sz**   Average I/O request size in sector (half KB)
- **avgqu-sz**   Average disk queue size
- **await**   Average I/O latency in milliseconds (including service time + time in queue)
- **svctm**   Average I/O service time in milliseconds
- **%util**   Device bandwidth utilization (0–100 percent)

Exachk

Exachk is a tool designed to audit important configuration settings within an Oracle Exadata Database Machine. The components examined are database servers, storage servers, InfiniBand fabric, InfiniBand switches, and Ethernet networks. The tool audits configuration settings within the following categories:

- Hardware and firmware

- OS kernel parameters

- OS packages

- Many other OS configuration settings important to RAC

- CRS/grid infrastructure

- RDBMS

- ASM

- Database and ASM initialization parameters

- Many other database configuration settings important to RAC

- Maximum Availability Architecture (MAA) Scorecard

- Database upgrade module with pre- and post-upgrade function

Exachk also provides a listing of firmware, software versions, and patches for comparison. It should be executed at least monthly and before and after any system configuration changes in the Exadata Machine. Although exachk is a minimal impact tool, it is a best practice to execute it during times of least load on the system.

The tool automatically runs a daemon in the background to monitor command execution progress. If for any reason one of the commands run by the tool should hang or take longer than anticipated, the monitor daemon kills the hung command after a configurable timeout so that main tool execution can progress.

The Exadata health-check plug-in is designed to raise alerts for the following checks automatically:

- Verify the disk cache policy on the database server

- Verify that database server disk controllers use Write-Back Flash Cache

- Verify RAID controller battery condition (database server)

- Verify RAID controller battery temperature (database server)

- Verify database server virtual drive configuration

- Verify database server physical drive configuration

- Exachk not running

- Results and exception file(s) missing

Exachk assumes that the secure sockets (SSH) connectivity between the nodes is already established; if not, exachk offers to set it up either temporarily or permanently.

The exachk utility can be downloaded from My Oracle Support from Note 1070954.1.

TIP & TECHNIQUE
Exachk is constantly being enhanced, so it should be redownloaded regularly. Exachk embodies one of the most important features of Exadata, which is the support model. Oracle can "find once, fix many" because of this tool and because every Exadata machine is the same as others in the field at other customer sites.

Download the exachk.zip in your local machine and then transfer it to the compute node of the Exadata Machine as the RDBMS owner, usually "oracle." Unzip the zip file and run the following command:

```
./ exachk -a
The option -a (All performs best practice check and recommended patch check)
```

You need root password or sudo root access to obtain the system-level metrics. If you don't have root access, those metrics will be skipped.

You don't have to run exachk from all the compute nodes; you need to run it only from one node of each cluster. Exachk makes remote connectivity using SSH to all other nodes and gathers the required data.

It prompts for answers to the following questions:

```
./ exachk -a

CRS stack is running and CRS_HOME is not set. Do you want to set CRS_
HOME to /u01/app/11.2.0/grid? [y/n] [y]

Type "y" and press the return key, or just press the return key.
```

```
Checking ssh user equivalency settings on all nodes in cluster
Node exa10db01 is configured for ssh user equivalency for oracle user

Searching for running databases . . . .

List of running databases registered in OCR
1. visow
2. psft9
3. ebs12c
4. All of above
5. None of above

Searching out ORACLE_HOME for selected databases. . . .

Checking Status of Oracle Software Stack - Clusterware, ASM, RDBMS . .
. .

---------------------------------------------------------------------
--------
Oracle Stack Status
---------------------------------------------------------------------
--------
Host Name CRS Installed ASM HOME RDBMS Installed CRS UP ASM UP RDBMS UP
DB Instance Name
---------------------------------------------------------------------
--------
exa10db01 Yes Yes Yes Yes Yes Yes visow1
exa10db02 Yes Yes Yes Yes Yes Yes visow2
---------------------------------------------------------------------
--------

root user equivalence is not setup between exa10db01 and STORAGE SERVER
exa10cel01.
1. Enter 1 if you will enter root password for each STORAGE SERVER when
prompted.
2. Enter 2 to exit and configure root user equivalence manually and re-
run exachk.
3. Enter 3 to skip checking best practices on STORAGE SERVER.
Please indicate your selection from one of the above options[1-3][1]:-

Is root password same on all STORAGE SERVER[y/n][y]

Enter root password for STORAGE SERVER :-
101 of the included audit checks require root privileged data
collection on DATABASE SERVER. If sudo is not configured or the root
password is not available, audit checks which require root privileged
data collection can be skipped.
```

1. Enter 1 if you will enter root password for each on DATABASE SERVER host when prompted
2. Enter 2 if you have sudo configured for oracle user to execute root_exachk.sh script on DATABASE SERVER
3. Enter 3 to skip the root privileged collections on DATABASE SERVER
4. Enter 4 to exit and work with the SA to configure sudo on DATABASE SERVER or to arrange for root access and run the tool later.

Please indicate your selection from one of the above options[1-4][1]:-

Is root password same on all compute nodes?[y/n][y]

Enter root password on DATABASE SERVER:-

9 of the included audit checks require nm2user privileged data collection on INFINIBAND SWITCH.

1. Enter 1 if you will enter nm2user password for each INFINIBAND SWITCH when prompted
2. Enter 2 to exit and to arrange for nm2user access and run the exachk later.
3. Enter 3 to skip checking best practices on INFINIBAND SWITCH
Please indicate your selection from one of the above options[1-3][1]:-

Is nm2user password same on all INFINIBAND SWITCH ?[y/n][y]

Enter nm2user password for INFINIBAND SWITCH:-

*** Checking Best Practice Recommendations (PASS/WARNING/FAIL) *** Log file for collections and audit checks are at
/home/oracle/exachk_215/20140619/exachk_196014_19030/exachk.log
==
Node name - exa10db01
==
Collecting - ASM Diskgroup Attributes
Collecting - ASM initialization parameters
Collecting - Database Parameters for visow database
Collecting - Database Undocumented Parameters for visow database

When exachk is finished, it generates a detailed report. A scorecard is generated on the top of the HTML page, similar to "System Health Score is 88 out of 100." A health-check score of more than 85 is considered good. Any item that fails needs to be revisited. Parts of the sample report are shown in Figures 8-29 and 8-30.

E-Business Suite

Status	Type	Message	Status On	Details
FAIL	SQL Check	One or more Workflow Error Items found	All Databases	View
PASS	SQL Check	No Workflow Notification Preferences are disabled	All Databases	View

Top

Findings Passed

Database Server

Status	Type	Message	Status On	Details
PASS	Database Check	There are no duplicate parameter entries in the database init.ora(spfile) file	All Databases	View
PASS	OS Check	Database server disk devices tune2fs check interval is set to 0	All Database Servers	View
PASS	ASM Check	You have enough space in all diskgroups to reestablish redundancy after a single cell failure	All ASM Instances	View
PASS	ORACLE_HOME Check	Same bundle patch is installed on GRID_HOME and RDBMS_HOME	All ORACLE_HOME's	View
PASS	ASM Check	You have enough space in all diskgroups to reestablish redundancy after disk failure	All ASM Instances	View
PASS	OS Check	Database Server InfiniBand network MTU size is 7000	All Database Servers	View
PASS	OS Check	The service exachkcfg is configured to autostart	All Database Servers	View
PASS	OS Check	Exadata Storage Server GI software version meets requirement for rolling cell patching	All Database Servers	View
PASS	ORACLE_HOME Check	Exadata Storage Server RDBMS software version meets requirement for rolling cell patching	All ORACLE_HOME's	View
PASS	OS Check	Exadata database server GI software version meets requirement for rolling RAC patching	All Database Servers	View
PASS	ASM Check	ASM griddisk,diskgroup and Failure group mapping is as recommended	All ASM Instances	View
PASS	OS Check	Berkeley Database location points to correct GI_HOME	All Database Servers	View
PASS	OS Check	Address Resolution Protocol (ARP) is configured properly on database server.	All Database Servers	View
PASS	OS Check	ExaWatcher is running.	All Database Servers	View
PASS	SQL Parameter Check	Database initialization parameter PFILE is set to recommended value	All Instances	View
PASS	OS Check	vm.min_free_kbytes is set as recommended.	All Database Servers	View
PASS	ASM Check	There was no ASM corruption found.	All ASM Instances	View

FIGURE 8-29. *Exachk report showing E-Business Suite and database settings*

Infiniband Switch

Status	Type	Message	Status On	Details
PASS	Switch Check	There were no opensm logs found containing AutomaticHighErrorRate messages	All Infiniband Switches	View
PASS	Switch Check	sminfo_polling_timeout is set to recommended value of 300	All Infiniband Switches	View
PASS	Switch Check	polling_retry_number is set to recommended value of 2	All Infiniband Switches	View
PASS	Switch Check	Subnet manager daemon is running	All Infiniband Switches	View
PASS	Switch Check	sm_priority is set to recommended value	All Infiniband Switches	View
PASS	Switch Check	Infiniband switch firmware version is compatible with Exadata software version	All Infiniband Switches	View
PASS	Switch Check	DNS Server ping time is in acceptable range	All Infiniband Switches	View
PASS	Switch Check	Infiniband switch software version meets the recommendation	All Infiniband Switches	View
PASS	Switch Check	controlled_handover is set to recommended value of TRUE on infiniband switch metissw–iba01	All Infiniband Switches	View
PASS	Switch Check	log_flags is set to recommended value of 0x03	All Infiniband Switches	View
PASS	Switch Check	routing_engine is set to recommended value of ftree	All Infiniband Switches	View
PASS	Switch Check	NTP configuration has been changed from default	All Infiniband Switches	View
PASS	Switch Check	HOSTNAME is set in /etc/sysconfig/network	All Infiniband Switches	View

Cluster Wide

Status	Type	Message	Status On	Details
PASS	Cluster Wide Check	CRS home has same number of patches installed across the cluster	Cluster Wide	–
PASS	Cluster Wide Check	RDBMS home /u01/app/oracle/product/11.2.0.3/dbhome_1 has same number of patches installed across the cluster	Cluster Wide	–
PASS	Cluster Wide Check	RDBMS home /u01/app/oracle/product/11.2.0.3/dbhome_2 has same number of patches installed across the cluster	Cluster Wide	–
PASS	Cluster Wide Check	Firmware version matches on all Infiniband switches	Cluster Wide	View
PASS	Cluster Wide Check	Localtime configuration matches on all Infiniband switches	Cluster Wide	View
PASS	Cluster Wide Check	All database and storage servers are synchronized with NTP server	Cluster Wide	View
PASS	Cluster Wide Check	NTP server matches across all database and storage servers	Cluster Wide	View
PASS	Cluster Wide Check	cellinit.ora matches across database servers	Cluster Wide	View
PASS	Cluster Wide Check	/etc/localtime matches across database servers	Cluster Wide	View

FIGURE 8-30. *Exachk report showing InfiniBand and cluster-related settings*

Summary

In this chapter you learned how to monitor all the components of an Exadata Machine. Oracle Enterprise Manager is the recommended tool for monitoring Exadata since everything can be monitored from a single console. OEM enables you to monitor everything from apps to disk. If you are using any of the Oracle applications (E-Business Suite, PeopleSoft, JD Edwards, Siebel, and so on), plug-ins exist for all these applications, so you can perform end-to-end monitoring using OEM.

If you don't have OEM, you can still monitor the Exadata Machine in the traditional way by using command-line tools and custom script.

Exachk is a very helpful tool to diagnose any problems in the Exadata Machine. It is recommended that you run exachk at least once a month to make sure the Exadata Machine is running optimally.

CHAPTER
9

Managing Exadata

Exadata Database Machine is similar to other hardware platforms—it is built on x86-based architecture with an Intel chipset, and it runs Oracle Database with Real Application Clusters (RAC) and Automatic Storage Management (ASM). It's a bit different from others, however, because it introduces Exadata Storage Server and Exadata storage software, which is specific to Exadata systems. An Exadata Machine includes a predefined configuration that is designed, engineered, and certified to run without making any deviations from the standard configuration. This makes the Exadata architecture simple and facilitates easy administration. In fact, the administration tasks required for an Exadata Machine are typically 30 percent less than those required for a non-Exadata platform. Exadata is also "pre-architected," which means customers perform much less work in building a technical machine architecture, selecting proper components, and other similar tasks.

Because the database running on Exadata runs on ASM, and in majority of cases customers use it with RAC, a DBA should have a minimum understanding of RAC and ASM to administer an Exadata Machine. Recovery Manager (RMAN) is the only way to back up the database running in an Exadata Machine, so it is important that the DBA is aware of RMAN as well.

Administering Exadata involves managing all the components running in an Exadata Machine. The installation and setup are done for you by Oracle Advanced Customer Support (ACS) or a certified partner, who takes care of configuring all the aspects of the machine according to your requirements. This includes installing Oracle Enterprise Linux, installing the Grid Infrastructure, configuring ASM disk groups, creating a starter database (typically a RAC database), and integrating compute nodes, InfiniBand, and storage cells, among other tasks. Once the machine is configured by ACS (or a certified partner), configuration is complete, and all that is required is mainly administering and maintaining the Exadata Machine, the focus of this chapter.

Starting and Stopping Exadata Machine

After the Exadata Machine is configured by ACS, you will rarely be required to shut it down completely and restart. Although the Exadata Machine will recover from an ungraceful shutdown, it is recommended that you shut down the machine properly if possible. Many customers run their Exadata Machines for years without restarting. If it becomes necessary to restart the Exadata Machine—for example, if you are migrating a data center or moving the machine from one floor to another in the data center, you should follow the proper shutdown procedures, discussed next.

Shut Down the Machine

One reason for shutting down the machine is to test whether it will start cleanly. Everything installed and configured by ACS or a partner should start cleanly. However, you may make modifications, such as adding third-party monitoring agents, creating additional databases, adding services, and so on. In this case, you may need to shut down and restart the machine. Here's how to do it:

1. Stop all the databases running in the Exadata Machine, preferably using **srvctl**:

   ```
   srvctl stop database -d <database_name>
   ```

2. After the database nodes have been shut down, stop the Cluster Ready Services (CRS). This will stop the Automatic Storage Management (ASM) instance as well. Run the following from each compute node:

   ```
   crsctl stop crs
   ```

3. In the storage server, shut down all the services by running this command:

   ```
   CellCLI> alter cell shutdown services all
   ```

4. Shut down the Management Server, Restart Server, and Cell Services one by one; use the following commands:

   ```
   CellCLI> alter cell shutdown services MS
   CellCLI> alter cell shutdown services RS
   CellCLI> alter cell shutdown services CELLSRV
   ```

5. Shut down the storage servers and then the database compute nodes. Because you access the storage servers' nodes via the compute nodes, you need to shut down the storage servers first, unless you are going via the Integrated Lights Out Manager (ILOM) route. Shut down the storage servers and the database servers as root using the following command:

   ```
   shutdown -h now
   ```

6. Shut down all the network interfaces.

You have successfully shut down the Exadata Machine.

Start Up the Machine

Start the machine by following these steps:

1. Power on all the network interfaces.

2. Power on the storage server.

3. Power on the database compute nodes. Switching on the compute nodes will automatically start the CRS, ASM instance, and all the databases and listeners registered with the CRS. Ideally, you shouldn't have to start anything manually. If some component does not start, you'll need to troubleshoot and start it manually.

Operational Commands

The compute nodes of the Exadata Machine run on Oracle Enterprise Linux (OEL) and host the Grid Infrastructure, ASM, and database instances. The Exadata Storage Cells also run OEL and the Exadata storage software. All the Linux operational commands work in the Exadata compute node. In this section, we will run some operational commands you will need for day-to-day maintenance of the machine.

Commands Related to Power Off/Reboot

The Intelligent Platform Management Interface (IPMI) enables you to administer the Exadata Machines remotely. IPMI is an open-standard hardware management interface specification that defines a specific way for embedded management subsystems to communicate. IPMI information is exchanged through baseboard management controllers (BMCs) that are located on IPMI-compliant hardware components.

Using low-level hardware intelligence instead of the operating system has two main benefits: this configuration allows for out-of-band server management, and the operating system is not burdened with transporting system status data. The command for launching the tool is **IPMITOOL**. Note that the IPMI tool is not an Exadata-specific feature, but is also available on non-Exadata systems.

You can access detailed information about command usage and syntax for the IPMI tool package from the main page that is installed. From a command line, type this command:

```
man ipmitool
```

To power on a cell or database server, issue this command from a remote server:

```
#ipmitool -H exa10cel01-ilom -U root chassis power on
```

NOTE
All the commands related to shutdown and reboot must be run as root user.

To stop a server, use the **shutdown** command. Because the compute node runs on a Linux operating system, all the Linux commands for shutdown and start activities are valid.

```
# shutdown -h  now
```

To reboot the machine, run this command:

```
#reboot
```

Commands Related to InfiniBand

InfiniBand is an open-standard–based backplane networking technology introduced in the Exadata Machine. Since InfiniBand is new, a DBA may not be familiar with all the commands related to its maintenance. Following is a list of InfiniBand commands:

```
# cd /usr/sbin
# ls ib*
ibaddr              ibchecknode         ibcheckstate        ibdatacounters
ibhosts             ibnetdiscover       ibprintca.pl        ibqueryerrors.pl
ibstatus            ibtracert           ibcheckerrors       ibcheckport
ibcheckwidth        ibdatacounts        ibis                ibnodes
ibprintrt.pl        ibroute             ibswitches          ibcheckerrs
ibcheckportstate    ibclearcounters     ibdiagnet           iblinkinfo
ibping              ibprintswitch.pl    ibrouters           ibswportwatch.pl
ibchecknet          ibcheckportwidth    ibclearerrors       ibdiscover.pl
iblinkinfo.pl       ibportstate         ibqueryerrors       ibstat
ibsysstat
```

> **TIP & TECHNIQUE**
> *All the command/scripts related to InfiniBand are located at the /usr/sbin directory.*

Most of these commands are self-explanatory, but we'll describe a few important commands here. The following command checks to see if there are any issues with the IB port:

```
# ibcheckstate

## Summary: 18 nodes checked, 0 bad nodes found
##          78 ports checked, 0 ports with bad state found
```

To check the status of the IB switch, run the command **ibstatus** or **ibstat**:

```
#ibstatus
Infiniband device 'mlx4_0' port 1 status:
        default gid:    fe80:0000:0000:0000:0010:e000:0133:c571
        state:          4: PORT_ACTIVE
        phys state:     5: LINK_UP
        sm lid:         0x3
        base lid:       0x10
        rate:           40 Gb/sec (4X)
        link_layer:     IB

Infiniband device 'mlx4_0' port 2 status:
        default gid:    fe80:0000:0000:0000:0010:e000:0133:c572
        state:          4: PORT_ACTIVE
        phys state:     5: LINK_UP
```

```
              sm lid:        0x3
              base lid:      0x11
              rate:          40 Gb/sec (4X)
              link_layer:    IB

# ibstat
CA 'mlx4_0'
        CA type: 0
        Number of ports: 2
        Firmware version: 2.11.2010
        Hardware version: 176
        Node GUID: 0x0010e0000133c570
        System image GUID: 0x0010e0000133c573
        Port 1:
                State: Active
                Physical state: LinkUp
                Rate: 40
                Base lid: 16
                LMC: 0
                SM lid: 3
                Capability mask: 0x00000030
                Port GUID: 0x0010e0000133c571
                Link layer: IB
        Port 2:
                State: Active
                Physical state: LinkUp
                Rate: 40
                Base lid: 17
                LMC: 0
                SM lid: 3
                Capability mask: 0x00000030
                Port GUID: 0x0010e0000133c572
                Link layer: IB
```

As you can see, the output of this command shows whether or not the port is active. The physical state shows whether the link is up or down. You can see that both ports are active and the link is up.

To find detailed information about the port, such as where the port is connected at the other end and so on, use the command **iblinkinfo**:

```
#iblinkinfo
Switch 0x0010e0406766a0a0 SUN DCS 36P QDR exa10-ibs0 172.20.40.25:
       3    1[  ] ==(                    Down/Disabled)==>              [  ] "" ( )
       3    2[  ] ==(                    Down/Disabled)==>              [  ] "" ( )
       3    3[  ] ==(                    Down/Disabled)==>              [  ] "" ( )
       3    4[  ] ==(                    Down/Disabled)==>              [  ] "" ( )
       3    5[  ] ==(                    Down/Disabled)==>              [  ] "" ( )
       3    6[  ] ==(                    Down/Disabled)==>              [  ] "" ( )
       3    7[  ] ==(                    Down/Disabled)==>              [  ] "" ( )
       3    8[  ] ==(                    Down/Disabled)==>              [  ] "" ( )
       3    9[  ] ==(                    Down/Disabled)==>              [  ] "" ( )
       3   10[  ] ==(                    Down/Disabled)==>              [  ] "" ( )
       3   11[  ] ==(                    Down/Disabled)==>              [  ] "" ( )
       3   12[  ] ==(                    Down/Disabled)==>              [  ] "" ( )
       3   13[  ] ==(                    Down/Disabled)==>              [  ] "" ( )
```

```
    3   14[  ] ==(                  Down/Disabled)==>           [  ] "" ( )
    3   15[  ] ==(                  Down/Disabled)==>           [  ] "" ( )
    3   16[  ] ==(                  Down/Disabled)==>           [  ] "" ( )
    3   17[  ] ==(                  Down/Disabled)==>           [  ] "" ( )
    3   18[  ] ==(                  Down/Disabled)==>           [  ] "" ( )
    3   19[  ] ==( 4X 10.0 Gbps Active/  LinkUp)==>      1   32[  ] "SUN DCS 36P QDR
exa10-ibs0 172.20.40.27" ( )
    3   20[  ] ==(                  Down/Disabled)==>           [  ] "" ( )
    3   21[  ] ==( 4X 10.0 Gbps Active/  LinkUp)==>      2   32[  ] "SUN DCS 36P QDR
exa10-ibs0 172.20.40.26" ( )
    3   22[  ] ==(                  Down/Disabled)==>           [  ] "" ( )
    3   23[  ] ==(                  Down/Disabled)==>           [  ] "" ( )
    3   24[  ] ==(                  Down/Disabled)==>           [  ] "" ( )
    3   25[  ] ==(                  Down/Disabled)==>           [  ] "" ( )
    3   26[  ] ==(                  Down/Disabled)==>           [  ] "" ( )
    3   27[  ] ==(                  Down/Disabled)==>           [  ] "" ( )
    3   28[  ] ==(                  Down/Disabled)==>           [  ] "" ( )
    3   29[  ] ==(                  Down/Disabled)==>           [  ] "" ( )
    3   30[  ] ==(                  Down/Disabled)==>           [  ] "" ( )
    3   31[  ] ==(                  Down/Disabled)==>           [  ] "" ( )
    3   32[  ] ==(                  Down/Disabled)==>           [  ] "" ( )
    3   33[  ] ==(                  Down/Disabled)==>           [  ] "" ( )
    3   34[  ] ==(                  Down/Disabled)==>           [  ] "" ( )
    3   35[  ] ==(                  Down/Disabled)==>           [  ] "" ( )
    3   36[  ] ==(                  Down/Disabled)==>           [  ] "" ( )
Switch 0x0010e040671da0a0 SUN DCS 36P QDR exa10-ibs1 172.20.40.27:
    1    1[  ] ==( 4X 10.0 Gbps Active/  LinkUp)==>     31    2[  ] "exa10cel02
C 192.168.60.7,192.168.60.8 HCA-1" ( )
    1    2[  ] ==( 4X 10.0 Gbps Active/  LinkUp)==>     25    2[  ] "exa10cel01
C 192.168.60.5,192.168.60.6 HCA-1" ( )
    1    3[  ] ==( 4X 10.0 Gbps Active/  LinkUp)==>     28    1[  ] "exa10cel04
C 192.168.60.11,192.168.60.12 HCA-1" ( )
    1    4[  ] ==( 4X 10.0 Gbps Active/  LinkUp)==>     27    2[  ] "exa10cel03
C 192.168.60.9,192.168.60.10 HCA-1" ( )
    1    5[  ] ==(                  Down/ Polling)==>           [  ] "" ( )
    1    6[  ] ==(                  Down/ Polling)==>           [  ] "" ( )
    1    7[  ] ==( 4X 10.0 Gbps Active/  LinkUp)==>      9    2[  ] "exa10db01 S
" ( )
    1    8[  ] ==( 4X 10.0 Gbps Active/  LinkUp)==>     23    2[  ] "exa10-h1-
storadm PCIe 1" ( )
    1    9[  ] ==( 4X 10.0 Gbps Active/  LinkUp)==>     19    2[  ] "MT25408
ConnectX Mellanox Technologies" ( )
    1   10[  ] ==(                  Down/ Polling)==>           [  ] "" ( )
    1   11[  ] ==(                  Down/ Polling)==>           [  ] "" ( )
    1   12[  ] ==(                  Down/ Polling)==>           [  ] "" ( )
    1   13[  ] ==( 4X 10.0 Gbps Active/  LinkUp)==>      2   14[  ] "SUN DCS 36P
QDR exa10sw-iba0 172.20.40.26" ( )
    1   14[  ] ==( 4X 10.0 Gbps Active/  LinkUp)==>      2   13[  ] "SUN DCS 36P
QDR exa10sw-iba0 172.20.40.26" ( )
```

You can find errors related to the InfiniBand switch by running the command **ibqueryerrors**. Another command, **ibcheckerrors**, tells you whether any errors occurred at a particular port, but it doesn't provide output as detailed as that provided by **ibqueryerrors**, as shown next.

```
# ibqueryerrors
Suppressing:
Errors for 0x10e0000133c584 "MT25408 ConnectX Mellanox Technologies"
    GUID 0x10e0000133c584 port 2: [PortXmitWait == 51126433]
Errors for 0x10e0406766a0a0 "SUN DCS 36P QDR exa10-ibs0 172.20.40.25"
    GUID 0x10e0406766a0a0 port ALL: [PortRcvSwitchRelayErrors == 699] [PortXmitWait ==
49795]
    GUID 0x10e0406766a0a0 port 0: [PortRcvSwitchRelayErrors == 699] [PortXmitWait ==
49795]
Errors for 0x10e0000132bf64 "sbcdbadm03 S "
    GUID 0x10e0000132bf64 port 1: [PortXmitWait == 407959815]
    GUID 0x10e0000132bf64 port 2: [PortXmitWait == 3163215656]
Errors for 0x10e0000132dbac "MT25408 ConnectX Mellanox Technologies"
    GUID 0x10e0000132dbac port 2: [PortXmitWait == 1987508]
Errors for 0x10e00001450710 "MT25408 ConnectX Mellanox Technologies"
    GUID 0x10e00001450710 port 1: [PortXmitWait == 1]
    GUID 0x10e00001450710 port 2: [PortXmitDiscards == 1]
Errors for 0x10e0000132c014 "MT25408 ConnectX Mellanox Technologies"
    GUID 0x10e0000132c014 port 2: [PortXmitWait == 5722831]
Errors for 0x10e0000132d24c "sbcdbadm04 S "
    GUID 0x10e0000132d24c port 1: [PortXmitWait == 60789104]
Errors for 0x10e0000133c57c "MT25408 ConnectX Mellanox Technologies"
    GUID 0x10e0000133c57c port 2: [PortXmitWait == 59020155]
Errors for 0x10e040671da0a0 "SUN DCS 36P QDR sbcsw-ibb0 172.20.40.27"
    GUID 0x10e040671da0a0 port ALL: [LinkErrorRecoveryCounter == 50]
[PortRcvSwitchRelayErrors == 603] [PortXmitDiscards == 359] [PortXmitWait ==
3752321463]
    GUID 0x10e040671da0a0 port 0: [PortXmitWait == 50905]
    GUID 0x10e040671da0a0 port 1: [LinkErrorRecoveryCounter == 18]
[PortRcvSwitchRelayErrors == 30] [PortXmitDiscards == 29] [PortXmitWait ==
1513392767]   GUID 0x10e040671da0a0 port 2: [LinkErrorRecoveryCounter == 1]
[PortRcvSwitchRelayErrors == 79] [PortXmitDiscards == 19] [PortXmitWait ==
1553630794]   GUID 0x10e040671da0a0 port 3: [LinkErrorRecoveryCounter == 14]
[PortRcvSwitchRelayErrors == 49] [PortXmitDiscards == 3] [PortXmitWait ==
1274516122]   GUID 0x10e040671da0a0 port 4: [LinkErrorRecoveryCounter == 16]
[PortRcvSwitchRelayErrors == 61] [PortXmitDiscards == 11] [PortXmitWait == 1424053407]
    GUID 0x10e040671da0a0 port 7: [PortXmitDiscards == 42] [PortXmitWait == 25363779]
    GUID 0x10e040671da0a0 port 8: [PortXmitDiscards == 24] [PortXmitWait == 3]
```

In normal circumstances, you won't have to run these commands. If you have network connectivity issues or if the AWR report shows an issue with the network, your first task should be to check whether any issues exist with the IB switches.

Tools and Commands for Managing the Grid Infrastructure, ASM, and Database

The compute nodes of the database server run the Grid Infrastructure (GI) and host Oracle Clusterware and the ASM instance. In this section we will learn the CRSCTL, SRVCTL, ASMCMD, and SQLPLUS utilities and their corresponding commands.

CRSCTL

CRSCTL enables you to perform check, start, and stop operations on the cluster. You can run these commands from any node in the cluster or on all nodes in the cluster, depending on the operation. The CRSCTL utility is located in <GI ORACLE HOME>/ bin. CRSCTL is used to run the following operations:

- Starting and stopping Oracle Clusterware resources

- Enabling and disabling Oracle Clusterware daemons

- Checking the health of the cluster

- Managing resources that represent third-party applications

- Integrating IPMI with Oracle Clusterware to provide failure isolation support and ensure cluster integrity

- Debugging Oracle Clusterware components

Most of the commands related to CRSCTL need to be run as a root user (such as starting or stopping the CRS). A few commands for verifying the cluster health check or checking the status of a particular service can be run as oracle user as well.

To stop and start the cluster running in all the compute nodes, run the following command:

```
# crsctl stop/start cluster -all
```

To verify the status of all the components running in the cluster, run the command **crsctl status resource -t**:

```
[oracle@exa10db01 ~]$ crsctl status resource -t
--------------------------------------------------------------------
Name            Target  State        Server          State details
--------------------------------------------------------------------
Local Resources
--------------------------------------------------------------------
ora.DBFS_DG.dg
                ONLINE  ONLINE       exa10db01       STABLE
                ONLINE  ONLINE       exa10db02       STABLE
                ONLINE  ONLINE       exa10db03       STABLE
                ONLINE  ONLINE       exa10db04       STABLE
                ONLINE  ONLINE       exa10db05       STABLE
                ONLINE  ONLINE       exa10db06       STABLE
                ONLINE  ONLINE       exa10db07       STABLE
                ONLINE  ONLINE       exa10db08       STABLE
```

```
ora.ELIZ_DATA.dg
              ONLINE   OFFLINE       exa10db01       STABLE
              ONLINE   OFFLINE       exa10db02       STABLE
              ONLINE   OFFLINE       exa10db03       STABLE
              ONLINE   OFFLINE       exa10db04       STABLE
              ONLINE   OFFLINE       exa10db05       STABLE
              ONLINE   OFFLINE       exa10db06       STABLE
              ONLINE   OFFLINE       exa10db07       STABLE
              ONLINE   OFFLINE       exa10db08       STABLE
ora.ELIZ_DBFS.dg
              ONLINE   OFFLINE       exa10db01       STABLE
              ONLINE   OFFLINE       exa10db02       STABLE
              ONLINE   OFFLINE       exa10db03       STABLE
              ONLINE   OFFLINE       exa10db04       STABLE
              ONLINE   OFFLINE       exa10db05       STABLE
              ONLINE   OFFLINE       exa10db06       STABLE
              ONLINE   OFFLINE       exa10db07       STABLE
              ONLINE   OFFLINE       exa10db08       STABLE
ora.LISTENER.lsnr
              ONLINE   ONLINE        exa10db01       STABLE
              ONLINE   ONLINE        exa10db02       STABLE
              ONLINE   INTERMEDIATE  exa10db03       Not All Endpoints
                                                     Registered,STABLE
              ONLINE   ONLINE        exa10db04       STABLE
              ONLINE   ONLINE        exa10db05       STABLE
              ONLINE   ONLINE        exa10db06       STABLE
              ONLINE   ONLINE        exa10db07       STABLE
              ONLINE   ONLINE        exa10db08       STABLE
ora.LISTENER_EBS12C.lsnr
              ONLINE   OFFLINE       exa10db01       STABLE
              ONLINE   OFFLINE       exa10db02       STABLE
              ONLINE   OFFLINE       exa10db03       STABLE
              ONLINE   OFFLINE       exa10db04       STABLE
              ONLINE   OFFLINE       exa10db05       STABLE
              ONLINE   OFFLINE       exa10db06       STABLE
              ONLINE   ONLINE        exa10db07       STABLE
              ONLINE   ONLINE        exa10db08       STABLE
ora.LISTENER_EXA10EBS.lsnr
              ONLINE   ONLINE        exa10db01       STABLE
              ONLINE   ONLINE        exa10db02       STABLE
              ONLINE   ONLINE        exa10db03       STABLE
              ONLINE   ONLINE        exa10db04       STABLE
              ONLINE   ONLINE        exa10db05       STABLE
              ONLINE   ONLINE        exa10db06       STABLE
              ONLINE   ONLINE        exa10db07       STABLE
              ONLINE   ONLINE        exa10db08       STABLE
--------------------------------------------------------------------
Cluster Resources
--------------------------------------------------------------------
```

```
ora.LISTENER_SCAN1.lsnr
      1           ONLINE  ONLINE        exa10db02          STABLE
ora.LISTENER_SCAN2.lsnr
      1           ONLINE  ONLINE        exa10db08          STABLE
ora.LISTENER_SCAN3.lsnr
      1           ONLINE  ONLINE        exa10db04          STABLE
ora.MGMTLSNR
      1           ONLINE  ONLINE        exa10db08          169.254.130.200 192.
                                                          168.13.8 192.168.13.
                                                          37,STABLE
ora.atg.db
      1           ONLINE  ONLINE        exa10db05          Open,STABLE
      2           ONLINE  ONLINE        exa10db06          Open,STABLE
ora.atg.rac_atgproduction.svc
      1           ONLINE  ONLINE        exa10db06          STABLE
ora.atg.rac_atgpublishing.svc
      1           ONLINE  ONLINE        exa10db06          STABLE
ora.atg.rac_atgswitchinga.svc
      1           ONLINE  ONLINE        exa10db06          STABLE
ora.atg.rac_atgswitchingb.svc
      1           ONLINE  ONLINE        exa10db06          STABLE
ora.cvu
      1           ONLINE  ONLINE        exa10db01          STABLE
ora.dbm.db
      1           OFFLINE OFFLINE                          STABLE
      2           ONLINE  OFFLINE                          STABLE
ora.delt.db
      1           ONLINE  ONLINE        exa10db03          STABLE
      2           ONLINE  ONLINE        exa10db04          STABLE
ora.ebs03cl.db
      1           ONLINE  ONLINE        exa10db07          Open,STABLE
      2           ONLINE  ONLINE        exa10db08          Open,STABLE
ora.ebs04cl.db
      1           ONLINE  OFFLINE                          Instance Shutdown,ST
                                                          ABLE
      2           ONLINE  OFFLINE                          Instance Shutdown,ST
                                                          ABLE
```

It is assumed that the DBA is already aware of RAC and ASM, and therefore we won't go into further details on this topic. For more details on a particular topic regarding crsctl you can run the command **crsctl <option> -h**:

```
[oracle@exa10db01 ~]$ crsctl add -h
Usage:
  crsctl add {resource|type|serverpool|policy} <name> <options>
where
  name         Name of the CRS entity
  options      Options to be passed to the add command
```

```
    See individual CRS entity help for more details

  crsctl add crs administrator -u <user_name> [-f]
where
  user_name      User name to be added to the admin list or "*"
  -f             Override user name validity check
```

Table 9-1 lists the options of the CRSCTL utility.

Option	Description
crsctl add	Add a resource, type, or other entity.
crsctl backup	Back up voting disk for CSS.
crsctl check	Check a service, resource, or other entity.
crsctl config	Output autostart configuration.
crsctl debug	Obtain or modify debug state.
crsctl delete	Delete a resource, type, or other entity.
crsctl disable	Disable autostart.
crsctl discover	Discover the DHCP server.
crsctl enable	Enable autostart.
crsctl get	Get an entity value.
crsctl getperm	Get entity permissions.
crsctl lsmodules	List debug modules.
crsctl modify	Modify a resource, type, or other entity.
crsctl query	Query service state.
crsctl pin	Pin the nodes in the node list.
crsctl relocate	Relocate a resource, server, or other entity.
crsctl replace	Replace the location of voting files.
crsctl release	Release a DHCP lease.
crsctl request	Request a DHCP lease.
crsctl setperm	Set entity permissions.
crsctl set	Set an entity value.
crsctl start	Start a resource, server, or other entity.
crsctl status	Get the status of a resource or other entity.
crsctl stop	Stop a resource, server, or other entity.
crsctl unpin	Unpin the nodes in the node list.
crsctl unset	Unset an entity value, restoring its default.

TABLE 9-1. *Options of the CRSCTL Utility*

SRVCTL

The SRVCTL utility is used to administer the RAC databases. Use SRVCTL to start and stop the database and instances, manage configuration information, and move or remove instances and services. You can also use SRVCTL to add services and manage configuration information.

Some SRVCTL operations store configuration information in the Oracle Cluster Registry (OCR). SRVCTL performs other operations, such as starting and stopping instances, by sending requests to the Oracle Clusterware process (CRSD), which then starts or stops the Oracle Clusterware resources.

The SRVCTL can be run as an oracle user or as the owner of the Oracle software. Members of the DBA group can also run SRVCTL commands.

The SRVCTL tool is located at the $ORACLE_HOME/bin directory. Always use SRVCTL from the ORACLE_HOME for the databases that you are administering. SRVCTL does not support concurrent executions of commands on the same object. Therefore, run only one SRVCTL command at a time for each database, service, or other object.

Start and stop databases running in an Exadata Machine using the SRVCTL utility only. The commands for starting and stopping the database using SRVCTL are shown here:

```
srvctl start database -d <db_unique_name> [-o <start_options>] [-n
<node>]
srvctl stop database -d <db_unique_name> [-o <stop_options>] [-f]

srvctl start database -d PFSTDB -n exa10db01,exa10db02
srvctl stop database -d PFSTDB -o immediate
```

The start options refer to various options such as startup no mount, mount, and so on. Similarly, stop options refer to options such as abort, immediate, and so on.

Table 9-2 lists the options for the SRVCTL utility.

To see more details on each specific task, run the command **srvctl –h** at the command prompt:

```
[oracle@exa10db01 ~]$ srvctl -h
Usage: srvctl [-V]
Usage: srvctl add database -d <db_unique_name> -o <oracle_home> [-c {RACONENODE |
RAC | SINGLE} [-e <server_list>] [-i <inst_name>] [-w <timeout>]] [-m <domain_name>]
[-p <spfile>] [-r {PRIMARY | PHYSICAL_STANDBY | LOGICAL_STANDBY | SNAPSHOT_STANDBY}]
[-s <start_options>] [-t <stop_options>] [-n <db_name>] [-y {AUTOMATIC | MANUAL |
NORESTART}] [-g "<serverpool_list>"] [-x <node_name>] [-a "<diskgroup_list>"] [-j
"<acfs_path_list>"]
Usage: srvctl config database [-d <db_unique_name> [-a] ] [-v]
Usage: srvctl start database -d <db_unique_name> [-o <start_options>] [-n <node>]
Usage: srvctl stop database -d <db_unique_name> [-o <stop_options>] [-f]
Usage: srvctl status database -d <db_unique_name> [-f] [-v]
Usage: srvctl enable database -d <db_unique_name> [-n <node_name>]
Usage: srvctl disable database -d <db_unique_name> [-n <node_name>]
```

Option	Description
srvctl add	Add the node applications, database, database instance, ASM instance, or service.
srvctl remove	Remove the node applications, database, database instance, ASM instance, or service.
srvctl config	List the configuration for the node applications, database, ASM instance, or service.
srvctl enable	Enable the database, database instance, ASM instance, or service.
srvctl disable	Disable the database, database instance, ASM instance, or service.
srvctl start	Start the node applications, database, database instance, ASM instance, or service.
srvctl stop	Stop the node applications, database, database instance, ASM instance, or service.
srvctl modify	Modify the node applications, database, database instance, or service configuration.
srvctl relocate	Relocate the service from one instance to another.
srvctl status	Obtain the status of the node applications, database, database instance, ASM instance, or service.
srvctl getenv	Display the environment variable in the configuration for the node applications, database, database instance, or service.
srvctl setenv unsetenv	Set and unset the environment variable in the configuration for the node applications, database, database instance, or service.

TABLE 9-2. *Options of the SRVCTL Utility*

ASMCMD

The Grid Infrastructure also hosts the ASM instance. ASM disk groups can be managed by ASMCMD, a command-line utility that you can use to manage Oracle ASM instances, disk groups, file access control for disk groups, files and directories within disk groups, templates for disk groups, and volumes.

Launch the ASMCMD utility by setting the environment variable, pointing to the Grid Infrastructure ORACLE_HOME and ORACLE_SID to ASM instance. For details about the ASM disk groups, run the command **lsdg** from ASMCMD:

```
[oracle@exa10db01 ~]$ asmcmd
ASMCMD> lsdg

State    Type    Rebal Sector Block AU      Total_MB Free_MB  Req_mir_free_MB
Usable_file_MB  Offline_disks  Voting_files  Name
MOUNTED NORMAL N     512    4096  4194304 3280640  352200   298240            26980
0              Y  DBFS_DG/
```

```
MOUNTED NORMAL N     512    4096  4194304 12902400 3126328  4300800       -587236
0            N   Q1DATA/
MOUNTED NORMAL N     512    4096  4194304 6587136  6309748  2195712       2057018
0            N   Q1RECO/
MOUNTED NORMAL N     512    4096  4194304 25804800 23654928 4300800       9677064
0            N   SIBDATA/
MOUNTED NORMAL N     512    4096  4194304 13174272 12254212 2195712       5029250
0            N   SIBRECO/
MOUNTED NORMAL N     512    4096  4194304 14745600 10669156 4915200       2876978
0            N   WSDATA/
MOUNTED NORMAL N     512    4096  4194304 4743936  4697040  1581312       1557864
0            N   WSRECO/
ASMCMD>
```

You can browse within the file system inside the ASM disk group by running basic UNIX commands such as **ls**, **cd**, and so on. You can even copy the files that are residing in an ASM disk group to a regular file system by issuing a **cp** command.

To determine the space consumed by each file, issue the **ls –ls** command:

```
ASMCMD> pwd
+Q1DATA/OTM
ASMCMD> cd datafile
ASMCMD> ls -ls
Type        Redund  Striped  Time          Sys  Block_Size  Blocks     Bytes
Space   Name
DATAFILE  MIRROR  COARSE   AUG 13   2013  Y        8192   122881 1006641152
2034237440  SYSAUX.264.819662765
DATAFILE  MIRROR  COARSE   AUG 13   2013  Y        8192    98561  807411712
1631584256  SYSTEM.732.819662765
DATAFILE  MIRROR  COARSE   AUG 13   2013  Y        8192     6401   52436992
109051904   UNDOTBS1.682.819662765
DATAFILE  MIRROR  COARSE   AUG 13   2013  Y        8192     9601   78651392
159383552   UNDOTBS2.262.819662839
DATAFILE  MIRROR  COARSE   AUG 13   2013  Y        8192      641    5251072
16777216    USERS.288.819662765
ASMCMD>
```

To see a complete listing of all the ASMCMD commands, use **help**:

```
ASMCMD [+] > help
        commands:
        --------
        md_backup, md_restore
        lsattr, setattr
        cd, cp, du, find, help, ls, lsct, lsdg, lsof, mkalias, mkdir, pwd, rm,
rmalias
        chdg, chkdg, dropdg, iostat, lsdsk, lsod, mkdg, mount, offline, online,
rebal, remap, umount
        dsget, dsset, lsop, shutdown, spbackup, spcopy, spget, spmove, spset,
startup
        chtmpl, lstmpl, mktmpl, rmtmpl
        chgrp, chmod, chown, groups, grpmod, lsgrp, lspwusr, lsusr, mkgrp, mkusr,
orapwusr, passwd, rmgrp, rmusr
        volcreate, voldelete, voldisable, volenable, volinfo, volresize, volset,
volstat
```

To get help about a specific command, use **help <Command>**:

```
ASMCMD> help cp
cp
        Copy files between Oracle ASM disk groups on local
        instances to and from remote instances.

Synopsis
        cp [--service <name>] [--port <port>] <[connect_str:]src_file...> <[connect_
str:]tgt_file>

Description
        The options for the cp command are described below.
        --service    - name of the ASM instance name if not default +ASM.
        --port       - Listener port number, default is 1521.
        connect_str  - The connection string to be used with a remote
                       instance copy.
        src_file     - Name of the source file to copy.
        tgt_file     - A user alias for the created target file name or
                       alias directory name.
        cp cannot copy files between two remote instances. The local Oracle ASM
instance must be either the source or the target of the operation.
        You can use the cp command to:
             Copy files from a disk group to the operating system
             Copy files from a disk group to a disk group
             Copy files from the an OS File system to a disk group
        Some file types cannot be the source or destination of the cp command.
These file types include OCR, OCR backup and SPFILE file types.
To back up, copy, or move an ASM SPFILE, use the spbackup, spcopy, or spmove
commands. connect_str is not required for a local instance copy, which is the
default case. In the case of a remote instance copy, you must specify the connect
string and Oracle ASM prompts for a password in a non-echoing prompt. The
connect_str is in the form of:
                user@host.SID
user, host, and SID are required in the connect_str parameter. The
default port number is 1521.
        --service    - name of the ASM instance name if not default +ASM.
        connect_str  - The connection string to be used with a remote instance
        src_file must be either the a fully qualified file name,
        system-generated name, or Oracle ASM alias.
The cp command performs a binary copy without any data transformation.

Examples
        The following are examples of the cp command.
        The first example shows a copy of a file in the data disk group to a file
on the operating system.
        The second example shows a copy of a file on the operating system to the
DATA disk group.

ASMCMD [+] > cp +data/orcl/datafile/EXAMPLE.265.691577295
                /mybackups/example.bak
        copying +data/orcl/datafile/EXAMPLE.265.691577295 ->
                /mybackups/example.bak
```

```
ASMCMD [+] > cp /mybackups/examples.bak
                +data/orcl/datafile/myexamples.bak
        copying /mybackups/examples.bak -> +data/orcl/datafile/myexamples.bak
```

SQLPLUS

The databases running on an Exadata Machine can be administered by the SQLPLUS utility. The SQLPLUS utility is located in the $ORACLE_HOME/bin directory and can be invoked by sourcing the ORACLE_HOME and SID of the database. It is assumed that the reader is aware of SQLPLUS for administering the database, so we are not going to cover SQLPLUS in this book.

Administering Storage Cells

Exadata introduces storage cells, a feature unique to Exadata systems. The Exadata Storage Server stores all the physical disks and Flash cards. The server runs on a Linux OS and has its own CPU and memory. Exadata Storage Server runs the Exadata Storage software. Oracle does not allow you to install any other software into the Exadata Storage Cells. Under no circumstances should any software be installed into the Exadata Storage Cells.

By default, two users are created for logging into the Exadata Storage Server:

- **Celladmin** The administrative user that can perform all administrative activity in the storage cell

- **Cellmonitor** A read-only user that can monitor the various metrics related to the cell

Exadata Storage Server can be accessed only from the database compute nodes. It cannot be accessed from any other servers externally. The cellmonitor user can be SSH-ed to the Exadata Storage Cells from the database compute nodes without any password:

```
[oracle@exa10db01 ~]$ hostname
exa10db01.us.oracle.com
[oracle@exa10db01 ~]$ ssh cellmonitor@exa10cel01
Last login: Sun Jun 29 00:53:02 2014 from exa10db01.us.oracle.com
[cellmonitor@exa10cel01 ~]$
```

TIP & TECHNIQUE
Because the Exadata Storage Cells run on OEL, all
Linux commands work in Exadata Storage Cell.

CellCLI

Use the cell command-line interface (CellCLI) utility to manage the cell resources. The CellCLI utility can be invoked only by the celladmin or cellmonitor user. Cellmonitor is a read-only user and cannot make any changes. To make any changes, log in as the celladmin user. If you have integrated Enterprise Manager with the Oracle Exadata Machine, you can run all the commands related to CellCLI from the OEM as well.

CellCLI can be invoked by typing the **CELLCLI** command at the UNIX prompt from Exadata Storage Cells:

```
[celladmin@exa10cel01 ~]$ cellcli
CellCLI: Release 12.1.1.1.0 - Production on Sun Jun 29 03:17:47 EDT 2014

Copyright (c) 2007, 2013, Oracle.  All rights reserved.
Cell Efficiency Ratio: 24

CellCLI>
```

The commands for CellCLI are very similar to those of SQLPLUS, with a few minor differences. Typing **help** displays syntax and usage descriptions for all CellCLI commands. You can quit the CellCLI session by typing **quit** or **exit**, and you can also exit by pressing CTRL-C or CTRL-D. Similar to SQLPLUS, you can use **Spool** for spooling the output to a text file, use **SET** for setting parameter options in the CellCLI prompt, use **START** or @ for running the CellCLI commands in the specified script file, and use **DESCRIBE** for displaying the attribute.

As mentioned, there are a few minor differences between the CellCLI and SQLPLUS utilities, including the following: The most common command used in SQL queries is **Select**. In CellCLI, there is no select command; you use **LIST** instead. Similarly, in CellCLI there is no FROM keyword, which is most commonly used in SQLPLUS queries. A SQLPLUS query ends by putting a semicolon (;) at the end of the query, where CellCLI doesn't use the semicolon. When your CellCLI query ends, you can simply press the RETURN key to get the output. When you write long and complex queries using CellCLI that span multiple lines, you can use a hyphen (-) at the end of each line to continue the query.

Table 9-3 shows various options that can be used with the CellCLI utility.

Typing **help** at the CellCLI prompt gives you all the commands that can be run from the CellCLI tool:

```
CellCLI> help

 HELP [topic]
   Available Topics:
        ALTER
        ALTER ALERTHISTORY
        ALTER CELL
```

Option	Description
-n	Runs the CellCLI utility in non-interactive mode. This option suppresses the command prompt and disables the command-line editing features.
-m	Runs CellCLI monitor (read-only) mode.
-xml	Causes output to be displayed in XML format for the Oracle Enterprise Manager.
-v, -vv, and -vvv	Sets the log level. The -v option is for fine, -vv is for finer, and -vvv is for the finest level.
-x	Suppresses the banner.

-e *command*	Runs the specified **CELLCLI** command. CellCLI exits after running the command. For example:
	`$ cellcli -e list cell detail`
	`$ cellcli -e "list celldisk attributes name where name like '.*cell01'"`

TABLE 9-3. *CellCLI Options*

```
ALTER CELLDISK
ALTER FLASHCACHE
ALTER GRIDDISK
ALTER IBPORT
ALTER IORMPLAN
ALTER LUN
ALTER PHYSICALDISK
ALTER QUARANTINE
ALTER THRESHOLD
ASSIGN KEY
CALIBRATE
CREATE
CREATE CELL
CREATE CELLDISK
CREATE FLASHCACHE
CREATE FLASHLOG
CREATE GRIDDISK
CREATE KEY
CREATE QUARANTINE
CREATE THRESHOLD
DESCRIBE
DROP
DROP ALERTHISTORY
DROP CELL
```

```
        DROP CELLDISK
        DROP FLASHCACHE
        DROP FLASHLOG
        DROP GRIDDISK
        DROP QUARANTINE
        DROP THRESHOLD
        EXPORT CELLDISK
        IMPORT CELLDISK
        LIST
        LIST ACTIVEREQUEST
        LIST ALERTDEFINITION
        LIST ALERTHISTORY
        LIST CELL
        LIST CELLDISK
        LIST DATABASE
        LIST FLASHCACHE
        LIST FLASHCACHECONTENT
        LIST FLASHLOG
        LIST GRIDDISK
        LIST IBPORT
        LIST IORMPLAN
        LIST KEY
        LIST LUN
        LIST METRICCURRENT
        LIST METRICDEFINITION
        LIST METRICHISTORY
        LIST PHYSICALDISK
        LIST QUARANTINE
        LIST THRESHOLD
        SET
        SPOOL
        START
CellCLI>
```

CellCLI commands can be divided into four major categories:

- **ALTER**   Used for modifying a cell disk, cell, grid disk, Flash Cache, LUN, IORM plan, and so on

- **CREATE**   Used for creating cell disk, cell, Flash Cache, grid disk, and so on

- **DROP**   Used for dropping a cell, cell disk, grid disk, Flash Cache, Flash Log, and so on

- **LIST**   Used for listing the various metrics, configurations, alerts, settings, and so on

To run **ALTER**, **CREATE**, and **DROP** commands from the CellCLI, you need to log in as celladmin, since these commands are related to administrative tasks. You can run all the commands under LIST categories as cellmonitor user.

Notice in the "help" output that other commands such as **CREATE KEY**, **ASSIGN KEY**, **CALIBRATE**, **EXPORT CELLDISK**, and **IMPORT CELLDISK** can be run from the CellCLI interface as well. Let's take a quick look at what these commands do:

- **CREATE KEY**   Displays a random hexadecimal security key.

- **ASSIGN KEY**   Assigns a security key for a database or ASM client.

- **CALIBRATE**   Runs raw performance tests on cell disks. Run this command when the CELLSRV is down. Running this command on a live database will cause severe performance issues.

- **EXPORT CELLDISK**   Prepares a cell disk before moving (importing) to a different cell.

- **IMPORT CELLDISK**   Reinstates exported cell disks on a cell where you moved the physical drives that contain the cell disks.

The *cell object type* refers to the object that can be manipulated or queried using the **CELLCLI** command. We can divide the objects into three main categories:

- **Resource-related object types (representing hardware and software configuration)**   CELL, CELLDISK, GRIDDISK, IORMPLAN, KEY, LUN, and PHYSICALDISK

- **Performance metric object types**   ACTIVEREQUEST, METRICCURRENT, METRICDEFINITION, and METRICHISTORY

- **Alert object types**   ALERTDEFINITION, ALERTHISTORY, THRESHOLD

Every object has attributes, or a list of options for that particular object. The attributes are often filtered using the WHERE clause. Use the List Detail option to display all the attributes.

Thus, **CELLCLI** commands are in the following format:

```
<verb> <object-type> [ALL |object-name] [<options>]
```

Generic verbs ALTER, CREATE, DROP, and LIST are used to change, create, remove, and display objects, respectively. DESCRIBE is another verb used to get more information about a particular object. Here's an example:

```
LIST CELLDISK DETAIL
CREATE  GRIDDISK  ALL
LIST PHYSICALDISK ATTRIBUTES ALL
```

In **CELLCLI** commands, you can use a WHERE clause for filtering the attributes. An example is shown here:

```
CellCLI> list celldisk attributes name where disktype=harddisk;
```

Similar to SQLPLUS, you can write queries with "not equal to" in CellCLI. So the query with negation would look similar to the following example:

```
CellCLI> list celldisk attributes name where disktype !=harddisk;
```

Let's discuss some of the important operations that can be done from the CellCLI.

Managing Disks

When the Exadata Machine is installed and configured by Oracle ACS, all the ASM disk groups are also created. You may never need to re-create a disk group, but it is important that you understand the concept and it is good to know how to create one, just in case.

As discussed, a cell disk is the physical Logical Unit (LUN). Thus, we can say for each cell disk, there is a physical disk associated with it. The cell disk can be divided into multiple logical partitions, and these partitions are called *grid disks*, which are used to create the ASM disk groups. The grid disk is exposed as an ASM disk to the database host.

In a cell, there are 12 physical disks. You can check the 12 physical disks from the CellCLI by running the command **list physicaldisk**. You can even check the LUNs by running the command **list luns**. You can create a cell disk from the physical disks by running the following command from CellCLI:

```
CellCLI > create celldisk all harddisk
CellDisk CD_00_exa10cel01 successfully created
CellDisk CD_01_exa10cel01 successfully created
CellDisk CD_02_exa10cel01 successfully created
CellDisk CD_03_exa10cel01 successfully created
CellDisk CD_04_exa10cel01 successfully created
CellDisk CD_05_exa10cel01 successfully created
CellDisk CD_06_exa10cel01 successfully created
CellDisk CD_07_exa10cel01 successfully created
CellDisk CD_08_exa10cel01 successfully created
CellDisk CD_09_exa10cel01 successfully created
CellDisk CD_10_exa10cel01 successfully created
CellDisk CD_11_exa10cel01 successfully created
```

This command converts all the physical disks (LUNs) into cell disks. If the size of the physical disk is 4TB, then the size of the cell disk would be 4TB. You can now carve out grid disks from the cell disk for creating the ASM disk groups.

From one cell disk, you can create multiple grid disks of different sizes. The sum total of all the grid disks created from a cell disk can't exceed the size of that cell disk. Thus,

Size of a cell disk = (Size of first grid disk + Size of second grid disk +....Size of *n*th grid disk)

Let's look at an example. Suppose we want to create two disk groups, say DATA and RECO, with the ratio 60:40, and we also want to keep 1TB of free space in each cell disk for the future. In that case, the space available to us in each cell disk for creating the DATA and RECO disk groups would be 3TB (4TB – 1TB). If we need to give 60 percent to the DATA disk group, the size we need to allocate is 60 percent of 3TB, which translates to 1.8TB. Then for the RECO disk group, we will allocate 40 percent of 3TB from each cell disk, which would be 1.2TB. Therefore, we need two separate grid disks from each cell disk: one of size 1.8TB for the DATA disk group and another of size 1.2TB for the RECO disk group.

To create the grid disks for the DATA disk group, we run the following command:

```
CellCLI> create griddisk all prefix=DATA, size=1800G
GridDisk DATA_CD_00_exa10cel01 successfully created
GridDisk DATA_CD_01_exa10cel01 successfully created
GridDisk DATA_CD_02_exa10cel01 successfully created
GridDisk DATA_CD_03_exa10cel01 successfully created
GridDisk DATA_CD_04_exa10cel01 successfully created
GridDisk DATA_CD_05_exa10cel01 successfully created
GridDisk DATA_CD_06_exa10cel01 successfully created
GridDisk DATA_CD_07_exa10cel01 successfully created
GridDisk DATA_CD_08_exa10cel01 successfully created
GridDisk DATA_CD_09_exa10cel01 successfully created
GridDisk DATA_CD_10_exa10cel01 successfully created
GridDisk DATA_CD_11_exa10cel01 successfully created
```

Similarly, to create a separate set of grid disks for the RECO disk group, we run the following command:

```
CellCLI> create griddisk all prefix=RECO, size=1200G
GridDisk RECO_CD_00_exa10cel01 successfully created
GridDisk RECO_CD_01_exa10cel01 successfully created
GridDisk RECO_CD_02_exa10cel01 successfully created
GridDisk RECO_CD_03_exa10cel01 successfully created
GridDisk RECO_CD_04_exa10cel01 successfully created
GridDisk RECO_CD_05_exa10cel01 successfully created
GridDisk RECO_CD_06_exa10cel01 successfully created
GridDisk RECO_CD_07_exa10cel01 successfully created
GridDisk RECO_CD_08_exa10cel01 successfully created
GridDisk RECO_CD_09_exa10cel01 successfully created
GridDisk RECO_CD_10_exa10cel01 successfully created
GridDisk RECO_CD_11_exa10cel01 successfully created
```

After you create grid disks, they are immediately available to create the ASM disk groups. You can use all the grid disks with the prefix *DATA* for creating the DATA disk group and the grid disks with the prefix *RECO* for creating the RECO disk group. After creating the grid disks, you can verify the same by running the command **list griddisk** from CellCLI:

```
CellCLI> list griddisk
        DATA_CD_00_exa10cel01          active
        DATA_CD_01_exa10cel01          active
        DATA_CD_02_exa10cel01          active
        DATA_CD_03_exa10cel01          active
        DATA_CD_04_exa10cel01          active
        DATA_CD_05_exa10cel01          active
        DATA_CD_06_exa10cel01          active
        DATA_CD_07_exa10cel01          active
        DATA_CD_08_exa10cel01          active
        DATA_CD_09_exa10cel01          active
        DATA_CD_10_exa10cel01          active
        DATA_CD_11_exa10cel01          active
        RECO_CD_00_exa10cel01          active
        RECO_CD_01_exa10cel01          active
        RECO_CD_02_exa10cel01          active
        RECO_CD_03_exa10cel01          active
        RECO_CD_04_exa10cel01          active
        RECO_CD_05_exa10cel01          active
        RECO_CD_06_exa10cel01          active
        RECO_CD_07_exa10cel01          active
        RECO_CD_08_exa10cel01          active
        RECO_CD_09_exa10cel01          active
        RECO_CD_10_exa10cel01          active
        RECO_CD_11_exa10cel01          active
```

You can also run the command **list griddisk detail** or **list griddisk <GRID_DISK_ NAME> detail** to obtain information about the grid disks.

In our example, we have 1TB free space in cell disks that we can use for creating other disk groups in the future. Suppose we want to create the DBFS disk group with the remaining space; we could run the following command:

```
CREATE GRIDDISK ALL PREFIX=DBFS
```

Note that if you don't indicate the size when creating the grid disk, CellCLI will use all the remaining free space available at the cell disk.

Managing Flash

Similar to managing physical disks, the Flash Cache can be managed using the CellCLI interface. The Flash disks are also presented to the Exadata Storage Cells as cell disks.

You may not be required to run this command because this is configured for you by Oracle ACS. However, if you want to delete all the default Flash configurations and reconfigure them again using a different configuration, you can drop the existing Flash Cache by running the following command:

```
CellCLI> drop flashcache
Flash cache exa10cel01_FLASHCACHE successfully dropped
```

You can create cell disks of all the Flash disks by running the following command:

```
CellCLI> create celldisk all flashdisk
```

This will create a cell disk using all the available Flash in the storage cell. At this point, you have two choices: use all the available Flash to create the Exadata Smart Flash Cache or use a portion of the Flash to create the Flash-based ASM disk group and use the remaining for creating the Exadata Smart Flash Cache, although we don't recommend creating a Flash-based ASM disk group. Flash Write Back Cache does more or less the same thing and reduces the size of Flash available to Exadata Smart Flash Cache.

If you don't want to create a Flash-based ASM disk group, you can use all the Flash now available as a cell disk to create the Exadata Smart Flash Cache by running the following command:

```
CellCLI> create flashcache all
Flash cache exa10cel01_FLASHCACHE successfully created
```

To create a portion of the Flash for creating the ASM disk group, you need to make a grid disk out of the cell disk, exactly as we did earlier for the physical drive, and use it for the Flash-based ASM disk group. Suppose you want to carve out 150GB from each Flash card to create the grid disk. You'd use the following command:

```
CellCLI> create griddisk all prefix=FLASH, size=150G
```

Now you can use the remaining Flash to create the Exadata Smart Flash Cache by running the following command:

```
create flashcache all
```

Multiple options are available for creating the Exadata Smart Flash Cache. You can use only a few cell disks, or you can specify the size of the Exadata Smart Flash Cache in the command itself.

To use only a certain cell disk, use this command:

```
CellCLI> create flashcache celldisk='FD_00_exa10cel01'
Flash cache cell01_FLASHCACHE successfully created
```

To specify a certain size, use this command:

```
CellCLI> create flashcache all size=500G
```

Monitoring Using CellCLI

The CELLSRV process manages the Exadata Storage Server and collects all the metrics related to various components running inside the Exadata Storage Cells, such as CPU activity, memory usage, activity on the Flash Cache, disk-based activities, I/O-related activities, IORM, and so on. Management Server (MS) captures these metrics from CELLSRV and writes them to internal disk, where all the metrics are stored. By default, all the metrics are stored for seven days, but you can change this to any value as needed.

To change the default number of days to a higher value, you can run the following command:

```
CellCLI> alter cell metricHistoryDays=30
Cell exa10cel01 successfully altered
CellCLI> list cell attributes metricHistoryDays
    30
```

Keep in mind that increasing the metric history days to a higher number can cause the local file system in the Exadata Storage Cells to fill quickly.

To understand metrics, you should also understand the various definitions associated with the metrics collection. The metrics related to a particular object are displayed with abbreviations separated by underscores: CD_IO_RQ_R_SM.

The attribute value usually starts with the abbreviation of the object type, like so:

- CL_ represents cell

- CD_ represents cell disk

- GD_ represents grid disk

- FC_ represents Flash Cache

- DB_ represents database

- CG_ represents consumer group

- CT_ represents category

- N_ represents network

After the abbreviation of the object type, most of the name attributes contain one of the following combinations to identify the operation:

- IO_RQ (number of requests)

- IO_BY (number of MB)

- IO_TM (I/O latency)

- IO_WT (I/O wait time)

Next could be _R or _W, for read or write. Following that in the name attribute value may be _SM or _LG to identify small or large blocks, respectively. At the end of the name is _SEC to signify per seconds or _RQ to signify per request.

Here are some examples of attribute names:

- CD_IO_RQ_R_SM is the number of requests to read small blocks on a cell disk.

- GD_IO_TM_W_LG is the microseconds of I/O latency writing large blocks on a grid disk.

You can use LIST METRICCURRENT or LIST METRICHISTORY to capture the current or historical metrics. You can filter the metric according to object—CELL, CELLDISK, CELL_FILESYSTEM, GRIDDISK, IORM_CATEGORY, IORM_DATABASE, IORM_CONSUMER_GROUP, or HOST_INTERCONNECT.

```
CellCLI> LIST METRICCURRENT WHERE objectType = CELL_FILESYSTEM
        CL_FSUT    "/"                63 %
        CL_FSUT    "/boot"            45 %
        CL_FSUT    "/dev/shm"          0 %
        CL_FSUT    "/opt/oracle"      63 %
        CL_FSUT    "/var/log/oracle"  12 %

CellCLI> list metriccurrent gd_io_rq_w_sm
        GD_IO_RQ_W_SM    DBFS_DG_CD_02_exa10cel01    112,198,119 IO requests
        GD_IO_RQ_W_SM    DBFS_DG_CD_03_exa10cel01    99,649 IO requests
        GD_IO_RQ_W_SM    DBFS_DG_CD_04_exa10cel01    86,880 IO requests
        GD_IO_RQ_W_SM    DBFS_DG_CD_05_exa10cel01    6,145 IO requests
        GD_IO_RQ_W_SM    DBFS_DG_CD_06_exa10cel01    93,784 IO requests
        GD_IO_RQ_W_SM    DBFS_DG_CD_07_exa10cel01    95,141 IO requests
        GD_IO_RQ_W_SM    DBFS_DG_CD_08_exa10cel01    5,433 IO requests
        GD_IO_RQ_W_SM    DBFS_DG_CD_09_exa10cel01    6,271 IO requests
        GD_IO_RQ_W_SM    DBFS_DG_CD_10_exa10cel01    102,443 IO requests
        GD_IO_RQ_W_SM    DBFS_DG_CD_11_exa10cel01    4,398 IO requests
        GD_IO_RQ_W_SM    Q1DATA_CD_00_exa10cel01     8,672,769 IO requests
        GD_IO_RQ_W_SM    Q1DATA_CD_01_exa10cel01     9,331,560 IO requests
        GD_IO_RQ_W_SM    Q1DATA_CD_02_exa10cel01     8,847,801 IO requests
```

```
GD_IO_RQ_W_SM      Q1DATA_CD_03_exa10cel01       21,493,131 IO requests
GD_IO_RQ_W_SM      Q1DATA_CD_04_exa10cel01        8,394,078 IO requests
GD_IO_RQ_W_SM      Q1DATA_CD_05_exa10cel01        8,795,662 IO requests
GD_IO_RQ_W_SM      Q1DATA_CD_06_exa10cel01        8,989,702 IO requests
GD_IO_RQ_W_SM      Q1DATA_CD_07_exa10cel01        8,756,546 IO requests
GD_IO_RQ_W_SM      Q1DATA_CD_08_exa10cel01        8,952,387 IO requests
GD_IO_RQ_W_SM      Q1DATA_CD_09_exa10cel01        8,987,333 IO requests
GD_IO_RQ_W_SM      Q1DATA_CD_10_exa10cel01       17,652,597 IO requests
GD_IO_RQ_W_SM      Q1DATA_CD_11_exa10cel01        8,774,468 IO requests
GD_IO_RQ_W_SM      Q1RECO_CD_00_exa10cel01        1,346,142 IO requests
GD_IO_RQ_W_SM      Q1RECO_CD_01_exa10cel01        6,062,850 IO requests
GD_IO_RQ_W_SM      Q1RECO_CD_02_exa10cel01        1,171,038 IO requests
GD_IO_RQ_W_SM      Q1RECO_CD_03_exa10cel01          985,152 IO requests
GD_IO_RQ_W_SM      Q1RECO_CD_04_exa10cel01        1,758,764 IO requests
GD_IO_RQ_W_SM      Q1RECO_CD_05_exa10cel01        1,490,915 IO requests
GD_IO_RQ_W_SM      Q1RECO_CD_06_exa10cel01        1,324,112 IO requests
GD_IO_RQ_W_SM      Q1RECO_CD_07_exa10cel01        1,237,607 IO requests
GD_IO_RQ_W_SM      Q1RECO_CD_08_exa10cel01        1,135,078 IO requests
GD_IO_RQ_W_SM      Q1RECO_CD_09_exa10cel01        1,584,782 IO requests
GD_IO_RQ_W_SM      Q1RECO_CD_10_exa10cel01        2,044,893 IO requests
GD_IO_RQ_W_SM      Q1RECO_CD_11_exa10cel01        1,120,146 IO requests
```

For an OLTP system, Flash plays a very important role, so it is important that you monitor the metrics of the Exadata Smart Flash Cache. All the metrics related to Exadata Smart Flash Cache are presented in Addendum 9.1 at the end of this chapter. Similarly, you may want to monitor the metric of the Smart Flash Log to see if the default size of the Smart Flash Log is good enough or you may need to increase it. The metrics related to Smart Flash Log are given in Addendum 9.2.

A list of various CellCLI commands is compiled in Addendum 9.3 so that you can run those commands and learn more details.

Distributed Command Line Interface (DCLI)

The Distributed Command Line Interface (DCLI) is used to run CellCLI commands across multiple cells at the same time from one location. Using DCLI, you don't have to log in to each and every cell to run commands. You can run all the commands from a single cell only. With DCLI, you can issue only *one* command on *one* host and get the result from all the targeted cells.

DCLI assumes that the SSH setup is already done across the cells, since it makes a remote call to the cell where you want to execute the CellCLI commands. The DCLI is written in Python script.

You can run the **dcli** command in multiple cells using the option -c. Here's an example:

```
[oracle@exa10db01 ~]$ dcli -c exa10cel01,exa10cel02,exa10cel03 'cellcli
-e list cell detail'
celladmin@exa10cel01's password:
```

```
celladmin@exa10cel02's password:
celladmin@exa10cel03's password:
exa10cel01: exa10cel01 online
exa10cel01: exa10cel01 online
exa10cel01: exa10cel01 online
```

Instead of typing all the names of the cells, you can create a text file with the names of all the cells and use the -g option. For example, in the following, we have created a file called cell_names, and we will run the same command using the option -g:

```
[oracle@exa10db01 ~]$ dcli -g cell_names 'cellcli -e list cell detail'

#cat cell_names
exa10cel01
exa10cel02
exa10cel03
```

Note that DCLI can be used to run any UNIX commands remotely. The scope of DCLI is not just limited to CellCLI. You can even use DCLI to shut down multiple storage cells:

```
# dcli -l root -g cell_names  shutdown -h -y now
```

Similarly, you can use DCLI for running any other UNIX commands. The various options for DCLI are listed in Table 9-4.

Option	Description
-c *cells*	Specifies a comma-delimited list of target cells to which commands are sent.
-d *destfile*	Specifies the target destination directory or file on remote cells to be used when copying files or directories using the -f option.
-f *file*	Specifies the files or file template to be copied to the cells. These files are not run. They can be script files to be run later. The files are copied to the default home directory of the user on the target cell.
-g *groupFile*	Specifies a file containing a list of target cells to which commands are sent. The cells can be identified by cell names or IP addresses.
-h, --help	Displays help text and then exits.
--hidestderr	Hides standard error messages (STDERR) for commands run remotely using SSH.
-k	Sets up SSH user-equivalence for the current user to the cells specified with the -c or -g option by appending public key files to the authorized_keys file on cells.

(continued)

TABLE 9-4. *DCLI Options*

Option	Description
-l *userId*	Identifies the user to log in as on remote cells. The default is the celladmin user.
-n	Abbreviates non-error output. Cells that return normal output (return code of 0) have only the cell name listed. The -n and -r options cannot be used together.
-r *regexp*	Abbreviates the output lines that match a regular expression. All output lines with that pattern are deleted from output, and the cell names from those output lines are listed on one line. The -r and -n options cannot be used together.
-s *sshOptions*	Passes a string of options to SSH.
--scp= *scpOptions*	Passes a string of options to scp if different from *sshOptions*.
--serial	Serializes the process over Oracle Exadata Storage Servers.
--showbanner, --sh	Shows the banner of the remote node when using SSH.
-t	Displays the target cells that are named with the -c option or in the *groupfile* identified by the -g option.
--unkey	Drops keys from the target authorized_keys file on Oracle Exadata Storage Servers.
-v	Prints the verbose version of messages to stdout.
--version	Shows the version number of the program and then exits.
--vmstat=VMSTATOPS	Displays view process, virtual memory, disk, trap, and CPU activity information, depending on the switches.
-x *execFile*	Specifies the command file to be copied and run on the cells. The specified file contains a list of commands. A file with the .scl extension is run by the CellCLI utility. A file with a different extension is run by the operating system shell on the cell. The file is copied to the default home directory of the user on the target cell.

TABLE 9-4. *DCLI Options*

Summary

In this chapter you have learned how to start and stop the Exadata Machine and how to manage all the components of the Exadata Machine. Because the operating system running in an Exadata Machine is Oracle Enterprise Linux, all the Linux commands can be used to administer the Exadata compute nodes and the storage cells.

We discussed how to manage the various components running in the Exadata Machine. In the database compute nodes, all the regular Linux commands can be used for Exadata administration.

The Grid Infrastructure can be managed using the CRSCTL and SRVCTL utilities. The RAC databases should be managed using the SRVCTL utility. All the database administration activity can be done using the SQLPLUS tool. Any administrative task within an ASM disk group can be done using the ASMCMD utility. The administrative tasks within an ASM instance can be done using SQLPLUS, as well by connecting to the ASM instance.

Exadata Storage Servers are completely unique to Exadata. The Exadata Storage Servers can be managed by the CellCLI and DCLI tools. You can monitor all the components within a storage cell (cell disk, grid disk, Exadata Smart Flash Cache, Exadata Smart Flash Log, and so on) using the CellCLI utility.

Addendum 9.1: Flash Cache Metrics and Descriptions

Metric	Description
FC_BY_ALLOCATED	The number of megabytes allocated in Flash Cache.
FC_BY_DIRTY	The number of megabytes in Flash Cache that are not synchronized to the grid disks.
FC_BY_STALE_DIRTY	The number of megabytes in Flash Cache that cannot be synchronized because the cached disks are not accessible.
FC_BY_USED	The number of megabytes used in Flash Cache.
FC_BYKEEP_OVERWR	The number of megabytes pushed out of Flash Cache because of the space limitation for keep objects.
FC_BYKEEP_OVERWR_SEC	The number of megabytes per second pushed out of Flash Cache because of space limitation for keep objects.
FC_BYKEEP_USED	The number of megabytes used for keep objects on Flash Cache.
FC_IO_BY_ALLOCATED_OLTP	The number of megabytes allocated for OLTP data in Flash Cache.
FC_IO_BY_DISK_WRITE	The number of megabytes written from Flash Cache to hard disks.
FC_IO_BY_DISK_WRITE_SEC	The number of megabytes per second written from Flash Cache to hard disks.
FC_IO_BY_R	The number of megabytes read from Flash Cache.
FC_IO_BY_R_ACTIVE_SECONDARY	The number of megabytes for active secondary reads satisfied from Flash Cache.
FC_IO_BY_R_ACTIVE_SECONDARY_MISS	The number of megabytes for active secondary reads not satisfied from Flash Cache.
FC_IO_BY_R_ACTIVE_SECONDARY_MISS_SEC	The number of megabytes per second for active secondary reads not satisfied from Flash Cache.
FC_IO_BY_R_ACTIVE_SECONDARY_SEC	The number of megabytes per second for active secondary reads satisfied from Flash Cache.
FC_IO_BY_R_DW	The number of megabytes of DW data read from Flash Cache.
FC_IO_BY_R_MISS	The number of megabytes read from disks because not all requested data was in Flash Cache.

Metric	Description
FC_IO_BY_R_MISS_DW	The number of megabytes of DW data read from disks because not all requested data was in Flash Cache.
FC_IO_BY_R_MISS_SEC	The number of megabytes read from disks per second because not all requested data was in Flash Cache.
FC_IO_BY_R_SEC	The number of megabytes read per second from Flash Cache.
FC_IO_BY_R_SKIP	The number of megabytes read from disks for I/O requests that bypass Flash Cache.
FC_IO_BY_R_SKIP_FC_THROTTLE	The number of megabytes read from disk for I/O requests that bypass Flash Cache due to heavy load on Flash Cache.
FC_IO_BY_R_SKIP_FC_THROTTLE_SEC	The number of megabytes read per second from disk for I/O requests that bypass Flash Cache due to heavy load on Flash Cache.
FC_IO_BY_R_SKIP_LG	The number of megabytes read from disk for I/O requests that bypass Flash Cache due to the large I/O size.
FC_IO_BY_R_SKIP_LG_SEC	The number of megabytes read per second from disk for I/O requests that bypass Flash Cache due to the large I/O size.
FC_IO_BY_R_SKIP_NCMIRROR	The number of megabytes read from disk for I/O requests that bypass Flash Cache as the I/O is on a non-primary, non-active secondary mirror.
FC_IO_BY_R_SKIP_SEC	The number of megabytes read from disks per second for I/O requests that bypass Flash Cache.
FC_IO_BY_W	The number of megabytes written to Flash Cache.
FC_IO_BY_W_FIRST	The number of megabytes that are first writes to Flash Cache.
FC_IO_BY_W_FIRST_SEC	The number of megabytes per second for first writes to Flash Cache.
FC_IO_BY_W_OVERWRITE	The number of megabytes that are overwrites to Flash Cache.
FC_IO_BY_W_OVERWRITE_SEC	The number of megabytes per second that are overwrites into Flash Cache.
FC_IO_BY_W_POPULATE	The number of megabytes for population writes into Flash Cache due to read misses.
FC_IO_BY_W_POPULATE_SEC	The number of megabytes per second that are population writes into Flash Cache due to read misses into Flash Cache.
FC_IO_BY_W_SEC	The number of megabytes per second written to Flash Cache.
FC_IO_BY_W_SKIP	The number of megabytes written to disk for I/O requests that bypass Flash Cache.
FC_IO_BY_W_SKIP_FC_THROTTLE	The number of megabytes written to disk for I/O requests that bypass Flash Cache due to heavy load on Flash Cache.
FC_IO_BY_W_SKIP_FC_THROTTLE_SEC	The number of megabytes written per second to disk for I/O requests that bypass Flash Cache due to heavy load on Flash Cache.
FC_IO_BY_W_SKIP_LG	The number of megabytes written to disk for I/O requests that bypass Flash Cache due to the large I/O size.
FC_IO_BY_W_SKIP_LG_SEC	The number of megabytes written per second to disk for I/O requests that bypass Flash Cache due to the large I/O size.
FC_IO_BY_W_SKIP_NCMIRROR	The number of megabytes written to disk for I/O requests that bypass Flash Cache as the I/O is on a non-primary, non-active secondary mirror.

Metric	Description
FC_IO_BY_W_SKIP_SEC	The number of megabytes written to disk per second for I/O requests that bypass Flash Cache.
FC_IO_BYKEEP_R	The number of megabytes read from Flash Cache for keep objects.
FC_IO_BYKEEP_R_SEC	The number of megabytes read per second from Flash Cache for keep objects.
FC_IO_BYKEEP_W	The number of megabytes written to Flash Cache for keep objects.
FC_IO_BYKEEP_W_SEC	The number of megabytes per second written to Flash Cache for keep objects.
FC_IO_ERRS	The number of I/O errors on Flash Cache.
FC_IO_RQ_DISK_WRITE	The number of requests written from Flash Cache to hard disks.
FC_IO_RQ_DISK_WRITE_SEC	The number of requests per second for Flash Cache writing data to hard disks.
FC_IO_RQ_R	The number of read I/O requests satisfied from Flash Cache.
FC_IO_RQ_R_ACTIVE_SECONDARY	The number of requests for active secondary reads satisfied from Flash Cache.
FC_IO_RQ_R_ACTIVE_SECONDARY_MISS	The number of requests for active secondary reads not satisfied from Flash Cache.
FC_IO_RQ_R_ACTIVE_SECONDARY_MISS_SEC	The number of requests per second for active secondary reads not satisfied from Flash Cache.
FC_IO_RQ_R_ACTIVE_SECONDARY_SEC	The number of requests per second for active secondary reads satisfied from Flash Cache.
FC_IO_RQ_R_DW	The number of read I/O requests of DW data read from Flash Cache.
FC_IO_RQ_R_MISS	The number of read I/O requests that did not find all data in Flash Cache.
FC_IO_RQ_R_MISS_DW	The number of read I/O requests of DW data read from disks because not all requested data was in Flash Cache.
FC_IO_RQ_R_MISS_SEC	The number of read I/O requests per second that did not find all data in Flash Cache.
FC_IO_RQ_R_SEC	The number of read I/O requests satisfied per second from Flash Cache.
FC_IO_RQ_R_SKIP	The number of read I/O requests that bypass Flash Cache.
FC_IO_RQ_R_SKIP_FC_THROTTLE	The number of requests read from disk that bypass Flash Cache due to heavy load on Flash Cache.
FC_IO_RQ_R_SKIP_FC_THROTTLE_SEC	The number of requests per second read from disk that bypassed Flash Cache due to heavy load on Flash Cache.
FC_IO_RQ_R_SKIP_LG	The number of read I/O requests that bypass Flash Cache due to the large I/O size.
FC_IO_RQ_R_SKIP_LG_SEC	The number of read I/O requests per second that bypass Flash Cache due to the large I/O size.
FC_IO_RQ_R_SKIP_NCMIRROR	The number of requests read from disk that bypass Flash Cache as the I/O is on a non-primary, non-active secondary mirror.
FC_IO_RQ_R_SKIP_SEC	The number of read I/O requests per second that bypass Flash Cache.

Metric	Description
FC_IO_RQ_REPLACEMENT_ATTEMPTED	The number of requests that attempted to find space in the Flash Cache.
FC_IO_RQ_REPLACEMENT_FAILED	The number of requests that failed to find space in the Flash Cache.
FC_IO_RQ_W	The number of I/O requests that resulted in Flash Cache being populated with data.
FC_IO_RQ_W_FIRST	The number of requests that are first writes into Flash Cache.
FC_IO_RQ_W_FIRST_SEC	The number of requests per second that are first writes into Flash Cache.
FC_IO_RQ_W_OVERWRITE	The number of requests that are overwrites into Flash Cache.
FC_IO_RQ_W_OVERWRITE_SEC	The number of requests per second that are overwrites into Flash Cache.
FC_IO_RQ_W_POPULATE	The number of requests that are population writes into Flash Cache due to read misses.
FC_IO_RQ_W_POPULATE_SEC	The number of requests per second that are population writes into Flash Cache due to read misses.
FC_IO_RQ_W_SEC	The number of I/O requests per second that resulted in Flash Cache being populated with data.
FC_IO_RQ_W_SKIP	The number of write I/O requests that bypass Flash Cache.
FC_IO_RQ_W_SKIP_FC_THROTTLE	The number of requests written to disk that bypass Flash Cache due to heavy load on Flash Cache.
FC_IO_RQ_W_SKIP_FC_THROTTLE_SEC	The number of requests written to disk per second that bypass Flash Cache due to heavy load on Flash Cache.
FC_IO_RQ_W_SKIP_LG	The number of requests written to disk that bypass Flash Cache due to the large I/O size.
FC_IO_RQ_W_SKIP_LG_SEC	The number of requests written to disk per second that bypass Flash Cache due to the large I/O size.
FC_IO_RQ_W_SKIP_NCMIRROR	The number of requests written to disk that bypass Flash Cache as the I/O is on a non-primary, non-active secondary mirror.
FC_IO_RQ_W_SKIP_SEC	The number of write I/O requests per second that bypass Flash Cache.
FC_IO_RQKEEP_R	The number of read I/O requests for keep objects from Flash Cache.
FC_IO_RQKEEP_R_MISS	The number of read I/O requests for keep objects that did not find all data in Flash Cache.
FC_IO_RQKEEP_R_MISS_SEC	The number of read I/O requests per second for keep objects that did not find all data in Flash Cache.
FC_IO_RQKEEP_R_SEC	The number of read I/O requests per second for keep objects satisfied from Flash Cache.
FC_IO_RQKEEP_R_SKIP	The number of read I/O requests for keep objects that bypass Flash Cache.
FC_IO_RQKEEP_R_SKIP_SEC	The rate that is the number of read I/O requests per second for keep objects that bypass Flash Cache.
FC_IO_RQKEEP_W	The number of I/O requests for keep objects that resulted in Flash Cache being populated with data.
FC_IO_RQKEEP_W_SEC	The number of I/O requests per second for keep objects that resulted in Flash Cache being populated with data.

Addendum 9.2: Exadata Smart Flash Log Metrics and Descriptions

Metric	Description
FL_ACTUAL_OUTLIERS	The number of redo writes written to Flash and disk that exceeded the outlier threshold.
FL_BY_KEEP	The number of redo data bytes saved on Flash due to disk I/O errors.
FL_DISK_FIRST	The number of redo writes first written to disk.
FL_DISK_IO_ERRS	The number of disk I/O errors encountered by Oracle Exadata Smart Flash Log.
FL_EFFICIENCY_PERCENTAGE	The efficiency of Oracle Exadata Smart Flash Log expressed as a percentage.
FL_EFFICIENCY_PERCENTAGE_HOUR	The efficiency of Oracle Exadata Smart Flash Log over the past hour expressed as a percentage.
FL_FLASH_FIRST	The number of redo writes first written to Flash.
FL_FLASH_IO_ERRS	The number of Flash I/O errors encountered by Oracle Exadata Smart Flash Log.
FL_FLASH_ONLY_OUTLIERS	The number of redo writes written to Flash that exceeded the outlier threshold.
FL_IO_DB_BY_W	The number of megabytes written to hard disk by Oracle Exadata Smart Flash Log.
FL_IO_DB_BY_W_SEC	The number of megabytes written per second to hard disk by Oracle Exadata Smart Flash Log.
FL_IO_FL_BY_W	The number of megabytes written to Flash by Oracle Exadata Smart Flash Log.
FL_IO_FL_BY_W_SEC	The number of megabytes written per second to Flash by Oracle Exadata Smart Flash Log.
FL_IO_W	The number of writes serviced by Oracle Exadata Smart Flash Log.
FL_IO_W_SKIP_BUSY	The number of redo writes that could not be serviced by Oracle Exadata Smart Flash Log because too much data had not yet been written to disk.
FL_IO_W_SKIP_BUSY_MIN	The number of redo writes during the last minute that could not be serviced by Oracle Exadata Smart Flash Log because too much data had not yet been written to disk.
FL_IO_W_SKIP_LARGE	The number of large redo writes that could not be serviced by Oracle Exadata Smart Flash Log because the size of the data was larger than the amount of available space on any Flash disk.
FL_IO_W_SKIP_NO_BUFFER	The number of redo writes that could not be serviced by Oracle Exadata Smart Flash Log due to lack of available buffers.
FL_PREVENTED_OUTLIERS	The number of redo writes written to disk that exceeded the outlier threshold. These writes would have been outliers if not for Oracle Exadata Smart Flash Log.

Addendum 9.3: Sample Commands Related to CellCLI

The commands are presented here to help you better understand the CellCLI tool and how to use it. In no circumstances should you run commands related to **ALTER**, **CREATE**, and **DROP** in a live production system if you do not understand what the command does. The author assumes no responsibility in case any damage happens to your system by running these commands. Some of the commands may work for you; some of the commands may not work for you, depending on the context.

Sample Commands Related to ALTER

```
CellCLI> alter cell shutdown services ALL
CellCLI> alter cell restart services ALL
CellCLI> alter cell shutdown services CELLSRV
CellCLI> alter cell restart services CELLSRV
CellCLI> alter cell shutdown services RS
CellCLI> alter cell restart services RS
CellCLI> alter cell shutdown services MS
CellCLI> alter cell restart services MS
CellCLI> alter cell led off
CellCLI> alter cell led on
CellCLI> alter alerthistory 8 examinedby="Prod_DBA"
CellCLI> alter physicaldisk all serviceled on
CellCLI> alter physicaldisk all serviceled off
CellCLI> alter physicaldisk harddisk serviceled on
CellCLI> alter physicaldisk all serviceled on
CellCLI> alter celldisk all flashdisk comment='Flash'
CellCLI> alter griddisk DATA_CD_01_exa10cel01 comment='ASM DATA DG'
CellCLI> alter griddisk all active
CellCLI> alter griddisk DATA_CD_01_exa10cel01 active
```

Sample Commands Related to CREATE

```
CellCLI> create celldisk all harddisk
CellCLI> create celldisk all flashdisk
CellCLI> create griddisk all prefix=DATA
CellCLI> create griddisk all prefix=RECO
CellCLI> create griddisk all flashdisk prefix=FLASH
CellCLI> create griddisk all harddisk prefix=DATA
CellCLI> create griddisk all prefix=RECO, size=1200G
CellCLI> create griddisk all harddisk prefix=DATA, size=500g
CellCLI> create flashcache all
CellCLI> create flashcache all size=800G
CellCLI> create flashcache celldisk='FD_00_exa10cel01'
```

Sample Commands Related to DROP

```
CellCLI> drop cell
CellCLI> drop cell force
CellCLI> drop celldisk all
CellCLI> drop celldisk harddisk
CellCLI> drop celldisk flashdisk
CellCLI> drop celldisk all flashdisk force
CellCLI> drop celldisk CD_01_exa10cel01
CellCLI> drop celldisk CD_01_exa10cel01 force
CellCLI> drop griddisk all
CellCLI> drop griddisk DATA_CD_01_exa10cel01
CellCLI> drop griddisk DATA_CD_01_exa10cel01 force
CellCLI> drop griddisk prefix=DATA
CellCLI> drop flashcache
```

Sample Commands Related to LIST

```
CellCLI> LIST ACTIVEREQUEST DETAIL
CellCLI> LIST ALERTHISTORY DETAIL
CellCLI> LIST ALERTDEFINITION DETAIL
CellCLI> LIST CELL attributes status, cellnumber
CellCLI> LIST CELL DETAIL
CellCLI> LIST CELLDISK CD_00_exa10cel01 DETAIL
CellCLI> LIST CELLDISK where freespace > 500M
CellCLI> LIST DATABASE DETAIL
CellCLI> LIST FLASHCACHE DETAIL
CellCLI> LIST FLASHCACHECONTENT DETAIL
CellCLI> LIST FLASHLOG DETAIL
CellCLI> LIST GRIDDISK where size > 500G
CellCLI> LIST GRIDDISK <gd_name> DETAIL
CellCLI> LIST IBPORT DETAIL
CellCLI> LIST IBPORT WHERE status='Active' ATTRIBUTES name, lid,
portNumber DETAIL
CellCLI> LIST IORMPLAN DETAIL
CellCLI> list metriccurrent
CellCLI> list metriccurrent where objecttype='celldisk'
CellCLI> list metriccurrent cl_cput, cl_runq detail
CellCLI> list metriccurrent where alertState ! = 'normal'
CellCLI> list metriccurrent where metricObjectName = '<Cell_DISK_NAME>'
ATTRIBUTES name,metricValue
CellCLI> LIST LUN where celldisk = null
CellCLI> LIST LUN DETAIL
CellCLI> LIST METRICDEFINITION DETAIL
CellCLI> LIST METRICDEFINITION ATTRIBUTES ALL
```

```
CellCLI> list metrichistory CL_CPUT where collectionTime > ' 2014-04-
28T13:32:13-07:00'
CellCLI> list metrichistory DB_IO_WT_SM_RQ where alertState ! =
'normal' AND - collectionTime > ' 2014-04-28T13:32:13-07:00'
CellCLI> list metrichistory where metricObjectName like 'CD.*' AND -
                     collectionTime > ' 2014-04-28T13:32:13-07:00'
                     AND -
                     collectionTime < ' 2014-04-28T15:32:13-07:00'
CellCLI> LIST PHYSICALDISK DETAIL
CellCLI> LIST QUARANTINE  DETAIL
    LIST QUARANTINE where comment like 'added.*'
CellCLI> LIST THRESHOLD  DETAIL
CellCLI> LIST THRESHOLD where name like 'db_io.*'
```

CHAPTER
10

Exadata Backup and Recovery

Y ou already have an established way of performing backups with your existing system, such as backup to tape or to a device such as a data domain. Now you're wondering whether you can use the same backup methods with the Exadata Machine. With Exadata, you can use your existing backup methods, or you can revisit and change your overall backup strategy.

If you are using the Oracle-recommended method, Recovery Manager (RMAN), to back up your databases, you'll need to make only a few changes in your existing scripts so that they work with Exadata. If you are using Oracle Enterprise Manager (OEM) to manage the backup, you can leverage it to back up databases running in Exadata. If you are not using RMAN for backup, you can quickly learn how to use it; RMAN is the only supported tool that can be used to back up the databases running in Exadata Machine, and this is the backup method we'll discuss in this chapter.

In addition to the database, other components on your Exadata Machine need to be backed up. Several options are available for backing up the various components of the Exadata Machine. This chapter will explore the backup options for the following components:

- Database

- Storage cells

- Compute nodes

- InfiniBand switch

Database Backup

Any database backup strategy is mainly governed by the recovery requirements. Following are the most critical factors that play a role in determining your recovery objectives:

- **Recovery time objective (RTO)**   This mainly governs how quickly you can recover your database.

- **Recovery point objective (RPO)**   This governs whether there is data loss and how much data loss the business can sustain. Some businesses can't sustain data loss even for a minute, while others can bear data loss for a few hours or one or two days.

- **Performance**   Often, whenever a backup kicks in, system performance is degraded. Does your OLTP take a hit when the backup kicks in? Do you need to minimize the impact of the backup on the running application because you need the application to be available 24/7?

■ **Retention** What is the backup retention policy? How many backups need to be stored on disks before they can be transferred to tape, archive, or a different tier storage?

Depending on your business's RTO and RPO, Exadata provides lots of choices for storing backup files. Before we discuss these choices, however, you need to get familiar with the fast recovery area (FRA).

Fast Recovery Area (FRA)

An FRA is a disk location where you can store recovery-related files such as control files and online redo log copies, archived redo log files, Flashback logs, and RMAN backups. If you plan to back up files for the Exadata Machine, use of the FRA is strongly recommended. Consider configuring an FRA as a first step in implementing a backup strategy.

Files in the FRA are *permanent* or *transient*. Permanent files are active files used by the database instance. All files that are not permanent are transient; in general, Oracle Database eventually deletes transient files after they become obsolete according to the backup retention policy or after they have been backed up to tape.

The FRA is enabled by setting two initialization parameters—DB_RECOVERY_FILE_DEST_SIZE, where the size of the FRA is specified, and DB_RECOVERY_FILE_DEST, where the location of the FRA is specified. In Exadata Machines the value of the parameter is RECO: DB_RECOVERY_FILE_DEST='+RECO'. To set these parameters, you do not need to shut down the database.

To calculate the size of the FRA, add up the space requirements for all the files that reside in the FRA:

```
FRA Size =
Size of a copy of database  +
Size of an incremental backup +
Size of (n+1) days of archived redo logs +
Size of (y+1) days of foreign archived redo logs (for logical standby) +
Size of control file +
Size of an online redo log member * number of log groups +
Size of flashback logs (based on DB_FLASHBACK_RETENTION_TARGET value)
```

In addition, allow some extra room for application growth, as well as for disk or cell failures. When sizing archived redo logs, consider the busiest interval in your application workload cycle.

If the calculation seems too difficult, you can follow the standard rule of thumb for Exadata (see the next section for more about DATA and RECO):

- **For disk-based backups:** 40 percent DATA, 60 percent RECO
- **For tape-based backups:** 80 percent DATA, 20 percent RECO

Tape-based (80/20) backups are not stored on the Exadata disk. Those backups can be stored on disk, but off the machine, such as on a ZFSSA, NetApp, or another file system. Use 40/60 for backups in the FRA or 80/20 for backups outside of the FRA.

Physical Storage Options for Backups

Let's evaluate the various options of physically storing the database backup files in a Exadata Machine.

Exadata Storage Cells

You can point the FRA inside the Exadata Storage Cells so that the database backup files can be kept in the Exadata Storage Cells; this is the fastest way of backing up a database running on an Exadata Machine. If the RTO is very short, this is probably the best storage option for backups. Depending on your requirements, one or two copies of the backup can be stored in the storage cells before moving them to a different location.

Exadata comes with two disk groups by default: DATA and RECO. The DATA disk group stores database files, and the RECO disk group contains the recovery-related files for the FRA. You can also use the FRA to store copies of the database control files, online redo log files, archive log files, and database backup files.

Exadata Storage Expansion Rack

If the RTO is short and Exadata Storage Cells can't be used for storing the backup of the database files due to space constraints, you can use the Exadata storage expansion rack to store the database backup files. The Exadata storage expansion rack is connected with the Exadata Machine using InfiniBand and provides even better backup and restore rates than backing up at the Exadata Storage Cells. You can either create a separate ASM disk group, such as DATA2, in the Exadata storage expansion rack for keeping the copies of the backup, or you can expand the existing ASM disk groups with the storage cells of the expansion rack. In both cases, you need to point the FRA to the location where you want to keep the database backup files.

Creating a separate disk group, such as DATA2, with the storage cells of the storage expansion rack offers a few advantages in storing the backup files: Because there is no contention for disks, the backup and restore rates are even faster. The DATA disk group can grow larger since the backup files move out of the RECO disk group. The Exadata storage expansion rack supports multiple database machines. The hard drive of the Exadata storage expansion rack can belong to a different category than the actual Exadata server. So, for example, if the Exadata server has high-performance disks, the Exadata storage expansion rack can be purchased with high-capacity drives. You need to make sure that the ASM disk groups are separate for the high-capacity and high-performance disks. You can back up onto an expansion rack using "image copy" backups to a separate set of disks (DATA2), leaving the FRA for storage of REDO only (on the RECO disk group).

ZFS Storage Appliance (ZFSSA)

ZFSSA is a cost-effective way of storing backup files if the Exadata Storage Cells or Exadata storage expansion rack cannot be used. ZFSSA can be connected to the Exadata Machine using InfiniBand or over 10-Gig Ethernet. ZFSSA provides snapshot and cloning capabilities, with which database snapshots can be created in seconds, and can be used to provision testing and development environments. The ZFSSA offers large amounts of usable space for storing backups, snapshots, and clones. It also supports database and non-database files. The ZFSSA can be connected to two different database machines' fabrics via InfiniBand. When configured with 10-Gig Ethernet, ZFSSA provides a centralized backup and recovery solution for the enterprise. Backup to ZFSSA (now called ZS3) is similar to a backup to an NFS mount point.

StorageTek Tape Library

The Exadata Machine can be integrated with the Oracle StorageTek tape library, which can backup database files as well as non-database files. In this case, StorageTek is connected via 10-Gig Ethernet instead of InfiniBand. StorageTek can run concurrent backups of multiple databases.

You cannot back up from Exadata directly to any tape library. You must go through a backup agent that is called by RMAN. The backup agent can be any of a wide variety of agents, including TSM (Tivioli Storage Manager), Simpana CommVault, EMC NetWorker, HP Data Protector, Symantec NetBackup, Oracle Secure Backup (OSB), and so on.

The tape library is physical hardware. You can also back up to third-party tape hardware libraries, which is functionally the same as using StorageTek.

Third-Party Backup Solutions

The third-party solutions such as NetBackup, NetWorker, Data Protector, and CommVault can be integrated with Exadata for backup and recovery. Make sure that the third-party solution can integrate with RMAN and is certified for Oracle

Database 11*g*R2. With third-party solutions, you should be able to apply all the Exadata backup and restore best practices.

Recovery Manager (RMAN)

Use RMAN to back up the databases running on the Exadata Machine. RMAN performs backups to disk, but with integrated media management software such as OSB, RMAN can also perform tape backups.

You can use RMAN to take full or incremental backups of the database. A full backup can occur online, with the database open, or offline, with the database in mounted state. There are two types of full backup. *Image copies* reside on disk storage and are approximately the same size as the database. The temp files are not taken into consideration in image copies. *Backup sets* can reside on disk or tape and are smaller because only the data is backed up, rather than the entire data file; the backup can also be compressed.

To configure an image copy, use the following command at the RMAN prompt:

```
RMAN> CONFIGURE DEVICE TYPE DISK BACKUP TYPE TO COPY; # image copies
```

To configure backup sets, use the following command at the RMAN prompt:

```
RMAN> CONFIGURE DEVICE TYPE DISK BACKUP TYPE TO BACKUPSET; #
```

RMAN uses two types of block compression when creating backup sets:

- **Unused block compression**   Supports disk backup and Oracle Secure Backup tape backup. RMAN does not check each block. Instead, it reads the bitmaps that indicate what blocks are currently allocated and then reads only those blocks.

- **Null block compression**   Supports all backups. RMAN checks every block to see if it has ever contained data. Blocks that have never contained data are not backed up. Blocks that have contained data, either currently or in the past, are backed up.

RMAN also provides the flexibility of taking incremental backups of the database. Incrementally updated backups reside on disk and offer typically a one- to seven-day rolling recovery window. A combination of full and incremental backup sets can reside on disk or tape and can also be compressed for longer retention windows. Incremental backups reduce the backup window to a shorter period of time with less overhead on the servers. Incremental backups can be stored as-is or applied to an image copy.

Incremental backups can be either level 0 or level 1. A level 0 incremental backup, which is the base for subsequent incremental backups, copies all blocks containing data, backing up the data file into a backup set just as a full backup would. Thus, level 0 incremental backup is often referred to as full backup. The only difference between a level 0 incremental backup and a full backup is that a full backup is never included in an incremental strategy.

A level 1 incremental backup can be either of the following types:

- A *differential* backup, which backs up all blocks changed after the most recent incremental backup at level 1 or 0

- A *cumulative* backup, which backs up all blocks changed after the most recent incremental backup at level 0

Incremental backups are differential by default.

We recommend an RMAN backup to the FRA and then an RMAN backup of the backup to tape. That solution keeps RMAN in control of both backups (locally on disk and to tape), which allows RMAN to handle the full restore, regardless of the source. Sweeping to tape outside control of RMAN requires a two-step restore: restore once from tape to disk, and then restore again to the database (a much longer process). If the backup resides in the FRA on Exadata, the customer can't use native OS tools or generic tape management utilities to back it up to tape. Instead, RMAN will be required, which means buying the agents.

There is no method to "sweep-to-tape" outside control of RMAN while using the FRA on Exadata. If customers back up to an NFS mount, they could possibly use an external sweep-to-tape process. That might be done on a network-attached storage (NAS) filer (such as ZFSSA) using NDMP or another method, but it's not recommended to do this outside of RMAN.

The FRA should *not* be placed on an NAS device. If you use an NAS device, it should be a user-managed storage area.

You can use multiple channels in RMAN to parallelize the backup operation. The number of parallel channels will vary depending on how busy the system is. For an X4-2 machine, two or three channels per node is a good start; for X4-8 machines, eight channels per node is a good start. The channels can be modified by the following commands.

For configuring parallel channel for disk backups:

```
RMAN>CONFIGURE DEVICE TYPE DISK PARALLELISM 12
```

For configuring parallel channel for tape backups:

```
RMAN> CONFIGURE DEVICE TYPE SBT PARALLELISM 8  ;

new RMAN configuration parameters:
CONFIGURE DEVICE TYPE 'SBT_TAPE' PARALLELISM 8 BACKUP TYPE TO BACKUPSET;
new RMAN configuration parameters are successfully stored
```

A simple backup strategy using RMAN would maintain an incremental level 0 backup (image copy) and an incremental level 1 backup on disk at all times and on a nightly basis:

1. Roll forward the previous night's level 1 backup to the image copy.

2. Take a new incremental level 1 backup to disk.

3. Copy the current day's archived redo logs to tape.

This will ensure quick access to a full backup (level 0) on disk that is less than 48 hours out-of-date. More than one incremental backup (level 1) is never needed to bring the database to less than 24 hours out-of-date. The current day's archived redo logs allow complete or point-in-time recovery up to available logs (archived and online).

> **TIP & TECHNIQUE**
> *Backups should be regularly tested, and you should be able to restore using the backups. If you are storing backups on tapes, the tapes should be regularly tested.*

It is recommended that you create an Oracle service to run against all database servers in the cluster. The service is used by the RMAN **BACKUP** command. RMAN automatically spreads the backup load evenly among the target instances offering the service:

```
$ srvctl add service -d <db_unique_name>  -s <service_name> \
-r <list of preferred instances>
$ srvctl start service -d <db_unique_name> -s <service_name>
```

Connect to RMAN using the service name:

```
$ rman target sys/<sys_password>@<service_name>
```

It is also recommended that you configure the automatic backup of the control file. It can be done by running the following command at the RMAN prompt:

```
RMAN > CONFIGURE CONTROLFILE AUTOBACKUP ON;
old RMAN configuration parameters:
CONFIGURE CONTROLFILE AUTOBACKUP OFF;
new RMAN configuration parameters:
CONFIGURE CONTROLFILE AUTOBACKUP ON;
new RMAN configuration parameters are successfully stored
```

Backing Up to Disks

As discussed previously, the fastest method is to back up to disk and then transfer the backup to tape. For backing up to disk, you should configure FRA and store the backups there. Perform an initial full backup (RMAN level 0) followed by daily incremental backup (RMAN level 1). A full backup can be taken every week if possible.

Enable RMAN block change tracking for fast incremental backups. *Block change tracking* allows RMAN to avoid scanning blocks that have not changed when performing incremental backups. Block change tracking should be enabled irrespective of the backup being taken to disk or to tape. Exadata Storage Server also offloads block inspection from the database servers.

When backing up to disk, configure the device type as DISK in RMAN. The command **show all** at the RMAN prompt displays the list of current configurations.

Run the following command at the RMAN prompt to configure the device type to disk:

```
RMAN > CONFIGURE DEFAULT DEVICE TYPE TO DISK;
new RMAN configuration parameters are successfully stored
```

Use the following script to take a full backup on the weekend:

```
run {
backup full database include current controlfile plus archivelog ;
}
```

To take a daily incremental backup, use the following script:

```
run {
backup cumulative incremental level 1 database;
backup archivelog all not backed up;
}
```

RMAN can take care of recovering and restoring the database from the backups. A sample script is shown here:

```
run {
restore database;
recover database;
}
```

Backing Up to Tape

Backing up the database to tape safeguards the backup in case a fault occurs in the Exadata Storage Cells. Tape backups can be done either directly to tape or in a two-step approach: first back up to storage cells in FRA, and then move the backup to tape. We recommend using RMAN backup to the FRA, and then RMAN backup of the backup to tape. That solution keeps RMAN in control of both backups (locally on disk and to tape), which allows RMAN to handle the full restore regardless of the source. Sweeping to tape outside the control of RMAN means you'll have a two-step restore.

Tape backups cannot really be stored for an "indefinite" period. Tape media degrades, and tapes must be migrated for use with newer tape drives. If you keep old tapes for too long, you'll need a museum full of tape drives to read them!

As mentioned, the sweep to tape (for backup to NFS mounts, for example) is outside the control of RMAN. You should not put the FRA on non-Exadata storage, and you cannot access Exadata storage without RMAN.

Management software is needed for tape backups, and Oracle's media management software is OSB, which can easily be integrated with RMAN. With OSB, the unused-block optimization capability is enabled. If the backup is made directly to tape using a third-party media management product, unused-block optimization is not available.

For tape-based backup solutions, the recommended strategy is to perform the following backups:

- Weekly RMAN level 0 (full) backups of the database

- Daily cumulative RMAN incremental level 1 backups of the database

- Daily backups of the Oracle Secure Backup catalog (if OSB is used)

Change the device type to tape at the RMAN prompt. Also check the number of parallel channels and modify them if needed:

```
RMAN> CONFIGURE DEFAULT DEVICE TYPE TO SBT;
RMAN > CONFIGURE DEVICE TYPE SBT PARALLELISM 8;
```

(SBT refers to secure backup tape.)

The following backup scripts can be used for backing up to tape. Here is the RMAN script for weekly backups:

```
run {
backup incremental level 0 database;
backup archivelog all not backed up;
}
```

Here is the RMAN script for daily backups:

```
run {
backup cumulative incremental level 1 database;
backup archivelog all not backed up;
}
```

Backing Up the Oracle Secure Backup Catalog

The OSB catalog maintains backup metadata, scheduling, and configuration details for the backup domain. Just as it is important to protect the RMAN catalog or control files, the OSB catalog should be backed up on a regular basis. In OSB, the catalog backup has been preconfigured:

- **Media family**   OSB_Catalog_MF writes all catalog backups to the same tape or tapes.

- **Job summary**   OSB-CATALOG-SUM sends e-mail showing a daily report status of the catalog backup to users.

- **Dataset**   OSB-CATALOG-DS defines all directories and files to back up for file system backups.

- **Schedule**   OSB-CATALOG-SCHED shows the schedule for the catalog backup.

The primary catalog backup configuration settings have been defined with only one step remaining, which requires user intervention: Edit the OSB-CATALOG-SCHED triggers to specify when to perform the backup.

Storage Cells Backup

The Exadata Storage Cells contain the physical disk drive where the database files are stored. The backup of the storage cells does not involve backing up the data, because we use RMAN to back up the database files. The backup of the storage cells refers to the backup of software that is running in the Exadata Storage Cell.

Storage cell backup needs to occur before you apply any patch to the storage cells. Exadata Storage Cells or Storage Servers run on a Linux operating system and run the Exadata storage software. By default, Oracle automatically performs backups of the OS and cell software on each storage cell.

The backups are located at /opt/oracle.cellos/iso on each storage cell:

```
[root@exa10cel01 ~]# cd /opt/oracle.cellos/iso
[root@ exa10cel01 iso]# ls
boot.cat  cellbits  imgboot.lst                        initrd.img
isolinux.cfg    memtest        trans.tbl  vmlinuz-2.6.39-400.126.1.el5uek
boot.msg  image.id  initrd-2.6.39-400.126.1.el5uek.img  isolinux.bin
lastGoodConfig  splash.lss  vmlinuz
```

The lastGoodConfig directory stores copies of the latest cell boot images and cell server software.

The backup of Linux OS (system volumes) is also located at the CELLBOOT USB Flash drive, an internal USB drive located at /dev/sdm1. You can verify this by running the **imageinfo** command:

```
[root@ exa10cel01 ~]# imageinfo

Kernel version: 2.6.39-400.126.1.el5uek #1 SMP Fri Sep 20 10:54:38 PDT 2013 x86_64
Cell version: OSS_11.2.3.3.0_LINUX.X64_131014.1
Cell rpm version: cell-11.2.3.3.0_LINUX.X64_131014.1-1

Active image version: 11.2.3.3.0.131014.1
Active image activated: 2014-03-04 14:10:12 -0800
Active image status: success
Active system partition on device: /dev/md5
Active software partition on device: /dev/md7

In partition rollback: Impossible

Cell boot usb partition: /dev/sdm1
Cell boot usb version: 11.2.3.3.0.131014.1
```

It can be backed up to an external USB drive or device using the script

```
'/opt/oracle.SupportTools/make_cellboot_usb'
```

The following steps are required to back up the CELLBOOT USB Flash drive to an external USB drive. (Note that backing up to an external USB drive is required only if you want to make a bootable disk. You can use another device for creating the bootable disk if you don't want to use a USB drive, because in many enterprise-class data centers, the USB may not be realistic.)

To back up the CELLBOOT USB Flash drive to an external USB drive, follow these steps:

1. Log in to the cell as the root user.

2. Attach a new USB Flash drive with a capacity of at least 1GB, and up to 8GB.

3. Remove any other USB Flash drives from the system.

4. Run the following commands:

```
cd /opt/oracle.SupportTools
./make_cellboot_usb -verbose -force
```

If the system disks fail, the OS has a corrupt file system, or there is damage to the boot area, the system can be rescued from the CELLBOOT USB Flash drive. Follow the next steps to rescue the CELLBOOT USB Flash drive. (Note: Use the rescue procedure with extreme caution. Incorrectly using the procedure can cause data loss. Ideally, you should use the rescue procedure only with assistance from Oracle Support Services.)

1. Connect to the Exadata Storage Server using the console.

2. Boot the Exadata Storage Server, and as soon as you see the Oracle Exadata splash screen, press any key on the keyboard. The splash screen remains visible for only five seconds.

3. In the displayed list of boot options, scroll down to the last option, CELL_USB_BOOT_CELLBOOT_usb_in_rescue_mode, and press ENTER.

4. Select the rescue option, and proceed with the rescue.

5. Do the following when prompted to restart the system or enter the shell at the end of the first phase of the rescue:

    a. Choose to enter the shell. Do not choose to restart the system.

    b. Log in to the shell using the rescue root password.

    c. Run the reboot command from the shell.

    d. Press F8 as the cell restarts and before the Oracle Exadata splash screen appears. Pressing F8 accesses the boot device selection menu.

    e. Select the RAID controller as the boot device. This causes the cell to boot from the hard disks.

You must reconfigure the cell after a successful rescue. If you chose to preserve the data, import the cell disks. If you chose not to preserve the data, create new cell disks and grid disks for any disks that were replaced during the rescue procedure.

Having to perform the rescue process is very rare, and you may never face it unless the system disk fails or there is corruption in the boot device of the OS running on the Exadata Storage Cells. In some cases, the rescue may not be needed—for example, if the system disk fails, you can recover from the mirror copy. But if both the original and mirror copy fail, rescue would be necessary.

TIP & TECHNIQUE
It is recommended that you work with Oracle Support whenever you perform rescue operations in an Exadata Storage Cell.

1. Use the following command to import grid disks on all disks other than those that failed and were replaced during the rescue procedure:

```
CellCLI> IMPORT CELLDISK ALL FORCE
```

2. Re-create the cell disks and grid disks for any disks that were replaced during the rescue procedure.

3. Log in to the Oracle ASM instance, and set the disks to ONLINE using the following command for each disk group:

```
SQL> ALTER DISKGROUP disk_group_name ONLINE DISKS IN FAILGROUP
cell_name WAIT;
```

4. Re-create the Flash Cache using the **CREATE FLASHCACHE** command.

5. Reconfigure the cell using the **ALTER CELL** command. Following is an example of the most common parameters:

```
CellCLI> ALTER CELL smtpServer='my_mail.example.com',
smtpFromAddr='john.doe@example.com', smtpToAddr='jane.smith@
example.com', notificationPolicy='critical,warning,clear',
notificationMethod='mail,snmp'
```

6. If any I/O resource management plans were created previously, they need to be re-created, as well as the cell metric thresholds.

Compute Nodes Backup

The Exadata compute node has three main software components: the OS, ORACLE_HOME for the databases and Grid Infrastructure ORACLE_HOME. All of this software can be backed up using a traditional backup method—making a zip or tar archive and then copying it to disk or tape.

Some amount of "user data" will be included in the file system, such as scripts owned by the oracle user. When backing up the ORACLE_HOME, the DBA should include all those files, including scripts created as a part of the user data.

In an Exadata Machine, the ORACLE_HOME is owned by the oracle user, which is used by DBAs. Depending on the system configuration, the GRID_HOME may be owned by the oracle user, the grid user, or some other user. If the DBA has the appropriate privilege, he can create the backup of the GRID_HOME; if not, the UNIX system administrator should create the GRID_HOME backup. The UNIX system administrator should create the backup of the OS.

In most cases, the only users logging into the OS would be the DBA. The DBA should rarely work directly from the OS login prompt on the Exadata Machine and should use a workspace on another platform. Backups can be created over either 1-Gig or 10-Gig Ethernet. InfiniBand can be used with a ZFS appliance. An additional network, NET3, can be used as a backup network if required.

Ideally, the backup of the compute node should be a part of the weekly backup. If that is not possible, a backup should be made before and after every significant change to the software on the database server, such as upon application of OS patches or Oracle patches, upgrading the Grid Infrastructure, changing or reconfiguring critical operating parameters, or installation or reconfiguration of third-party software.

Snapshot-Based Backup

You can also create snapshot-based backups of the compute nodes for both customized and non-customized partitions. (If the partitions of the database server were not changed from their original shipped configuration, these are in the *non-customized* partition category; if the partition of the database server was modified from the original shipped configuration, it is known as a *customized* partition.)

Follow these steps to create a snapshot-based backup of the compute node. Note that this is a great method if you have deployed backup to a ZFS storage appliance or a ZFS backup appliance.

1. Identify the file system to which you want to store the backup. It should be a writable NFS location. If it is a non-customized partition, then 150GB of space is enough; if it's a customized partition and you have multiple ORACLE_HOMEs, you need to plan for space accordingly.

2. As root user, create a mount point for the NFS share using the following command:

    ```
    mkdir -p /root/snapshot_backup
    ```

3. As root, mount the NFS share. In the following command, ip_address is the IP address of the NFS server and nfs_location is the NFS location:

    ```
    mount -t nfs -o rw,intr,soft,proto=tcp,nolock ip_address:/nfs_
    location/ /root/snapshot_backup
    ```

4. As root user, make a snapshot-based backup of the /(root), /u01, /boot directories, and any customized partitions you have created. First create a snapshot named root_snap for the root directory by running the following command:

    ```
    lvcreate -L1G -s -n root_snap /dev/VGExaDb/LVDbSys1
    ```

5. Label the snapshot by running the following command:

    ```
    e2label /dev/VGExaDb/root_snap DBSYS_SNAP
    ```

6. Mount the snapshot by running the following command:

    ```
    mkdir /root/mnt
    mount /dev/VGExaDb/root_snap /root/mnt -t ext3
    ```

7. Create a snapshot named u01_snap for the /u01 directory using the following command. If you have a customized partition, say /u02, do the same for /u02 or any other customized partition that you have in the compute nodes.

    ```
    lvcreate -L5G -s -n u01_snap /dev/VGExaDb/LVDbOra1
    ```

8. Label the snapshot by running the following command. Run this command for each customized partition.

```
e2label /dev/VGExaDb/u01_snap DBORA_SNAP
```

9. Mount the snapshot by running the following command:

```
mkdir -p /root/mnt/u01
mount /dev/VGExaDb/u01_snap /root/mnt/u01 -t ext3
```

10. Change to the directory for the backup:

```
cd /root/mnt
```

11. Create the backup file using one of the following commands.

If the system does not have NFS mount points:

```
# tar -pjcvf /root/snapshot_backup/mybackup.tar.bz2 * /boot -
exclude\
snapshot_backup/mybackup.tar.bz2 > /tmp/backup_tar.stdout 2>
/tmp/backup_tar.stderr
```

If the system has NFS mount points:

```
# tar -pjcvf /root/snapshot_backup/mybackup.tar.bz2 * /boot
--exclude \
snapshot_backup/mybackup.tar.bz2 --exclude nfs_mount_points > \
/tmp/backup_tar.stdout 2> /tmp/backup_tar.stderr
```

In the preceding command, nfs_mount_points are the NFS mount points. Excluding the mount points prevents the generation of large files and results in long backup times.

12. Check the /tmp/backup_tar.stderr file for any significant errors. Errors about failing to tar open sockets and other similar errors can be ignored.

If you want to unmount the snapshots and remove the snapshots for the root and /01 directories, use the following commands as root user:

```
cd /
umount /root/mnt/u01
umount /root/mnt
/bin/rm -rf /root/mnt
lvremove /dev/VGExaDb/u01_snap
lvremove /dev/VGExaDb/root_snap
```

You can unmount the NFS by running the following command as root:

```
umount /root/tar
```

Restore Using Snapshot-Based Backup

You might need to restore the compute node after severe disaster conditions affect the database server, or when all the hard drives are replaced together. In this section you'll learn how to restore the compute nodes using the snapshot-based backups.

The recovery procedures use the diagnostics.iso image as a virtual CD-ROM to restart the database server in rescue mode using the Integrated Lights Out Manager (ILOM). It consists of the following steps:

1. Re-create the following:

   ■ Boot partitions

   ■ Physical volumes

   ■ Volume groups

   ■ Logical volumes

   ■ File system

   ■ Swap partition

2. Activate the swap partition.

3. Ensure that the /boot partition is the active boot partition.

4. Restore the data.

5. Reconfigure the GNU Grand Unified Bootloader (GRUB).

6. Restart the server.

Recovering Compute Nodes with Non-customized Partitions

In this section you will learn how to recover compute nodes from a snapshot-based backup when using non-customized partitions. The following procedure is applicable when the layout of the partitions, logical volumes, file systems, and their sizes are equal to the layout when the database server was initially deployed—that is, no modifications to the file system have been made since the install deployment.

1. Prepare the NFS server to host the backup archive mybackup.tar.bz2. The NFS server must be accessible by IP address. For example, on an NFS server with the IP address nfs_ip, where the directory /export is exported from NSF mounts, put the mybackup.tar.bz2 file in the /export directory.

2. Attach the /opt/oracle.SupportTools/diagnostics.iso file from any other compute node as virtual media to the ILOM of the database server to be restored. The following is an example of how to set up a virtual CD-ROM using the ILOM interface:

   a. Copy the diagnostics.iso file to a directory on the machine using the ILOM interface.

   b. Log in to the ILOM web interface.

   c. From the Remote Control tab, select Remote Console to start the console.

   d. Select the Devices menu.

   e. Select the CD-ROM image option.

   f. Navigate to the location of the diagnostics.iso file.

   g. Open the diagnostics.iso file.

   h. From the Remote Control tab, select Host Control.

   i. Select CDROM as the next boot device from the list of values.

   j. Click Save. When the system is booted, the diagnostics.iso image is used.

3. Restart the system from the iso file by choosing the CD-ROM as the boot device during startup. You can also preset the boot device using the **ipmitool** command from any other machine that can reach the ILOM of the database server to be restored, instead of selecting the boot device manually during boot up, using the following commands:

```
ipmitool -H ILOM_ip_address_or_hostname \
-U root_user chassis bootdev cdrom

ipmitool -H ILOM_ip_address_or_hostname \
-U root_user chassis power cycle
```

   The ILOM_ip_address_or_hostname needs to be replaced with the IP address or the hostname of the ILOM.

4. Answer as follows when prompted by the system:

```
Choose from following by typing letter in '()':
 (e)nter interactive diagnostics shell. Must use credentials from Oracle
support to login (reboot or power cycle to exit the shell),
 (r)estore system from NFS backup archive,
Select:r
Are you sure (y/n) [n]:y
```

```
The backup file could be created either from LVM or non-LVM based
compute node
versions below 11.2.1.3.1 and 11.2.2.1.0 or higher do not support LVM
based partitioning
use LVM based scheme(y/n):y

Enter path to the backup file on the NFS server in format:
ip_address_of_the_NFS_share:/path/archive_file
For example, 10.10.10.10:/export/operating_system.tar.bz2
NFS line:nfs_ip:/export/mybackup.tar.bz2
IP Address of this host:IP address of the DB host
Netmask of this host:netmask for the above IP address
Default gateway:Gateway for the above IP address
```

The login screen appears when the recovery is complete.

5. Log in as the root user and run the **dsetach** command on the diagnostics.iso file.

6. Use the **reboot** command to restart the system. The restoration process is complete.

7. Verify that all Oracle software can start and function by logging in to the database server. The **/usr/local/bin/imagehistory** command indicates that the database server was reconstructed. An example is shown here:

```
imagehistory

Version : 11.2.2.1.0
Image activation date : 2010-10-13 13:42:58 -0700
Imaging mode : fresh
Imaging status : success

Version : 11.2.2.1.0
Image activation date : 2010-10-30 19:41:18 -0700
Imaging mode : restore from nfs backup
Imaging status : success
```

Recovering Oracle Linux Database Server with Customized Partitions

In customized partitions, changes have been made to the file system after it was installed that differ from the standard installation template. You may need to create customized partitions depending on your security requirements. For example, if you are planning to run PeopleSoft, JD Edwards, and Demantra in your Exadata Machine and your security standards require that you have a separate file system for each application's ORACLE_HOME, you may end up installing three ORACLE_HOMEs in /u01, /u02, and /u03 file systems. This differs from the standard installation and is considered a *customized partition*.

The following procedure describes how to recover an Oracle Linux database server from a snapshot-based backup when using customized partitions. The steps are the same as those for restoring non-customized partitions, until you are prompted to enter the interactive diagnostics shell and restore the system from NFS backup archive after booting the database server using diagnostics.iso.

1. Choose to enter the diagnostics shell, and log in as the root user.

2. If required, use /opt/MegaRAID/MegaCli/MegaCli64 to configure the disk controller to set up the disks.

3. Ensure that you create a primary boot partition of a size at least 128MB to be mounted at /boot. The boot area cannot be an LVM partition.

4. Create an LVM partition after creating the boot partition by running the following commands:

```
umount /mnt/cell
fdisk /dev/sda
```

The interactive shell appears. Use the following steps to respond to the system prompts:

   a. Enter **d** to remove the partitions that will be re-created.

   b. Enter **n** to create a new partition.

   c. Enter **1** for the partition number.

   d. Enter **1** for the first cylinder

   e. Enter **15** for the last cylinder.

   f. Enter **t** and then **82** to select the type of Linux. The t toggles the partition number, and 82 selects the type of Linux.

   g. Enter **a** to set the bootable flag for the boot partition.

5. Create a second primary partition as follows:

   a. Enter **n** to create a new partition.

   b. Enter **2** for the partition number.

   c. Enter **16** for the first cylinder.

   d. Press ENTER to select the default for the last cylinder.

Note that if customized or additional partitions need to be created, the value for the last cylinder may change.

    e. Enter **t** and then **8e** to select LVM.

    f. Enter **p** to print the new partition information.

    g. Enter **w** to write the information to disk.

6. Use the **/sbin/lvm** command to re-create the customized LVM partitions and **mkfs** to create file systems on them. The detailed steps are listed next.

    a. Create the physical volume, volume group, and logical volumes as shown here:

```
lvm pvcreate /dev/sda2
lvm vgcreate VGExaDB /dev/sda2
```

    b. Create the logical volume for the /(root) directory, a file system, and label it:

```
lvm lvcreate -n LVDbSys1 -L40G VGExaDb
mkfs.ext3 /dev/VGExaDb/LVDbSys1
e2label /dev/VGExaDb/LVDbSys1 DBSYS
```

    c. Create the logical volume for the swap directory, and label it:

```
lvm lvcreate -n LVDSwap1 -L24G VGExaDb
mkswap -L SWAP /dev/VGExaDb/LVDbSwap1
```

    d. Create the logical volume for the root/u01 directory, and label it:

```
lvm lvcreate -n LVDbOra1 -L100G VGExaDb
mkfs.ext3 /dev/VGExaDb/LVDbOra1
e2label /dev/VGExaDb/LVDbOra1 DBORA
```

    e. Create a file system on the /boot partition, and label it:

```
mkfs.ext3 /dev/sda1
e2label /dev/sda1 BOOT
```

For all the customized file system layouts, additional logical volumes need to be created. For customized layouts, different sizes may be used.

7. Create mount points for all the partitions to mirror the original system, and mount the respective partitions. For example, assuming /mnt is used as the top-level directory for this, the mounted list of partitions may look like the following:

```
/dev/VGExaDb/LVDbSys1 on /mnt
/dev/VGExaDb/LVDbOra1 on /mnt/u01
/dev/sda1 on /mnt/boot
```

The following is an example of how to mount the root file system and create two mount points:

```
mount /dev/VGExaDb/LVDbSys1 /mnt -t ext3
mkdir /mnt/u01 /mnt/boot

mount /dev/VGExaDb/LVDbOra1 /mnt/u01 -t ext3
mount /dev/sda1 /mnt/boot -t ext3
```

You'll need to create additional mount points for customized file systems during this step.

8. Bring up the network, and mount the NFS server where you have the backup as follows.

   a. Run the following command to bring up the network:

   ```
   ifconfig eth0 ip_address_for_eth0 netmask netmask_for_eth0 up
   route add -net 0.0.0.0 netmask 0.0.0.0 gw gateway_ip_address
   ```

   b. Mount the NFS server with IP address nfs_ip and then export it as /export to the backup location using the following commands:

   ```
   mkdir -p /root/mnt
   mount -t nfs -o ro,intr,soft,proto=tcp,nolock nfs_ip:/export
   /root/mnt
   ```

9. Restore from backup using the following command:

   ```
   tar -pjxvf /root/mnt/mybackup.tar.bz2 -C /mnt
   ```

10. Unmount the restored file systems, and remount the /boot partition:

    ```
    umount /mnt/u01
    umount /mnt/boot
    umount /mnt
    mkdir /boot
    mount /dev/sda1 /boot -t ext3
    ```

11. Set up the boot loader. For the following, /dev/sda1 is the /boot area:

    ```
    grub
    find /I_am_hd_boot (1)
    root (hdX,0)
    setup (hdX)
    quit
    ```

    In the preceding commands, (1) finds the hard disk hdX that has the file I_am_hd_boot, such as (hd0,0).

12. Detach the diagnostics.iso file.

13. Unmount the /boot partition:

```
umount /boot
```

14. Restart the server to complete the restoration procedure:

```
reboot
```

InfiniBand Switch Backup

You can back up the InfiniBand switch from the ILOM for the newer versions of the InfiniBand firmware. Before backing up the InfiniBand, you need to find the version of the firmware. Depending on the firmware version, you may be required to perform additional steps for each version backup. Back up the InfiniBand switch whenever there is a planned firmware upgrade.

To find the firmware version, log in as root to the IP address of the InfiniBand switch and run the command **version**.

```
[root@exa10-ib1 ~]# version
SUN DCS 36p version: 2.1.3-4
Build time: Aug 28 2013 16:25:57
SP board info:
Manufacturing Date: 2013.10.01
Serial Number: "NCDCK0456"
Hardware Revision: 0x0007
Firmware Revision: 0x0000
BIOS version: SUN0R100
BIOS date: 06/22/2010
```

You can see that the firmware version in this example is 2.1.3-4.

- If the version is later than 1.1.3.-2, follow steps 1–5.

- If the firmware version is 1.1.3-2, follow steps 1–7.

- If the firmware version is 1.0.1, follow only steps 6 and 7; do not follow steps 1–5.

To begin the backup of the InfiniBand switch, open the ILOM URL from a browser:

http://exa10-ib1.osc.us.oracle.com

Log in as the ilom-admin user and perform the following steps:

1. Select the Maintenance tab.

2. Select the Backup/Restore tab.

3. Select the Backup operation and the Browser method.

4. Enter a passphrase. This is used to encrypt sensitive information, such as user passwords, in the backup.

5. Click Run, and save the resulting XML file in a secure location. Figure 10-1 shows the backup of an XML file using ILOM.

6. Log in to the InfiniBand switch as root user.

7. Copy the following files using scp:

   ■ **Network configuration** /etc/sysconfig/network-scripts/ifcfg-eth0

   ■ **DNS information** /etc/resolv.conf

   ■ **NTP information** /etc/ntp.conf

   ■ **Time zone information** /etc/localtime

   ■ **openSM settings** /etc/opensm/opensm.conf

   ■ **Host name** /etc/sysconfig/network. If the hostname information is not in this file, make a note of it and save it somewhere.

Make a note of the passwords of the root and nm2user users. If you need to restore the InfiniBand switch, you must restore the old passwords.

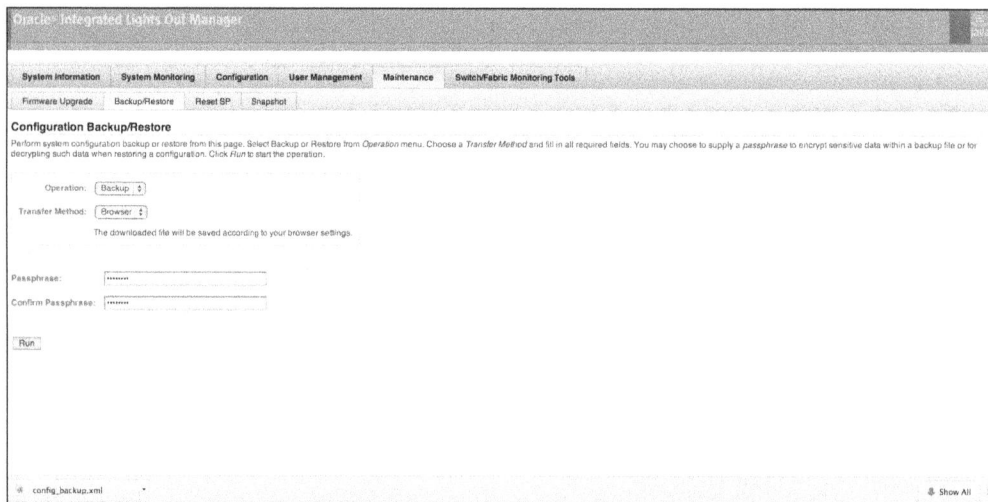

FIGURE 10-1. *InfiniBand backup using ILOM*

Restore an InfiniBand Switch

Like the backup, you can restore the InfiniBand switch via ILOM for versions of InfiniBand firmware prior to 1.1.3-2.

- For versions later than 1.1.3-2, follow steps 1–9.

- If the firmware version is 1.1.3-2, follow steps 1–13.

- If the firmware version is 1.0.1, follow only steps 10–13; do not follow steps 1–9.

Open the ILOM URL from a browser:

http://exa10-ib1.osc.us.oracle.com

Log in as the ilom-admin user and perform the following steps:

1. Select the Maintenance tab.

2. Select the Backup/Restore tab.

3. Select the Restore operation and the Browser method.

4. Click Browse, and select the XML file that contains the switch configuration backup. Figure 10-2 shows an example.

5. Enter the passphrase that was used during the backup.

6. Click Run to restore the configuration.

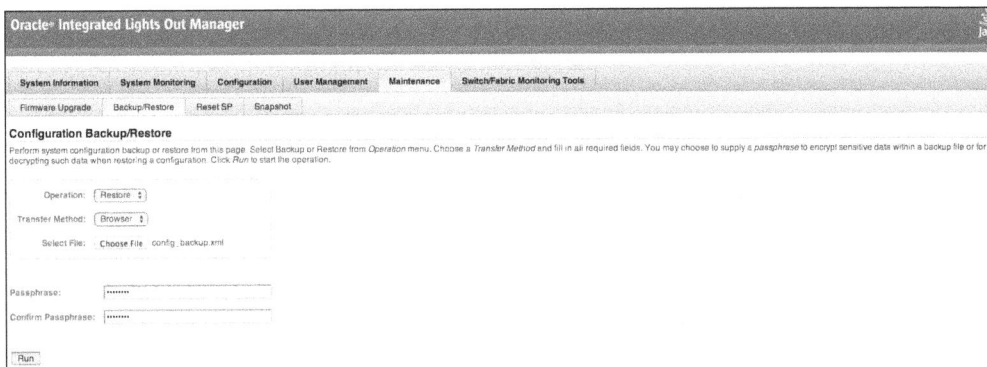

FIGURE 10-2. *InfiniBand switch recovery*

7. Restart Open Subnet Manager (openSM) from the switch command line using the following commands:

```
disablesm
enablesm
```

8. Log in as the root user.

9. Restart the switch.

10. Restore the following files:

   - **Network configuration**   /etc/sysconfig/network-scripts/ifcfg-eth0

   - **DNS information**   /etc/resolv.conf

   - **NTP information**   /etc/ntp.conf

   - **Time zone information**   /etc/localtime

   - **openSM settings**   /etc/opensm/opensm.conf

   - **Host name**   /etc/sysconfig/network. If the hostname information is not there, enter **HOSTNAME=switch_host_name**.

11. Restore the passwords of the root and nm2user users using the **passwd** command.

12. Run the following commands in the order shown to restart the services and openSM:

```
service network restart
service ntpd restart
disablesm
enablesm
```

13. Reboot the switch as root.

Summary

For any organization, data is critical, so it's very important to protect it. Databases running on an Exadata Machine can be backed up to the internal storage cells, storage expansion rack, tape drive, ZFS storage appliance, or any third-party storage device. In addition to the database backup, you should back up the compute node, storage cells, and InfiniBand switch.

Index

A

active database duplication, 157–159
active users in predictive sizing, 136
ad hoc reports in predictive sizing, 138
ADMINISTER_RESOURCE_MANAGER privilege, 210
administration reduction
    ASM, 9
    Exadata, 22
Advanced Compression Option, 53
advanced supply chain planning (ASCP)
    environments, 108–109
aggressive consolidation scenario, 204
Alert History metric, 247, 252
alert object types, 289
allocation directive, 227
ALTER command in CellCLI, 288–289
ALTER CELL command
    backups, 320
    events, 69
    Flash Cache Compression, 107
    WBFC, 100
ALTER FLASHCACHE command, 106
ALTER IORMPLAN command, 226–227, 229–230
ALTER SESSION commands, 55
ALTER TABLE commands
    Exadata Smart Flash Cache, 84
    HCC, 56–57, 59–60
ALTER TABLESPACE command, 59
AMM (Automatic Memory Management), 117
anti-indexes, 67
application growth in predictive sizing, 138
application services in predictive sizing, 136–137
applications
    consolidating. *See* consolidation
    migrating. *See* migrating applications
architecture, 5
    configurations, 15–19

    database servers, 5–11
    Exadata Storage Expansion rack, 19–20
    Exadata Storage Servers, 11–14
    InfiniBand, 14–15
archival compression, 53–54
ARCHIVE HIGH compression mode, 55
ARCHIVELOG files
    application migration, 184
    backups, 154, 157
    disk groups, 9
ARCHIVELOG mode
    Data Guard, 183
    DBFS, 190
ASCP (advanced supply chain planning)
    environments, 108–109
ASM. *See* Automatic Storage Management (ASM);
    Automatic Storage Management (ASM) disk groups
ASMCMD utility, 282–285, 299
ASR (Auto Service Request), 22
ASSIGN KEY command, 289
auque1.sql file, 160
auque2.sql script, 160
Auto Service Request (ASR), 22
auto setting in IORM, 225, 229
Automatic Memory Management (AMM), 117
Automatic Storage Management (ASM)
    application migration, 150
    grid disks, 13–14, 85
    managing, 276–285
    overview, 8–10
    for redundancy, 130, 133
    stopping, 271
Automatic Storage Management (ASM) disk groups,
    9, 85
    administrative tasks, 299
    creating, 63, 88, 90, 290–293
    DBFS file system, 131
    default, 233–234

333

Linux operating system (*Cont.*)
  memory, 235, 244, 260
    Oracle Database Machines, 3–4
    power off commands, 272
    storage cells, 12, 285, 317–318
LIST command in CellCLI, 286, 288–289
LIST CELL ATTRIBUTES command, 107
LIST FLASHCACHE command, 86
LIST FLASHCACHE ATTRIBUTES command, 108
LIST FLASHCACHECONTENT command, 91
LIST FLASHLOG command, 102–105
LIST GRIDDISK command, 292
LIST IORMPLAN command, 228
LIST METRICCURRENT command, 92, 104, 295
LIST METRICHISTORY command, 295
LIST PHYSICALDISK command, 290
listeners
    application migration, 185
    database duplication, 158
    InfiniBand, 109, 111–114
local disks
    Exadata Storage Servers, 35
    X4-2 servers, 30
    X4-8 servers, 33
localization in predictive sizing, 138
LOG_ARCHIVE_CONFIG parameter, 184
LOG_ARCHIVE_FORMAT parameter, 184
LOG_ARCHIVE_MAX_PROCESSES parameter, 184
log_file_name_convert parameter, 186
Logical Units (LUNs), 13, 290
logs in application migration, 162, 184, 186
low_latency option, 224
LRU (Least Recently Used) algorithm
    Exadata Smart Flash Cache, 81
    WBFC, 98–99
LSO (Large Send Offload), 37
LUNs (Logical Units), 13, 290
lvcreate command, 321–322
LZO (Lempel-Ziv-Oberhumer) compression
    algorithm, 52

M

M-Values, 125
Main Least Recently Used algorithm, 81
maintenance in consolidation, 199
manageability in consolidation, 198–199
Management Server (MS), 12, 294
Manager module in GoldenGate, 188
media family configuration in OSB catalogs, 317
medium concurrently active users in predictive
    sizing, 136
medium consolidation scenario, 204
MemFree metric, 260
memory
    comparative sizing, 125–128
    consolidation, 234–235
    Exadata Storage Servers, 35
    HugePages, 116
    monitoring, 242, 244, 260
    storage cells, 60
    X4-2 servers, 30
    X4-8 servers, 33
Memory Details page, 244
MEMORY_MAX_TARGET parameter, 117
Memory Scan Rate metric, 244
MEMORY_TARGET parameter, 117
Memory Utilization % metric, 244
metadata in Smart Scans, 64
Metric and Collection metrics, 246
Metric Collection Errors metric, 246, 252
metrics. *See* monitoring
migrating applications
    Data Guard, 182–187
    Data Pump Export, 159–161
    Data Pump Import, 161–162
    factors, 150–151
    GoldenGate, 187–192
    planning and preparing, 151–153
    RMAN, 153–159
    transportable database, 163–168
    TTS, 168–176
    XTTS, 176–182
mirroring
    ASM, 10
    comparative sizing, 130
monitoring
    with CellCLI, 294–296
    compute nodes, 240–247
    CPU utilization, 259–260
    databases, 254–256
    DBRM, 221–222
    Enterprise Manager. *See* Enterprise
        Manager monitoring
    Exachk for, 263–268
    flash usage, 91–93
    ILOM, 247–248, 260–261
    InfiniBand networks, 252–253
    IORM, 230–231
    memory utilization, 260
    Smart Scans, 75–76
    SQL, 256–259
    storage cells, 248–252, 261–262
    system log, 259
month-end batch jobs in predictive sizing, 137
mount points
    application migration, 160
    Linux database server recovery, 327–328
    TTS migration, 171
MS (Management Server), 12, 294

N

N_ attributes in CellCLI, 294
nature of applications in application migration, 150
negative indexes in Smart Scans, 67

O

P

Join the Largest Tech Community in the World

Download the latest software, tools, and developer templates

Get exclusive access to hands-on trainings and workshops

Grow your professional network through the Oracle ACE Program

Publish your technical articles – and get paid to share your expertise

Join the Oracle Technology Network
Membership is free. Visit oracle.com/technetwork

@OracleOTN   facebook.com/OracleTechnologyNetwork

ORACLE®

Reach More than 700,000 Oracle Customers with Oracle Publishing Group

Connect with the Audience that Matters Most to Your Business

Oracle Magazine
The Largest IT Publication in the World
Circulation: 550,000
Audience: IT Managers, DBAs, Programmers, and Developers

Profit
Business Insight for Enterprise-Class Business Leaders to Help Them Build a Better Business Using Oracle Technology
Circulation: 100,000
Audience: Top Executives and Line of Business Managers

Java Magazine
The Essential Source on Java Technology, the Java Programming Language, and Java-Based Applications
Circulation: 125,000 and Growing Steady
Audience: Corporate and Independent Java Developers, Programmers, and Architects

For more information or to sign up for a FREE subscription: Scan the QR code to visit Oracle Publishing online.

ORACLE®

Beta Test Oracle Software

Get a first look at our newest products—and help perfect them. You must meet the following criteria:

✔ Licensed Oracle customer or Oracle PartnerNetwork member

✔ Oracle software expert

✔ Early adopter of Oracle products

Please apply at: pdpm.oracle.com/BPO/userprofile

ORACLE®

If your interests match upcoming activities, we'll contact you. Profiles are kept on file for 12 months.

www.ingramcontent.com/pod-product-compliance
Lightning Source LLC
Chambersburg PA
CBHW080715220326
41598CB00033B/5426